THE S. MARK TAPER FOUNDATION

IMPRINT IN JEWISH STUDIES

BY THIS ENDOWMENT

THE S. MARK TAPER FOUNDATION SUPPORTS

THE APPRECIATION AND UNDERSTANDING

OF THE RICHNESS AND DIVERSITY OF

JEWISH LIFE AND CULTURE

The publisher gratefully acknowledges the generous support of the
Jewish Studies Endowment Fund of the University of California
Press Foundation, which was established by a major gift
from the S. Mark Taper Foundation

Rabbis, Sorcerers, Kings, and Priests

Rabbis, Sorcerers, Kings, and Priests

The Culture of the Talmud in Ancient Iran

Jason Sion Mokhtarian

UNIVERSITY OF CALIFORNIA PRESS

University of California Press, one of the most distinguished university presses in the United States, enriches lives around the world by advancing scholarship in the humanities, social sciences, and natural sciences. Its activities are supported by the UC Press Foundation and by philanthropic contributions from individuals and institutions. For more information, visit www.ucpress.edu.

University of California Press
Oakland, California

First Paperback Printing 2021

Library of Congress Cataloging-in-Publication Data

Mokhtarian, Jason Sion, author
Rabbis, sorcerers, kings, and priests : the culture of the Talmud in ancient Iran / Jason Sion Mokhtarian.
p. cm.
Includes bibliographical references and index.
ISBN 978-0-520-28620-7 (cloth, alk. paper) — ISBN 978-0-520-96154-8 (electronic) -- ISBN 978-0-520-38572-6 (pbk. : alk. paper)
1. Talmud—Iranian influ ences. . 2. Judaism—History—Talmudic period, 10–425. 3. Judaism—History—Medieval and early modern period, 425–1789. I. Title.
BM501.M65 2015
296.1'2506—dc23 2014049394

This book is dedicated to my grandparents,
Aghajan and Akhtar Mokhtarian
and Sion and Khorshid Assil,
and to my parents,
Mehran and Shahla Mokhtarian

CONTENTS

List of Abbreviations *ix*
Note on Translations, Transcriptions, and Manuscripts *xi*
Acknowledgments *xiii*

Introduction *1*

1. The Sources and Methods of Talmudic and Iranian Studies *7*
2. Comparing Sasanian Religions *22*
3. Rabbinic Portrayals of Persians as Others *43*
4. Rabbis and Sasanian Kings in Dialogue *74*
5. Rabbis and Zoroastrian Priests in Judicial Settings *94*
6. Rabbis, Sorcerers, and Priests *124*

Conclusion: Rabbis, Sorcerers, Kings, and Priests in Sasanian Iran *145*

Notes *153*
Bibliography *229*
Index of Sources *259*
General Index *267*

ABBREVIATIONS

RABBINIC SOURCES

B. or *b.*	Babylonian Talmud
BT	Babylonian Talmud
M. or *m.*	Mishnah
Y. or *y.*	Yerushalmi (Jerusalem) Talmud

TALMUDIC TRACTATES

ʿAbod. Zar.	*ʿAbodah Zarah*
ʿArak.	*ʿArakin*
B. Bat.	*Baba Batra*
B. Meṣiʿa	*Baba Meṣiʿa*
B. Qam.	*Baba Qamma*
Bek.	*Bekorot*
Ber.	*Berakot*
ʿErub.	*ʿErubin*
Giṭ.	*Giṭṭin*
Ḥag.	*Ḥagigah*
Hor.	*Horayot*
Ḥul.	*Ḥullin*
Ketub.	*Ketubbot*
Meg.	*Megillah*
Moʿed Qaṭ.	*Moʿed Qaṭan*
Naz.	*Nazir*

Ned.	*Nedarim*
Nid.	*Niddah*
Pesaḥ.	*Pesaḥim*
Qidd.	*Qiddušin*
Roš Haš.	*Roš Haššanah*
Sanh.	*Sanhedrin*
Šabb.	*Šabbat*
Šebu.	*Šebuʿot*
Taʿan.	*Taʿanit*
Yebam.	*Yebamot*
Zebaḥ.	*Zebaḥim*

LANGUAGES

Aram.	Aramaic
Av.	Avestan
Heb.	Hebrew
JBA	Jewish Babylonian Aramaic
Mand.	Mandaic
MIr.	Middle Iranian
MP	Middle Persian
NP	New Persian
OP	Old Persian
Syr.	Syriac

NOTE ON TRANSLATIONS, TRANSCRIPTIONS, AND MANUSCRIPTS

Citations of the Babylonian Talmud are from the standard printed edition (Vilna, 1880–86), unless indicated otherwise. Manuscript variants listed are adopted from the Sol and Evelyn Henkind Talmud Text Databank of the Saul Lieberman Institute of Talmud Research of the Jewish Theological Seminary of America. The transcription of Hebrew and Aramaic words, as well as the abbreviations for biblical and rabbinic texts, follow the conventions of the *Society of Biblical Literature Handbook of Style for Ancient Near Eastern, Biblical, and Early Christian Studies*, edited by Patrick H. Alexander and others (Peabody, Mass.: Hendrickson, 2011). Middle Persian transcriptions follow David Neil MacKenzie, *A Concise Pahlavi Dictionary* (Oxford: Oxford University Press, 1971), with some exceptions.

ACKNOWLEDGMENTS

This book would not have been possible without the support of my mentors, colleagues, and family. It is a revised and expanded version of my doctoral dissertation completed in the Department of Near Eastern Languages and Cultures at the University of California, Los Angeles, under the direction of Carol Bakhos. Carol was the best advisor I could have asked for, as she guided me to figure out for myself who I am as a scholar of ancient Judaism, while also training me rigorously in rabbinic literature. I owe her a great deal for this. I hope that this book makes her proud. I also wish to thank the other members of my doctoral committee—Ra'anan Boustan, William Schniedewind, Rahim Shayegan, and Richard Kalmin (Jewish Theological Seminary), each of whom acted as a generous mentor and contributed something unique and crucial to my education. I would be remiss if I did not also express my gratitude to Hossein Ziai, who was responsible for bringing me to UCLA and whose door was always open to me.

The rewriting of my dissertation into this book took place at Indiana University, Bloomington, under the auspices of the Borns Jewish Studies Program and Department of Religious Studies. I am very fortunate to work in such an intellectually stimulating and collegial environment. I want to thank the former and current directors of the Jewish Studies Program, Jeffrey Veidlinger and Mark Roseman, for their unwavering support for my research, and for working so hard to make Bloomington one of the most lively centers of Jewish Studies in America, which I get to be a part of daily. I also wish to thank Winnifred Sullivan, chair of the Department of Religious Studies, who has been a generous mentor and true supporter of my goals. I am particularly grateful to Shaul Magid for reading the entire manuscript of this book and for making suggestions that made me reconsider some central parts of its arguments and methods. My colleagues here in the Ancient Mediterranean and Near Eastern Religions program—Jamsheed Choksy, R. Kevin Jaques, Eva Mroczek, and Jeremy Schott—all played a formative role for this book in different ways, offering insightful comments and always being open to conversation. I thank them, and likewise all my colleagues at Indiana University, for creating such a wonderful atmosphere in which to write and teach. Many other people also deserve acknowledgment for helping me write this book, including Touraj Daryaee, who served as a reader for the press and offered some new insights that I ended up expanding on at some length in my revisions, and Prods Oktor Skjærvø, who invited me to study with him at Harvard as I was writing my dissertation and gave me some critical guidance at early stages in this project. I would also like to extend my sincere gratitude to Richard Kalmin for his consistent intellectual mentorship and encouragement, and for taking the time to teach me Talmud in various settings in New York and Los Angeles. This book has also benefitted from my conversations over the years with other scholars who helped me conceptualize the study of the Talmud in its Iranian context, including Yaakov Elman, Isaiah Gafni, Geoffrey Herman, and Shaul Shaked.

While writing this book I received the support of various institutions, including the Lady Davis Foundation and the Hebrew University of Jerusalem, the Foundation for Jewish Culture, the Memorial Foundation for Jewish Culture, the UCLA Department of Near Eastern Languages and Cultures, and the UCLA Jewish Studies Program. Indiana's Jewish Studies Program also provided financial support for the completion of this book.

An abbreviated version of chapter 4 of this monograph was published as "Authority and Empire in Sasanian Babylonia: The Rabbis and King Shapur in Dialogue," in the *Jewish Studies Quarterly* 19 (2012): 148–80.

I appreciate all the hard work that the University of California Press staff put into producing this book. Eric Schmidt was an excellent editor and conversation partner, and approached my book with care and attention. I would also like to recognize Cindy Fulton and Maeve Cornell-Taylor of the press for their assistance. Paul Psoinos, the book's copyeditor, showed patience, humor, and generosity toward me, a first-time author, in this process, and saved me from many errors—for which I thank him.

My family means the world to me, and they deserve the most credit for any successes that I may ever have. My parents, Mehran and Shahla Mokhtarian, have always given me unconditional love and support, and all that I have ever wanted to do is to make them proud—I hope that I have succeeded in that. My passion for Iranian Jewish history comes from the way that they raised me. Many thanks, too, to Melody, the entire Mokhtarian family, the Assil family, and the Greenbergs for everything they do for me. Finally, to my patient and beautiful wife, Stefanie, and to baby Eliana: words cannot express how grateful I feel to have both of you in my life—I am so proud of the family that we are creating together.

Introduction

For over four centuries in late antiquity, the rabbis who produced the vast compendium of Jewish laws and narratives called the Babylonian Talmud, or Bavli, resided in the Sasanian Empire (224–650 C.E.). The Babylonian sages who composed the Talmud, which to this day forms the basis of normative Jewish behavior, formed one of numerous religious groups located in Babylonia, a cultural and administrative heart of the Persian Zoroastrian Empire. This geographic area and its surroundings were replete with diverse religions, political movements, languages, and ethnicities in contact with one another. In this book, I read the Talmud in its broader Sasanian context by exploring its relationship to Persian society and culture, broadly defined. What impact did the Persian Empire, as both a real historical force and imaginary interlocutor, have on rabbinic identity and authority as expressed in the Talmud?

This general question regarding the influence that the Persian world exerted on rabbinic culture and history permeates each chapter of this monograph. But what does it mean to study the Talmud in its Sasanian context in the first place, and how does one do so when the extant evidence is so often problematic? This book engages these questions by utilizing common tools in the history of Judaism, especially philological and historical ones, as a means of investigating the complex ties between religions and societies in western Sasanian Iran. Given the fact that the Bavli is the single richest source of information for research on the Jews of ancient Persia, the majority of this book's data naturally emanates from this extraordinary corpus of oral Torah. A sustained examination of how Sasanian cultural, historical, and social landscapes influenced the Babylonian rabbis is the present book's contribution to the field of Talmudic studies, as it interprets anew Talmudic texts that explicitly depict the Persians. This book has another objective in mind as well—namely, to integrate Talmudic studies further into the field of religious studies, of which Jewish studies represents one branch.

Although the internal, exegetical tendencies of the Talmud leave contemporary readers with the impression that the ancient sages were uninterested in the cultural horizon outside the rabbinic academies, this was indeed not always the case. In fact, the Babylonian rabbis were integrated into a sociocultural network of religious and ethnic groups in late antique Mesopotamia. As this book shows, the rabbis constructed their group identity in a heterogeneous environment that welcomes comparison with non-Jewish contexts. Before the achievements of Talmudist Yaakov Elman in the past decade, Talmudic studies had yet to systematically grapple with the consequential question of the impact of the Iranian context on the Talmud.[1] Elman's research agenda comparing Talmudic and Middle Persian sources, facilitated by a partnership with ancient Iranist Prods Oktor Skjærvø, sparked a much-needed dialogue about these weighty topics, opening the door for books such as this one and Shai Secunda's *The Iranian Talmud: Reading the Bavli in Its Sasanian Context*.[2] In twentieth-century historiography, this subfield in rabbinics, once dubbed "Talmudica Iranica" by E.S. Rosenthal (1982), experienced several false starts despite influential individual contributions to the topic.[3] Regrettably, even with the recent surge in interest in the field, scholarly discourse on the subfield has been inadequate, a desideratum that is all the more conspicuous when compared with the vast secondary literature that exists on the Greco-Roman and early Christian contexts of Palestinian rabbinism.[4] There are numerous explanations for why rabbinics has been more aligned with Roman contexts of late antique Judaism than with Iranian ones. To begin with, as Seth Schwartz has asserted, the fact that there is a relatively deficient material record for Babylonian Jews, as well as a limited non-Talmudic corpus originating from this community, adversely affects the task of researching social history.[5] By contrast, the study of Greco-Roman Jewry does not have such barriers. Moreover, the insufficient role that ancient Iranology has played in the field of Talmudic studies can also be attributed to the former field's recondite status in North American academies, especially relative to classics, a trend buoyed up by Iranists' proclivities for linguistic inquiry. This book acknowledges these obstacles in researching the Talmud in its Iranian context and, in light of them, advances pragmatic historical and philological approaches that promote mutual fruition between Iranian and Talmudic studies, two historically distinct disciplines.[6]

TALMUDIC PORTRAYALS OF PERSIANS, SASANIAN KINGS, AND ZOROASTRIAN PRIESTS

This book analyzes the Babylonian Talmud's portrayals of three categories of Persian others—namely, the Persians, the Sasanian kings, and the Zoroastrian priests.

Although some of these texts are short and anecdotal, many of them are sustained legal commentaries or narratives on a wide scope of topics, offering insight into rabbinic attitudes toward Persians and how the Jewish sages defined their group identity vis-à-vis the Persian world. Comparative insights notwithstanding, these dozens of Bavli texts on their superficial level tell us something meaningful about the rabbis' attitudes toward Persians.[7] Palestinian Midrashim and the Jerusalem Talmud also contain numerous traditions about Persians, some of which lay the foundation for later Babylonian adaptations, though as we shall see it is more frequently the case that the Bavli's passages about the Persians are products of Babylonia.

This book's focus on the images of Persians as others is a familiar strategy in rabbinics. Numerous scholars have utilized questions of otherness as a fruitful interpretive framework in which to investigate the formation of rabbinic identity. Previous studies have zeroed in on all types of internal and external others, such as non-rabbinic Jews and heretics, or Egyptian pharaohs and Ishmael.[8] Drawing from anthropology and critical theory, these studies illuminate how the rabbis invoke others in an us/them dialectic in order to construct the boundaries of their group identity in a world replete with non-Jews. This book adds to this established line of inquiry by tailoring past models of research on rabbis and others in Greco-Roman and Christian contexts to the evidentiary and historical idiosyncrasies of the Talmud's Sasanian context.

THE COMPARATIVE METHOD

One question that this book addresses is how scholars should compare the Talmud with other sources from Sasanian Persia, including imperial inscriptions and seals, Middle Persian Zoroastrian literature, and the Jewish Aramaic bowl spells. Although in this book I do not wish to reject outright the value of constructing terminological parallels between primary texts of different communities, I believe that such methods of comparison should not form the basis of historical arguments regarding interactions between Jews and Persians. Instead, comparativists should focus their research on the diversity itself—that is to say, how the peoples and religions in Mesopotamia (such as the rabbis, non-rabbinic Jews, Persian Zoroastrians, and others) interfaced with one another structurally in social or institutional contexts.[9] This book focuses on the social settings of courts of law and popular magic. One of the benefits of comparing the Bavli with non-Talmudic sources as external, second-order evidence is that to do so allows scholars to problematize the rabbis' internal claims to legal authority and literary representations of their past and present.[10] In other words, by probing Sasanian history deeply, scholars can begin to interpret Talmudic or other texts as internal expressions of a given group's culture and power relations with others within societal and institutional systems. The rabbis' portrayals of Persia are, therefore, politics of representation aimed at bolstering their social power. Accordingly, the comparative study of Talmudic Judaism and Zoroastrianism is effective when it revolves around queries of institutions, identity, or authority, with an emphasis on the sociohistorical complexities regarding interactions,[11] while simultaneously undertaking the source-critical work that is required to unravel the literary features of texts.

THE PROGRAM OF THIS BOOK

Chapters 1 and 2 in this book explain why and how comparativists can study the Talmud in its Sasanian context. In chapter 1, I justify contextual research as a necessary counterbalance to source-critical, literary, and exegetical approaches toward Talmudic texts. When up-to-date methods are applied, contextual research on the Bavli can avoid many of the past flaws associated with Talmudic history, or the reconstruction of the supposed true tale or historical kernel behind rabbinic texts. The first chapter concludes with a discussion of the ramifications for Talmudists of the widely acknowledged fact that late antique Persia was teeming with diverse elite, sectarian, and popular social groups whose identities cut across linguistic, political, and religious axes. In chapter 2, I draw from the fields of comparative religion and ancient Iranian studies to offer an overview of the sources of this study and the prospects and pitfalls of comparing Talmudic and Middle Persian primary sources.

Chapter 3 of this book is a survey of rabbinic literature's portrayals of Persians, an ethnic and imperial appellation. The Talmud describes the Persians in all types of contexts, including sex, cuisine, law, magic, and festivals. These passages are sprinkled throughout the various tractates in the Talmud on a redactional level. In general, the rabbis depict Persians as others in order to clarify rabbinic self-definition and claims to authority in relation to the imperial world. After analyzing the sources, I take an intermediary position in the debate, dating from Jacob Neusner's skepticism in the 1960s to Yaakov Elman's current optimism, over how much Persian culture existed in Jewish Babylonia. Chapter 3 also considers the value of Iranian loanwords in researching the impact of Iranian culture on the Jews of Babylonia.

Chapter 4 of this book contextualizes the Talmud's portrayals of the Sasanian kings Shapur I, Shapur II, and Yazdegird I in light of discourses about authority and empire among Jews and Persians in late antiquity. This chapter argues that the Sasanian kings became symbols of authority, a reputation that is paralleled in Middle Persian historiographical and propagandistic traditions. The chapter also pays close attention to the pseudo-dialogues found in the Talmud between the Babylonian rabbis and Persian kings.

Chapter 5 explains the philological background to the Talmud's two titles for Zoroastrian priests (*amgûšā* and *ḥabarei*) and compares the roles of the rabbis in

Jewish society to those of the Zoroastrian priests (especially *mowbeds* and *hērbeds*) in Persian society. Among other topics, this chapter is concerned with the context of the judiciary and the Sasanians' policies toward non-Zoroastrians and non-Persians. The chapter analyzes in detail several important Talmudic texts that illustrate the ties between the Jewish and Sasanian courts, including *b. Sanh.* 4b–5a, which delineates the legal authority of the public expert; *b. Ber.* 58a, where R. Shila receives authority from the Persians to execute the guilty; and *b. Sanh.* 98a, where Rav Pappa decries the Persian priests in comparison with Jewish judges.

Chapter 6 of this book continues the inquiry into the Talmud's portrayals of the Zoroastrian priests, but from a different angle. This final chapter delves into the complicated social and cultural ties between the Babylonian rabbis and Jewish sorcerers who produced the Aramaic magical bowls in late Sasanian Mesopotamia. Magic was a context wherein social and epistemic competition and exchange between Jews, Christians, Zoroastrians, and Mandaeans were frequent. By comparing the Bavli and the bowls, scholars can cultivate polythetic definitions of Babylonian Judaism that bring to light alternative Jewish identities external to the rabbis.

1

The Sources and Methods of Talmudic and Iranian Studies

This book engages the complex interface between texts and contexts, a longstanding problem in the field of rabbinics. When scholars research ancient corpora such as the Talmud, the word "context" denotes a wide range of possible meanings. For instance, rabbinic literature is fruitfully analyzed, often simultaneously, within interrelated literary, cultural, and sociohistorical contexts.[1] Indeed, academic debates in rabbinics are constantly reinvigorated by the inherent tensions and interdependencies that exist between rabbinic texts and contexts, with scholarly methods falling along a spectrum according to which type of context a given researcher emphasizes.[2] On this spectrum of approaches, this book on rabbinic culture in Sasanian Iran intentionally foregrounds the ties between Talmudic texts and Sasanian sociohistorical contexts.

In Talmudic studies, there exists a mutual interdependency between source-critical and historical approaches toward the Bavli. As Richard Kalmin and Geoffrey Herman have illustrated in recent books, the continued advancements in Talmudic textual criticism and historical methodologies necessitate a rewriting of the Babylonian Jewish history done by earlier generations of scholars.[3] Improvements in source-critical methods offer social and cultural historians of Babylonian Jewry requisite insights into the texts on which they base conclusions. More specifically, source-critical approaches toward the Talmud, including Stammaitic theory,[4] help to delineate a given sugya's hermeneutical logic, provenance, and more accurate dating of Tannaitic, Amoraic, and anonymous strata. For historians, the viability of chronological inquiry depends upon this ability to distinguish between datable dicta and geographical origins.[5] Literary scholarship, in other words, renders historical analysis possible. Yet despite the clear value of text-based approaches for historians, Talmudists who utilize source-critical methodologies disagree on core questions regarding the formation of the Bavli,[6] such as: What is the role of the redactors in a given sugya? Should Amoraic or Tannaitic sayings be dated according to the rabbis to whom they are attributed,[7] or did the editors rework them too thoroughly? And finally, is it the case that anonymous materials are always the products of the later Stammaim or Saboraim?

In engaging these questions, many Talmudists in the past several decades have subscribed to the general theory that through source-criticism one can deconstruct a sugya into Amoraic dicta versus the work of later anonymous editors who created dialectical argumentation based upon the earlier traditions.[8] This theory is perhaps best exemplified by the works of the Talmudists Shamma Friedman and David Weiss Halivni.[9] For his part, Halivni argues that one can recover Amoraic traditions through careful readings of the texts. Over the course of his career, Halivni has revised his dating of the rabbinic movement, recently placing the Amoraic period circa 200–550 C.E. (marked by a century of decline between 450 and 550 C.E.) and Stammaitic-Saboraic activity circa 550–750 C.E.[10] In this chronology, the final redaction of the Talmud thus straddles the late Sasanian and early Islamic periods. As Halivni's own modifications to the dating of the Talmud show,[11] scholars continue to debate the possibilities and ramifications of the separation of memrot from anonymous editorial traditions, a discussion with far-reaching implications for our ability to periodize Talmudic history. For example, taking a radically different position than Halivni on this issue, Yaacov Sussmann contends that the later producers of the Talmud played such a dominant role in how Amoraic materials are presented that the original statements of the Amoraim are transformed beyond recovery. As Adiel Schremer remarks in an important article on the utility of Stammaitic theory for writing history, for Sussmann "separation is impossible."[12] To quote Sussmann in his own words, the author explains that the Geonim and Saboraim altered the structure and meaning of Amoraic statements:[13]

> The Talmud of the early Amoraim . . . continued to be discussed by many generations of Savoraim and Geonim, who added new insights about the statements of their predecessors. During the long period of free and open oral transmission, not only were the structure and explanation of the sugyot reworked and frequently changed, but the new understanding necessarily affected the formulation of the sayings themselves. And just as it is not always possible to distinguish between early and late, between *svara* and "later addition," so too the lines between the structure of the sugya and the body of a dictum, between the interpretation of a saying and its very wording, become increasingly blurry.

From this perspective, the recovery of genuine Amoraic statements is problematic. The notion that historians, using literary techniques, can recover Amoraic traditions therefore does not go unchallenged.

More recent scholarship has begun to call into question some of the basic premises upon which Stammaitic theory are based. In a 2014 monograph entitled *Tradition and the Formation of the Talmud*, Moulie Vidas proposes that the layered structure of the Talmud does not represent a chronological phenomenon but is rather a "literary gap." Vidas calls into question the notion that the anonymous editorial traditions were later additions that were "woven around" earlier apodictic statements.[14] On this topic, Vidas concludes as follows:[15]

> Our ability to separate the words of the Talmud's creators from the traditions they quote depends on the omnipresent literary distinction in the Bavli between the anonymous literary framework and the attributed traditions embedded in it. Most scholars today believe this distinction reflects the Talmud's literary history: the dicta were produced first and the *stam* was woven around them by later scholars.
>
> This chapter explores the possibility that this distinction is constructed, that it is a strategy pursued by the Talmud's creators. The distance between the dicta and the *stam*, I argue, is not simply a reflection of their different provenances. Rather, it may also be the outcome of a particular pattern of organization and technique of differentiation that was maintained throughout the Talmud and even imposed on materials in which it did not exist. We will see in this chapter how the Bavli takes Palestinian texts and divides them into layers, assigning dynamic, narrative, and deliberative material to the anonymous layer and static and apodictic material to the dicta. . . . The gap between the two layers is not the mark of a historical gap that the Talmud's creators tried to overcome, but a literary gap that these scholars produced.

Unlike Halivni and Friedman, who presume that the layers of the Bavli were natural products of the centuries that passed between earlier sources and later exegeses, Vidas argues that the layers are an intentional literary design that was not simply the product of transmission. This revisionist theory unsettles current judgments regarding the dating of Talmudic texts and, by consequence, our ability to use them historically. The seeming chronological gaps between strata may not be solid foundations upon which scholars should construct historical claims.

In sum, this brief survey of the complicated issue of the implications of Stammaitic theory on the study of history demonstrates how the wide range of scholarly opinions regarding the separation of Amoraic apodictic statements from anonymous editorial traditions reflects poorly on the feasibility of dating texts to precise epochs. With little consensus on these matters, historians are left to contemplate whether a major part of their procedure—namely, the alignment of rabbinic traditions, attitudes, and trends with external historical happenings—is even feasible.[16] In the face of such difficulties, however, it is nonetheless important to bear in mind that temporal or chronological considerations of textual data are but one aspect of historical research, which can instead address questions of cultural or religious development over long periods of time.

In addition to the ubiquitous use of textual approaches toward Halakhah, literary approaches have also been prioritized in the study of Aggadah. For example, both Shamma Friedman and Jonah Fraenkel have in their own ways asserted that the quest for the literary kernel must precede historical analysis.[17] According to this viewpoint, it is not until source-critical questions are resolved that one can use the Talmud for historical purposes, since these types of data are foundational to the task of the historian, who is reliant upon the literary evidence. Fraenkel argued that because rabbinic stories are highly crafted works of literature that were produced separately from the influences of the outside world, a scholar's literary analysis should precede historical interpretation. Fraenkel explains that "the historian of the Talmudic Era cannot begin to use aggadic stories until the literary critic has completed the literary analysis . . . (but) historians are not willing to commit to this procedure."[18] Utilizing literary theory and philology, Fraenkel focuses his attention on the literary features of rabbinic stories, such as parallelism, plot, and narration.[19] Fraenkel was not compelled to connect rabbinic stories to historical events or specific provenances, and accordingly he underestimated the function of society in the construction of traditions.[20]

There are well-founded reasons why many Talmudists today utilize internal, literary, and exegetical approaches of scholarship. As is well known, the Talmud is first and foremost an exegetical commentary on the Mishnah, produced by rabbis for rabbis. Technical in style, Talmudic law demonstrates a more explicit concern with Jewish traditions than with the gentile world. Its exegetical function lends itself to textual study, inviting its readers to participate in its hermeneutical processes. The fact that the rabbis appear uninterested in the non-Jewish world contributes to the ostensible insularity of the Talmud, raising the specter that Talmudists studying Persian influences on rabbinic culture may care more about such influences than the ancient Jewish sages themselves did. This difficulty of reading the Talmud in its Persian context has undermined our attempts for historical analysis, instead appealing to internal approaches.

TALMUDIC HISTORY AND THE QUEST FOR THE TRUE TALE

Acting as a counterbalance to Talmudists' source-critical orientation, historians of Babylonian Jewry dating back decades have contextualized the rabbis from a variety of perspectives, some more successfully than others.[21] More specifically, social or institutional histories of Babylonian Jewry are attested, albeit rarely.[22] Jewish historians of late antiquity agree that rabbinic sources are challenging to use as documents of social history for Babylonian Jewry,[23] though there have been advances in this area of inquiry. For example, the current research agendas of Kalmin and Herman explore aspects of Babylonian Jewish society using well-balanced historical and literary models that avoid the reductionist and positivistic pitfalls found in the previous generations of historians,[24] including those from the *Wissenschaft des Judentums* school of thought, as well as Jacob Neusner's multivolume work on Babylonian Jewry from nearly half a century ago.[25] These prior shortfalls in the study of Babylonian Jewish history have been described by the author of the best synthetic history of Jewish Babylonia,[26] Isaiah Gafni, who, trained in the *Wissenschaft des Judentums* tradition, laments the flaws of the earlier generations' quest for the purportedly true tale:[27]

> As a disciple of teachers trained in the classical historical-philological methodology established by the luminaries of *Wissenschaft des Judentums*, I was weaned on the assumption that the "true tale" (give or take some obvious legendary embellishments) can be uncovered once the text has undergone critical scrutiny. This would entail a careful analysis of the relevant talmudic manuscripts and parallel traditions, language, comparisons with external information of both a literary and physical nature, and the proper insertion of each case into a known historical context. Thus, by establishing something considered fairly close to the original, "authentic," text, we are that much closer to the "things" that these texts describe.

According to this school of thought, the unraveling of the true tale assumes a dependency on the literary elements of a tale whose historicity stems from our recovery, through source-criticism, of its authentic or original versions: that is, if we can recover the tale's transmission and geographical origins, then history somehow becomes more discernible. At core, this type of scholarly hermeneutic presumes that the rabbis were reacting to the happenings around them through exegesis or narrative. In a similar vein, the writings of Joseph Heinemann, such as his book *Aggadah and Its Development* (1974) and other works, argue that the rabbis produced what Heinemann calls "creative exegesis" in response to the events of their time.[28] He writes that "the Aggadah represents a creative reaction to the upheavals suffered by Israel" and that the rabbis try "to develop new methods of exegesis designed to yield new understandings of Scripture for a time of crisis and a period of conflict, with foreign cultural influence pressing from without and sectarian agitation from within."[29] Although Heinemann's lachrymose vision of Jewish history draws too simple a causal connection between texts and history, the notion that rabbinic stories and laws are in some ways responses to historical events as the rabbis experienced them is a reasonable perspective to the extent that such texts are ideologically situated within a general time and space—that is to say, even though Talmudic texts are of limited use for writing history, scholarly attention paid to broader historical contexts can nevertheless help to elucidate those texts' attitudes and cultural contents. It is well known that the rabbis' view of history was not rooted in a desire to understand "what really happened,"[30] a feature of rabbinic thought that leaves historically minded scholars frustrated by the seemingly impossible task of reconstruction. In building upon these past points of view, in this monograph I wish to redefine and revamp the study of Talmudic history[31] by moving away from an interpretive model whose aim is to try to recover the historicity of evasive rabbinic texts to one that avails itself of non-Talmudic sources and secondary literature that offer a wider frame of reference for understanding rabbinic culture.[32] The most productive route out of the pitfalls of historical reductionism, the limits of source-criticism, and the search for the true tale is to open up Talmudic studies to Sasanian studies. Above all else, studies of Talmudic culture and history require contextualization and comparison.

EXEGETICAL APPROACHES TOWARD TALMUDIC TEXTS

One influential book in Talmudic studies that emphasizes internal perspectives toward the development of Halakhah is Christine Hayes's *Between the Babylonian and Palestinian Talmuds* (1997). In this erudite work which examines legal differences between tractate *'Abodah Zarah* in the two Talmuds, Hayes argues that the rabbis' hermeneutical mind-set dominated the production of rabbinic laws. Like the positions of Friedman and Fraenkel with respect to Aggadah, Hayes's method foregrounds the exegetical features of halakhic texts prior to any attempt at historical analysis. For researchers holding this sort of viewpoint, which is particularly prevalent in the Israeli academy today, scientific critical editions of primary texts are the necessary first step and foundation of research. With respect to the development of Halakhah in *'Abodah Zarah,* Hayes maintains that a scholar should grapple with "the canons of interpretation and legal argumentation that have produced" a passage before attempting to interpret its historical or cultural significance.[33] In a relevant passage, reproduced here at length, Hayes summarizes her position on the internal-external divide in Talmudic studies:[34]

> Reductive historical analyses fail to recognize that in the rabbinic world of late antiquity the reading and interpretation of sacred or authoritative texts were real and powerful forces in the construction of culture, and in the generation of halakhic developments—as real and powerful as famines and wars. Rabbinic texts are, certainly formally speaking, fundamentally exegetical. The two Talmuds are more or less a literature of interpretation, development, and analysis of Mishnah. Thus, unless we understand rabbinic reading practices and canons of interpretation, unless we appreciate the degree to which and the specific way in which rabbinic literature is generated and shaped by the reading of other texts, we run the risk of subjecting this literature to reductive historical analysis. Historical forces and events, socioeconomic pressures, and so on may be hypothesized in an effort to account for phenomena that may in fact be partly or fully explained as a response to exegetical stimuli. At the same time, however, one must guard against a kind of exegetical reductionism

> that would parody rabbinic texts as the dry and pedantic production of a scholastic elite cut off from (or simply ignoring) the realities of everyday life.

In this passage, Hayes argues that for the rabbis of late antiquity the exegesis of authoritative texts was a historical act in and of itself. Rabbinic interpretive practices were key inspirations in the production of law and culture. The author continues her discussion by insisting that scholars should investigate the exegetical features of halakhic development before turning to historical interpretations, and by warning against "the dual dangers of reductive historical and exegetical analyses":[35]

> In sum, any study of talmudic literature, any reading of rabbinic readings, must do justice to the complex exegetical and historical forces that interact in the formation of rabbinic culture of late antiquity—or in that piece of rabbinic culture available to us: the texts in question. In this work, I endeavor to avoid the dual dangers of reductive historical and exegetical analyses. I argue that before we approach a passage of Talmud as cultural or religious historians, we must first understand the canons of interpretation and legal argumentation that have produced the passage before us. Subsequent historical and cultural analysis, if any, will be the more reliable for this approach. Why more reliable? Only with a proper understanding of talmudic strategies of interpretation, argumentation, and rhetoric is one equipped to recognize precisely those places in which these strategies are violated, to spot interpretations of a mishnah or early tradition that diverge from interpretive norms, to sense when a rabbinic reading is a reading against the grain. And it is precisely where the exegetical element is muted or compromised or deformed that the text may be susceptible to analysis in cultural-historical terms.

For Hayes, the quality of historical analysis increases once a scholar parses the exegetical contents of a particular sugya. In the last line of this passage, Hayes claims that it is only after Talmudists determine that the "exegetical element" of a text is "muted" or "deformed"—that is, that it does not follow rabbinic rules of logic or interprets an earlier tradition "against the grain"—that we can then perform cultural or historical analysis. In this outlook, historical analysis of Talmudic law comes into play when scholars who possess "a proper understanding of talmudic strategies of interpretation, argumentation, and rhetoric" are able to determine when Talmudic laws "diverge from interpretive norms." It is, in other words, in cases when exegetical normalcy is violated that culture becomes reified and open to academic interpretation. For proponents of this exegesis-first persuasion, history and culture are secondary stages of scholarly evaluation.

Although prioritizing hermeneutics, Hayes does not ignore the potential of historical analysis, acknowledging on multiple occasions that everyday life plays a role in the evolution of Talmudic law. The author cites as an example the sale of weapons to non-Jews, as seen in *b. ʿAbod. Zar.* 15b–16a, where Rav Ashi states that

Jews may sell weapons "to the Persians who protect us."[36] Using this and other cases as specimens, Hayes clarifies that she is "not suggesting that the rabbis were hermetically sealed off from events around them."[37] As we saw in the passage cited above, Hayes prudently warns against exegetical reductionism just as she critiques the reductive historical studies of Louis Ginzberg and Gedalyahu Alon.[38] In the book's chapters on extratextual influences on Halakhah, Hayes does not proffer a road map for how scholars can introduce nonreductionist historical methods to avoid the danger of exegetical reductionism, leaving such a project to others. In a sense, the field of Irano-Talmudica fills this need by emphasizing historical context as much as Hayes does hermeneutics, and thus it offers an important supplement needed to counterbalance exegetical studies.

In addition to Hayes's important book, the research of David Weiss Halivni is also germane to a discussion of the relationship between source-critical and historical approaches toward the Talmud. Halivni's decades of research on the anonymous editorial strata and his multivolume commentary on individual tractates revolutionized Talmudic research. Halivni's work reconstructs ur-texts using textual source-criticism, with attention paid to manuscript variants, synoptic parallels, and redactional features. A major concept in Halivni's work is the forced explanation: that is, instances when the Talmud interprets earlier traditions in ways that do not follow their simple sense.[39] Jeffrey Rubenstein describes forced explanations as cases in which "the flow of the Talmudic discourse often does not read smoothly, exhibiting gaps and incongruities between questions and their answers or comments and their referents such that the sequence of statements must be read in a 'forced' way in order to be understood."[40] According to Halivni, these gaps and incongruities are the natural result of centuries of oral transmission, among other factors. Halivni's approach implies that there existed an original Talmud composed of what he calls sources, or rabbinic utterances in their original form, and traditions, which were transformed versions of those sayings that were altered in the course of transmission and that later tradents interpreted. His research aims to recover these original sources from our corrupted traditions. From this point of view, distortions in Talmudic logic and strained resolutions are problems that modern scholars explain through recourse to other rabbinic traditions and knowledge of rabbinic hermeneutics.

In one of his writings, Halivni lays out the five stages of analyzing a sugya.[41] The first stage is to read the text alongside Rashi and the medieval commentaries. The second through fourth stages involve determining whether a passage is a case of a forced explanation; if it is not, then there is no problem; but if it is, then several additional steps are needed, including scrutinizing intertextual parallels in the rabbinic corpus. In the final stage of analysis, Halivni mentions the role of historical factors in his methodology which has as its overarching goal the explication of rabbinic hermeneutics:[42]

> Fifth stage: If we find that the text is correct and yet the Bavli's explanation seems forced, then we must assess the reasoning that led the interpreter to offer the explanation in case the cause resulted from historical factors or from the lack of the requisite information.

For Halivni, history is employed in the service of exegesis: a scholar should turn to historical factors in order to explain the exegetes' logic that led to a forced explanation. History is, in other words, utilized in cases of, and in order to resolve, hermeneutical problems and disjunctions. In his autobiography, Halivni says that his emphasis on internal methods is motivated by a dissatisfaction with the lack of attention that rabbinists studying the Greco-Roman context of Palestinian texts pay to the textual features of the Talmud (or what he calls "text-immanent studies"), with Saul Lieberman being an exception; research that elucidates the unidirectional influences of external Greek, Roman, or Arabic cultures on Jewish civilization "induces a sense of inferiority," he writes.[43] Halivni's research agenda is therefore in part intended to offset what he deems to be the failure of past studies of rabbinic texts within Greco-Roman contexts. The highly influential author's disaffection with contextual models, however warranted, has moved the field away from the consideration of the Iranian context.

UR-TEXTS, TALMUDIC COMMENTARIES, AND THE PROBLEMS OF WRITING HISTORY

Internally oriented and source-critical approaches toward Talmudic texts presuppose an ideal structure of recoverable ur-texts that were altered or corrupted through oral transmission or the impact of varying historical (gentile) contexts. The presupposition of Talmudic ur-texts is, however, problematic on several fronts and rightly debated.[44] With respect to contextual investigation, Irano-Talmudists should problematize the logic that naturally flows from methods that prioritize source-critical analysis—namely, that in cases when Talmudists show how the Bavli deviates from or creatively expands upon Palestinian rabbinic precedents, including the Mishnah; and Talmudists trained in Iranian studies trace similarities of these idiosyncratic Babylonian elements, construed as otherwise inexplicable deviations in law, in Middle Persian sources; then what we have are Persian influences on the Talmud, presumably through historical contact. But this logic of analysis falls into one of the traps of comparative inquiry by assuming that there exists an authentic form of legal or narrative traditions that digressed or deviated as a result of the beneficial or polluting influence of the cultural horizon outside the rabbinic academies.[45]

The methods of harmonizing traditions or juxtaposing sources were performed by later Talmudic commentators, including the Geonim (7th–11th centuries C.E.),

Rashi (*fl.* 1040–1105 C.E.), the Tosafists (12th–14th centuries C.E.), as well as some medieval and modern Yeshivot.[46] In general, a distinguishing feature between the Tosafistic and academic perspectives is that the former is conceptual and presumes ideal structures, whereas the latter is literary and historical. Similarly, for traditional Yeshivot the study of history is a minor concern. On this point, Michael Rosensweig clarifies the differences between the study of Talmud in universities versus in Yeshivot:[47]

> The primary goal of academic investigation is to deconstruct the various historical and geographic layers of the talmudic text and to examine the potential role of the historical context. In sharp contrast, traditional *yeshivah* learning is concentrated on the continuing relevance of the substantive topics developed in the Talmud. It evinces little interest in historical issues and regards the different layers of the Talmud as ongoing debate within the integrated whole.

The academic study of the Talmud is thus defined by its dual goals of literary and historical reconstruction. Nevertheless, these divisions between commentarial frames of reference, which carry authority in traditional learning settings, and academic study is not so unambiguous as the quotation above from Rosensweig may suggest. In actuality, as some Talmudists rightly maintain, it is difficult for modern researchers to detach themselves from the outlook that Tosafistic approaches promote.[48] Some Talmudists today favor conceptual or phenomenological methodologies that share an intellectual heritage with medieval and early modern commentators.[49] Talya Fishman, citing Robert Brody and Haym Soloveitchik, sums up the "tosafization" of the Talmud as follows:[50]

> In short, the "tosafization" of Talmud obscured earlier cultural realities. In Brody's words, "We are bound by a very specific perspective of the talmudic material—which springs from our talmudic education and draws upon Rashi and the tosafists in particular. It is difficult for us to free ourselves from this perspective." Or, as Haym Soloveitchik put it, it is difficult to think "in a mode other than Tosafist" when approaching issues of Jewish law.

If turning to the medieval commentaries is, as we saw with Halivni's first stage of reading a sugya, a governing practice in the academic discipline of Talmudic studies, then it is easy to understand why the study of the Talmud in its Sasanian setting has been slower to develop. Indeed, historians of late antique Persian Jewry must contend with the fact that the early medieval European commentators of the Talmud were geographically, chronologically, and culturally far removed from the Persian world in which the Babylonian rabbis flourished. Further cultivating this trend in scholarship away from Iran and toward medieval commentaries is the unique history of the Talmud as a normative guidebook for Jewish behavior up until today. For historians, the notion of the Bavli as a living[51] guidebook to Jewish behavior is at risk of imposing uniqueness onto a document and the historical knowledge that flows from it.[52] As Brody spells out in his definitive history of the Geonim, it is not clear that the Amoraim intended to create the normative canonical work that the Bavli became in subsequent generations. Brody explains the status of the Talmud in the Geonic period as follows:[53]

> We have no way of knowing to what extent, if at all, the "editors" of the Talmud—as distinct from the authors of the legal dicta embedded within it—intended to create a normative legal work rather than an academic or literary corpus. . . . On the face of it, the authors and editors of this Talmud could have hoped at best that their work would be accepted as authoritative within Babylonia and its immediate environs; and even within Babylonia, it is difficult to estimate the degree of influence exercised by the talmudic rabbis over the Jewish populace.
>
> The situation in the Geonic period was fundamentally different. On the one hand, the Talmud was now perceived as a closed corpus. As far as the Geonim were concerned, the Savora'im who preceded them had added whatever finishing touches were needed to the Talmud which they inherited from the Amoraic period. . . . This is not to say that the rule was perfectly observed in practice: a considerable number of glosses crept into the text, as did a modest number of more substantial additions. . . . The ambitions which the Geonim entertained on behalf of the Talmud were probably greater than those of its creators.

As Brody's account makes clear, the status of the Talmud changed from the rabbinic to Geonic eras, a rupture marked by its closing and canonization. Although it is known that the Geonim transmitted and implemented the Bavli, scholars continue to debate to what extent Jews and rabbis practiced Talmudic laws in Sasanian Babylonia. As a point of comparison, the Zoroastrian priests in ninth- and tenth-century Fārs, working around the same time as the Geonim, were similarly managing comparable transitions from orality to textuality,[54] though one difference between the Talmud and the Pahlavi corpus is the fact that the Bavli was closed earlier, whereas the writing down and redaction of the Pahlavi sources took final shape in the ninth and tenth centuries. As a consequence of this lateness, both the Talmud and Pahlavi sources are challenging to use for the writing of Sasanian-era history in that the impression of orthodoxy that they leave is anachronistic and does not necessarily reflect the heterogeneous and heterodox qualities of Sasanian religions. Given all these factors, the early medieval influences on the history of Talmudic scholarship impede an accurate rendering of the sociohistorical environment in late antique Jewish Babylonia. Scholars who wish to research the *Sitz im Leben* of the Babylonian rabbis in late antiquity should avail themselves of the sources and secondary literature available for understanding Sasanian society.

What are the ramifications for historical scholarship when one employs analytical frameworks derived from the Talmud's internal discourses and methods, including medieval commentaries? Even if there is no doubt that as scholars of religion we need to utilize internal and commentarial perspectives in our studies, we must be equally cognizant of the "seductive congruence between analytical and indigenous categories."[55] As the editors of a recent volume on anthropology and history in Jewish studies report, "analytical categories derived from normative Jewish discourse" are "limiting," because "approaches that see Jewish law as the reflection of actual behavior, or even as a set of authoritative ideals, often fail to account for the fact that authority is not an imminent property of canonical texts but rather an emergent effect of the social institutions and practices in which they are embedded."[56] According to this perspective, studies of Talmudic texts that fail to explore Jewish Babylonian society and institutions, and their ties to the Sasanian context, potentially misconstrue our understanding of rabbinic authority. Part of what external sources provide are correctives to academic appropriations of rabbinic self-descriptions that are not always grounded in historical actualities.[57] The use of exclusively exegetical or redactorial methods toward Talmudic texts thus wrongly dissolves the link between Babylonian texts and the social situations of their agents, the rabbis of Sasanian Babylonia.[58] To the detriment of the field, internal methods in Talmudic studies often assume in an unbalanced way that the rabbis' ties to their past and contemporaneous Jewish traditions were the primary catalysts in rabbinic cultural production and that the social presence of non-Jewish others was of secondary influence. Such internal approaches interpret Babylonian rabbinic Judaism according to a sugya's similarities and differences with antecedent Palestinian rabbinic sources and other Jewish cultures rather than according to the rabbis' relationship with the outside world. In doing so, internal approaches toward the Talmud mistakenly yield the logic of historical time and space to the reconstruction of Jewish chains of tradition and, ultimately, intracultural conclusions.[59] Without attention paid to non-Jewish cultural contexts, endogenous modes of textual analysis cannot account for the influence of Babylonian realities on Babylonian rabbinic culture, instead continuously assigning the continuities and discontinuities in Babylonian rabbinic Judaism to rabbinic Judaism itself. Exemplifying this deficiency, the research methods of Fraenkel and Halivni, for instance, do not account for the broader cultural background of Talmudic texts' symbols, concerns, or values.[60] Research on Talmudic culture that does not fully engage non-Jewish contexts brings to light the question whether one is overlooking an essential component in the formation of Talmudic culture without recourse to non-Jewish Sasanian contexts.

Studies of the Talmud that ignore the impact of the gentile world on Babylonian rabbinic culture are also contradicted by the historical evidence emanating from Sasanian Iran. Ancient Iranology documents that Sasanian Mesopotamia, the diasporic exilic homeland for the Jews of ancient Persia, was full of hybrid identities and is thus as ripe for the multicultural turn as other ancient Jewish cultures that scholars have contextualized according to broader landscapes.[61]

INSULAR RABBIS IN A MULTICULTURAL WORLD?

Studies of Talmudic culture that assume rabbinic insularity from the gentile world stand in stark contrast to the picture of Sasanian culture that the field of Iranian studies paints. Ancient Iranists have proven that Sasanian Mesopotamia was composed of a spectrum of intersecting identities that cut across ethnic, linguistic, social, political, and religious lines.[62] Late antique Mesopotamia was a multicultural environment replete with elite, subelite, sectarian, and popular movements, all of which intermingled in various social contexts. This diversity dates back more than a millennium before the early Sasanians came to power and inherited a cultural legacy steeped in Akkadian, Achaemenid, Parthian, and Avestan expressions. The eastern provinces of the Roman Empire also play a central role in understanding the culture and society in Jewish Babylonia, especially beginning in the fourth century C.E., as Richard Kalmin maintains in several publications.[63] Additionally, such political and military events as the large-scale transfer of prisoners to certain regions, as for example those of Shapur I, affected the stratification of populations in Mesopotamia. Indeed, in royal inscriptions the Sasanian monarchy itself praises and promotes the image of the empire as a mixture of citizens.

In the Sasanian era, the fertile region surrounding the Tigris and Euphrates rivers was home to an array of Aramaic-speaking religious groups, including Jews, Mandaeans, and Christians. These groups' writings share linguistic and cultural affinities with one another to such an extent that some scholars have argued that together they may have formed an Aramaic linguistic or cultural koiné. This is especially true in the realm of magic, a topic that I treat in chapter 6 of this book. Each Aramaic group's relationship with the other groups was distinctive, depending on whether they lived as neighbors, shared scriptural writings, spoke dialects of the same language and could perhaps communicate orally, or possessed higher or lower forms of social standing or institutional organization. The Persian Zoroastrian elements in Mesopotamia, particularly near the Sasanian capital of Ctesiphon, were equally complex: in spite of the fact that there was a strong imperial presence in the area, there was neither a large Zoroastrian population nor a major fire temple located there.[64] The Zoroastrian kings and administrative priesthood, ruling from a region inhabited by numerous Aramaic-speaking non-Zoroastrians, were uniquely situated parties in the mélange of social and religious groups. It is, as a result, Persian imperial culture that impacts the rabbis more than it is the Zoroastrian religion.

The major centers of rabbinic activity were located near the administrative center of the Persian Empire. The region of Āsōristān (Aram. *bēt aramāyē*), a province considered the heart of the empire, had borders proportional to Babylonia.[65] As the material and literary sources bear out, the population of this area was largely Semitic, with an Iranian administrative class.[66] Seals of Zoroastrian priests and other titles exist for Weh-Ardashir, demonstrating the Persian governmental presence near the Jewish sages.[67] As Geoffrey Herman has concluded, "the administrative divisions of the Sasanian Empire impacted upon the inner-Jewish territorial hierarchy just as this seems to have occurred with the Christians."[68] The rabbinic academies in Pumbedita and Nehardea were located approximately fifty kilometers[69] west of the urban center of the Sasanians' winter capital, Ctesiphon, where the founder of the dynasty, Ardashir, constructed a palace in the early third century.[70] Over the course of late antiquity the Sasanians expanded the area of Ctesiphon, leading to the development of various cities and suburbs around the Tigris River.[71] The river separated Weh-Ardashir and Maḥoza, on its western side, from Ctesiphon, which was to its east. Numerous scholars have demonstrated the significance of the proximity to Ctesiphon of Maḥoza, which had large Jewish and Christian populations.[72] As Yaakov Elman has emphasized in numerous publications, Maḥoza was home to Rav Naḥman and Rava, two rabbis acculturated to Persian norms who were impacted by the culture of the Persian urban elite.[73] The city, with its many proselytes according to *b. Qidd.* 73a, was also a central locale for the exilarch.[74] These broad geographic and ethnic boundaries demonstrate the rationale behind researching further the rabbis in a Sasanian context.

THE LOGIC OF STUDYING THE TALMUD IN ITS SASANIAN CONTEXT

In this chapter I have demonstrated the multiple ways in which Talmudic studies would benefit by adopting ancient Iranology as an analytic category of comparison. Research on the Talmud in its Sasanian context acts as a needed counterbalance to the field's predilection for source-critical and exegetical approaches. It is, in fact, the very sophistication of Talmudic studies' collective inquiries on the literary aspects of Talmudic texts—especially when considered in relation to scholarship on Syriac, Middle Persian, or Mandaic literature—that I believe warrants and legitimizes an opening up of the field to questions regarding the impact of the Sasanian context on rabbinic culture. In order to do comparative work, however, our historical methods need to become as refined as our literary ones. Pushing back against the isolationist nature of our sources, one essential contribution that comparative work makes toward understanding social history is that it deemphasizes the normative claims in religious traditions and unlocks new pathways to reconstructing institutions and social structures of one group in light of another. Rabbinic culture and society are in some ways inherently comparative. In sum, it is through contextualization that historians of Babylonian Jewry can eschew the flaws of Talmudic history's quest for the true tale or historical kernel of ahistorical texts and contribute to a healthier distribution between hermeneutics and history.

Although this book highlights the Persian and Zoroastrian contexts of the Talmud, its goal can be similarly applied to Sasanian Mesopotamia's other religious traditions, especially Syriac Christianity,[75] Manichaeism, Mandaeism, popular magic, and early Islam. It is only once all these sources and contexts are exploited simultaneously that the field of Talmudic studies can arrive at a better understanding of the Talmud in its Sasanian context. Some of these interfaces are certainly more constructive than others, and each of them poses unique methodological challenges. This book's study of Persian culture is in the end but one fruitful avenue of contextualizing the Talmud in its Sasanian setting, albeit an important one given the Persians' imperial standing.

2

Comparing Sasanian Religions

In chapter 1 of this book, I laid out the rationale for why scholars of Babylonian Judaism should aim to contextualize the Talmud in its Sasanian context by adopting ancient Iranology as an additional lens of study. If this is indeed a sound proposition, then a question that naturally arises is how one goes about contextualizing the Talmud in Sasanian Iran using balanced methodologies that avoid the common pitfalls of comparative inquiry. Although a majority of Talmudists would agree in principle that there exists a relationship between Talmudic texts and the Persian world, they continue to debate the appropriate scope and methods of tracing it. As decades of scholarship demonstrate, comparative research is a necessary methodological framework through which scholars make sense of ancient materials, albeit one fraught with challenges. In this chapter, I draw from the discipline of comparative religion in order to map out the major prospects and pitfalls of juxtaposing the Talmudic and Middle Persian corpora.

The best comparative approaches toward Talmudic and Middle Persian literatures—as well as toward the rabbis, Persian priests, and other groups who authored them—are those that seek a nuanced application of sameness and difference between them. Attention paid to differences, as articulated in postmodern thought, is of central importance in the comparison of Sasanian religions.[1] In an influential book on comparative religions, Jonathan Z. Smith expresses the necessity for comparativists to point to the differences between two religions rather than the drawing up of simple similarities: "What is required is the development of a discourse of 'difference', a complex term which invites negotiation, classification and comparison, and, at the same time, avoids too easy a discourse of the 'same.'"[2] With Smith's arguments in mind, in what follows I would like to outline the differences between the Talmud and the Middle Persian corpus before proceeding to locate specific areas where comparative inquiry can be productive.

One problem that comparativists in this field face is the interpretive question of how one uses textual comparisons as evidence of intercultural influences between Jews and Persians. From the outset, the analytical categories "intercultural" and "influence" are not straightforward and require scrutiny.[3] Scholars of the Iranian context of the Talmud should try to neutralize the goal of discovering intercultural influences via primary textual comparisons by self-consciously employing academic skepticism that considers seriously the differences between the elements of comparison. This need for scholarly circumspection is especially heightened in the case of Talmudic and Middle Persian texts, since neither corpus necessarily lends itself to analysis of intercultural relations; instead, these corpora express exclusivist ideologies that downplay the presence of other cultures by ignoring, generalizing, or denigrating them in what Albert de Jong calls "a rhetoric of insularity." The author explains one of the main challenges in the study of Sasanian religions:[4]

> This leads to some of the most crucial problems in the writing of the religious history of the Sasanian empire. Zoroastrian, Jewish, Christian, and Mandaean texts all reflect what one could call a "rhetoric of insularity." This means that they present a vision of their own community as being self-contained and autonomous.

Internally oriented texts are challenging to use for researching interculturality. The way that I deal with this interpretive problem of the insularity of Talmudic texts is not by placing them in dialogue with Middle Persian texts, as Shai Secunda advocates in his book *The Iranian Talmud: Reading the Bavli in Its Sasanian Context*,[5] but rather by explaining why and how they are insular in a noninsular cultural and social environment. To be sure, this common form of late antique writing—of obfuscating others—creates quandaries of interpretation for modern researchers of group interactions in Sasanian Iran, for if the Talmud and Middle Persian texts themselves limit their explicit engagement with other cultures, how then do we today justify tracing interculturality through the comparison of primary texts?[6]

Scholars who compare Talmudic and Middle Persian sources bear the burden of proof in demonstrating which excavated literary affinities or shared legal concerns serve as corroborated evidence of the impact of Persian civilization on rabbinic Judaism, as opposed to which are merely phenomenological similarities between two ancient religions in contact. How, in other words, do we avoid misinterpreting universal congruities as historical interculturalism? In my opinion, the comparative study of Judaism and Zoroastrianism in late antiquity needs to counterbalance the trap of textual parallelomania,[7] encouraging a nuanced understanding of rabbinic and Sasanian history and society. It is, in other words, through historical insights that comparativists can differentiate between universal congruities and intercultural activity. And herein lies the real interpretive obstacle for the study of the Talmud in its Iranian context: for comparative research to demonstrate that similarities between the Bavli and Middle Persian texts are the result of centuries of interaction between Jews and Persians requires a sophisticated engagement with history and society; and yet it is exactly this type of engagement that is hindered by the internal, ahistorical nature of the literary sources upon which our reconstructions of history and society depend. No doubt, writing social history on the basis of literary sources is difficult, a situation exacerbated by the complex dialectic between comparative methods and historical knowledge. Such circularity makes the study of the Talmud in its Iranian context a frustrating field.

Although the late antique East is ripe for comparative inquiry, there are flaws in methods of analysis that thrive on the juxtaposition of literary sources from diverse communities. Given these limitations, scholars invoking literary parallels need to address on a text-by-text basis what constitutes a suitable parallel and why it does so. Scholars should continue to debate the value of any given textual comparison, and it is counterproductive to try to assign a single standard. In carving out areas of consensus, scholars who research Sasanian religions can avert some of the common methodological fallacies in comparative work by drawing from the decades of pertinent research on comparative religions. Where does the study of the Talmud in its Sasanian context fall on the spectrum in the field of comparative religion?

COMPARISONS AND COMPARATIVISTS IN THE STUDY OF SASANIAN RELIGIONS

The field of comparative religion frequently debates the question of to what extent a scholar does and should play a role in the comparison of two religious traditions. On one end of the spectrum, comparativists who deploy approaches in the mold of Mircea Eliade argue that scholars can compare patterns and concepts about the sacred across time and space in order to gain insight into a reified essence of religious phenomena. Since its inception, the discipline of the history of religions has been flooded with phenomenological and morphological studies comparing the world's religions, which need not have been in historical contact with one another for the comparison of their sacred structures to be of value. By downplaying history, or at least reducing it to a simplistic notion of time and space, morphological and transhistorical hermeneutics compare "variations on structures—like cosmogonic myths—in order to amplify the meaning of the structure."[8] For Eliade specifically, the scholarly quest for reconstructing the universal elements of religions using "creative hermeneutics" qua spiritual technique also had humanistic motivations.[9]

Critics of this form of scholarship justifiably argue that transhistorical approaches toward comparative religion are problematic on several fronts. For instance, critics have rightly faulted such methods for not championing a sophisticated notion of history.[10] In a book entitled *The Ideology of Religious Studies,* Timothy Fitzgerald has critiqued the field of religious studies, especially its phenomenological heritage, as a form of theology in how it reifies religion as a sui generis concept.[11] In the history of comparative religion, phenomenological inquiry has often focused upon the similarities between two religions and has been an easy target of criticism for historically minded scholars who instead prefer to spotlight differences. As noted by David Gordon White, there is a general division in religious studies between two sorts of comparisons—one oriented toward universalism and sameness, exemplified by the phenomenological heritage of Eliade, and the other toward history and difference.[12]

Scholars of Sasanian religions face a unique set of circumstances regarding the role of sociohistorical contexts in comparative inquiry. In the case of Sasanian Mesopotamia, comparativists are able to research religious groups that were undoubtedly in social and historical contact with one another. This is, in fact, one of the basic premises in accordance with which the study of the Talmud in its Sasanian context is a worthwhile course of research. Comparative studies of Talmudic Judaism, Zoroastrianism, and Syriac Christianity need not be criticized for Eliadean antihistoricism, since scholars agree that these groups resided in the same time and place. The justification of contextualizing the Bavli in Sasanian Persia is therefore as follows: since the study of texts in contexts is an accepted and logical mode of inquiry, and given the fact that the rabbis and Persians lived in a heterogeneous world where social contact between groups occurred, then there must be fruitful areas of comparative inquiry to be unearthed between their literatures.

Although there is something to be gained from undertaking research based on these premises, it behooves comparativists to be equally cautious of such logic and ask how the well-established fact of historical contact between groups in Sasanian Persia affects how they compare the evidence. The interactive historical context is certainly a boon to scholars interested in researching the sociocultural interactions between the groups of the time period. Nevertheless, it is essential to note the potential downside to this boon—namely, when it leads to scholarly overreach. As rewarding as the fact of interaction seems, it can mislead comparativists into methods of inquiry that read too far against the grain of the internal source material in a desire to find intercultural influences. Once given the green light by history, textual comparativists feel protected in classifying literary parallels as evidence for social interactions. But this approach can sometimes lead us astray. In this book, I push back against this method and instead argue that scholars of Sasanian religions should be all the more circumspect in their comparisons of primary texts precisely because of the ease of drawing textual similarities in light of the historical boon of interaction. The historical asset of Sasanian Mesopotamia is real, but its complexity requires us to make it the focus of our research rather than to interpret it as blanket permission to trace similarities and influences between texts that also exhibit differences.

THE IMPORTANCE OF EMPHASIZING DIFFERENCES BETWEEN SASANIAN RELIGIONS

Further explaining the challenges of comparison, Jonathan Z. Smith explains that historical contiguity is a flawed category of inquiry for scholars who overemphasize similarities between religions. For Smith, comparison qua differences and similarities is a scholarly enterprise that is not necessarily rooted in historical realities.[13] Although this limitation does not preclude the value of comparisons, it requires comparativists to be sensitive to principles of interpretive neutrality.[14] If anything, scholars of Sasanian religions should let differences dominate, offsetting such universalist and essentialist discourses as are common in comparative inquiries.[15] In numerous publications, Smith criticizes comparative methods that emphasize similarities at the expense of differences and make no attempt to answer why patterns matter.[16] In Smith's words, "*comparison has been chiefly an affair of the recollection of similarity. The chief explanation for the significance of comparison has been contiguity.*"[17] The author adds elsewhere that "the perception of similarity has been construed as the chief purpose of comparison; contiguity, expressed as historical 'influence' or filiation, has provided the explanation."[18] In these two statements Smith chooses his words of caution carefully: "recollection" and "perception" refer to the cognitive processes of comparativists. Perhaps utilizing encyclopedic knowledge,[19] comparativists may recall that they have seen something similar to what is presently before them. A comparison that focuses on similarities is a positivistic act whereby scholars construe contiguity in terms of historical influence or genealogy. Humanistic research, especially in the field of comparative religion, tends toward positivism since scholarship devalues negative arguments emanating from research that concludes that there existed a lack of interaction between groups.

In a well-known quote, Smith calls flawed comparisons magic rather than science:[20]

> In the vast majority of instances in the history of comparison, this subjective experience is projected as an objective connection through some theory of influence, diffusion, borrowing, or the like. It is a process of working from a psychological association to an historical one; it is to assert that similarity and contiguity have causal effect. But this, to revert to the language of Victorian anthropology, is not science but magic.

Comparativists can manifest their "subjective experience" of "recollecting similarity" by making the fallacious move of working "from a psychological association to an historical one." The field of comparative religions is prone to the encroachment of subjective perspectives. For these and other reasons, comparativists are at risk of confusing subjective readings with objective links, usually at the expense of historical understanding.[21] Automatic recourse to theories of influence, borrowing, genealogy, or psychic unity[22] permits comparativists to make such confused interpretive transitions and connections, which are sometimes apologetic.[23] With these problems in mind, comparativists of Sasanian religions need to police themselves with respect to how much their desire for similarities and influences intrudes into the comparative analysis. The tendency toward the drawing up of similarities for the sake of one's core discipline is common in the study of Sasanian religions, wherein each subfield has developed and worked in relative isolation. Scholars trained in one religious tradition should therefore be careful not to transpose internal categories onto other traditions' data,[24] or to perceive similarities based on what they may see as "intuitive familiarities . . . in traditions different from their own."[25] As Smith warns about such connections, "one may derive arresting anecdotal juxtapositions or self-serving differentiations, but the disciplined constructive work of the academy will not have been advanced, nor will the study of religion have come of age."[26] In the end, comparisons between Talmudic and Middle Persian texts are problematic if their main aim is to analyze or harmonize one (internal) tradition in light of another (external) tradition via a discourse of sameness.

Another potential flaw in the comparison of Sasanian religions is its tacit participation in centuries of identity politics.[27] As is often acknowledged, the origins and methods of comparative religion are bound up with the history of Western imperialism and colonialism.[28] The reception of Iranian languages and religions in European and American universities from the seventeenth through the twentieth century plays a vital role in the development of religious studies as practiced today. Irano-Semitic studies have been susceptible to polemics and apologetics. Viewed more specifically, the field of Irano-Judaica as conceived by early European scholars helped to orientalize and biblicize Zoroastrianism by tracing seeming Iranian influences in the Hebrew Bible, Dead Sea Scrolls, and Babylonian Talmud through an emphasis on sameness. In a brilliant study of this topic, Guy Stroumsa describes how the seventeenth-century orientalist and humanist Thomas Hyde sparked a debate regarding Zoroastrianism's dualistic and monotheistic tendencies as a means of espousing sympathetic views of the Persian religion. Hyde's research is paradigmatic of the problems in the historiography of comparisons of Judaism and Zoroastrianism. Describing Hyde, Stroumsa writes:[29]

> It was pure monotheism, then, that Zoroaster had preached, and the dualism reflected by the Greek sources and the Islamic heresiographers reflected a later stage of the religion, when the original cult was misunderstood. One advantage of presenting Zoroastrianism as an essentially monotheistic tradition was obvious: it permitted its

sympathetic treatment, as a religion akin to that of Israel. The original religious teaching of humankind thus remained within the biblical *Heilsgeschichte;* Israel's religion (and, ipso facto, Christianity) retained its chronological as well as its ontological supremacy.

The study of Zoroastrianism as a potential form of monotheism served Hyde's apologetics. According to Stroumsa, Hyde brought Zoroastrianism into the fold of the Abrahamic religions, thereby biblicizing it. By arguing that Noah and Seth were "the forefathers of the religion later preached by Zardusht," Hyde maintained, "like other great scholars of the seventeenth century, the original unity of humankind."[30] In another study that draws attention to how the personal judgments of scholars in Irano-Judaica affected the field, Jacques Duchesne-Guillemin characterizes Hyde in similar terms:[31]

> To Hyde, Zoroaster not only had been the preceptor of Pythagoras: he had prophesied about Christ and borrowed from Ezra and other Jewish prophets. . . . Thus, in his portrayal of Zoroaster and his religion, Hyde is bent on showing them in the light most favourable to Christian eyes. Zoroastrians were always monotheists.

A humanist, Hyde maintained "the existence of deep Jewish influences on the religion of Iran" as "a way to affirm his sympathy with Zoroastrianism."[32] Hyde's universalist perspective on the purported similarities between Judaism and Zoroastrianism represents a major rupture in the history of religious studies in the past several centuries. Stroumsa explains:[33]

> By insisting on the universal patterns of religious transformation, across time and around the world, the orientalists were effecting a dramatic "de-theologizing" (one could speak, in Bultmanian fashion, of an *Enttheologisierung*) of the study of religious phenomena. It is there, mainly, that one can detect the paradigm shift that permitted the birth of the modern study of religion.

In the centuries since Hyde, there have been both Iranists and scholars of Jewish studies, including throughout the twentieth century, who researched the Iranian-Jewish nexus using problematic, even polemical, methods of comparisons qua similarities.[34] Contemporary scholars engaged in the comparison of Sasanian religious traditions should be cautious not to recycle these earlier flawed models of Irano-Judaica, which aimed to emphasize the similarities between Semitic and Iranian religions as a means of harmonization for humanistic purposes.[35]

THE RECONDITE STATE OF MIDDLE PERSIAN STUDIES

Another hurdle that scholars comparing Talmudic and Middle Persian sources face is the recondite state of ancient Iranian studies. There are several reasons why the study of ancient Iran has, in my view, not kept pace with analogous disciplines.

Over the course of the past century, this field has been dominated by philology, a trend that contributes to the field's inaccessibility to nonspecialists, including Talmudists. According to one school of thought among Iranian philologists, expertise in Middle Persian language and literature requires knowledge of numerous other Iranian languages, including Avestan, Old Persian, and modern Persian. The emphasis on philology has indeed been one of necessity for the discipline, since the semantics and syntax of many Avestan and Middle Persian works remain elusive and debated. Pahlavi manuscripts are also late, corrupt, and in some cases produced by scribes whose knowledge of the Middle Persian language was deficient, making their decipherment difficult.[36] The exertion of scholarly resources on critically editing and translating Middle Persian texts has hampered the field's progress on source-critical or historical interpretations of these works of literature, a tension between the prerequisites of philology and the challenges of history that should be familiar to Talmudists. In addition to linguistic issues, Iranology's frequent lack of consensus on basic questions stems from Sasanian historians' disagreements regarding the use of literary sources for writing history.[37] This lack of consensus not only exacerbates the isolation of ancient Iranian studies from other disciplines, but it also makes it crucially important that students of Iran do not rely upon earlier secondary literature and instead critically engage anew the primary sources. Paradoxically, however, the study of ancient Iran, at least in the United States, has been marginalized and co-opted by other disciplines interested in comparative research, such as history of religions, Indo-European studies, archaeology, classics, and, more recently, Talmudic and Syriac studies, a trend that can result in an underspecialization in Iranian philology as a core research area.

Thankfully, Iranists today, in North America, Europe, and Israel, are dramatically improving the discipline by rectifying gaps in our knowledge through the publication of up-to-date critical editions of key primary texts (e.g., the *Hērbedestān*, *Pahlavi Vīdēvdād*, and *Bundahišn*), comprehensive transcriptions and dictionaries, and synthetic histories of Sasanian Iran.[38] There are recent monographs devoted to the topic of the Zand's dating, translation techniques, and literary strata such as, to name but two examples, Carlo Cereti's work on the *Zand ī Wahman Yasn*, and a rich study of the *Hōm Yašt* by Judith Josephson.[39] Research on Sasanian glyptics is also of high value to the reconstruction of social history. These and other important advances in the field will continue to open the door for nonspecialists to engage with Sasanian imperial and Zoroastrian sources.

DIFFERENCES IN THE TRANSMISSION OF TALMUDIC AND MIDDLE PERSIAN SOURCES

One difference between the Talmud and Middle Persian sources is the way in which the two corpora were transmitted circa the third through the tenth century

C.E.[40] The fact that both literatures developed from an originally oral context is a significant though not necessarily distinctive feature in late antique compositions.[41] Although Middle Persian works contain datable authorities such as Sōšāns and Abarag,[42] they do not necessarily betray an entrenched system of attribution, followed by later editorial anonymity, that parallels the development of oral Torah or Islamic Hadith. As I discuss below, many extant Pahlavi sources have a transmission history that is complex and poorly understood.[43] The fact that Jews and Zoroastrians of late antiquity did not share scriptural writings, as did Jews and Christians, significantly limits any connection between rabbinic texts and the Zand.[44] This type of incongruity makes Jewish-Zoroastrian polemics unlikely to be expressed via competing exegeses of the same scriptural lemma. Moreover, each group's ties to its own past scriptures were idiosyncratic: whereas the Aramaic-speaking rabbis of Babylonia had access to the Hebrew Bible and Mishnah as the basis of their exegetical study, the Persian priests produced the Zand, a Middle Persian translation-*cum*-exegesis of the Avestan canon composed in an archaic eastern Iranian language.

The Talmud and the Middle Persian corpus are different compositions in other ways as well. For its part, the Bavli is a unified corpus collectively produced by members of the rabbinic class over the course of late antiquity. Driven by an exegesis of the Mishnah, Talmudic sugyot are reworkings of earlier traditions in increasingly dialectical modes of thought. The Talmud's editors fuse together Tannaitic, Amoraic, and anonymous layers in an intentional way, homogenizing its composite genres and original sources, which range from Second Temple traditions to local folklore. In contrast, the Middle Persian corpus is a scattered collection of books and inscriptions that contains no clear counterpart to the Bavli, not even the *Dēnkard*. Middle Persian literature is made up of independent genres and styles, ranging from the religious treatises called *Rivāyat*s to epic poetry to apocalypses to secular how-to manuals, and each Pahlavi work has a distinctive transmission history and purpose. Except for the Zand, most Middle Persian legal works do not have a hermeneutical focus on earlier traditions in the same manner that the Talmud concentrates on the Mishnah. As a point of similarity, it is worth noting that Middle Persian literature, such as *Dēnkard* Book 9, does evince intertextual ties with other Zoroastrian works,[45] a feature that it has in common with other religious scriptural writings of late antiquity.

THE MIDDLE PERSIAN CORPUS

Middle Persian literature contains numerous works that are of value to Talmudists interested in contextual research. In what follows, I would like to synopsize this rich and diverse corpus, with some attention paid to which resources Talmudists can exploit. One concern here is Iranists' ability (or inability) to date accurately

Middle Persian texts to the Sasanian era, when the rabbis were active. Sources that unambiguously date to this period include material remains and epigraphica (e.g., seals, magical bowls, inscriptions), as well as sundry Middle Persian texts that were composed in the late Sasanian period, including works of law and exegesis. The use of the Pahlavi books from the ninth and tenth centuries C.E. is more complicated. Although there is widespread agreement among experts in the field that in some fashion or another much of these books' contents are based on or are conservative renderings of traditions or materials from the pre-Islamic period, Middle Persian studies as a whole has not yet applied source-critical methods to the corpus text by text with the hope of disentangling early and late layers.[46] The most suitable approaches toward this goal are likely to be found in the linguistic features of each text, as well as in references to external and internal figures or events (e.g., to Muslims or named Zoroastrian jurists). In the end, even though there may still be more questions than answers about the dating of Middle Persian texts, we must proceed as best we can on the basis of available information.[47]

The Middle Persian law book known as the *Mādayān ī Hazār Dādestān* (*Book of a Thousand Judgements*) is the single richest source for Sasanian law.[48] This work is a seventh-century compilation of records from cases that were potentially adjudicated in imperial courts. As such, it reflects the legal opinions of key Sasanian jurists and contains discussions of a range of civil matters, including guardianship, inheritances, and ownership. Absent from this work is any serious engagement with questions of religious practice. Although the *Mādayān ī Hazār Dādestān* does not mention Jews explicitly, and rarely references Christians, it is the indispensable resource for understanding the inner workings of Sasanian courts of law in the seventh century.

In addition to the *Mādayān ī Hazār Dādestān*, the Middle Persian corpus contains numerous works that are translations of or related to the Avesta, including the *Pahlavi Yasna*, the *Zand ī Xorde Avesta* (*The Small Avesta*), and several *Yašts* (Hymns).[49] Even though produced in late antiquity and the early medieval periods, the Zand-Avesta (i.e., the Middle Persian translation of the canon of Zoroastrian holy scriptures, the Avesta) records ancient materials from the Avestan oral tradition dating back millennia. In general, works of Zand are composed of verbatim Pahlavi translations of Avestan texts alongside exegetical glosses. In comparison with the Jewish canon, the Zand's model of exegesis is more similar to the Aramaic translations, or Targums, of the Bible than to the Bavli.[50] For Talmudists interested in comparative law, much of the Zand treats matters of purity, as for example the *Pahlavi Vīdēvdād* (*Laws against the Demons*)[51] and the sixth-century *Zand ī Fragard ī Juddēvdād* (*A Commentary on Chapters of the Vīdēvdād*),[52] which delineate regulations regarding corpses, menstruation,[53] and noxious creatures. In addition to these works, the *Hērbedestān* (*Priestly-Scholar School*) and the *Nērangestān* (*Book of Ritual Directions*) are two priestly-scholar study manuals together offering a raw perspective on the details of scholarly and ritual practices in the late Sasanian or the early Islamic era.[54] Unfortunately, there is no consensus among Iranists regarding the transmissional backgrounds and dates of most of these works, each of which would benefit from a reexamination using up-to-date tools. Some experts suggest that the Zand began to be composed and even written circa the third century C.E., with subsequent updates in the time of Khusrow I (531–79 C.E.).[55] The late writing down and redaction of Pahlavi sources deflate this dating, however. In a key study of the Zand, Alberto Cantera dates the redaction of the *Hērbedestān*, *Nērangestān*, and *Pahlavi Vīdēvdād* to roughly the sixth century C.E., the *Pahlavi Yasna* to the eighth and ninth centuries, and the *Zand ī Xorde Avesta* to various time periods.[56] If Cantera's dates are correct, then the first set of these Middle Persian works emanating from the sixth century could justifiably be dated to the same general time frame as the Talmud. Finally, there are other religious works in the Middle Persian corpus whose authors build on and cite works of Zand. For instance, *Šāyest nē Šāyest* (*Proper and Improper*), which could have been compiled in the late Sasanian period, though a later date is also possible, obsesses over pollutions, rituals, and repentance.[57] For Talmudists interested in comparative law and exegesis, the Zand is the most fertile part of the Middle Persian corpus to exploit.

In addition to imperial law books and the Zand-Avesta, Middle Persian literature also contains national narratives dating to the late Sasanian era. The most famous of these is the romance describing the exploits of the founding monarch of the Sasanian Empire, entitled *The Book of the Deeds of Ardashir, the Son of Pābag* (*Kārnāmag ī Ardaxšēr ī Pābagān*), a work from Fārs, some of which was composed in the time of Khusrow I.[58] This dating is complicated by the fact that the work clearly underwent different stages of editing, perhaps even as late as the ninth century. For Talmudists, this narrative offers value in comparison with Aggadah, as demonstrated in several articles by Geoffrey Herman and Jeffrey Rubenstein.[59]

Another central genre in the Middle Persian corpus is *andarz* (wisdom literature), which offers testimony to Zoroastrian sensibilities regarding how to live a proper life.[60] Topics in such works include guidance on how much to eat and drink, on the value of prayer and rituals, and on core beliefs. Although many of these works, such as the *Memorial of Wuzurgmihr* (*Ayādgār ī Wuzurgmihr*)[61] and *Selected Precepts of the Ancient Sages* (*Čīdag Andarz ī Pōryōtkēšān*),[62] are attributed to well-known Sasanian authorities in the fourth century and onward, it is hard to accept so early a dating. A different work in this genre, known as *The Spirit of Wisdom* (*Mēnōg ī Xrad*), is an extraordinary question-and-answer dialogue between personifications of Wisdom.[63] Regrettably, except for Ahmad Tafazzoli's Persian translation, there exists no reliable translation nor either any critical edition in English since Edward West's version (1871).

The Middle Persian corpus also includes several apocalyptic and eschatological works. Two of these are the *Memorial of Zarēr* (*Ayādgār ī Zarērān*)[64] and the

Memorial of Jāmāsp (*Ayādgār ī Jāmāspīg*),[65] both short works. The *Memorial of Zarēr* is one of the few extant Middle Persian remnants of the Iranian epic tradition, reporting the story of the battle between the heroes Wištāsp (who was converted to the Good Religion by Zarathustra)[66] and his brother Zarēr versus the sorcerer Wīdrafš. It may contain Parthian materials, and if so it would be a rare example of so early a literary specimen. The *Memorial of Jāmāsp* contains a dialogue between Wištāsp and Jāmāsp and is a part of apocalyptic tradition in Pahlavi, a genre that also includes the seventh- or eighth-century *Zand ī Wahman Yasn*,[67] and the spiritual voyage to heaven and hell described in *The Book of Wirāz the Just* (*Ardā Wirāz Nāmag*).[68] These two latter works probably date from the seventh to the ninth or even the tenth century, but they seem to contain earlier materials.

THE PROBLEM OF ANACHRONISM

The most significant impediment to the comparison of Talmudic and Middle Persian literature is the potential for anachronism as a result of the latter's early Islamic context of production. Indeed, major Zoroastrian books such as the *Dēnkard* (*Acts of the Religion*), the cosmological tract *Bundahišn* (*Primal Creation*),[69] and the apocalyptic work the *Zand ī Wahman Yasn* were redacted in the ninth and tenth centuries C.E., and thus centuries after the Bavli. Dating to an even later time, two well-known political treatises ascribed to the Sasanian founding monarch, Ardashir, the *Testament of Ardashir* and the *Letter of Tansar*,[70] are extant only in later Persian and Arabic recensions.[71] The fact that we do not have a copy of the original Middle Persian *Xwadāy-Nāmag* (*Book of Lords*), the Iranian national history, epitomizes the problem of lateness in the study of the Middle Persian literary tradition. Shapur Shahbazi dates the earliest compilations of *The Book of Lords* to the fifth century, with later editing and additions in the sixth and the early seventh century.[72] But it is difficult to reconstruct the Sasanian work based on today's remnants, which are "Arabic and Persian adaptations of the ninth to eleventh centuries,"[73] including most famously in Ferdowsi's tenth-century *Book of Kings* (*Šāhnāme*).

Complicating the task of dating Middle Persian sources is the question regarding what impact the Arab conquests may have had on the ninth- and tenth-century Zoroastrian priests in Fārs who compiled or authored many of the Pahlavi books.[74] In my opinion, a drastic change in the structures and role of the priesthood occurred in the two centuries between the fall of the Sasanian Empire and the editing of the Pahlavi books. The roles in society of the *mowbeds*, *hērbeds*, *rads*, *dastwars*, and other priestly posts and titles were transformed by the transition of their status from administrators of the Persian Empire to subjects of an Islamic one. Pahlavi literature's explicit engagement with Islam and heightened concern for apostasy and conversion reflects this less favorable environment. For this reason, one must be judicious in using post-Sasanian sources as accurate representations of Sasanian-era priestly society, such as researching priestly titles, rituals, hierarchy, or authority. Comparative studies on rabbis and Persian priests should avoid using only Pahlavi literature as a source. In post-Sasanian Iran, the Zoroastrian priests' authority, stripped of its imperial status, became more focused on ritual law. In several definitive articles,[75] Philip Kreyenbroek explains the challenges of researching the Zoroastrian priesthood using Pahlavi sources such as the *Dēnkard* or Arabic sources about the scholar-priests:[76]

> The difficulty in interpreting these data is that, although the anecdotes may well be based on an old oral tradition . . . they were written down in their present form in the 10th century, so that it is impossible to tell whether their terminology reflects Sasanian or post-Sasanian usage, i.e. whether such priests would indeed have been called *hērbed* in Sasanian times.

The titles and social positions of the Zoroastrian priests changed over time, with the Islamic conquests being a particularly transformative moment of rupture that resulted in the reduction of administrative authority. As Albert de Jong has spelled out, Pahlavi sources erase from discussion the position of the *mog*, a title that is so prominent on Sasanian seals.[77] In the same article cited above, Kreyenbroek explains how the later works of Manūščihr discontinued a deep engagement with the priestly tradition of administration and instead turned to the scholar-priests as the leaders of the community:[78]

> Given the radically altered position of the Zoroastrian Church in post-Sasanian Iran, it is hardly surprising to find signs of change and decay in the later use of administrative titles. Thus the title *mōbedān mōbed* had been replaced by *hudēnān pēšōbāy*, "leader of the faithful" (a title reminiscent of the Islamic *amīr al-mu'minīn*).

In the post-Sasanian Pahlavi writings, the *dastwar* succeeded earlier administrative titles used in imperial contexts.[79] The fact that the post-Sasanian Pahlavi sources, written by the priests themselves, often retroject concerns and knowledge from an early Islamic standpoint into their recordings of the past, while posing a difficulty for scholars of comparison, actually offers Iranists an opportunity to differentiate between pre- and post-Islamic contents using source-critical methods. In the end, however, comparativists interested in the rabbinic-priestly interface must take into account the fact that the later Pahlavi corpus does not accurately represent the social fabric of the Sasanian-era priesthood.[80]

Another example of the difficulty of dating Pahlavi texts from the early Islamic period will suffice—namely, the case of *Dēnkard* Book 3.[81] The *Dēnkard* is a compilation in nine distinctive tomes of Zoroastrian law, theology, narrative, exegesis, and polemics that was redacted in the ninth and tenth centuries. By far the lengthiest of the nine volumes, *Dēnkard* Book 3 is a trove of polemics against others, such as heretics, Jews, and Muslims, and thus constitutes a particularly valuable resource for understanding intercultural dialogues. Despite its potential merit, the date of this notoriously cryptic work, of which there exists no modern critical edition, is still unclear and debated.[82] On both the macro and the micro level, the redaction of the work's hundreds of loosely related chapters is imperfectly understood. Is there any organizational logic to the sequence of its chapters? Are there common literary features throughout the work, such as introductory formulas, that can be attributed to later redactors? And which chapters or traditions originate from the Sasanian era and were left unaltered? Until such questions are resolved, *Dēnkard* Book 3 remains of limited and controversial value for understanding Zoroastrianism of the pre-Islamic era and, by extension, its ties to Talmudic Judaism.

Further highlighting Middle Persian literature's early Islamic context, the *Bundahišn, Dēnkard,* and *Ayādgār ī Jāmāspīg,* among other works, explicitly reference Islam and the Arab conquests, including in apocalyptic terms.[83] For instance, a later chapter in the dense cosmological work the *Bundahišn* expresses the anguish felt by the rise of the Arabs (Middle Persian *tāzīg*), explaining:[84]

> Iran was left to the Arabs and they have made that law of evil religion current, many customs of the ancients they destroyed and the religion of the Mazdā worshipping religion was made feeble and they established the washing of the dead, burying the dead, and eating the dead. And from the primal creation of the material world till today, a heavier harm has not come, because of their evil behavior, misery and ruin and doing violence and evil law, evil religion, danger and misery and other harm have become accepted.

In addition to these explicit testimonies, Zoroastrian apocalypticism is a literary expression of the despondent mood felt by a priesthood in decline. With respect to Islam, the ninth-century polemical work the *Škand Gumānīg Wizār* (*The Doubt-Dispelling Exposition*),[85] written in Pāzand (Pahlavi transcribed in Avestan characters), devotes several of its chapters to safeguarding the faith against the intrusion of the new religion, as well as against Judaism,[86] Christianity, and Manichaeism. The *Škand Gumānīg Wizār* was written by Mardānfarrox son of Ohrmazddād in response to the inquiries of a man named Mihrayār ī Mahmadān, whom Maria Macuch identifies as perhaps "a Zoroastrian from a family of Muslim converts."[87] Although much more research needs to be done on this fascinating work's history of composition, it appears that it was intended for internal consumption by Zoroastrians living under Islam.[88]

Finally, other Pahlavi works from the ninth and the tenth century, especially the *Rivāyat*s, attest their authors' heightened concern with Islam through more restrictive laws against interactions with non-Zoroastrians and apostates. As Yuhan Vevaina has shown, hermeneutics and history were intertwined phenomena in late antique Iran, especially when it came to the Islamic conquests. The author explains that:[89]

> This powerful hermeneutic assumption of "Omnisignificance," which I have written about elsewhere, is activated by the narrative of the four ages in the *Sūdgar Nask* of *Dēnkard* Book 9, which clearly acknowledges a period of social challenges faced by the Zoroastrian tradition. This period of difficulty appears to me to primarily reflect the social challenges of the early Islamic era, and the "memories of much hardship" appear to acknowledge the changing socio-economic conditions facing the Zoroastrian communities of Iran. . . . It seems to me that the entire narrative of the four ages was mobilized by the Zoroastrian priests to explain the contemporary challenges they faced in a new era dominated by non-Iranian—Arab—elites and an ever-increasing number of apostates.

The social setting of the Pahlavi priestly writers in early Islamic Iran plays a vital role in the production of the literature at our disposal. Notwithstanding Macuch's argument that the *Rivāyats*, such as the *Rivāyat ī Ēmēd ī Ašawahištān*,[90] named after a high priest from the middle of the tenth century, contain useful information for the reconstruction of Sasanian law, because of their lateness these works should be sparingly juxtaposed with the Bavli.[91]

Middle Persian works composed in the ninth and tenth centuries do not represent the diversity of pre-Islamic Zoroastrianism. This misrepresentation is a result not only of the texts' lateness but also of the fact that many of them were produced by a single priestly family from Fārs, a region where Zoroastrianism persisted into the tenth century. The final two editors of the *Dēnkard* come from this priestly line.[92] The first of these figures, Ādurfarnbag ī Farroxzādān, was the chief priest, or *mowbedān mowbed*, during the reign of the caliph al-Ma'mūn (813–33 C.E.) who redacted *Dēnkard* Books 3–5 and helped to preserve earlier religious literature. The purported author of *andarz* and a *rivāyat*, Ādurfarnbag ī Farroxzādān is also the protagonist of a court drama entitled *The Accursed Abalish* (*Gizistag Abāliš*), wherein before al-Ma'mūn he debates a disaffected Zoroastrian convert to Islam. Given its early Islamic milieu, this work has little historical value for understanding the interactions between Jews and Zoroastrians in late antiquity.[93] Approximately a century after Ādurfarnbag another priest, named Ādurbād Ēmēdān, whose life story is obscure, continued the task of his predecessor by completing the redaction of the final four books of the *Dēnkard*. Decades later, in the late ninth century, descendants of Ādurfarnbag ī Farroxzādān,[94] brothers named Manūščihr and Zādspram,[95] authored other important Pahlavi works. Caught in a brotherly struggle, Manūščihr wrote works reflecting a new genre entitled the *Religious Judgments* (*Dādestān ī Dēnīg*)[96] and the *Epistles of Manūščihr* (*Nāmagīhā ī Manūščihr*)[97] while acting as the *rad* and *pēšag-framādār* of Fārs and Kirman circa the 880s, and Zādspram, located in Sirgan, was attracted to astrology and medicine as seen in the *Selections of Zādspram* (*Wizīdagīhā ī Zādspram*).[98] These two brothers, leaders of their communities, expressed themselves in writings that were inspired not only by a desire to preserve and draw upon earlier Zoroastrian traditions to which they had access but also by the realities of their lives in the ninth century.

This brief background of the authors of our later Pahlavi sources points to several difficulties for scholars who are interested in using them as the basis of researching Sasanian Zoroastrianism and its similarities to the Talmud. In the first place, the location of these authors is not in Mesopotamia, a geographical difference with the Talmud that should not be ignored. A more urgent consideration is that scholars should be wary of interpreting ninth- and tenth-century Pahlavi texts as reflecting late antique Zoroastrianism, which in reality was legally and theologically more diverse than what the sources depict. Later Pahlavi works represent only one branch of ancient Iranian religions, and they tend to ignore or to polemicize against the numerous divisions or sects that existed alongside them.[99] The Sasanian priesthood and monarchy faced heretical and sectarian challenges, chief among them Manichaeaism, Zarduštagan,[100] and Mazdakism. The heterodoxy of Iranian religions in late antiquity is illustrated by the worship of Mithra and Anahita and other polytheistic trends that are not recorded in the Pahlavi corpus.[101] Pointing to the limitations of evidence regarding the eclecticism of Sasanian-era Zoroastrianism, Shaul Shaked's assessment is correct when he writes that scholars "can only manage to reconstruct a small portion of the variegated religious heritage of ancient Iran."[102] In sum, the Pahlavi corpus is not at all representative of the diversity of Iranian religions and Zoroastrian beliefs in the Sasanian period.[103]

The study of Middle Persian literature would benefit from reassessing the conventional wisdom that Pahlavi writings from the ninth and tenth centuries emanate ultimately from the era of Khusrow I, whose reign lasted for about half of the sixth century. Carlo Cereti synopsizes the main question of the dating of Pahlavi literature in the following passage:[104]

> The bulk of it was compiled in the ninth and the tenth centuries A.D. and some texts date from even later. Though most of these works contain much earlier material, this material was influenced by the religious tradition to such an extent that it often cannot be entirely trusted. In passing, it may be said that the greatest part of the historical evidence present in such works can, with all probability, be traced back to the reign of Xōsrōē I (531–572 A.D.) or even later.

This monarch is well known for instituting military and fiscal reforms and promoting the centralization of the empire. It is also possible that the Avesta was written down sometime during or around his reign, although this claim is still conjectural.[105] There is a common view among Iranists that the Pahlavi texts, despite their lateness, are in some way either from or representative of the late Sasanian period, thanks to the "diligent priestly copyists who preserved the literary remains of their ancestors," as Macuch writes (see below). The Zand-Avesta in particular records religious traditions that date to the first or second millennium B.C.E. These features of Zoroastrian preservation and conservatism were championed by Mary Boyce, whose normative perspectives have since been critiqued.[106] Frustrated by the lack of extant literature produced in late antiquity proper, Sasanian historians sometimes fall into the trap of reading Pahlavi literature as reflective of earlier centuries. Maria Macuch has described the nuance with which a scholar must approach the use of religious and minstrel Pahlavi materials as conservative records of ancient Zoroastrian traditions:[107]

> Although the loss of these different genres leaves a deplorable gap in our knowledge of Pahlavi literature, we still have reason to be thankful to the generations of diligent priestly copyists who preserved the literary remains of their ancestors over long periods of oppression and persecution. The surviving works, tedious and conservative as they may partly seem, are nonetheless of eminent importance for the social and cultural history of ancient and medieval Iran, since they not only reflect the beliefs and convictions of the late period in which they were put to writing, but also ancient traditions of the Zoroastrians from time immemorial. As has been repeatedly observed, it is mainly due to the tenacity of this tradition that a chronological survey of Pahlavi writings seems impossible. Individual works from the ninth century may contain material from a much earlier period, transmitted across numerous centuries, whereas a composition from the sixth or seventh century may reflect only the circumstances and conditions of its own time.

Macuch notes here the difficulty of chronologizing Pahlavi literature, which comprises Zoroastrian traditions dating from the Avestan period to the tenth century C.E. The more that Iranists can date specific traditions or chapters of Pahlavi works to the reign of Khusrow I in the sixth century C.E., the higher their potential value for comparison with the latest Amoraic stratum of the Bavli, since this was the general time frame in which the Talmud underwent its transition from Amoraic attributions to anonymity.

THE MATERIAL REMAINS OF SASANIAN PERSIA: SEALS, INSCRIPTIONS, AND ARAMAIC BOWLS

In addition to Middle Persian literature, scholars of Sasanian Persia can utilize epigraphic and material sources. These types of evidence include Sasanian administrative seals, the imperial inscriptions, the Aramaic magical bowls from Mesopotamia, and other remains such as coins.[108] Philippe Gignoux and other Iranists have justifiably promoted epigraphic remains and Talmudic, Syriac, and Manichaean sources as the best resources to study Sasanian society, in part because they challenge the literary evidence of Middle Persian sources.[109] The material remains of the Zoroastrian priesthood are firmly datable to the Sasanian era. Historiographically considered, the study of ancient Iranian history from the Achaemenids through the Sasanians has been political or social history,[110] in part because of the archaeological evidence available. With respect to Sasanian seals, Rika Gyselen has noted that the seals "are the only objects to have been handled by all levels of society, as well as by the administration,"[111] which certified the transactions recorded by the seals. Sasanian seals "functioned as a guarantee of a sealed document in commercial transactions and in administrative records."[112] The personal and administrative seals offer insight into the roles and the personal names of Zoroastrian priests who engaged in commercial or administrative transactions.[113] The Sasanians produced the seals beginning in the late fifth and the early sixth century.[114] Seals are attested on local, district, provincial, and regional administrative levels, including near Babylonia. One seal, for instance, records the presence of a *mowbed* in Mesene, southern Mesopotamia ("Baffarag, *mowbed* of Meshun").[115] Material sources are on-the-ground testimony to the functions of the Zoroastrian priesthood in Sasanian society.

Of particular value to the study of the Talmud in its Sasanian context are the Jewish Aramaic magical bowls from late Sasanian Mesopotamia.[116] Unfortunately, the precise provenance of a great number of these magical bowls is unknown, though some are from Nippur, a city between the two rivers approximately 125 kilometers southeast of Ctesiphon in the region of Mesene. Some bowls include the names of geographical locales that are near Pumbedita and Maḥoza,[117] and still others mention Babylonia. The apotropaic incantations written on these bowls were produced by Jewish magicians individually for both Jewish and gentile clients and were intended to ward off evil spirits, diseases, and bad luck. Other spells serve other purposes, such as for success in business.[118] Most sorcerers used efficacious words that kept demons and illnesses away from the bodies and residences of clients. In Sasanian Mesopotamia the belief in both white magic, which protected someone from harm and evil spirits, and black magic, which brought evil upon an enemy, was ubiquitous. Extant bowls are written in various Aramaic dialects, and there also exist around twenty cryptic bowls in Pahlavi.[119] As I discuss later in this book, these archaeological relics, which record the names of the clients, demonstrate popular forms of religious syncretism that overlap in both harmony and tension with the Talmudic tradition. Although known for a long time as a potential resource for historians of Babylonian Jewry, scholars have yet to fully exploit the valuable corpus of spell texts.[120] The recent and forthcoming publication of hundreds of new bowls,[121] alongside the surge in interest in the Talmud's Iranian context, makes the comparative inquiry of the Bavli and bowls relatively untapped territory.

THE LIMITS OF PARALLELING TALMUDIC AND MIDDLE PERSIAN TEXTS

Historiographically speaking, one reason that the study of the Talmud in its Iranian setting has not been fully integrated into the academic study of late antique Judaism is because of a lack of robust dialogue. As more scholars populate this small subfield, our understanding of the Bavli in its Iranian context will be enriched by the carving out of a consensus on basic questions, as well as by the fostering of debates over controversial issues. With the publication of several monographs and many articles on Irano-Talmudica in recent years, the discipline of Irano-Talmudica is becoming increasingly accepted. This monograph's emphasis on the historical context of the Babylonian rabbis, and the differences between the Talmud and the Pahlavi corpus, is in part a response to some of the current trends in this subfield. For instance, Shai Secunda's monograph *The Iranian Talmud: Reading the Bavli in Its Sasanian Context* lays out a path forward in this field of study, offering up a solid justification for researching the Talmud in Sasanian Iran. Although Secunda and I agree on multiple key issues, including the idea of a world of discourse shared between groups in Sasanian Mesopotamia, and the notion that the internal rhetoric of the Bavli gives the wrong impression of rabbinic cultural segregation,[122] there are also methodological, evidentiary, and argumentative differences between our researches that are worth noting. One distinction between Secunda's *Iranian Talmud* and this book is how each monograph employs the comparative method. Secunda's book prioritizes the excavation of similarities and textual parallels between the Bavli and Middle Persian literature.[123] For Secunda, the way to offset the problem of the internal nature of these texts and "the apparent lack of intersection between the Bavli and Middle Persian literature" is by undertaking "a more traditional examination of influences," which illuminates "certain kinds of historical 'encounters' between Jews and Persians, namely, between their literatures."[124] Scholars reconstruct plausible conversations between Jews and Zoroastrians by paralleling their literatures or examining the portrayals of their interactions.[125] Secunda advocates bringing Talmudic and Middle Persian texts, including those with no internal markers of cultural dialogue, "into conversation with one another as a kind of reenactment of late antique historical encounters."[126] Comparison is justified when one demonstrates that the Zoroastrians and rabbis "shared common geographic space, assumptions, and experiences."[127] In this approach, Secunda intentionally reads against the grain of rabbinic internality by putting the Bavli into dialogue with Middle Persian sources as part of a broader "text-scape" of Sasanian Iran. The author describes the idea as follows:[128]

> To conceive of these forms of textual interactions, one might imagine a kind of late antique (and early medieval) "text-scape" across Iranian lands that included, among other groups, Aramaic-speaking rabbis and Persian-speaking Zoroastrians. Using

> the notion of "text-scape" may help account for related articulations appearing in different textual and cultural formations. It also implies that these phenomena might even represent a type of textual interaction. In a sense, the current attempt to read the Bavli and Middle Persian literature together by placing them in conversation with one another is not an entirely unreasonable exercise, as it can be seen as parallel to the original textual work of late antique Jews and Zoroastrians. . . . The approach that I am outlining focuses on moments when texts from one tradition directly intersect with those of another.

For Secunda, one of the values of juxtaposing Talmudic and Middle Persian sources is that this procedure "can be seen as parallel to the original textual work of late antique Jews and Zoroastrians." In this perspective, the comparativist's act of putting texts into dialogue with each other mimics ancient authors' textual processes. In Secunda's work, the theory of a Sasanian "text-scape," buttressed by the historical premise of interaction, transcends the internal nature of the sources, which do not offer unambiguous data regarding interactions between Jews and Persians. In another passage in *The Iranian Talmud*, Secunda describes further his text-centered approach:[129]

> I would like to suggest a different strategy, in which scholars initially approach the reading of the Bavli and Middle Persian literature *qua* texts, and as a result look at the intersections between them first and foremost as *textual* intersections. By honing in on the very textuality of the parallels between the Bavli and Zoroastrian literature, it is possible to highlight examples of textual and literary interactions between these two corpora that can be considered apart from—and in the hermeneutical process "prior" to—the intermingling of flesh and blood rabbis and Zoroastrian priests. My intention here is not to flee to the cocoon of philological research, nor to ignore the agency of the people and communities that created the texts. Rather, my purpose is to construct an interpretative structure built on an alternative order of operations wherein the textual nature of the sources is acknowledged first, even when considering questions of cultural intersection. Subsequently, this textuality can inform comparative research.

Advocating a notion of "textual intersections," Secunda argues that comparativists should focus on "the very textuality of the parallels" between the Bavli and Middle Persian sources. Secunda concludes that the elite scholastic groups who produced our literature communicated with one another orally and textually, exchanging religious traditions through various channels such as religious disputations (e.g., *bei abeidan*), translation projects, and study houses.[130] Moreover, the Babylonian rabbis possessed knowledge of Persian priestly traditions, because they studied with them in oral fashion.[131] On this point Secunda contends that "direct study with Zoroastrian priests could have constituted one mode by which Zoroastrian texts entered rabbinic society"[132] and that Talmudists can find "instances in which explicit traces and even entire passages of imperial, cosmological, and polemical

Middle Persian literature appear in the Bavli in the form of parallel taxonomies, loanwords, and calques of specific terminologies."[133] According to this point of view, comparativists will discover passages in the Bavli that contain traces of Middle Persian literary influence.

As I have outlined in this chapter, I believe that between the Bavli and Middle Persian texts there are differences in chronology, transmission, and geography that diminish the value of researching intercultural interactions through their juxtaposition. Although there exist some traceable fragments of Middle Persian textual influence on the Bavli, the bulk of the Bavli does not contain markers of textual interpenetration from outside sources that warrants strict juxtapositions. For these reasons, I disagree with Secunda's appraisal that entire passages from Middle Persian texts appear in the Talmud. Moreover, we do not need to regard the historical boon of interaction, proved by the totality of the evidence, especially from Iranology, as license to read against the grain of the insular rhetoric of Talmudic sources by putting them into conversation with Zoroastrian texts that were produced centuries later. Instead of inverting the rabbis' internality, I argue in this book that comparativists should try to explain why the rabbis constructed an insular ideology while residing in a diverse social environment. In other words, why were the rabbis insular in a heterogeneous environment? And why were their ideologies toward others what they were in light of the rabbinic movement's place within Sasanian society? It is these questions that the remaining chapters of this monograph will address.

POINTS OF MUTUAL FRUITION BETWEEN IRANIAN AND JEWISH STUDIES

In this chapter I have outlined a path forward in the study of the Talmud in its Persian context by drawing from the discipline of comparative religion in order to avoid some of the common pitfalls of comparative research. Methodologically, I argue that it is crucial for comparativists of Sasanian religions to accentuate and take seriously the differences between Jews and Persians, and between Talmudic and Middle Persian texts, alongside any similarities. To this end, one goal of this chapter has been to demonstrate how different and disconnected Talmudic and Pahlavi primary texts are from one another in terms of transmission, purpose, provenance, and chronology. These differences raise serious doubts about comparative methods that seek to juxtapose Talmudic and Zoroastrian sources without attention being paid to broader sociohistorical contexts. In this regard, studies of Sasanian history need to be exploited. Rather than engaging in textual parallelomania or comparative taxonomies, the rest of this book aims to contextualize the Bavli's portrayals of Persians, as well as rabbinic culture's insular ideologies toward others, by emphasizing as much as possible social and historical frames of reference in addition to those types of evidence that are most historically valuable.

3

Rabbinic Portrayals of Persians as Others

In one Talmudic sugya that illustrates the rabbis' complicated engagement with Persian culture, the two Babylonian Amoraim Rav Yosef and Abaye are engaged in a debate about the laws of preparing food for use in an *eruv*. Typically, the Talmud reports that one should prepare two meals' worth of food for an *eruv*, with some exceptions—such as, for instance, meals consumed with bread. As part of a lengthy commentary on *m. 'Erub.* 3:1, this passage appears in the Gemara's list and quantities of foods such as apples, onions, beer, and dates, which are considered suitable or unsuitable for use. In our excerpt, three Babylonian sages associated with Pumbedita reflect on how the status of roasted meat as food eaten with or without bread affects the needed amount. Rabbah and Rav Yosef disagree over whether roasted meat is in fact eaten with bread. In support of his position, Rav Yosef makes reference to the Persian practice of eating *ṭabhĕqei*,[1] a Middle Iranian loanword meaning "pieces of roasted meat" or "meat dish," without bread. The passage from *b. 'Erub.* 29b reads as follows:[2]

> Regarding roasted meat—Rabbah[3] said: As much as (is needed) to eat with (bread for two meals). And Rav Yosef said: As much as (is needed) to eat (two meals) from it. Rav Yosef said: Whence do I derive this? For the Persians [פרסאי] eat various types of *ṭabhĕqei* [טבהקי טבהקי] without bread. Abaye said to him: But are the Persians the majority of the world? But surely it has been taught in a baraita (regarding the laws of impurity for cloth):[4] Clothing of the poor are for the poor, and clothing of the rich are for the rich.

In a debate with Abaye, Rav Yosef backs up the position that one should prepare two meals' worth of roasted meat by citing the Persian custom of eating meat dishes without bread (Aram.: "the Persians eat various types of *ṭabhēqei* without bread"). Persian diet is a topic of discussion elsewhere in the Talmud, such as in *b. Pesaḥ.* 41a, where Rav uses a Middle Persian word in the voice of the Persians: "How is 'raw' [נא] (Exod. 12:9)[5] (explained)? Rav said: As the Persians say, אברנים." This final word is Middle Persian *abarnēm*, literally "halfway," but in this context it means "partly roasted."[6] Other relevant texts that substantiate rabbinic familiarity with Persian culinary culture include the Iranian loanwords אומצא (cf. MP *āmiz*, "side dish; vegetables"), used in reference to meat dishes with duck or deer, as well as כמכא (cf. MP *kāmag*, "soup"), perhaps a type of milk recipe.[7] In our passage cited above, Abaye rebuts Rav Yosef's conclusion that the law should accommodate the Persian custom of eating roasted meat. Rav Yosef's pupil, Abaye, in an uncommon instance of disrespect toward his master,[8] disagrees and questions whether the Persians in fact represent "the majority of the world."[9] The subsequent baraita backs up this claim by demonstrating that the practices of one class of people are not applicable to another class. For Abaye, Persian culinary habits cannot serve as the basis of Jewish behavior regarding the preparation of roasted meat for an *eruv*. This sugya's debate between Rav Yosef and Abaye over whether the Persians are the majority of the world and, if so, whether their customs should influence Jewish law encapsulates the complex attitude of the Jewish sages toward Persian culture. As we see many times in the Talmud's portrayals of Persians, rabbinic familiarity with and acculturation to Persian culture raise new legal possibilities with which the Babylonian rabbis must grapple.

HOW MUCH PERSIA IN JEWISH BABYLONIA? SCHOLARLY DEBATES FROM NEUSNER TO ELMAN

Contemporary Talmudists probe a question similar to what the Babylonian rabbis did in late antiquity: namely, what is the role, if any, of Persian culture in Jewish Babylonia? The past century of Talmudic and Iranological scholarship has witnessed a number of attempts at answering this question using various comparative and philological methodologies.[10] In the late nineteenth century Alexander Kohut published several comparative studies on demonology and legends of the first man in Iranian and Jewish sources.[11] Several decades later, in 1920, Isidor Scheftelowitz wrote a monograph, detailed for its time, entitled *Die altpersische Religion und das Judentum*, which concentrates on the similarities between Judaism and Zoroastrianism in the realms of demonology, magic, and customs, and in other areas.[12] In 1935, Zsigmond Telegdi wrote an article on the phonetics of Iranian loanwords, one example of the philological approach that used to predominate in the study of the Talmud in Iran.[13] More recent generations of scholars, including Joshua Heschel Schorr, Ezra Spicehandler, Daniel Sperber, E.S. Rosenthal, and Shaul Shaked have all declared in their own ways that the study of the Talmud in its Iranian context bears fruit.[14]

This approach has always had its skeptics. In 1941, for instance, Louis Ginzberg, in his *Introductory Essay to the Palestinian Talmud,* wrote:[15]

> A theory favored by many is that one of the characteristic distinctions between the two Talmuds is that the Babylonian Talmud, in contrast to the Palestinian, was greatly influenced by Persian law. In view of the new light shed on this question by the recent discovery of a Sassanian "Book of Laws"—so far the only one of its kind known—this theory can hardly be maintained. Fragmentary and obscure as this Persian Book of Laws is, it contains enough material to enable us to form an opinion on the relation of Jewish civil law in Babylonia to the Persian law in use in that country. Here too the observation made above is valid: the foreign elements in Jewish law date back to pre-talmudic, even to pre-mishnaic times. The parallels in the Sassanian Book of Laws to Jewish civil law are chiefly related to those parts of the latter which are also found in Palestinian sources such as the Mishnah and the Palestinian Talmud. If those parallels mean anything, they prove that in very early times, when Palestine was still a Persian province, old Persian law was not without influence upon the Jews of that country.

Ginzberg insisted that any connections between the *Mādayān ī Hazār Dādestān* (*Book of a Thousand Judgements*), which had come to the attention of scholars in his generation, and the Bavli emanate from an earlier—Second Temple and Achaemenid—context. Although Persian influences do exist in the Dead Sea Scrolls and Ezra-Nehemiah, among other pre-rabbinic Jewish texts,[16] Ginzberg's claims of Second Temple influence are anachronistic. Ginzberg's incorrect observations that "foreign elements" in Jewish law preceded the rabbinic period, and that the Bavli's seeming parallels with the *Mādayān ī Hazār Dādestān* can also be found in the Palestinian Talmud, mute the influence of Sasanian Persia on the rabbis. In another passage, not cited above, the author adds that the only law that the Talmud borrowed from Sasanian Persia was Rav Naḥman's oath of exoneration. Ginzberg's downplaying of the *Mādayān ī Hazār Dādestān*'s value was in part a result of the status of Iranian studies in the middle of the twentieth century and of the state of cooperation (or lack of it) between Iranists and Talmudists. In a quote that sums up the historical division between Talmudic studies and Iranology, Daniel Sperber begins a short article on *b. Sukkah* 18a published in 1968 with the following statement:[17]

> The Talmud is replete with material that can cast light on Sassanid Persia. But the average Talmudist, not being a trained Iranologist, is usually incapable of appreciating the significance of such passages. Conversely, the Iranologist on his own may not be competent to analyse Talmudic texts in a sufficiently critical manner. It is at this point that cooperation must be sought.

Sperber explains that Irano-Talmudica has failed to thrive because of a lack of interdisciplinary training and competence between Iranologists and Talmudists.

Sperber's explanation admirably focuses on the mutual responsibility and potential for fruition between the two fields of study and presumes that the Talmud is a source of information for Sasanian historians.[18]

In the 1960s Jacob Neusner published his five volumes of *A History of the Jews in Babylonia*. Although a milestone achievement of that generation, Neusner's work on the Persian context of the Talmud is outdated by today's standards. In this and other publications, Neusner expresses skepticism that the rabbis possessed intimate knowledge of Persian culture. He derives this conclusion in part from the fact that the Talmud's explicit depictions of Persians are uninformed and in some cases inaccurate. In his article entitled "How Much Iranian in Jewish Babylonia?" Neusner argues that the rabbis were not a part of Iranian civilization:[19]

> The rabbis do not seem to have known much about Iranian religion and culture, and the two minority-cults suggest the contrary was also the case. While one certainly may locate in rabbinic literature various motifs and images familiar in Iranian religions, one cannot suppose the authorities responsible for the inclusion of those motifs and images were aware of their origin, or, therefore, derived them directly, without mediation, from Iranian Magi or laity. Nor are we certain that such ideas as may be called Iranian were perceived by the rabbis or other Jews as uniquely or quintessentially Iranian at all. The rabbis give evidence of knowing what they should have known: those few aspects of Iranian culture, law, and religion, which impinged upon the practical affairs of the Jewish community. We do not know exactly how much Iranian the rabbis knew. . . . Professor Nina Garsoian observes that the Middle East of late antiquity was divided into three cultural units: Hellenistic-Roman, Iranian, and, in-between the two, the mixed 'third world' of Semites, Armenians, and other, smaller peoples. It was to this varied, complex third world, particularly the Semitic, Aramaic-speaking, part of it, that the Babylonian rabbis belonged, and not to the equally varied and complex Iranian civilization.

Despite vastly underestimating the existence of a civilization shared between the Aramaic and Iranian communities in Sasanian Mesopotamia, Neusner's passage is telling in that it rejects interpreting the presence of Iranian motifs in rabbinic literature as evidence for Iranian influence. Neusner's dismissal of such influences stems from his assumption that the rabbis were unaware of the origins of any impact that Iran had on them. The rabbis, he continues, possessed knowledge of the Iranian world only to the extent that it "impinged upon" their "practical affairs." The rabbis had no innate interest in understanding their neighbors beyond the inevitability of political relations. In another essay, Neusner explains that the rabbis were interested in Iranian law only to the extent that it had a bearing on Jewish life: "The only matters of Iranian law that interested them had to do with taxes and real estate transactions, laws they had to enforce in their own courts."[20] In totality, then, Neusner downplays the Iranian context and admits only limited subconscious and political forms of rabbinic knowledge of Persia. Neusner's work, including his inauspicious attempts to compare the Bavli with the Pahlavi *Rivāyats* and to translate the *Škand Gumānīg Wizār*,[21] has cast a negative shadow over the comparative field of inquiry until only recently, with the emergence of new research models for the study of the late antique East.[22]

Moving beyond Neusner's unwarranted skepticism, scholars in the past decade have begun to view the Jews of Babylonia as part and parcel of the Iranian cultural orbit. Most notably, the research of Yaakov Elman presumes rabbinic acculturation to elite Persian norms.[23] With optimism in regard to excavating Persian influences on the Talmud, Elman's research represents the opposite end of the spectrum from Neusner. What distinguishes Elman from Talmudists before him is his direct and sophisticated engagement with Pahlavi literature and his utilization of ancient Iranian studies, as well as his partnership with the Iranist Prods Oktor Skjærvø, in many ways fulfilling Sperber's call for cooperation and interdisciplinarity. In one of his early articles on the Talmud in Iran, Elman writes as follows about the *Mādayān ī Hazār Dādestān* with respect to the rabbinic idea of the rebellious wife:[24]

> The parallels between the two compilations extend beyond the verbal and explicit, but also to institutions, problems, and habits of mind that betray the results of twelve hundred years of close contact between Babylonian Jews and Iranians.
>
> Thus, the rabbinic institution of the "rebellious wife," the *moredet*, finds its exact counterpart in *atarsagāyīh*, "insubordination," to which an entire chapter of the *Mādayān* is devoted, with similar definitions (refusal of marital relations and "work") and penalties. In this case, as in others, the differences are sometimes as illuminating as the similarities, and historians of Jewish law ignore them at their peril.

Elman performs a parallel taxonomy of the Talmudic and Zoroastrian legal practices of *moredet* and *atarsagāyīh*, highlighting the similar definitions of a wife's insubordination and also alluding to the differences between these two corresponding legal practices. In other writings, the author explains why Jews and Iranians may have emphasized their differences:[25]

> True, the operation of the sociological/psychological principle of the "narcissism of small differences" would have inspired leaders of both religions to stress their differences rather than similarities; but as the evidence preserved in the Babylonian Talmud indicates, Jewish acculturation to the Persian way of life, mores, and culture was high.

Elman's statement here maneuvers around the problem of rabbinic insularity by understanding the rabbis' emphasis on differences as a type of response to acculturation. Elman's tantalizing claim suggests that the rabbis' and the Persian priests' belaboring of their differences is a result of the deep integration of Persian culture into Jewish life. In this view, the differences between the rabbis and Persians sit atop a foundation of sameness and interconnection.

Elman's comparative work does not necessarily rely on explicit markers of cultural dialogue, such as loanwords, portrayals of Persians, or history,[26] and often examines comparative law and intellectual history by juxtaposing primary texts concerning comparable issues such as impurity legislation or civil law. Other Irano-Talmudists, especially Shai Secunda and Yishai Kiel, have also contributed comparative studies on purity legislation, especially menstruation and defilement.[27] Part of what is at stake in this type of research is the extent to which scholars believe that Jewish-Persian interculturality manifests itself in unconscious or latent expressions of acculturation.[28] Indeed, this question of whether rabbinic acculturation—if such a conceptual framework is even apt—occurred over long periods of time with or without the conscious recognition of the rabbis or Jews is central to how we scholars interpret the evidence, since when as comparativists we reconstruct such latent cultural transformations, in a sense we do so doubly removed from our subject matter: that is, we are trying to recover ancient peoples' modes of acculturation, of which they themselves were not cognizant. In other words, the distance between our ancient subjects and us today becomes even greater when we derive conclusions of latent acculturation through parallel taxonomies and—too often devised—our reconstructions of nonextant urtexts. Although rabbinic acculturation is a valuable research paradigm, it also has certain flawed presuppositions regarding how the process of "Persianization" (or "Iranization") occurred in Mesopotamia. As the editors of a volume on the politics of religious synthesis explain, it is fair to critique notions of acculturation that promote "teleological and quantitative assumptions, such that if a person is placed in a new cultural setting he or she will acculturate progressively, proceeding along a continuum towards some ultimate completion."[29] In the case of Babylonian Jewry, we know so little regarding the origins of rabbinic culture—which, circumstantially it seems, emerged contemporaneously with the transition from the Hellenized Parthians to Persian Sasanians—that it remains difficult to trace the natural ebbs and flows of Persian influences. Still, it is possible that source-critical demarcations between early and late strata of the Bavli can help track cultural trends from the third through the seventh century that move closer toward or farther away from Zoroastrianism or Persian culture. In the end, however, scholars today are better poised to research questions of rabbinic authority in a Sasanian context rather than acculturation to Persian norms; as Elman himself has written: "We are not yet able to determine the degree of acculturation of the typical Babylonian Jew, though we may be better placed to describe the Babylonian rabbinic authority."[30]

In addition to the contribution of Elman, there exists a wave of studies by both Iranists and Talmudists that collectively corroborate the existence of Persian influences on Jewish Babylonia. For instance, the Iranist Maria Macuch has analyzed several Sasanian legal terms in the Talmud, such as *dastwar(īh)*, "the right or title to a certain object," proving that the rabbis possessed knowledge of the technical implications of such terms.[31] Administrative loanwords have proved an area worthy of exploitation, as have words for objects of everyday life, especially items of clothing and food. The onomastic evidence of the Aramaic magical bowls serves as archaeological testimony to the fact that the Jews in Babylonia interacted with gentiles in business, marriage, and magic in the late Sasanian era.[32] Further stimulating cultural interchange between Jews and Zoroastrians was the authoritative status of oral communication in preference to the written word, which may have facilitated the sharing of narrative genres and motifs attested in, for instance, the Bavli's tales of Rav Kahana or of the sea voyages of Rabbah bar bar Ḥanah, both of which exhibit Persian features.[33] These studies validate that Persian motifs and genres penetrate some Babylonian aggadot.[34] In other research, Isaiah Gafni and Daniel Sperber have delineated the emergence of the Talmud's pro-Babylonian rhetoric and polemic against Palestinian rabbis as meant to assert the superiority of Babylonian learning, effectively turning Babylonia into Israel.[35] When evaluated in totality, all these past studies on the Talmud in its Persian context confirm that Irano-Talmudists are on solid ground in their research.

PORTRAYALS OF PERSIANS IN RABBINIC LITERATURE

The Babylonian Talmud is the best source of information for researching the representations of Persians in ancient Judaism. This is true not only in terms of the number of texts at our disposal but also because, unlike the Palestinian sages, Babylonian rabbis depict the Persians from a domestic slant. Although scholars have identified other late antique Jewish works that circulated or originated in Babylonia, such as the *Targum Onqelos* and the minor tractates, the Bavli is still by and large the best resource for ancient Iranian Jewish history and Jewish attitudes toward Persia.[36] The portrayals of Persians in the Bavli appear in a wide array of literary contexts, ranging in topics from the coming of the Messiah to property laws.[37] The Talmud displays better knowledge of imperial culture and law than of Zoroastrian theology or rituals, of which only several, such as remaining silent during meals,[38] are named—a fact that devalues studies that target the Zoroastrian-rabbinic interface as opposed to the imperial-rabbinic one. In addition to references to "Persian law" or other adjectival usages,[39] the appellation "Persian" in the Babylonian Talmud refers to the Achaemenid, the Parthian, or the Sasanian Empire, or to Persian people as an ethnic class. The correct identification of references to Persians as the Achaemenids often stems from a given text's exegesis of a biblical verse (e.g., from the books of Esther or Ezra) or concern with current or past events such as the rebuilding of the Second Temple. Scholarly determinations that texts about Persians are references to either the Parthians or Sasanians are made in various other ways, such as based on whether the rabbis in a given passage are Tannaim or Amoraim, or via the dates of other figures mentioned. For instance, one example of a source about Parthians is the widely circulated legend cycle, appearing in both Palestinian and Babylonian versions, about how the Hasmonean king Yannai, reigning from 103 until 76 B.C.E., receives Persian (i.e., Parthian) officials asking the whereabouts of Shimon ben Shetaḥ, who had fled after bad relations with the king.[40] In the end, even though rabbinic texts in general conflate the Persians, past and present, into a homogenized entity, there are, especially in the Bavli, also passages that express specificities as well.

Rabbinic texts from Palestine also contain numerous portrayals of Persians that prove useful in both source-critical and historical trajectories. In contrast to the domestic outlook of the Bavli, these sources tend to depict Persians as external others located in Babylonia. As we shall see below, in the Jerusalem Talmud and classical Midrashim references to Persians are to either Persian Jews or, more commonly, to Persian gentiles in Babylonia.[41] These sources often portray Persians interacting with Babylonian sages, especially Rav and Shmuel, hinting at their possible Babylonian origins. Although the flow of influence in the Amoraic era was primarily from west to east, there are bits of evidence to suggest that Babylonian traditions ended up influencing some texts in later Midrashim such as *Ecclesiastes Rabbah.*

In terms of general attitude toward the Persians as an ethnic group, the Babylonian Talmud is, as Sacha Stern has remarked, "remarkably benign," depicting them as "at worst ridiculous and gluttonous" and as "at best polite and worthy of emulation."[42] As with other "others" in rabbinic literature, the Talmud's depictions of the Persians tend not to provide ethnographic information but rather focus on their imperial status:[43]

> Rabbinic sources are not ethnographically inclined. Their attention is drawn somewhat to the Persians, the Arabs and the Romans, but no more. Remarkably, they appear to ignore their immediate neighbours, the non-Jewish peoples amongst whom they lived—there is no reference, in rabbinic sources, to 'Syrians' or to 'Babylonians'. The attention given to Persians, Arabs and Romans reflects, I would surmise, the central political role which they held in the Late Roman Levant: Persian and Roman empires controlling either side of the Fertile Crescent, and Arab tribes controlling its semi-desertic fringe.

The Talmud's portrayals of Persians often relate to their imperial connections. Stern's observation that the rabbis "appear to ignore their immediate neighbours" corroborates Albert de Jong's notion of the "rhetoric of insularity" prevalent in Sasanian religions. One recurring motif found in the Talmud is the status of the Jewish people under the Persian and the Roman Empire.[44] The history surrounding the restoration of the Second Temple, erected by the Persians and destroyed by the Romans, becomes a focal point of comparison. On several occasions the rabbis associate the Achaemenid Persians with the Sasanians, a point that is noteworthy for the debate among Iranists about how much memory the Sasanians had of their forebears.[45] In *b. Yoma* 10a, for instance, the rabbis compare the future of their Sasanian overlords ("Persia is destined to fall into the hands of Rome") with the Achaemenids' policies of rebuilding the Second Temple ("Will the builders [of the Temple] fall into the hands of the destroyers?"). As evidenced in what is likely the only extant Midrash from Amoraic Babylonia called the *Babylonian Esther Midrash* (*b. Meg.* 10b–17a), the Babylonian sages were particularly invested in understanding the biblical events surrounding Cyrus the Great and the Achaemenids, including chronological issues. The sages' worldview was thus affected by an awareness of Babylon as their historical exilic homeland, a perspective that invited autochthonous traditions regarding Achaemenid figures such as Ezra, Esther, and Cyrus.[46]

In addition to the Talmud's association of Persians with empire, on several occasions the Bavli praises or denigrates Persian dietary and sexual habits. In the following text (*b. Ber.* 8b), for example, Rabban Gamaliel and Rav Yosef, a third-generation Amora active in Pumbedita, express differing attitudes toward Persian cultural mores:[47]

> (It is taught in a baraita:)[48] R. Akiva said, I like the Medes for[49] three things—when they cut meat they do so only on the table, when they kiss they do so only on the hand, and when they advise they do so only in the field. Rav Adda (bar Ahavah)[50] said: What is its verse? "Jacob had Rachel and Leah called to the field, where his flock was" (Gen. 31:4).
>
> It was taught in a baraita: Rabban Gamaliel says: I like the Persians [הפרסיים] for three things—they are modest in their eating, modest in the outhouse, and modest in sex.[51] It is written:[52] "I have summoned My consecrated guests" (Isa. 13:3).[53] Rav Yosef taught a baraita: This (refers to) Persians, who are consecrated for hell.

This text is embedded with both positive and negative attitudes toward the Persians. Mirroring R. Akiva's praise of three Median cultural habits, Rabban Gamaliel commends the Persians for their modesty in how they eat, micturate, and have sex.[54] This editorial juxtaposition is not unusual since rabbinic texts commonly conflate the Persians and the Medes.[55] Rabban Gamaliel's theme of Persian modesty also appears in *b. Ketub.* 48a's description of Persian sexual humility, which says: "Rav Yosef taught (in a baraita): 'Her flesh' (Exod. 21:10) means closeness to flesh—that he should not treat her in the manner of the Persians [מנהג פרסיים], who have conjugal relations in their garments."[56] The first half our passage above from *b. Ber.* 8b is analogous to *Genesis Rabbah* 74.2, where Rabban Gamaliel (not R. Akiva) mentions that he likes the Medes for the same three reasons. In an interpretation of 1 Kings 5:9, *Ecclesiastes Rabbah* 7.23.1 contains the same tradition, except that it alludes to the "men of the East" instead of the Medes. An obvious difference between the Bavli text and its Palestinian counterparts is the inclusion of the Persians. In *b. Ber.* 8b Rabban Gamaliel's prooftext from Isaiah 13:3, about the fall of Babylon and universal judgment, implicitly praises the Persians as "consecrated guests." The connection of this biblical passage with the Medes (and by extension with the Persians) is actually later, in Isaiah 13:17, where God calls upon the Medes to destroy the evil Babylonians. In the final line of our text, however, Rav Yosef, whom other Talmudic sources connect with Zoroastrian demonology and the mother of King Shapur Ifra Hormizd,[57] reinterprets this verse, instead using it to denigrate the Persians as being consecrated for hell. The two sages interpret the same biblical verse in opposite ways in order to compliment and to insult the Persians. As illustrated in this text, one way that the Persians are cited in the Bavli is through baraitot attributed to Rav Yosef (see *b. Yoma* 9b–10a, *b. Qidd.* 72a, and *b. ʿAbod. Zar.* 2b). These Amoraic baraitot are difficult to date with accuracy to either the Tannaitic or the Amoraic era. It is conceivable, as Rashi states, that the introductory phrase of this baraita implies that it was a Tannaitic saying received and transmitted by Rav Yosef, though the fact that Tannaitic traditions regarding Persians are found exclusively in the Bavli, and not in parallel Palestinian sources, suggests Babylonian hands are at work.

The Babylonian Talmud's attitude toward the Persians is often construed according to the dialectic of modesty versus pride. A common leitmotif found in the Talmud's portrayals of Persians is their haughtiness or pride, terms borrowed from biblical verses such as Isaiah 13:3 and Zephaniah 3:11.[58] This description appears to be a negative polemic against the Persians' imperial standing. One description of the Persians as "haughty" appears in *b. Šabb.* 94a, translated below. The Talmud here comments on the legal principle in *m. Šabb.* 10:5, which permits carrying on the Sabbath a live person on a bed because the person contributes to the act of carrying. Our excerpt below is part of a legal debate between Ben Bathyra and R. Nathan over whether animals are to be included in this exemption. The discussion eventually digresses into a specific case introduced by R. Yoḥanan to explain a position of R. Nathan—namely, horses made for carrying birds, which the editors identify as "falconers" (באזיארן), a loanword from Iranian (MIr. **bāzyārān*).[59] The following text goes on to describe the Persians as haughty in the way that they ride horses:[60]

> But are there horses singled out for birds? Yes,[61] there are horses of falconers. R. Yoḥanan said: But R. Nathan agrees (that one is liable for labor) for tied up (animals). Rav Adda bar Mattenah[62] said to Abaye: But the Persians are as if bound (in how they ride). But R. Yoḥanan said (that) Ben Bathyra and R. Nathan said the same thing. (There,)[63] it is haughtiness that overcomes them, as when there was a certain officer[64] with whom the king was angry, and he ran three parasangs on foot.

This passage cites the Persian practice of falconry as providing an example of a horse made for carrying birds. Rav Adda bar Mattenah tells Abaye that the Persians ride as if they are tied up and therefore would be liable. The end of the passage explains, however, that this manner of riding is due to the Persians' haughtiness and is not to be used as an example of a case of immobility, as demonstrated in the concluding allusion to a high-ranking Persian officer who was forced to run on foot after angering the king.[65] As we have seen before, in this text the Talmud is probing whether Persian cultural phenomena are valid or invalid considerations for specific cases of rabbinic law.

The motif of Persians as haughty or proud also appears in a section of *Ecclesiastes Rabbah* 7.8.1's praise for men with patient spirits as opposed to haughty ones. Two recent studies of this Palestinian text have illuminated its implications for understanding the images of Persians in rabbinic literature. In a book on education in late antiquity, Marc Hirshman analyzes *Ecclesiastes Rabbah*'s ties to its intertexts found in *Avot de-Rabbi Nathan* and a baraita in *b. Šabb.* 31a.[66] Going against the thesis that the Babylonian sages were more interested in Persians than were their Palestinian counterparts, *Ecclesiastes Rabbah*'s version of the story is the only adaptation that uses a Persian other (whose desire to learn Torah may signal him as a potential convert from Zoroastrianism)[67] as its antagonist, and Rav and Shmuel as the protagonists, making Babylonia the theater of this drama. In this midrash, which probably dates to roughly the sixth through the eighth century, the Persian represents the gentile in Babylonia. By contrast, the baraita in *b. Šabb.* 31a invokes Hillel and Shammai, instead of Rav and Shmuel, and turns the text's message into an apologetic for the concept of the dual Torah. Let us now read the midrash on Ecclesiastes 7:8's reference to the "haughty spirit":[68]

> Better a patient spirit than a haughty spirit [מגבה רוח] (Eccl. 7:8)
> A Persian came to Rav and said to him: Teach me the Torah.
> He said to him: Say aleph.
> He replied: Who says this is aleph? Others would say it is not!
> He said to him: Say bet.
> He replied: Who says this is bet?
> Rav rebuked him and drove him out in anger.
> He went to Shmuel and said to him: Teach me the Torah.
> He said to him: Say aleph.
> He said: Who says this is aleph?
> He said to him: Say bet.
> He said: Who says this is bet?
> He took hold of his ear, and (the man) cried out: My ear! My ear!
> Shmuel said to him: Who says that this is your ear?
> He answered: Everyone knows that this is my ear!
> He said to him: In the same way, everyone knows this is aleph and that is bet.
> The Persian was immediately silenced and accepted it.
> Thus, "Better a patient spirit than a haughty spirit" (Eccl. 7:8).
> Better is the forbearance that Shmuel displayed with the Persian than the impatience that Rav showed toward him, for otherwise the Persian might have returned to his

> heathenism. It is thus about him that Scripture said, "Better a patient spirit than a haughty spirit."

This midrash describes a Persian asking Rav and then Shmuel to teach him Torah. As the story unfolds, Rav and Shmuel both react differently to the recalcitrant pride of the Persian man, who in the end does not trust the sages' teaching of the alphabet. Rav rebukes the Persian, whereas Shmuel is patient, but he violently tugs on the ear of the Persian to teach him a lesson. As Hirshman notes, this dialogue between the Persian and the Babylonian sages deals with "the epistemological basis of the teacher's knowledge."[69] The Persian, acting as other, does not trust the authority of the rabbis' teachings. The invocation of a Persian as a stubborn pupil unable to learn Hebrew, let alone Torah, touches on two of the main anxieties that rabbinic literature expresses toward Persian others—namely, questions of knowledge and authority.

As in *Ecclesiastes Rabbah,* Rav and Shmuel also appear in the Jerusalem Talmud's portrayals of Persians. For example, *y. Ber.* 6:2 (10b) tells a short story regarding "a Persian,"[70] presumably a Jew, who inquires of Rav whether he is reciting the prayer on bread correctly. The short exchange reads:[71]

> An affair of Rav says thus: A Persian (Jew) [חד פרסוי] came in front of Rav. Since I eat my bread and I do not know how to recite the blessing over it, and I say, "Blessed be He who created this bread." Do I fulfill my obligation? Rav said to him: Yes.

This Persian—whom Hirshman correctly notes "probably denotes a Jew who is barely acquainted with everyday Jewish observance"[72]—asks Rav whether he has fulfilled his obligation in reciting the blessing. This rare usage of the word פרסוי, which appears nowhere else in the rabbinic corpus, helps to express his liminal character: that is, he is a Jew, but one without command of blessings over bread. It is, in other words, due to his lack of knowledge of Jewish prayers that the Talmud designates him Persian—he is Jewish but still other, still Persian.[73] In contrast to *Ecclesiastes Rabbah,* Rav is lenient toward the Persian Jew here.

Elsewhere, the Jerusalem Talmud uses the word "Persian" with reference to gentiles. This story in *y. Šabb.* 16:8 (15d) describes an encounter between Shmuel and a Persian, who lights a lamp on the Sabbath. In both versions of the story below, the gentile is depicted as working on a document. Shmuel turns away, not wanting to benefit from the light, until he realizes that the Persian intended to use it for his own purposes:[74]

> (What is the law) for himself and for a Jew? Let us hear from this: Shmuel was received at a Persian's (house). The lamp went out. The Persian [פרסיי] went and wanted to light it. Shmuel turned his face away. When he saw (the Persian) working on his documents, (Shmuel) knew that (the light) was not for him, and Shmuel turned his face back.

We see a tradition related to this in *b. Šabb.* 122b, where Shmuel encounters a gentile instead of a Persian:[75]

> Shmuel visited the house of Abin of Toran. A gentile came and lit a lamp [שרגא]. Shmuel turned his face away. When he saw that he had brought documents and was reading them he said, he lit it for his own purposes. Shmuel turned his face to the lamp.

The differences between these two texts are illuminating. Whereas the Jerusalem Talmud reports an encounter between Shmuel and a gentile Persian at the Persian's house, the Bavli's protagonists are Shmuel and a gentile in the house of Abin of Toran. In spite of this muting of the Persian character, the Bavli's later version contains the ubiquitous Iranian loanword for "lamp" (שרגא; cf. MP *čirāg*)[76] instead of Aramaic בוציניא, "lamp," which is attested in *y. Šabb.* 16:8. As we see in the comparison of these two sources, as well as in the differences between *Ecclesiastes Rabbah* 7.8.1 and *b. Šabb.* 31a above, there are instances wherein despite common logic Palestinian texts invoke Persians but the Bavli's corresponding texts do not. Whereas in the one case (*Ecclesiastes Rabbah* and *b. Šabb.* 31a) the Palestinian texts include the Persians as distant gentile others, in the other (*y. Šabb.* 16:8 and *b. Šabb.* 122b) the Bavli substitutes a gentile for a Persian. The Bavli's engagement with the Persian world is nevertheless more discerning than the Jerusalem Talmud's, which is merely generic. The sages of Palestine invoked Persians as generic others as a rhetorical device.

In *b. Ta'an.* 24a we find another relevant tale regarding a poor Jew named Ilfa, who, living in a remote "district" (cf. MP *kust*), goes out of his way to acquire wine for Kiddush in order to help other Jews in his area fulfill their ritual duties. For this good act, Ilfa is rewarded with the power to produce rain and wind through prayer. The short story goes as follows:[77]

> Rabbi[78] decreed a fast, but no rain came. Then Ilfa—and some say R. Ilfai[79]—went down in (Rabbi's) presence. He said: "He makes the wind blow," and wind arose. He said: "He makes the showers fall," and rain came. Rabbi asked him: "What do you do (that you are worthy of this ability)?" He said to him: "I reside in a poor [or: 'distant'] district,[80] where there is no wine for Kiddush and Havdalah.[81] I take pains to obtain wine for Kiddush and Havdalah, and I cause them to fulfill their obligation."

By fulfilling the duties of Jewish law in the face of challenges, Ilfa's prayers turn into natural miracles. In this text the Middle Persian loanword reinforces the effect of Ilfa's remoteness in obtaining wine for Havdalah. As seen here, in certain manuscript traditions the Talmud often uses Middle Persian loanwords as a way of creating a dramatic mood expressing distance or otherness.

As noted earlier, the majority of the rabbinic traditions about Persians are in the Bavli. For instance, the Talmud contains several passages on Persian dress, especially on the use of the belt called a "girdle"[82] (המיינא) or an "ornamental belt" (קמרא).[83] The wearing of a belt in Persian society may be broadly related to the Zoroastrian ritual of wearing a *kustīg*, which marks the boundary between the upper and lower sections of the human body.[84] It is notable that *kustīg* is not the term that appears in Jewish Babylonian Aramaic, a fact implying a lack of rabbinic acculturation to Zoroastrian religious practices.[85] The Persian practice of wearing belts for authoritative purposes or as a vogue symbol of high social status was diffused among non-Persian inhabitants in Iran.[86] The example of belts demonstrates how Jews and other groups were part of a single cultural orbit, a trend also seen in the use of Persian names and dietary habits among Sasanian Jews.[87] As Shaul Shaked notes, Babylonian Jews actually expressed their identity as Iranians through the wearing of a girdle:[88]

> Whatever the origin of the occasional wearing of a girdle in Judaism of the Talmudic period, it became an element in the discourse between Jews and Iranians. It was also sometimes used to distinguish between Jews in Babylonia (who lived within the orbit of Iran) from Jews in other areas. A similar observation can be made, as we have seen, about the . . . Jewish custom . . . of avoiding talk at mealtime. Both practices are highly meaningful ritual requirements in Zoroastrianism, and both have no more than a social etiquette value in Judaism. Neither the one nor the other custom ever gained a status of legal requirement in Judaism.

As Shaked spells out, the Zoroastrian rituals of not talking during a meal and wearing a girdle enter Judaism not as Halakhah but rather as social etiquette or custom.

In addition to the girdle, the Talmud also mentions an ornamental belt, a lavish accessory, called *qamrā*. Geo Widengren has defined this type of belt as belonging to warriors and covered with jewels.[89] The political significance of this type of belt is documented in Middle Persian sources. For example, in the *Naqš-i Rostam* inscription, Hormizd I endows the high priest Kirder with a hat and belt (*kulāf ud kamar*) to mark his status.

The following sugya in *b. Šabb.* 59b discusses the prohibition against wearing tiaras and belts on the Sabbath in the context of stories about Levi's arrival in Nehardea. In this passage, Levi has come to Nehardea after a series of events that took place in Palestine. In that narrative, R. Ḥanina refuses to take over as a leader of the rabbinic academies after the death of Rabbi Judah the Prince, despite the latter's request. Instead, R. Afeis, an elder sage, takes over, while Levi goes to join R. Ḥanina in study. But R. Afeis eventually dies, leaving R. Ḥanina to take over the responsibilities and Levi to travel to Nehardea. An excerpt of this passage, which includes references to two and possibly three Iranian belts, reads as follows:[90]

> Levi[91] expounded in Nehardea (that) a tiara is permitted (on the Sabbath), (and) twenty-four tiaras came out in all of Nehardea (on the Sabbath). Rabbah bar Avuha[92]

expounded in Maḥoza (that) a tiara is permitted, (and) eighteen tiaras came out from one alley. Rav Yehudah said in the name of Shmuel:[93] A *qamrā* is permitted. There are some who say that (this is) a piece of cloth. And Rav Safra said: (It is permitted,) just as a cloak made of gold (is permitted). There are some who say that (it references) woven material. And Rav Safra said: (It is permitted,) just as a belt of kings (is permitted). Ravina said to Rav Ashi: What about wearing a *qamrā* over a *hamyānā?* He replied: Are you talking about two *hamyānā*s?! Rav Ashi said: In the case of a *rîsûqā,*[94] if it has fringes, then it is permitted; but if not, then it is prohibited.

Upon arriving in Nehardea, Levi expounds that "a tiara is permitted" to be worn on the Sabbath. After the sage declares this, the passage explains, twenty-four women in Nehardea follow Levi's dictum and go out on the Sabbath with tiaras. Mirroring Levi's tradition, our passage states that after Rabbah bar Avuha declared tiaras permissible in Maḥoza, eighteen women from a single alley wore them. This text is engaging the halakhic problem of whether a *qamrā* is considered a permissible ornament, with Rav Safra arguing that it is allowed because it is like a cloak of gold or belt of kings. At the end of the dialogue, Ravina queries what would happen if one put a *qamrā* on top of a *hamyānā:* that is to say, as an ornament. Rav Ashi's answer probes whether what Ravina meant was two *hamyānā*s before then expounding the case of what is probably a third Iranian belt, *rîsûqā,* which he describes as having fringes.[95] As we have seen multiple times, Persian culture, as in this case, enters into halakhic debate, with the rabbis using Iranian loanwords with knowledge of their precise cultural implications.

IRANIAN LOANWORDS IN THE BABYLONIAN TALMUD

According to my conservative estimate, the Babylonian Talmud contains approximately two hundred or so Iranian loanwords.[96] As other scholars have observed, there is no doubt that this number is paltry when compared to the thousands of Latin and Greek words that are found in rabbinic literature, as counted by Samuel Krauss at the end of the nineteenth century in his book *Griechische und lateinische Lehnwörter im Talmud, Midrasch und Targum.*[97] Despite this dearth in comparison with the Palestinian context, there is great value in researching the Bavli's Iranian loanwords as part of this book's study. From the outset, it is important to clarify that my tally of two hundred Iranian loanwords is complicated by the frequent uncertainty of defining what a loanword is. This determination is based on a variety of factors, not least of which is the fact that many of the words' etymologies involve linguistic reconstruction and guesswork. Indeed, the majority of the loanwords are reconstructed from Middle Iranian, a broad category that refers to Iranian languages in use from around the end of the Achaemenid period to the early Islamic era. Middle Iranian thus includes Middle Persian as well as, in the northern and eastern geographic regions, Parthian and Sogdian, among other languages.

Not all Iranian loanwords in the Bavli are extensions of Middle Persian, since one can trace the influence of various Iranian dialects, including Parthian, in certain words. Numerous loanwords in the Talmud are, in fact, rare attestations that have no extant or precise cognates in Middle Persian, thereby making them uniquely significant to Iranian linguists.

In addition to the reconstructive nature of etymological research, another problem that scholars face is attempting to calculate the time periods and channels through which specific Iranian words entered Jewish Aramaic. The borrowings and interpenetrations between languages in Iran are the result of centuries of contact, sometimes antedating the Sasanian era, and are not easy processes for scholars to trace.[98] Some Iranian loanwords in the Talmud clearly predate the rabbinic period, having penetrated official Aramaic during the Second Temple era through the intermediary of Old Persian or another language. The Achaemenid Empire's use of Aramaic for official administrative communications opened the door for Iranian-Aramaic interchanges. As one case in point, the loanword for "matter" (פתגמא) appears in its plural form in *b. B. Bat.* 136a in the phrase "in a record of the matters that were before us," yet it is already found, in Hebrew via Aramaic, in the Hebrew Bible (Esth. 1:20).[99] The appearance of this and other Iranian words in the Talmud is, therefore, not novel.

By contrast, other Iranian loanwords that crop up in the Talmud are words that were commonly used in multiple Aramaic dialects in late antique Persia. Although this fact offers scholars potentially useful comparative data by which to study interactions through the lens of language sharing, it simultaneously complicates scholarly claims that there existed direct avenues of Iranian linguistic penetration on the rabbis. Both the fluidity of exchanges between languages in proximity and the possibility of intermediary languages such as Syriac, Mandaic, and Armenian, in fact lessen the prospect of direct Iranian–Jewish Aramaic contact. For instance, the words אוונא, "station," and מרגא, "meadow," appear in many different languages of the late antique East.[100] Both the Bavli and Syriac texts, for their parts, contain a comparable range of Iranian words, as for example in the realm of food (e.g., "cinnamon") and government administration,[101] overlaps that suggest the possibility of other trends in Iranian penetration into different Aramaic dialects. As in the Talmud, a category of the Iranian loanwords in Syriac applies to everyday life, especially items of food, clothing, or the household (e.g., "nut," "artichoke," "wine," "silk," "apron," "shoe"). However, in comparison with the types of loanwords in the Talmud, those in the Syriac corpus exhibit a more intimate knowledge of the Zoroastrian religion and include the words "heretic," "Avesta," "barsom" (twigs), "kin marriage," and "Mazdean feast."[102] Taken at face value, this distinction intimates that Iranian languages impacted Christians more than Jews. In the end, it is difficult for scholars working today to determine to what extent ancient people who spoke different dialects of Aramaic were able to converse with each other, let alone across Iranian and Aramaic. In my view, even though the loanwords are signposts of interculturality between Persians and Jews, they do not necessarily imply that speakers of different language groups were able to communicate freely with one another.[103] Pending further research, this consequential question is outstanding.

My tally of two hundred Iranian loanwords in the Talmud is subject to change depending upon how one construes the exercise of counting. To be more specific, there are two determining factors that one must consider in a more precise enumeration—namely, the number of times that a loanword appears in the various manuscript witnesses of a given text, and the number of times that a single loanword appears in different passages throughout the entire Babylonian Talmud. For instance, there are Iranian loanwords that appear only once in the entire Talmud, such as דמינקא, "bellows," found in *b. Sanh.* 74b in reference to Zoroastrian fire rituals. There are also loanwords that materialize in only one (or sometimes several) of the manuscript witnesses of a given text. In these cases, the Iranian loanword typically appears in lieu of its Aramaic synonym. For example, the Florence manuscript of *b. Ber.* 40a uses the Iranian term גוווזא, "branch," in the spot where the Oxford manuscript refers to the common and expected Aramaic word אילנא, "tree."[104] These divergences between manuscripts may be the outcome of different oral performances or scribal practices of Jews who exhibited more or less comfort or familiarity with Iranian languages. More intensive study of such phenomena is needed in order to determine which manuscripts—as for example, as is often proposed, the Yemenite group—are more reliable in their renderings of Iranian words. Given the complexity of the transmission of the Talmud, it is hard to prove that Iranized rabbis, editors, or scribes were intentionally substituting Iranian loanwords for Aramaic terms in received traditions. Nevertheless, there are instances in which it is clear that the rabbis were cognizant of such exchanges in an exegetical context. On several occasions, the Talmud invokes an Iranian loanword as part of its exegesis of an equivalent or ambiguous biblical or mishnaic term. For example, in *b. Meg.* 12b the Talmud explicitly correlates the Persian word "lees" (דורדיא; cf. NP *durdī*) with Jeremiah 48:11's statement that Moab "is settled on his lees [שמר]." In a more complicated example of this phenomenon found in *b. Šabb.* 20b, the rabbis use wordplay to interpret an obscure word in the Mishnah by defining it as its Iranian homonym. The word under scrutiny is כלך (*m. Šabb.* 2:1), a type of wool. In seeking a definition for this word, the Bavli builds upon the Jerusalem Talmud's parallel tradition, which alludes to popular folklore. ("I inquired of all the sailors, and they told me that it is soft wool from goat's hair.") The Jerusalem Talmud contains the Persian loanword כולכא, meaning "soft wool from goat's hair" (cf. NP *kulk*). Remodeling this tradition to a Babylonian context, *b. Šabb.* 20b fleshes out the problem by giving at least one additional Iranian word, or perhaps two, as identifying the material.[105] An excerpt of *b. Šabb.* 20b, which includes a reference to the exilarch, reads: "Ravin and Abaye were sitting before

Rabbana Nehemiah, the brother of the exilarch. They saw that he was wearing silk. Ravin said to Abaye: 'This is the כלך that we learned in the Mishnah.' (Abaye) said: 'We call it פרנדא' ['silk'; cf. NP *parand*, 'silk']." In this sugya, the Babylonian Amora Abaye uses an Iranian loanword pertaining to everyday life ("silk") in order to distinguish between different grades of silk and helps to define an ambiguous term. This passage displays how the Talmud uses Iranian loanwords in an intentional and creative fashion for purposes of exegesis.

Although my total of two hundred Iranian loanwords in the Talmud is somewhat meager and in some respects disappointing, one must remember that there are in fact certain loanwords that surface upwards of a dozen times or more throughout the corpus. For example, the words אושפיזא, "lodging, inn," and its derivatives (cf. MP *aspinj*), and בגא, "rural area" (MP *bāg*) are ubiquitous.[106] Based on my conservative estimate, I believe that there are roughly seven hundred to eight hundred occurrences of the two hundred different loanwords throughout the entire corpus. Moreover, the grand total of Iranian loanwords in Jewish Babylonian Aramaic increases if one expands the dividing line to include words that are found in Geonic sources or the Aramaic bowls, only some of which are also in the Talmud.[107] In the end, this sum total of Iranian loanwords in the Talmud is still extremely small when put into perspective, since the only complete copy of the Talmud, the Munich manuscript, is comprised of around 1.4 million words (excluding the Mishnah).[108]

Iranian loanwords in the Talmud are usually either technical terms in the realm of Sasanian administration or law or, more commonly, words from everyday life, especially regarding fashion or food.[109] Some loanwords may have also been part of a standardization system among different language groups in realms of everyday life such as weights, measurements, food, and currency.[110] Shaked has aptly classified the Iranian loanwords in the Bavli according to those that relate to the state and administration, titles of office, justice, punishment, military, and textiles.[111] There are surprisingly few loanwords that have meaningful Zoroastrian religious or ritual connotations,[112] a fact that weakens research assuming Jewish-Persian interaction was in the realm of religious practice or theology. Talmudic Aramaic also absorbed Iranian adjectives, enclitics, prepositions, and adverbs as common as "black" (סייב or סיואה; cf. Middle Parthian *syāw*), "now, then" (זי; cf. NP *zī*), "also" (הם; cf. MP *ham*), and perhaps the common Middle Persian preposition *pad*, "at, to, on, by."[113] The existence of Aramaic verbs derived from Iranian loanwords—for example, אווש, "to make a sound" (MP *āwāz*) and הנדז, "to make equal, overlap" (MP *handāz*)—also certifies the deep penetration of Iranian languages into Jewish dialects.[114]

From a source-critical perspective Iranian loanwords can help scholars in multiple ways. They are patent indicators of rabbinic activity in Babylonia and perhaps even particular geographical locales and datings and can thus assist Talmudists in establishing the provenance of traditions.[115] With respect to manuscripts, the prominence or conservatism of Iranian loanwords in distinct manuscript traditions of certain tractates in the Bavli (e.g., a Yemenite manuscript of Sanhedrin) can help in the reconstruction of our sources by tracing which manuscripts are related to one another.[116] Loanwords can also point to specific tractates or generations of sages that were more acclimated to Persian culture. There are individual rabbis to whom loanwords are attributed more frequently, but also a wide range of sages who say Persian words in one form or another. In the passages treated at length in this book, Rav, Shmuel, Rav Naḥman, Rav Yosef, Rava, Ameimar, Rav Ashi, Ravina, and the anonymous editors all use loanwords. Finally, it behooves scholars to elucidate the potential significance, if there is any to be found, of the clustering of loanwords in certain sections of the Bavli, such as *b. B. Meṣiʿa* 83a–86a and *b. Taʿan.* 20a–24b: each of the two passages contains approximately seventeen Iranian words. In sum, more detailed studies of the Iranian loanwords can open up new paths of data for unraveling the formation of the Bavli.

Although there is value in comparing the Bavli's loanwords with their Middle Persian counterparts, it is important to note that such words do not always carry the same semantic meaning in Middle Persian as they do in Aramaic. A Middle Iranian word that entered Aramaic can have come to mean something different in the new host language. One example of this transformation is the expansion of the semantic range of the word בגא, which in the Bavli means "rural area adjoining a city," from Middle Persian *bāg*, meaning "garden."[117] Such differences in meaning may simply result from the passing of time or geographical disparities between their occurrences in our extant literature. They may also point to the independent mutation of borrowed words in a non-Persian society. This point can also be demonstrated in a study of the word פרדשנא, "gift in return for another gift" (cf. MP *pādāšn*, "gift, reward"), found in *b. ʿAbod. Zar.* 71a.[118] As in other Talmudic images of the Persians, Rav Ashi here explains that the cause of Persian cultural habits is their haughtiness (רמות רוחא). The legal context of this passage deals with how ownership over objects, including in transactions with non-Jews, is conferred through different modes of acquisition. In this case, the method by which the ownership of property is transferred is not through the exchange of money or a verbal contract but rather through the act of pulling (*mĕšîkâ*), wherein the buyer pulls the object in the presence of the seller. This mode of acquisition is also applicable in the case of gifts. In our passage below, Ameimar and Rav Ashi debate whether *mĕšîkâ* is a legitimate mode of acquisition with gentiles. Ameimar alludes to the Persian practice of sending gifts without return as evidence for his halakhah before Rav Ashi explains that the Persian practice is not an example of *mĕšîkâ* but rather a manifestation of Persian pride:[119]

> Ameimar said: *mĕšîkâ* with a gentile is acquisition. Know (this is so), for the Persians [פרסאי][120] send פרדישני[121] to each other in return, and (the senders) do not take them

back. Rav Ashi said: In fact[122] *měšîkâ* with a gentile is not acquisition. And the reason that they [i.e., the senders] do not take back (the gifts) is haughtiness that overcomes them.

In this text, Rav Ashi says that the Persians do not retract their gifts because of the pride that overcomes them. This phrase is also found in *b. Šabb.* 94a in reference to how the Persians ride horses. The Middle Persian word *pādāšn* is well attested in the *Dēnkard* and *Dādestān ī Dēnīg*, often as a reward of good deeds (*kirbag pādāšn*) or a reward of the righteous (MP *pādāšn ī ahlawān* or *ahlāyīh*).[123] It is essentially a reward for maintaining one's Zoroastrian beliefs. Thus, whereas the Bavli describes this word as a material gift, Pahlavi sources such as *Dēnkard* Book 6 explain that it is one's duty to seek the reward of good deeds from the spirits (*mēnōgān*) and not from the material world (*gētīg*). There is, therefore, a gap in meaning between the Bavli's loanword and its Middle Persian counterpart, with the Talmud's meaning something closer to Middle Persian *dāšn*, which also appears in the Talmud (*b. Sanh.* 94b). This example emphasizes the caution that scholars should use when trying to compare the Iranian loanwords in the Talmud with their Middle Persian counterparts. In short, there are several complicating factors in any comparison of Middle Persian and Talmudic texts using loanwords as the basis.

If we accept that Saul Lieberman's proposition—that "almost every foreign word and phrase have their '*raison d'être*' in rabbinic literature"[124]—applies not only to Greek and Latin loanwords but also to Iranian ones, then what purpose do the latter serve in the Bavli? At times the Talmud invokes Iranian loanwords intentionally, as a means of identifying Persians as others.[125] In other words, the use of Iranian loanwords sometimes indicates a conscious attempt on the part of the Talmudic tradents to allude to some aspect of the Persian world.[126] Technically speaking, one could debate whether these are in fact loanwords, since the rabbis were imitating Persian speech. In addition, Geoffrey Herman counts more than twenty Iranian loanwords in texts about the exilarch, an institution with ties to the Persian elite.[127] That the Bavli uses Iranian words in reference to Persians is evidence that the tradents were aware of the words' meanings or Persian origins. There were certain Jews in late antique Iran who possessed at least a minimal knowledge of spoken dialects of Middle Persian.[128] In an article on rabbinic culture, Isaiah Gafni has described Jewish knowledge of Middle Persian languages in the following manner:[129]

Babylonian Jews were clearly aware that other languages were also in use in their immediate vicinity, most significantly the Parthian and Pahlavi dialects of what is commonly called "Middle Persian." Although the literary heritage of this dialect was preserved primarily in Zoroastrian writings rooted in the Sassanian period but surviving primarily in products of the ninth and tenth centuries, it did serve as the vernacular of the Sassanians and would probably have been identified by the Babylonian rabbis as the language of the Iranian government and clergy. As such, the rabbis

> apparently attained some degree of familiarity with Middle Persian and even introduced it into their exegetical activity.

Babylonian Jews were exposed to the Middle Persian vernacular, the official language of the Sasanian Empire. It is fair to assume that the Jews of pre-Islamic Iran would have had greater exposure to Persian languages than subsequent generations when Arabic flourished. Robert Brody has explained the status of Persian among the Geonim as follows:[130]

> With regard to Persian, which had much deeper roots in Babylonia and continued to occupy an important position as the second language of Islam, the situation is less clear. There is good reason to believe that certain Geonim did not know Persian; these include Se'adyah Gaon, who repeatedly refers to "all the languages we know" in statements which apply only to Semitic languages. On the other hand, some responsa, especially those of Hayya Gaon, seem to reflect a knowledge of Persian, although there is no unequivocal evidence to this effect. It seems likely that some Geonim had some knowledge of this language, while others did not.

As I noted earlier, there are Iranian loanwords that are attested only in Geonic texts. If there were some Geonim who knew some Persian, then it seems likely that there were rabbis and Jews living in the Sasanian era who knew as much if not more of the language of their neighbors.

In the Talmud, the rabbis sometimes explicitly discuss the meaning of Middle Persian words.[131] The following text is *b. 'Abod. Zar.* 24b:[132]

> Rava[133] said: According to what do the Persians [פרסאי] call the scribe [סיפרא] *dibīr* [דביר]? From this: "the name of Debir [דביר] was formerly Kiriath-sefer [קרית ספר]" (Jud. 1:11). Rav Ashi said: According to what do the Persians call a menstruating woman דשתנה [cf. MP *daštān*]? From this: "for the period of women is upon me" [כי דרך נשים לי] (Gen. 31:35).

In these traditions of Rava and Rav Ashi, Persian words are given folk explanations through reference to biblical words that sound similar. Rava connects the Persian word for "scribe," *dibīr*, with biblical Debir, an ancient city near Hebron that the tribes of Judah conquered (see Judges 1:8-15), which used to be called Kiriath-sefer (literally "book city"). In other words, the text from Judges itself associates the place Debir, which sounds the same as the Middle Persian word *dibīr*, with the place Kiriath-sefer, the latter word of which contains the same root as the Aramaic word for "scribe" (*sefer*). Rava is, in other words, using a biblical verse to explain the reason behind the Persian word's phonology. After Rava's tradition, Rav Ashi performs a similar type of move, though it is less clear whether this exegesis is based on an acronym (e.g., the letters dalet and shin somehow represent Middle Persian *daštān*, "menstruant"), as Rashi suggests, or is an apology for Jewish menstruation rituals against similar Zoroastrian practices.[134]

Scholars have debated to what extent the rabbis understood, read, and wrote Middle Persian.[135] In practical terms, this question affected how the rabbis dealt with legal documents in non-Jewish languages like Persian.[136] In *b. Giṭ.* 19b, the rabbis deliberate over the proper action for dealing with legal documents and signatures in non-Jewish languages. This issue appears in a discussion of what to do when witnesses cannot read the documents that they need to sign. The status of divorce documents in such circumstances was of particular interest to the sages, hinting at the fact that divorce law was an area of rabbinic jurisdiction. Are divorce documents in Persian valid? In what follows, the fifth-generation Babylonian Amora Rav Pappa explains how to handle a Persian document produced in a gentile office:[137]

[A] Whenever a Persian document, produced in a gentile office, would come before Rav Pappa, he would have two gentiles read it (aloud), not in each other's presence, as if talking incidentally [i.e., without knowledge of the legal bearing],[138] and (if they agreed), he would (rely upon it to such an extent that he would even) collect (a debt) from mortgaged property.

[B] Rav Ashi said that Rav Huna bar Nathan told me that Ameimar said thus: that this Persian document upon which Jewish witnesses are signed—we would collect (a debt) with it from mortgaged property.

[C] But surely they [i.e., the witnesses] do not know how to read (it).

[D] When they do know.

[E] But surely we need writing that cannot be forged, but this is not (such a case).

[F] When it was processed with gallnut juice.

[G] But we require (the scribe) to repeat the matters of the document in the last line, but this is not (such a case).

[H] When it was recapitulated.

[I] But what is (Ameimar) trying to tell us? That any language is valid?

[J] We have learned [in *m. Giṭ.* 9:8]: A bill of divorce written in Hebrew with witnesses signed in Greek, or written in Greek with witnesses in Hebrew, is valid.

[K] If (the rule comes) from that (mishnah), I would say that these words (apply) in (only cases of) divorce documents; but in the case of other documents, no, (they cannot be written in a foreign language).

[L] It teaches us.

What does this text suggest about the status of Persian languages in Jewish Babylonia? At the beginning, Rav Pappa receives a Persian document produced in a gentile office. Rav Pappa's procedure for comprehending and verifying its contents is to have two gentiles who know the language read the document and then compare their readings. The implication here, if this interpretation of the text is correct,[139] is that Rav Pappa understood Persian and was wont to enforce such documents as valid and collect debts based on them. Line B introduces a tradition ascribed to Ameimar through the mouths of his contemporaries Rav Ashi and Rav Huna bar Nathan. Like Rav Yosef, Ameimar is one of the sages frequently cited in the Talmudic texts about Persia. A famous judge from the sixth generation, Ameimar considered rational thought and everyday circumstances in his legal rulings, sometimes at the expense of Tannaitic law.[140] In our text above, Ameimar declares that debts should be collected based on Persian documents with the signatures of Jewish witnesses. After this tradition, lines C and D begin a series of rhetorical questions and answers by probing whether this could be the law, given that these witnesses would not be able to read Persian documents—to which the answer is, it is the law in cases when the witnesses can read them. The same formula is then repeated about the threat of forgery and the recapitulation of the matter in the final line of the document (lines E–H).

The Iranian loanwords in the Talmud are frequently misspelled or defective as a result of scribal errors. Indeed, one of the challenges in determining to what extent the rabbis possessed knowledge of Persia lies in understanding how to interpret Talmudic passages that seem to contain inaccuracies regarding Persian words or culture. Are such inaccuracies indicative of the rabbis' lack of knowledge, or are they simply errors in transmission? Making particular reference to *b. 'Abod. Zar.* 11b's list of Persian festivals, a text that was a topic of early interest in the field of Irano-Talmudica,[141] Jacob Neusner argues that such inaccuracies prove how little the rabbis knew about their neighbors:[142]

> Furthermore, when the rabbinic literature refers to Iranian festivals, its information is garbled and inaccurate. In fact, the rabbis allude to only a few of the Iranian religious holidays, and of these, in particular, two were days on which taxes had to be paid. . . . What is most striking . . . first of all, is the absence of information on the correct names of the various festivals, all of which indicate lack of precise knowledge. Second, the Jewish sayings indicate little or no insight about the *meaning* of the festivals.

Neusner's interpretation of the Talmud's "garbled and inaccurate" information regarding Persian festivals as being evidence of a lack of rabbinic knowledge ignores the role of later copyists in the transmission of our manuscripts. The rabbis' renderings of Iranian loanwords fell victim to later transmitters who did not know the Persian language well or, for that matter, Talmudic Aramaic. In an article on Iranian linguistic influences on Jewish Middle Aramaic, Shaul Shaked explains this phenomenon in the following way:[143]

> Jewish Middle Aramaic, it may be recalled, came down to us largely in manuscripts copied by people for whom this was a dead literary language. As a result, Iranian words may often hide their true original identity because they lost some of their characteristic features through careless textual transmission.

The Talmud's list of Persian festivals in *b. ʿAbod. Zar.* 11b helps to illustrate this sort of transmittal error. This list of four Persian festivals, which has a parallel in the Jerusalem Talmud, occurs in a legal discussion regarding prohibitions on conducting business with gentiles during their festivals. Each witness contains a different spelling of the same Persian festival, with several letters consistently miscopied. Here is the passage, with some of the manuscript variants based on the Talmud text database:[144]

> And what are (the festivals) of the Persians?
> [MS Paris 1337] מוסדרי וטרייסקי מוהרקי ומחרוז
> [MS Munich 95] מוטיררי וטירייסקי מוהרסנקי ומוהרן
> [Vilna/Pesaro Print] מוטרדי וטוריסקי מוהרנקי ומוהרין

Of these four Persian festivals, only two have been clearly identified: מוסדרי as Nōwrōz and מוהרקי as Mihragān.[145] Some scholars have argued that טרייסקי is Tihragān,[146] but this is difficult to corroborate. Our inability to identify the other two with confidence is probably a result of the errors of transmission, or, potentially, a gap in our scholarly knowledge of the names of Iranian festivals.

The Jerusalem Talmud preserves a similar list of festivals, part of which it characterizes as Median. This text exhibits both similarities and differences with the list that appears in the Bavli. For instance, although it mentions three of the same festivals as the later Bavli pericope, it does so in Hebrew and under the heading of Media (not Persia). Furthermore, in contrast to the anonymous Aramaic list of the festivals in the passage from the Bavli, in the Jerusalem Talmud the Babylonian sage Rav Naḥman bar Yaakov, in the name of Rav Huna, also provides a precise phonetic rendering of the festival of Nōwrōz:[147]

> Three in Media: נוסרדי ותירייסקי ומהירקנה. Rav Huna said in the name of Rav Naḥman bar Yaakov: Nōwrōz [נרוס or נרוז] (is) on the second of Adar in Persia [בפרס], on the twentieth of Adar in Media.

Whether the tradition about Nōwrōz originated in Babylonia, as suggested by the presence of the two Babylonian Amoraim, is hard to determine based on extant evidence. In the end, these two texts bear witness to the fact that some of the Talmud's inaccuracies about Persia are the result of errors in transmission.

A MAGIAN'S TALE

Among the Talmud's few explicit references to Zoroastrianism is a dialogue in *b. Sanh.* 39a between a magian and Ameimar. In this short tale, which has been discussed at length by other scholars in the context of the ritual *kustīg* belt,[148] the Zoroastrian priest references how the upper and lower halves of the human body belong to Ohrmazd and Ahriman, respectively:[149]

> A certain magian [אמגושא] said to Ameimar: From your waist up belongs to Hormiz,[150] and from your waist down belongs to Ahriman.[151] Ameimar said to him:[152] Why does Ahriman allow Hormiz to pass water through his land?

This brief dialogue represents the rabbis' attempt to subvert a Zoroastrian concept. For the magian, the upper half of the body, which includes our heart and head, represents the deity Ohrmazd (here spelled Hormiz; sometimes also Hormin),[153] whereas the lower half, which includes our stomach, is Ahriman. The fifth-generation Babylonian sage Ameimar is seen here challenging a magian's logic connecting the duality of the body with the duality of the chief deities. Adding to the polemical tone of the sage's response, Ameimar's reference to water acts as a metaphor for urine, an impurity in Zoroastrianism. The spatial dualism implied in the magian's statement regarding the duality of the human body conforms to the macrocosm of Zoroastrian cosmogony, wherein at the beginning of time Ohrmazd from above and Ahriman from below battle each other from the polar opposites of the firmament. The first chapter of the *Bundahišn* explains that Ohrmazd "was forever the most high in his omniscience and goodness," whereas Ahriman "rose from the depths" and his "deep station" to challenge the creator.[154] This cosmogonic dualism led to physical dualism, which, as scholars have noted, was often symbolized among Zoroastrians by the wearing of the *kustīg* belt.

THE BIBLICAL ORIGINS OF THE PERSIANS

The Babylonian rabbis' memory of the past was projected through both biblical and social lenses. The exegetes interpreted biblical narratives, especially those related to the Babylonian diaspora in the sixth century B.C.E., in part on the basis of their lived experiences in Sasanian Babylonia. Biblical Babylon became a symbolic space in which the rabbis could discuss their identity as Babylonians one millennium removed.[155] For instance, the rabbis decoded biblical sites and genealogies, such as the Tower of Babylon and the Table of Nations, in light of their contemporary geographical locales. For the Jews of late antiquity, Babylonia was an exilic homeland entrenched in a lachrymose memory of diaspora, exemplified in Psalm 137's expression of loss and nostalgia: "By the rivers of Babylon, there we sat, sat and wept, as we thought of Zion." Yet centuries after the destruction of the Second Temple and the editing of the Jerusalem Talmud, Babylon became an asset to Persian Jewry's claims of legal authority over their Palestinian coreligionists.[156] The Babylonian Amoraim and editors of the Bavli often subvert the negative symbolism assigned to exilic Babylon, instead taking pride in local achievements. For instance, in several places the Talmud argues that the Torah and the Divine Presence were located in Babylonia, not Israel. To cite one example, a tradition attributed to Abaye in *b. Meg.* 29a explains that the Divine Presence went into exile with the Babylonian Jews and is found "in the synagogue of Ḥutzal and in the synagogue of Shaf ve-Yativ in Nehardea."[157] For the Babylonian rabbis, God was present in the synagogues in Babylonia, including presumably the one in Mata Meḥasya, near Sura, populated with scholars including Rav Ashi.[158]

Let us now turn to a lengthy sugya about the Persians in *b. Yoma* 9b–10a that illustrates how the Babylonian rabbis connected themselves and their biblical heritage to their contemporary surroundings. This passage is part of a collection of texts in rabbinic literature that comments on Genesis 10's Table of Nations from the line of Noah (10:1–12). Rabbinic literature identifies the origins of the Persians with Tiras, a descendant of Noah's son Japheth.[159] In its exegesis of Genesis 9:27 and 10:1–12, the editors connect some of the descendants of Noah with place names in Sasanian Iran, including Ctesiphon,[160] Kashkar, Hamadan,[161] and Inner and Outer Sakistan.[162] The use of these specific geographical toponyms demonstrates an awareness on the editors' part of the locales in other regions of Iran outside Babylonia. This passage highlights the equal roles played by both exegesis and historical context in the rabbis' engagement with Persia. An excerpt from this important text about the Persians reads as follows:[163]

[A] When (Resh Lakish) came in front of R. Yoḥanan, (R. Yoḥanan) said to him: Even if all (Jews) had immigrated, the Divine Presence would not have resided in the Second Temple, as it is written: "May God enlarge Japheth, and let him dwell in the tents of Shem" (Gen. 9:27). Although God enlarged Japheth, the Divine Presence resides only in the tents of Shem.

[B] And the Persians [פרסאי]: Where does it say that they are descended from Japheth?

[C] For it is written: "The descendants of Japheth: Gomer, Magog, Madai, Javan, Tubal, Meshech, and Tiras" (Gen. 10:2).

[D] Gomer is Germania. Magog is Gintiya. Madai is Macedonia. Yavan is meant in its literal sense. Tubal is Bait Unaiki. Meshech is Musia.

[E] Tiras is a matter of dispute between R. Simai and the rabbis. Others say: R. Simon and the rabbis—one said it is Traiki, and one said it is Persia.

[F] Rav Yosef taught a baraita: Tiras is Persia [פרס].

[G] "Sabtah, Raamah, and Sabteca" (Gen. 10:7). Rav Yosef taught: Inner Sakistan and Outer Sakistan. Between the two (is a distance of) one hundred[164] parasangs, and the circumference (of the outer one) is one thousand parasangs.

[H] "The mainstays of (Nimrod's) kingdom were Babylon, Erech, Accad, and Calneh" (Gen. 10:10).

[I] Babylon is meant in its literal sense. Erech is Orech. Accad is Kashkar.[165] Calneh is Nifar.

[J] "From that land Asshur went forth" (Gen. 10:11).
[K] Rav Yosef taught in a baraita: Asshur is Silak.
[L] "and built Nineveh, Rehoboth-ir, Calah" (ibid.).
[M] Nineveh is meant in its literal sense. Rehoboth-ir is Perat of Meishan.[166] Calah is Perat of Bursif.
[N] "and Resen between Nineveh and Calah, that is the great city" (Gen. 10:12).
[O] Resen is Ctesiphon.

This sugya begins with R. Yoḥanan explaining to Resh Lakish why the Divine Presence existed only in the First Temple of Solomon and not in the Second Temple that the Persian Achaemenids helped to rebuild. In support of this position, R. Yoḥanan cites Genesis 9:27, a reference to Japheth that rabbinic texts associate with Cyrus the Great. Additionally, *Genesis Rabbah* 36.8 interprets "May God enlarge Japheth" as referencing "Cyrus, who ordered the Temple to be rebuilt." After R. Yoḥanan's pro-Roman statement, the anonymous editors (line B) query what evidence exists that the Persians are descendants of Japheth, Noah's third son. The Talmud answers this query by explicating the biblical genealogy in Genesis 10:2, a line from the Table of Nations that lists Japheth's descendants, including, in the seventh and final slot, Tiras. In line D, the exegetes then go one by one through these biblical names, connecting them with present-day geographical locations: Gomer is Germania; Magog is Gintiya; and so forth. There are no historical facts behind such identifications. After defining the first six names of Japheth's descendants, the Bavli records a dispute between either R. Simai or R. Simon and the rabbis regarding the proper identification of Tiras—one says it is Traiki; another says it is Persia. Rav Yosef's baraita stating that Tiras is Persia resolves the debate.[167]

In our passage above, Rav Yosef identifies Akkad (Gen. 10:10) with the city of Kashkar (i.e., Bashkar). The city of Kashkar was located in the region of Mesene and was an important center of Christian *Catholikoi* in the fifth and sixth centuries.[168] Elsewhere in the Bavli, Kashkar, where it is said that no rabbis resided,[169] is mentioned as a location wherein a Persian "provincial chief" is seated. In *b. Giṭ.* 80b, several Babylonian Amoraim elaborate on the "provincial chief" (אסטנדרא; cf. MP *ōstāndār*) of Kashkar in a deliberation on the necessity of dating a divorce document to the year of the reigning kingdom. According to the Sasanian law book the *Mādayān ī Hazār Dādestān,* the *ōstāndār* was a post responsible for the property taxes transferred to the royal treasury.[170] The perciope of the mishnah upon which this text is based (*m. Giṭ.* 8:5) treats a case wherein, according to the Gemara and the explications of Rashi, a Jew in Babylonia writes a divorce deed according to the year of the Roman emperor as opposed to the year of the Persian monarch. As stated in the mishnah, a divorce deed should be dated according to the local kingdom. In the Gemara the Babylonian sage Ulla explains that this rule is intended "for the sake of peace with the kingdom." The passage then reads:[171]

> A certain divorce deed had written in it the name of the אסטנדרא[172] of Kashkar. Rav Naḥman bar Rav Ḥisda sent (it) to Rabbah:[173] What is (the law) in this case? (Rabbah) sent him (this reply): Even R. Meir agrees (that the divorce deed is valid). What is the reason? (The official) is from that kingdom. And why is this different from (the case of) a *santer* in the city? There, it is an insult to them; here, it is an honor to them.

This passage discusses the ramifications of having a divorce document that was dated according to the *ōstāndār* of Kashkar. Rabbah's answer is that R. Meir's position that such a document is valid holds true in this situation, since it is indeed completed in the name of the administrator in Persia. The subsequent inquiry regarding the question why this is different from the case of a *santer* refers back to an earlier dispute in the sugya, where the sages use the example of divorce document signed in the name of a *santer* as a case of an invalid document. Why, then, is the case of the *ōstāndār* valid? The difference, the editors explain, is that in the case of the *santer* the dating was an insult because the *santer* was not a high official, whereas in the case of the *ōstāndār* the act was seen as an honor, given the high status of this administrative post. This sugya typifies how the Babylonian rabbis reconsidered the validity of and updated earlier mishnaic laws based on the idiosyncrasies of their Persian setting.

Bavli Yoma 9b–10a's exegesis of the Table of Nations in light of Sasanian locales also includes a reference to Perat de-Borsif, a town located next to and, as seen in traditions in *b. Sukkah* 34a and *b. Šabb.* 36a, often interchanged with Babylon. Aharon Oppenheimer has shown how the rabbis, as well as Arabic sources, link the city of Borsif with the biblical events of the Tower of Babylon.[174] A passage in *b. 'Abod. Zar.* 11b also associates this location with the pagan temple of Nabu. The rabbis used this next story, found in *b. Sanh.* 109a, as a means for commenting upon their experiences in Sasanian Babylonia. The Talmud interprets *m. Sanh.* 10:3's condemnation of "the generation of the Dispersion" as having no share in the world to come, a passage that includes a line from Genesis 11:8, the Tower of Babylon story:[175]

> [*M. Sanh.* 10:3] "The generation of the Dispersion has no share in the world to come, as it is written: 'Thus the Lord scattered them from there', (Gen. 11:8) in this world; 'and from there the Lord scattered them' (Gen. 11:9) in the world to come." What did they do? They say in the academy of R. Shila: (They said) let us build a tower, ascend to the sky, and cleave it with hatchets so that its waters flow out. In the West they laughed at this: If it is so, let them build upon the length of a mountain.[176] R. Yeremiah b. Elazar said: They divided up into three parties. One said: Let us ascend and live there. And another said: Let us ascend and wage war. And another said: Let us ascend and worship idols.[177] The one that said, "Let us ascend and live there," it is

> written "and from there the Lord scattered them" (Gen. 11:9). And the one that said, "Let us ascend and wage war" were made into apes, demons, spirits, and liliths. And the one that said, "Let us ascend and worship idols," it is written "because there the Lord confounded (the speech of the whole earth)" (Gen. 11:9). It was taught in a baraita: R. Nathan said—and all of them were focused upon idolatry. It is written here: "to make a name for ourselves" (Gen. 11:4). And it is written there: "Make no mention of the names of other gods" (Exod. 23:13). Just as there ("name" means) idolatry, so here ("name" also means) idolatry. R. Yoḥanan said: A third of the tower was swallowed up, a third was burned, and a third still stands. Rav said: The air near the tower causes forgetfulness of study. Rav Yosef[178] said: Babylon and Borsif are evil signs for the Torah: "because the Lord confounded the speech of the whole earth" (Gen. 11:9). What is Borsif? R. Assi said: An empty well [בור שפת].

This passage explores why the generation of the Dispersion has no share in the world to come in light of the Tower of Babylon tale. According to the academy of R. Shila, there were three parties who expressed different idolatrous motivations for building the tower—one wanted to live in the heavens, another wanted to wage war, and another wanted to worship idols. Each of these groups, however, meets a terrible fate, either being "scattered" or "confounded" by the Lord as Genesis 11 describes, or being turned into apes and demons. After citing a baraita of R. Nathan, the passage gives R. Yoḥanan's explanation of the demise of the Tower of Babylon, continuing the text's motif of the number three: a third was swallowed up by the ground, a third was burned down, and a third remains standing. From here, the early Babylonian Amora Rav adds that, given the past iniquities of the Tower's history, "the air near the tower causes forgetfulness of study" in his own lifetime. Rav Yosef's subsequent statement reiterates the harmful portent of Babylon, now connecting it as well with Borsif, before the passage ends with R. Assi's play on words for this latter town.

PERSIANS AS BEARS IN DANIEL 7:5

In a lengthy exposition on the genealogical boundaries of Babylonia found in *b. Qidd.* 72a, Rav Yosef calls the Persians "bears" on the basis of an exegesis of Daniel 7:5, an Aramaic composition that describes Daniel's vision of four metaphorical beasts representing kingdoms that oppressed the Jews. The text reads:[179]

> "And with three fangs in its mouth among its teeth" (Dan. 7:5). R. Yoḥanan said: This is Halzon, Ḥadayab, and Nisibin, which it sometimes swallowed and sometimes spit up. "Then I saw a second, different beast, which was like a bear" (Dan. 7:5). Rav Yosef taught in a baraita: These are the Persians [פרסיים], who eat and drink like a bear, are shaggy like a bear, grow long hair like a bear, and are restless like a bear.[180] When R. Ammi saw a Persian [פרסאה],[181] he would say: This is a moving bear. Rabbi said to Levi: Show me the Persians. He said: They are like the House of David's armies. Show

> me the Zoroastrian priests [חברים].[182] He said to him[183] they are like the destroying angels. Show me the Ishmaelites. He said to him they are like the demons of the privy. Show me the scholars of Babylon. He said to him they are like the ministering angels.

According to R. Yoḥanan, the Persian Empire held sway over three areas, the second of which is Adiabene, and the third of which is Nisibis.[184] Rav Yosef's baraita goes on to describe the Persians as bears in their daily habits and appearance. Although this equation of the Persians with an animal is perhaps meant to be disparaging, its origins are exegetical. As Sacha Stern has correctly noted about this text, there is a difference between how Rav Yosef's baraita describes the Persians as "like" bears, in contrast to the Palestinian Amora R. Ammi's identification of them as "moving bears."[185] Overall the imagery of the Persians in this entire text is one of strength, a characterization that is extended to Levi's identification of the Persians with King David's powerful military. The exchange between these two Tannaim goes on to contrast the Zoroastrian priests as destroying angels, as opposed to the scholars of Babylon as ministering angels.

Another passage in which Rav Yosef's baraita about the Persians as bears appears is *b. ʿAbod. Zar.* 2b, which compares Persia with Rome. This passage is set up as a dialogue between God and the Kingdom of Persia, describing what takes place when the Persians come before the Jewish God for judgment:[186]

> The Kingdom of Persia enters after (Rome). For what reason? Because it is the next in importance after it. And from where do we know that it is next in importance after it? For it is written: "Then I saw a second, different beast, which was like a bear" (Dan. 7:5). And Rav Yosef taught in a baraita: These are the Persians, who eat and drink like a bear, are fleshy like a bear, grow hair like a bear, and are restless like a bear. The Holy One, Blessed be He, says to them: "With what have you busied yourselves?" They say to Him: "We built many bridges. We conquered many cities. We fought many wars. And we did all this only in order that Israel could busy themselves with Torah." The Holy One, Blessed be He, says to them: "Everything you did, you did for yourselves. You built bridges in order to collect tolls from them, cities in order to impose forced labor; I am responsible for war, as it says: "The Lord, the Warrior" (Exod. 15:3). Are there none among you who promulgated this? As it says, "Who among you declared 'this'?" (Isa. 43:9), and "this" refers to Torah, as it says: "This is the Torah that Moses set" (Deut. 4:44). Straightaway (the Persians) depart from Him dejectedly. And after the Kingdom of Rome entered and gained nothing, why did (Persia) approach? It reasons: They [Rome] destroyed the Temple, whereas we built it.

After the Roman Empire leaves God's presence, the Persian Empire enters to be judged. The biblical verse from Daniel 7:5 and Rav Yosef's baraita based on it are quoted as evidence for why the Persians enter after the Romans as next in importance in the empires. Standing before God, the Persians must account for their actions—What have they done to deserve His good favor? In response, the Persians boast about their military achievements and public works, claiming that they were all done “only in order that Israel could busy themselves with Torah.” According to the rabbinic imagination, the Persians try to convince God that their acts of self-benefit were intended for the Jews, in order for them to study Torah. Unsurprisingly, however, God is not convinced that these acts were done for the sake of the Jews, declaring that the Persians’ wars and public works were intended for their own material enrichment. The Persians, hearing God’s judgment, leave dejectedly. The last lines of this dialogue explain the reason why the Persians followed the Romans in attempting to convince God of their good intentions: they believed that they had an advantage, because they had built the Second Temple whereas the Romans had destroyed it. Whether this text’s negative portrayal of the Achaemenid Persians is a latent critique of the Sasanians is unfortunately challenging to answer, but it seems likely that the rabbis would make such an association. In any case, the rabbis believed that their Jewish God would judge the Persians harshly.

PERSIAN CULTURE IN THE TALMUD, OR TALMUDIC CULTURE IN PERSIA

How much Persian culture is there in the Talmud? This question has prompted a range of opinions from Jacob Neusner’s unwarranted pessimism to Yaakov Elman’s pioneering optimism. The correct answer is, I believe, somewhere between these two extremes. As we saw in this chapter, the Bavli contains dozens of rich texts that demonstrate a thoughtful engagement with the role of Persian culture, especially fashion and food, in Halakhah—or, more precisely, in Jewish customs. These texts accord with the fact that the Iranian loanwords found in the Bavli bear witness to the penetration into the Jewish vernacular of these same features of the Persians’ culture in daily life. The Talmud also contains many words related to the Sasanian administration, as we saw in the case of *ōstāndār*, exemplifying the rabbis’ familiarity with the inner workings of the ruling classes. The Talmud depicts the Persians as an ethnoimperial class, using several common leitmotifs—such as haughtiness, bears, or horsemanship—to express both positive and negative attitudes toward them and to mark Persians as others. Yet such portrayals did not emerge out of nothing, and it is important to highlight the role that biblical exegeses of Isaiah 13:3 and Daniel 7:5 played in the first two of these leitmotifs, as well as in the images of Persians as Achaemenids rather than as Sasanians. In the end, the totality of the evidence demonstrates that many of the Babylonian rabbis were quite knowledgeable about at least some aspects of Persian ethnic life—perhaps less so about Zoroastrianism—and that they utilized Persian otherness as a way to understand themselves and their place in the Sasanian world.

4

Rabbis and Sasanian Kings in Dialogue

The study of rabbis and others has contributed greatly to rabbinists' knowledge of late antique Jewish identity and culture, especially with respect to the Greco-Roman and Christian contexts of the rabbinic world. For decades now, scholars interested in Palestinian Judaism have published widely on the subject of the Jewish-gentile dichotomy as expressed in the Jerusalem Talmud and Midrash, drawing our attention to how rabbinic texts use internal and external others to construct identity and engage otherwise untreatable problems and anxieties. Rabbinic texts frequently narrate voices of others in order to place rabbinic ideas in relation to non-rabbinic ones, thereby enhancing the rabbis' own prestige over against these others' while simultaneously negotiating boundaries of self-identity through an us/them dialectic. Rabbinic texts employ non-Jews as characters, symbols, or icons in self-reflective narratives that explicate Jewish traditions and rabbinic issues. This inward tendency of course does not preclude the formative role that various historical and cultural contexts play in texts about rabbis and others, since these texts' rhetorical or ideological meanings are informed by the non-Jewish sociocultural systems in which they were produced. This interplay between text and context is particularly germane in dialogues in rabbinic literature between the sages and their imperial others in Rome and Persia, since such dialogues contain attitudes toward the ruling classes who tacitly promoted their own political propaganda and religious ideologies within broader sociocultural and political spheres of life in Roman Palestine and Sasanian Babylonia to which the Jews were subject.

This chapter explores Talmudic texts that depict the sages in dialogue with the Sasanian kings, with special attention paid to King Shapur I (241–72 C.E.). The Talmud contains references to both Shapur I and Shapur II (309–79 C.E.),[1] and the king to whom these texts refer is sometimes decipherable based on internal or external factors such as the rabbis involved, the historical events mentioned, the appearance of Ifra Hormiz (Shapur II's mother), or any combination of these. In a number of Talmudic texts, however, the reference to Shapur is too vague to be meant as referring to one of the two kings specifically; in these instances, the name "King Shapur" is used generically, not unlike the imperial ethnic appellation "Persians."[2] In addition to Shapur I and Shapur II, the other Persian kings to appear in the Talmud are the last Parthian monarch, Ardawān IV (216–24 C.E.), Yazdegird I (399–420 C.E.), and a brief reference to Peroz (459–84 C.E.).[3] The lack of information about the other Sasanian kings is conspicuous.

THE SASANIAN CONTEXT OF THE TALMUD'S IMAGES OF SHAPUR I

In the Talmud, King Shapur I is a positive figure who represents Persian imperial authority and whose Judaized words and deeds demonstrate or praise rabbinic thought. These texts about Shapur achieve this effect on both a formal level, in that the creators insert the sage-king encounters as constructive illustrations of the text's halakhic conclusions, and on the level of content—that is, in the king's pro-rabbinic stance. In the texts analyzed in this chapter, Shapur qua other cooperates as a manufactured interlocutor who is a symbol of a Persian (but not necessarily Zoroastrian) figure of imperial authority interested in hearing about, and in one case even performing, rabbinic law. For instance, in *b. B. Meṣiʿa* 119a the king praises Jewish law, and in *b. ʿAbod. Zar.* 76b he participates in a Jewish purity ritual while eating with sages. In these texts about the kings, the Babylonian rabbis could not only self-aggrandize their reputation as players on the Sasanian royal scene but also latently engage issues of authority and identity, including how they reckoned such issues vis-à-vis the Persian Empire.

That the rabbis chose Shapur I and not another Sasanian monarch to represent a non-rabbinic voice of authority can in part be explained by the fact that they and their audience who lived in Sasanian Babylonia both during and after Shapur's reign were exposed to Persian imperial propagandistic and Zoroastrian priestly traditions about the king. Although the sage-Shapur dialogues in the Talmud do not contain any direct citations from Middle Persian sources, the Sasanians' sustained control over Shapur's legacy in ways that promoted their hegemony should not be overlooked as a source of ambient cultural influence on the rabbis' literary creations. Even though it is true that Jewish and Persian societies in Sasanian Iran each maintained a unique notion of history and connection to the past, they also shared with each other an ideological plane of collective memory wherein one society's historical narratives were never fully isolated from those of other societies in its realm of social contact.[4] In the webs of memory among inhabitants who lived in a heterogeneous world, the Persian imperial ideology about its own kings and past played a significant and idiosyncratic role, driven by the empire's quest for authority over internal and external others.[5] Middle Persian sources of a wide variety offer insight into these aspects of Persian civilization. The logic behind the connection that I make in this chapter between the rabbis' representations of Persian kings and Sasanian imperial ideology and historiography thus presupposes a relationship between the Bavli as a literary corpus and western Sasanian society and culture, broadly defined.

My choice of Shapur I as a test case for contextualizing the Talmud in Sasanian Persia stems largely from the fact that both the Talmud and Middle Persian sources portray the monarch rather frequently. For Talmudists, the Persian Empire's inscriptions and Zoroastrian historiographical writings about Shapur I are additional research tools that delineate the broader frames of reference in relation to which the Talmudic authors operated. Not surprisingly, there are chronological problems with the comparison of Talmudic and Persian sources about Shapur I. The richest Middle Persian sources about this monarch are typically found either in early Sasanian inscriptions from the era of Ardashir and Shapur or just thereafter (ca. 230–300 C.E.) or in Pahlavi Zoroastrian historiographical narratives written from a post-Sasanian priestly perspective, the contents of which may or may not reflect Sasanian-era attitudes and traditions. Thus, the fact that there is a dearth of information in Middle Persian regarding the indigenous attitude toward Shapur emanating from the fourth through the sixth century C.E. lessens Middle Persian sources' evidentiary value to the project of contextualizing the Bavli's images of Shapur, since it was during this general time frame that there was prolific rabbinic activity. The textual comparisons are clearly chronologically challenged.

Despite this impediment, there is value in analyzing the Talmud's images of Shapur in light of Middle Persian epigraphic and historiographical sources. For example, included in the golden age of the official art form of Sasanian rock reliefs dating from the reign of Ardashir (224–41 C.E.) until the early fourth century[6] is the first lengthy Sasanian imperial narrative, attested in Shapur I's trilingual res gestae on the walls of the *Ka'ba-ye Zardušt*.[7] This inscription and others composed during the early Sasanian era, when combined with other material evidence from Shapur I's era, such as numismatic remains,[8] serve as testimony for the reconstruction of the early Persian Empire's ideological underpinnings and construction of an imperial identity. In addition, Middle Persian literary works such as the *Kārnāmag* and the *Dēnkard*, which were written from a sacerdotal perspective centuries after Shapur's reign, depict the monarch in historiographical narratives that reflect their late Sasanian or post-Sasanian attitudes toward the monarch's reign and era.[9] Both the epigraphic and the literary sources depict Shapur as the figure of early imperial authority par excellence and his era as one of self-definition resulting from the solidification of imperial and cultural institutions, the response to the Parthian heritage, and military gains over Rome.[10] Each of these historical developments played a part in the Sasanian construction of a dynastic identity that promoted its authority over its territories. For centuries after his reign, the early Persian monarch Shapur I remained a symbol of authority, including in the Babylonian Talmud.

SHMUEL, SHAPUR, AND QUESTIONS OF AUTHORITY IN SASANIAN MESOPOTAMIA

The Jewish sage in the Babylonian Talmud with whom King Shapur I most frequently interacts is the first-generation Amora Shmuel, in the early to mid-third century, probably during Shapur I's reign.[11] The Talmud portrays the king and his subject as having an affable relationship: in one text Shmuel juggles for the king's entertainment (*b. Sukkah* 53a). The line reads: "Shmuel (would juggle) in front of King Shapur with eight glasses of wine." This form of entertainment is in fact attested in a Middle Persian *andarz* work entitled *Xusrow and the Page,* which portrays the education of a boy in the court of Khusrow I, who tests the boy's knowledge. This work contains the word *tās-bāzī,* "juggling with cups,"[12] the act that Shmuel does for Shapur I, in a long list that the boy gives in his answer to the king's question about the best forms of entertainment. Another Talmudic passage that depicts Shmuel and Shapur in dialogue is *b. Sanh.* 98a, where the two men trade quips over the image in Zechariah 9:9 of the Messiah coming on a donkey, a text that the New Testament uses in reference to Jesus. R. Alexandri quotes R. Yehoshua b. Levi's explanation of a contradiction between Zechariah 9:9 and Daniel 7:13, which, after Daniel's vision of the four beasts, references the "son of man." The contradiction is explained in ethical terms: if he is worthy, he rides on the clouds of heaven; if he is not, he rides a donkey. In this dialogue, Shmuel uses several Middle Persian loanwords when talking to the king, a literary detail that highlights the sage's marked comfort with Persian culture.[13] Here is the tradition that discusses the coming of the Messiah:[14]

> R. Alexandri said: R. Yehoshua b. Levi demonstrated a contradiction—it is written, "One like a human being came with the clouds of heaven" (Dan. 7:13), but it is (also) written: "yet humble, riding on a donkey" (Zech. 9:9). If they are worthy, "with the clouds of heaven," (but) if they are not worthy, "yet humble, riding on a donkey." King Shapur said to Shmuel: You say the Messiah will come on a donkey?! Let me send him my horse [בהרג].[15] (Shmuel) said to him: Do you have a donkey of a thousand colors [כאר הזר גוונין]?

King Shapur's response to the R. Alexandri tradition counters the irony of the biblical text by offering up a horse instead of a humble donkey, thus precipitating the coming of the Messiah. As we have seen before, this Talmudic text uses horses as a common trope for Persians and invokes a Middle Persian loanword—"horse," from MP *bārag*—in the mouth of a Persian figure. Shmuel, too, as witnessed in the Yad Harav Herzog manuscript, speaks in Persian (MP *xar hazār gōnag*, "a donkey of a thousand colors") when addressing the king's response. The symbolic import behind Shmuel's retort asking for a donkey of a thousand colors may be an image of glorification, or it can be seen as a challenge to the monarch's abilities.

Whether Shmuel and Shapur were in reality ever acquainted is impossible to deduce from our evidence. It seems unlikely that any of the Shmuel-Shapur texts, which are often short and anecdotal, reflect historical encounters between the two men, though based on our knowledge of Sasanian history it is not completely unimaginable that the early Sasanian court, a place of *savoir-vivre* where intellectual culture was mediated and produced, could have called upon the renowned sage, "the judge of the Diaspora" (*b. Sanh.* 17b), to be a representative of the Jewish community. However, we should assume that these texts reflect not historical realities but rather the interactions that the sages imagined themselves having with the Persian monarch. Faced with the limits in our evidence regarding the historical relationship between Shmuel and Shapur, what we can know for certain is that the Talmud links these two contemporary figures because both represented rabbinic and imperial authority at the dawn of an expanding and transformative political order. In third-century Babylonia, the Jewish sages and Sasanian monarchy were both gradually becoming holders of power over their respective communities, organizing their legal hegemony via claims to authority by divine right, pure lineage, and authoritative chains of tradition. When the Talmud juxtaposes Shmuel with Shapur, it is concerned with this analogy between rabbinic and Persian authority.

On two occasions Rav Naḥman or the anonymous editors conflate Shapur and Shmuel into a single identity. As the following citations illustrate, the generations after Shmuel refer to the sage by the name King Shapur, invoking the Persian other as a voice of authority. The editors of the following text apply the name "King Shapur" to both Shmuel and Rava. Presumably, this text's equation of Shmuel with Shapur is meant as an allusion to Shapur I, whereas the equation of Rava with Shapur alludes to Shapur II. It reads:[16]

> But perhaps there were two people named Anah?[17] Rava said: I shall say something that King Shapur did not say. And who is (this)? Shmuel. There are those who say that Rav Pappa said: I shall say something that King Shapur did not say. And who is (this)? Rava.

In this text, Shapur is used to reference the two Amoraim. The passage explicitly spells out the Amoraic name swap, asking the rhetorical question "And who is (this)?" as a way to explain the meaningful conflation between the king and sage. This other text uses Shapur-as-Shmuel to connote the concept of authority, invoking the king as a means of indicating that two rabbis' opinions were equally authoritative:[18]

> (Rav Naḥman) said to (Rava): Have I not told you not to say anything to me while I sit in judgment? For Huna, our friend, said about me: King Shapur [i.e., Shmuel] and I are brothers regarding the law. This man is a well-known robber, and I want to punish him.

As seen here, Shapur I became absorbed into the rabbinic worldview as a designation for the sage Shmuel. One related leitmotif in the Talmud's representations of Shapur I and Shapur II is money, such as appears in the topics of charity and bribery. For example, in the course of an interpretation of Deuteronomy 31:7, *b. Ḥag.* 5a reports that the rabbis distrust Rava, who responds to them, "Do you know how much secretly I bribe King Shapur's court?" Despite attempts at appeasement, the text continues, Rava did not satisfy the monarch, who in turn sends royal officials to seize his possessions. As this text illustrates, the interactions between rabbis and monarchs deal with the topic of money, with the Jews often trying to appease the government through bribes or the acceptance of charity. Similarly, elsewhere in the Talmud (*b. B. Bat.* 10b), Rava is depicted as accepting four hundred dinars from Ifra Hormiz for the sake of charity, despite the fact that as a result the gentile queen may accrue merit in this world. Rava's reason for accepting the money? He wanted peace with the kingdom. Yet another Ifra Hormiz tale in *b. B. Bat.* 8a concentrates on the theme of royal charity, with Rav Yosef and Abaye debating which good deed one can use such money for. Finally, other, shorter texts mention Shapur's wealth (*b. B. Meṣi'a* 85a, *b. Šabb.* 113b), willingness to give charity to the poor (*b. B. Meṣi'a* 70b), and as a hypothetical lender (*b. B. Bat.* 172b).

In a sugya on the sin of leaving a corpse unburied, *b. Sanh.* 46b reports a dialogue between Shapur II and Rav Ḥama, a fifth-generation Babylonian Amora. It is well known that Jews and Zoroastrians in antiquity differed with respect to the proper treatment of corpses. Unlike the requirements for burial in the Jewish tradition, the common Zoroastrian practice was to expose the corpse in an exposed tomb, called a *daxmag*, rather than pollute the earth through interment. This Talmudic dialogue uses the Persian king to address these differences while engaging in an unsuccessful attempt at proving a biblical requirement for burying the dead. It reads as follows:[19]

> King Shapur said to Rav Ḥama: Where in the Torah is burial? Rav Ḥama was silent and did not say anything to him. Rav Aḥa bar Yaakov said: The world has been delivered into the hands of fools, for he should have said: "but you must bury (him on the same day)" (Deut. 21:23). (This could mean) that (only) a coffin must be made [as opposed to burial]. "You must bury him" (ibid.). (King Shapur) would not accept the reasoning. (Rav Ḥama) should have said: from the righteous who were buried. (Burial could be) merely a custom. From (when) the Holy One, Blessed is He, buried

Moses. (But maybe God did it,) so that there should not be a change from the custom.

The king initiates the conversation, asking for the Jewish text that supports the rite of burial. Rav Ḥama's initial silence, which Rav Aḥa bar Yaakov criticizes, may reflect the anxiety that the sage felt in proving in front of a king that the Jewish rite of burial was scripturally ordained. Rav Aḥa bar Yaakov offers as proof for the requirement of burial the repetition of the word *QBR* in Deuteronomy 21:23. Still, the Persian king does not accept the argument, leading the sugya to conclude that burial may simply be a custom rather than a law. This dialogue is another example of how the Talmud uses King Shapur as an imaginary interlocutor who raises challenges to the rabbis' exegeses.

Before moving on to explore other Talmudic sources, I would like to say more about the topic of legal authority in third-century Sasanian Babylonia, in particular the early Sasanian context of Shmuel's principle that "the law of the empire is the law" (*dînā de-malḥûtā dînā*).[20] Shmuel's principle, albeit cited in narrow civil cases,[21] is a rabbinic formulation on what I argue was one of the central problems with which Babylonian rabbis who lived in the early Sasanian era were forced to deal—namely, the interrelationship between Babylonian Amoraic rabbinic law and authority, and Sasanian imperial authority and policy over Jewish (and other non-Zoroastrian subjects') legal issues, especially in matters of civil law such as property ownership.[22] Early Sasanian Iran was a time of intense self-definition for Jewish, Sasanian, and Zoroastrian elites, all of which faced internal and external tensions on their group identity, including with respect to their legal authority. For the Babylonian rabbis, the fact that the transition from the Tannaitic to the Amoraic era roughly coincided in time with the changeover from a loosely centralized, Central Asian Arsacid rule to a Persian Empire, emanating from the same region (Fārs) and political tradition as the ancient Achaemenids, engendered a need for all parties to redefine their group identities and legal authority from various perspectives. The Sasanian Zoroastrian priesthood, whose clergymen functioned in various administrative, ritual, and scholarly capacities throughout the Sasanian era, also greatly contributed to the changing dynamics of structures of authority in late antique Iran.

Both the Jerusalem Talmud and the Babylonian Talmud contain positive portrayals of the final Parthian king, Ardawān IV, who in 224 C.E. was defeated by Ardashir, the first Sasanian ruler.[23] For instance, the following passage in *y. Pe'ah* 1:1 (15d) about Rabbi Judah the Prince's encounter with the Parthian king describes the two men as exchanging gifts, another manifestation of the money motif. Whereas the king sends a valuable pearl, the rabbi sends a mezuzah:[24]

Ardawān sent our holy teacher a priceless pearl. (Ardawān) said to him: Send me something of equal value. He sent him a mezuzah. (Ardawān) said to him: What is

> this? I sent you something invaluable, and you send me something worth a follarion. (Rabbi) said to him: Your desirable objects and my desirable objects "cannot compare to it."[25] Moreover, you have sent me something that I have to guard, whereas I sent you something that guards you when you sleep, as it is written: "When you walk it will lead you." (Prov. 6:22)

This text portrays the Parthian king as not understanding the significance of the ritual object that Judah the Prince sends him in return for the gift. The sage, however, eschews the materialism of the exchange, quoting from Proverbs 3:15, which says that wisdom and Torah study is more precious than rubies. The didactic message of this passage is that the value of Torah is greater than that of material objects of wealth. The choice of the Parthian king versus Rabbi is a narrative tool that helped the authors create the desired effect of a contrast between Jewish and gentile values.

Another encounter between a sage and Ardawān is also found in *b. ʿAbod. Zar.* 10b–11a, which scholars have interpreted in light of the change of empires from Parthians to Sasanians. Here, Rabbi Judah the Prince is connected to Antoninus, whereas Rav is tied to the Parthian monarch. The text reads: "Antoninus served Rabbi. Ardawān served Rav. When Antoninus died, Rabbi said: The cord is separated. When Ardawān died, Rav said: The cord is separated." As Alyssa Gray has correctly noted, the phrase "the cord is separated" expresses the sages' "sense of deep personal loss" and "some set order of events has now been disrupted."[26] After the change of empires, the Babylonian Amoraim, after centuries of near-silence, began to construct an ideology of Babylonian rabbinic authority that would allow their Jewish culture to persist and modernize in the new sociopolitical environment of Sasanian Babylonia.[27] One way that they achieved these goals was to appropriate symbols of Persian imperial authority as part of their own ideological project. Shmuel's principle of *dînā de-malḥûtā dînā*, combined with how the Talmud employs Shapur-as-other as part of a pro-Babylonian rhetoric, shows that the rabbis construe the authority of the early Sasanian Empire as upholding Babylonian rabbinic authority and identity.

The topics of religious and imperial authority were also of great interest to the early Sasanian kings. For the Mazdayasnian king Shapur I, policy decisions about the empire's sundry religions, including how the empire should define itself and exert Zoroastrianism, were as much if not more affected by political considerations as by religious zeal or fidelity.[28] With respect to the non-Mazdayasnian religious communities living under Sasanian rule, the early Sasanian policy appears to have been to allow the leaders of each to exercise jurisdiction over legal cases involving members of their own groups, thereby maintaining an umbrella of imperial authority over the Sasanian provinces while not spawning rebellions or resentment among the masses, a tactic reminiscent of the Persian Achaemenids' strategy as well. Taxes paid to the imperial government, among other services, were presumably central features of any such agreement.[29] Driven by political realities of a vast new imperial reign, the earliest Sasanian kings did not rule through the imposition of a universal religion on the masses. The consolidation of power or the establishment of institutions, or both, among the Zoroastrian elite likely gained momentum during but especially after the reign of Shapur I, a trend documented in the rise of the high priest Kirder,[30] who may or may not have attempted to spread Mazda worship and persecute Jews and others.

During his reign, Shapur I devised a political ideology that managed the diversity of religious communities in the empire. For instance, Shapur's military victories over Rome and his subsequent policy of deporting inhabitants of *Anērān,* including Hellenized Christians,[31] to various regions in the Persian Empire, including Mesopotamia, warranted the honorific inscribed on the king's res gestae and preserved as the figurative Sasanian title by subsequent Persian kings until the reign of Shapur III (383–88 C.E.): "Shapur, King of Kings of Iran and non-Iran" (MP *Šābuhr šāhān šāh Ērān ud Anērān*).[32] Shapur's third-century propagandistic epic defines the Sasanian King of Kings as the divinely administered imperial authority over all the provinces of his and his enemy's realm, regardless of ethnic or religious makeup.

In addition to Shapur's third-century epigraph, the Middle Persian narrative entitled the *Kārnāmag ī Ardaxšēr ī Pābagān* and Ferdowsi's eleventh-century New Persian epic *The Book of Kings* (*Šāhnāme*) also emphasize Shapur's role as the defining figure of imperial authority. These later works from the late Sasanian–early Islamic period use the third-century monarch in narratives championing the legitimacy of the Sasanians' claims to imperial authority through Ardashir's genealogical descent from the Parthian noble families of Ardawān and Mehrān.[33] In one romanticized narrative in the *Kārnāmag,* for instance, the Zoroastrian priests describe how the "chief priest of the empire" (MP *mowbedān mowbed*) goes against the orders of King Ardashir and saves Shapur I's mother, who is Ardawān's daughter and Ardashir's concubine, from execution after she attempts to poison Ardashir.[34] In the story, Shapur I represents the heroic boy who perpetuates the Sasanian imperial authority that was in fact almost lost with the recklessness of his father, Ardashir. In general, the ideological aim of this narrative represents a late Sasanian or post-Sasanian priestly construct that promotes a point of view supporting the legitimacy of the early Sasanian kings as rightful heirs of authority from the Parthians.

As we have seen, the third century C.E. was a time of great change in the Near Eastern world. In around thirty years of rule, Shapur I was able to manage the nascent empire in ways that promoted its imperial authority over rapidly expanding populations, including non-Iranians. This political process caused ruptures to the old structures of authority in Sasanian Babylonia, including ones that would influence the rabbis' conception of their own authority in relation to the Persian Empire. Shmuel's principle of *dînā de-malḥûtā dînā* in this way reflects third-century imperial culture. Moreover, the third-century transformations instigated by Shapur's reign continued to be a relevant topic of contemplation for later eras. In Jewish and Zoroastrian writings dating from the third through the tenth century, the second Sasanian king became a symbolic figure who stood for the issues of his transformative era—that is to say, as the Sasanian era unfolded, the Sasanian monarchy and its inhabitants reimagined and recalculated their own definitions of identity and authority vis-à-vis their predecessors, upon whose authoritative traditions and laws they relied and expanded. For the Babylonian rabbis, Shapur and Shapur's era thus became literary subjects that they could invoke in order to engage issues of Babylonian rabbinic identity and authority that were inextricably linked to earlier sages from Shapur's era like Shmuel. The three Talmudic texts discussed below about the sages and Shapur in dialogue will demonstrate how the Babylonian sages used Shapur as a Persian other in narratives in which they negotiated their group identity and their conception of authority.

THE AUTHORITY OF CODIFICATION: SHAPUR PRAISES RABBINIC LAW

The first sage-Shapur dialogue that we examine is in *b. B. Meṣi'a* 118b–119a and contains a brief, two-sentence dialogue in which the rabbis report their approval of R. Simon's halakhah to King Shapur, who then praises the Tanna using the Middle Persian loanword אפרין (< MP *āfrîn*, "praise, blessing") in a stately hortative construct ("Let us bring praise upon R. Simon!"). So far as I can tell, the specific civil law under discussion in this passage—ownership law in the case of neighboring gardens—does not carry any relevance for why Shapur appears in this text. In other words, there appears to be no specific Sasanian or Zoroastrian legal influence with respect to the Jewish civil case being discussed here that would cause the rabbis to invoke the Persian king. Instead, the author or editors of this sugya use the Shapur narrative in order to engage two specific issues of rabbinic legal approbation, the Palestinian Amora Resh Lakish's endorsement of R. Simon's ruling. In the following passage, the voice of the imperial other Shapur adds a second, Persian layer of approval to the Palestinian Amora Resh Lakish's endorsement of R. Simon's law:[35]

> [*M. B. Meṣi'a* 10:6] "(If there are) two gardens, one above the other, with vegetables between them, (who owns the vegetables)? . . . R. Simon said: Any (vegetables) that the owner of the upper garden can reach by hand and grab belong to him, and the rest belong to the owner of the lower garden."
>
> They said in R. Yannai's academy: Only if he does not strain himself. Rav Anan, and some say R. Yeremiah, asked: If he can reach the foliage but not the roots, or if

> he can reach the roots but not the foliage—what is the law (in this case)? Let it stand. Ephraim the Scribe, a disciple of Resh Lakish, said in the name of Resh Lakish: The law is in accordance with R. Simon. They reported (this) to King Shapur. (King Shapur) said to them: Let us bring praise [*āfrîn*][36] upon R. Simon!

After the law of R. Simon declaring that the upper garden's owner keeps whatever vegetables he can reach by hand, R. Yannai's academy is cited giving a stipulation on this practice—namely, that the upper garden's owner must not strain himself while reaching for the vegetables, a stipulation of R. Yannai that is also found in the Yerushalmi discussion to this mishnah. The text then raises Rav Anan's question regarding what the law is in the case of an owner who can reach the foliage of the vegetables but not their roots, a problem that the Talmud treats in detail earlier in the tractate (see *b. B. Meṣiʿa* 118b). In the last two lines, King Shapur appears as a figure of external imperial authority whose open-minded receipt and praise of a Tannaitic law empowers rabbinic legal decisions—for if the King of Kings approves of a law, then it must be righteous. The Persian monarch is depicted as recognizing rabbinic laws as legitimate. The creators of this text consciously invoke the discourse of the Persian ruler with the Middle Persian word *āfrîn*, "praise, blessing," a literary detail that reveals how the authors appropriated a foreign word as a way to accentuate Shapur's Persian alterity through linguistic representation. By having a Persian imperial other enunciate the final approval of a Tannaitic law, the creators of this sugya cast a specifically Babylonian rabbinic orientation for the authority figure praising and, by implication, supporting the law. Shapur's statement of praise leaves the audience with the impression that Persia is a place where the external authorities accept Tannaitic law and where the Babylonian rabbis' legal authority can thrive. The Babylonian editors use the voice of Shapur to recontextualize the location of authority over Tannaitic law as part of a pro-Babylonian rhetorical agenda meant to consolidate their image of authority. In sum, this text invokes Shapur as a figure of Persian imperial authority in a way that would be understood by the audience of Babylonian Jewry, whose familiarity with the reputation of the king and the issues of the king's time would allow the desired literary effects of self-aggrandizement, validation, and peroration.

SHAPUR AND THE CODIFICATION OF THE AVESTA ACCORDING TO *DĒNKARD* BOOK 4

In *b. B. Meṣiʿa* 119a, the Talmud depicts Shapur I as a ruler who is presented with and then venerates a Tannaitic law. This image of Shapur as a king who praises non-Mazdayasnian thought and oversees the codification of religious knowledge invites comparison with the king's reputation in Middle Persian literature. For example, in the 169,000-word synoptic digest of Zoroastrian thought called the

Dēnkard, which was redacted in the ninth and tenth centuries C.E., Shapur I is portrayed as a monarch who welcomes foreign knowledge into the Avestan canon.

In one rich narrative about the transmission of the Avesta, which may have originated in the reign of Khusrow I (531–79 C.E.),[37] King Shapur contributes to the long process of the canonization of the Avesta by "collecting" (*ō ham āwurd*) writings about science, philosophy, and other subjects from the edges of the Sasanian Empire as far as India and Rome. The passage that I cite here includes several details that may be interpreted as evidence that its contents originally stem from earlier Sasanian traditions. One of these details is the fact that the narrative, only a part of which is cited above, describes the reign of Khusrow I at much greater length and with greater concern than the other kings' reigns, even referring to the sixth-century king as "His present Majesty Khusrow" (*im bay Xusrōw*). In general, Sasanian historians often argue, based on the totality of the evidence, that Khusrow I's era was indeed one of prolific literary activity, making the attribution of this narrative in the *Dēnkard* to his time not implausible. From a philological point of view, the narrative shows signs of being a late form of Middle Persian; see, preliminarily, the three uses of the suffix *-īhā* as indicating a plural noun (MP *šahrīhā, nibēgīhā, zamīgīhā*), a grammatical development marking the transition from Middle Persian to New Persian. Further philological comparison of this passage's linguistic features with those in other Middle Persian texts could potentially yield a more accurate dating of its composition and decide the question whether it is recording older traditions verbatim. Given the general lateness of the Pahlavi sources that treat the history of the Avestan canon and the Avestan manuscripts themselves, Iranists continue to debate the Avesta's exact development and precise date of composition based on internal factors.[38] The following Pahlavi narrative is generally thought to have several historically corroborating claims, such as the existence of various regional traditions of the Avesta and the codification of the scriptures by the Sasanians and, pending more intensive study, could be convincingly interpreted as a tenth-century written record of what was originally a late Sasanian oral tradition. An excerpt of the well-known narrative reads as follows:[39]

I

walaxš ī aškānān abestāg ud zand čiyōn abēzagīhā andar āmad ēstād hammōg-iz ī aziš har čē az wizend ud āšuftgārīh ī aleksandar ud ēwār[40] ud rōb ī hrōmāyān andar ērānšahr pargandagīhā abar nibištag tā čē uzwān-abespārišnīg pad dastwar mānd ēstād andar šahr čiyōn frāz mad ēstād nigāh dāštan ō šahrīhā ayādgār kardan framūd.

Walaxš the Arsacid ordered that a memorandum be sent to the provinces (telling them) to keep, in the state in which it had come down in (each) province, whatever was pure in the Zand-Avesta, (and) the teaching derived from it—all of which, (having been) dispersed in the land of Iran by the havoc and turmoil of Alexander and the robbery and pillaging of the Romans, is written or preserved orally by an authority.

II

ōy bay ardaxšēr šāhān šāh ī pābagān pad rāst-dastwarīh tansar ān-iz hammōg ī pargandag hamāg ō dar xwāst tansar abar mad ān ī ēk[41] frāz padīriftan ud abārīg az dastwar hišt ud ēn-iz framān dād kū frāz ō amāh har nigēzišn ān ē bawēd az dēn māzdēsn čē nūn-iz āgāhīh ud dānišn aziš frōd nest.

His Lord Ardašīr, the King of Kings, son of Pābag, acting on the righteous authority of Tansar, requested that all those scattered teachings be brought to his court. Tansar took charge. He accepted one part of them, and he excluded the rest from authority. And he gave forth the following order: "Every exposition that shall be from the Mazdayasnian religion is restricted[42] to us, since (from) now on there is no deficiency[43] of understanding and knowledge from it."[44]

III

šābuhr šāhān šāh ī ardaxšērān nibēgīhā-iz ī az dēn bē abar bizeškīh ud starjumbišnīh[45] ud čandišn ud zamān ud gyāg ud gōhr jahišn[46] bawišn wināhišn jadagwihērīh ud gōwāgīh ud abārīg kirrōgīh[47] ud abzār andar hindūgān hrōm abārīg-iz zamīgīhā pargandag būd abāz ō ham āwurd ud abāg abestāg abāz handāxt har ān ī drust pačēn ō [ō][48] ganj ī *šaspīgān[49] dādan framūd ud ēstēnīdan ī hamāg hargestān(?)[50] abar dēn māzdēsn ō uskār kard.

Shapur, the King of Kings, son of Ardašīr, further collected nonreligious[51] writings on medicine, astronomy, movement, time, space, substance, accident, becoming, decay, transformation, logic, and other crafts and skills that were scattered among the Indians and in Rome (and) other lands, and he collated[52] them with the Avesta. He ordered each of the correct copies to be placed into the royal treasury, and he brought forth for consideration the establishment[53] of all the disciplines(?) upon the Mazdayasnian religion.

According to this Zoroastrian narrative, which may perhaps in some way reflect an oral tradition dating back to the time of Khusrow I, Shapur I orders "each of the correct copies" (*har ān ī drust pačēn*) of the Avesta, including its newly "collated" (*abāz handāxt*) scientific and philosophical writings that had been scattered around the world, to be deposited into a "treasury" (*ganj*) for safekeeping. As Michael Stausberg has correctly argued, against the previous readings of Mary Boyce, Ardashir's request that "all those scattered teachings be brought to his court" is not a reference to the Avesta itself.[54] In the picture painted in this text, the Avestan canon in Shapur's time contains not only the Zoroastrian priest Tansar's regional Avestan traditions, parts of which Tansar authorizes during Ardashir's reign in the third century C.E., but also all types of foreign knowledge. This view that the Avesta incorporates foreign knowledge is corroborated by other passages in the *Dēnkard* that express a similar openness toward procuring the divinely inspired writings of other regions of the world. With a permeable Avesta open to such topics as medicine, movement, and time, Shapur is able to establish an imperially authorized and authenticated encyclopedia of wisdom composed of both Zand-Avestan and non-Iranian scientific and philosophical thought, an amalgamation of knowledge that extant Zoroastrian texts attest took place. It is well known, for instance, that Sasanian Zoroastrian scholars actively sought and translated Greek writings, influences that are discernible in, among other texts, chapter 2 of the *Bundahišn.*[55]

On one level, the narrative in the *Dēnkard* about Ardashir and Shapur reflects back on the early Sasanian Empire's attempts to gain imperial authority over its internal (i.e., Arsacid predecessors, Zoroastrian heretics, et al.) and external (i.e., non-Zoroastrian) others through a systematic amalgamation of its emergent Sasanian Zoroastrianism with ancient, non-Iranian forms of knowledge. Rather than attempting to impose any universal Zoroastrianism on the masses, Shapur I broke down the us/them dichotomy with respect to the imperial canon's authority. From a political perspective, Shapur's Sasanian Avesta helped the early empire's ability to sustain its rule over its vast territories, since the canon simultaneously consolidated the empire's varieties of Zoroastrianism, accommodated foreign ideas, and put the monarchy and sacerdotal class in a position to manipulate, codify, and house a Sasanian encyclopedia of knowledge that suited their politico-religious needs. The intentional permeability of the Avestan canon was therefore one means by which the upper classes could gain control over knowledge in the empire and then assimilate it to their worldview, as seen in another passage in the *Dēnkard,* transcribed and translated by Shaki.[56] Once the canonization of the Avesta was complete in Shapur's era, the later Sasanian kings Shapur II (309–79 C.E.) and Khusrow I, according to the same narrative in *Dēnkard* Book 4, proceeded to rout all internal Zoroastrian heresies, hold disputations, rule against minorities' anti-Zoroastrian behavior when deemed necessary, and spare themselves the need to revisit others' ideas.[57]

This last goal summarizes what I believe to be the main ideological point of the passage—namely, that the Avesta was thought to subsume all foreign knowledge for the specific purpose of enhancing the empire's abilities to concentrate on examining and thus ruling in view of Zoroastrianism. In Shapur's worldview specifically, or more precisely Shapur's worldview according to the later priestly authors of the *Dēnkard,* part of the early empire's authority sprang from the controlled permeability of its Avestan canon to accommodate foreign knowledge. Of all the kings in the Sasanian period, it was Shapur I who remained the figurehead of this policy.

THE POWER OF RABBINIC KNOWLEDGE OVER THE FATE OF EMPIRES

The second sage-Shapur text that we investigate in this chapter is part of the Talmud's dream book in *b. Ber.* 55a–57b.[58] In our excerpt (55b–56a), King Shapur asks Shmuel to predict what he will see in his dream that evening. Shmuel responds that the king will dream about his capture by the Romans and personal humiliation in being forced to be a pig herder. Predictably, the king thinks about these images and then later that night dreams about them. Unlike *b. B. Meṣiʿa* 119a, where Shapur praises Jewish law, in this text Shapur is made to participate in his own domination through his inquiry into rabbinic wisdom about dream interpretation. The following passage invokes Shapur as a symbol of imperial authority in order to demonstrate the supremacy and efficacy of rabbinic knowledge over the fate of its rulers:[59]

> R. Shmuel bar Naḥmani said in the name of R. Yonatan: A man is shown nothing (in his dreams) except (the images) of his own thoughts, as it is said: "O King, as for you, your thoughts came upon your bed" (Dan. 2:29). Or, if you want, I can cite from here: "That you may know the thoughts of your heart" (Dan. 2:30). Rava said: Know that this is so—a man is never shown (in his dream) a date palm of gold, or an elephant going through the eye of a needle. Caesar said to R. Yehoshua b. R. Ḥanina: You Jews say that you are very wise. Tell me what I will see in my dream tonight. (R. Yehoshua) replied to him: You will see the Persians come and seize you, and they will make you grind date stones in a golden mill. (Caesar) thought about (this) all day, and he saw it. King Shapur said to Shmuel: You Jews say that you are very wise. Tell me what I will see in my dream. (Shmuel) replied to him: You will see the Romans come and seize you, and they will make you tend pigs with a golden staff. (King Shapur) thought about (this), and he saw it.

On a formal level, the R. Yehoshua–Caesar and Shmuel-Shapur dialogues function as aggadic illustrations of R. Yonatan's theory that a man dreams only what he thinks. The two biblical prooftexts cited (Dan. 2:29–30), one by R. Yonatan and the other by an anonymous first-person narrator, allude to the story in which Daniel saves all the wise men of Babylon from King Nebuchadnezzar's murderous wrath by successfully guessing (with God's assistance) and interpreting the king's dream, one that, just like Caesar's and Shapur's dreams, forecasts the end of his empire. In our text, these latter two figures of Roman and Persian imperial authority press the rabbis on their purported abilities ("You Jews say you are very wise"), thereby creating a literary tension through the monarchs' challenge to the rabbis' claims of interpretive power: Can rabbinic knowledge of dreams be translated into practice and transform the world order for the better? Never ones to disappoint, the rabbis exert dream control over the monarchs, putting the idea of personal humiliation into their minds and thus, as R. Yonatan's theory claims, into their dreams. With their knowledge of dreams, the rabbis boldly and consciously cause their imperial others to endure terrible nightmares. Dream interpretation, and by implication its prophetic nature, is a form of power that the rabbis can use to transform the world. Both dialogues use their imperial others as generic symbols of authority through whom the rabbis can demonstrate their own interpretive prowess.

The two dialogues in our text (Yehoshua-Caesar, Shmuel-Shapur) exhibit a strong formal parallelism with each other, repeating the same question-and-answer structure except for the images of punishment. In the descriptions of the two punishments, there is the adjective "golden" attached to the instrument of use ("golden mill," "golden staff") to create the effect of irony—the defeated monarchs should not be allowed to forget about their past glory during their enslavement. The motif of the personal capture of a king by the enemy is in fact quite common in the early Sasanian inscriptions, such as, for instance, the emphasis in Shapur's inscriptions of his capture of Valerian.[60] In contrast to other Talmudic texts, the juxtaposition of Rome and Persia here does not have any patriotic overtones, because each empire is depicted as being defeated by its martial other. But while this juxtaposition of narratives stems from the fact that the two empires were enemies, the link between Caesar and Shapur is not based on any chronological correspondence, since if this Caesar is Trajan or Hadrian, who "had strife with the Persians," as Rashi says, then his enemies would have been the Parthians, not the Sasanians. Instead, these two rulers represent two stock characters symbolizing imperial authority who give fabricated consent to the rabbis' mind games. In their fictional encounters with Shapur and Caesar, the rabbis imagine a world in which Jewish knowledge can be a tool used to defeat their rulers.

The scholar David Winston has noted a Zoroastrian parallel to Rava's statement in *b. Ber.* 55b–56a: "Rava said: Know that this is so—a man is never shown a date palm of gold, or *an elephant going through the eye of a needle.*"[61] Rava's statement serves as an elucidative reiteration of R. Yonatan's principle that a man sees in his dreams only what he has thought. Rava's aphorism implies that a man would never dream about an elephant going through an eye of a needle because he would never think of such a thing. Rava's image of a large animal going through the eye of a needle also appears in other religious literature, including the Gospels (e.g., Matthew 19:23–24)[62] and the Quran (Sura 7.40), both of which have the same tradition about a camel. Rava's case of an elephant going through the eye of a needle is more closely paralleled in the post-Sasanian Zoroastrian polemical treatise *The Doubt-Dispelling Exposition* (*Škand Gumānīg Wizār*), which dates to roughly the ninth century C.E. This parallel demonstrates that the Talmud and *Škand Gumānīg Wizār* contain a shared cultural aphorism ubiquitous in religious texts as an expression of epistemological or redemptive impossibility. These texts use the aphorism as a way to express the near-impossibility of an event or deed. Of these references, the Bavli's two usages[63] have more in common with the Zoroastrian parallel than with the others. For example, the Bavli and the *Škand Gumānīg Wizār* both apply the saying in the context of a discussion on the types and limits of knowledge, as well as how those limits are applied to aspects of everyday life, whereas the Christian and Islamic usages typically occur in discussions of eschatology and redemption.

The aphorism appears in the *Škand Gumānīg Wizār* in a chapter that attacks atheistic belief by asserting the types of knowledge that one can ascertain about God. After outlining three types of knowledge of anything—namely, necessary knowledge, knowledge by analogy, and knowledge according to what is possible—the *Škand Gumānīg Wizār* then uses the image of the elephant passing through the eye of a needle as an example of knowledge of nonexistent things:[64]

> Another form (of knowledge) besides those (is of) something that, at the limit of the necessary, did not exist (and) is not possible. For example, one can say that the world can be secretly placed inside an egg; or that an elephant can pass through an eye of a needle, as if one were to become bigger and (the other) smaller; or (that there exists a) substance without an origin, and a fight without limits, and a being that exists without containing time and space, or with unlimited space, and a movement that (exists) without emptiness. And to speak (and) think of other such things (is) vile, untrue, and impossible.

The general contention of this Zoroastrian discussion of epistemology is that one is forbidden to contemplate hypotheticals that are scientifically impossible, since no "good thought" (MP *humenišnīh*) or "good speech" (*hugōwišnīh*), two key ethical Zoroastrian precepts, can be produced from such thinking. In Zoroastrian theology, the comprehension of the sacred being is possible only through pure and truthful intellect, and therefore contemplating things not grounded in reality leads one astray. With respect to the existence of God, the Zoroastrian polemicists argue against atheism because knowledge of God can come through observing God's creations. To cite two of their examples, one can comprehend God by gaining "inevitable" and "analogical" knowledge based on observing the perfection of human physiology and elements of nature. In other words, the fact that the four natural elements—fire, water, air, and earth—exist in the world individually and in harmony is proof of the existence of the sacred being. Ruminating on objects or scenarios that are outside God's grand creation, such as an elephant going through the eye of a needle, does not, according to the *Škand Gumānīg Wizār*, lead one to gain proper knowledge of God. This literary and philosophical context of the motif of an elephant going through the eye of a needle is, in the end, different than Rava's usage as it pertains to dreams.

KING SHAPUR AS AN ARBITER OF BABYLONIAN RABBINIC IDENTITY

Our third and final Shapur narrative appears at the conclusion of tractate *'Abodah Zarah* in a Babylonian Amoraic discussion about the purification laws for a knife bought from a gentile. After a halakhic debate on the issue, the Persian king is depicted interacting with Rav Yehudah and the half-manumitted slave Bati bar

Tovi.[65] In this narrative, which is one of the Talmud's longest about either Shapur I or Shapur II, the Persian king performs the purification for Rav Yehudah but denies the same courtesy for Bati. When Bati complains to the king about the disrespectful treatment, Shapur responds that he was uncertain that Bati was Jewish because of his lack of Jewish morals. The Persian other, Shapur, thus functions in this story as the adjudicator of Babylonian Jewish identity, ultimately deciding which man is Jewish enough to warrant the purification rite. The authors of this narrative employ Shapur's voice as a means to engage their own internal anxieties over dietary and sexual mores in Sasanian Babylonia:[66]

> [*M. 'Abod. Zar.* 5:12] "And the knife (from a gentile)—one polishes it, and it becomes purified." Rav Huna said: One sticks it in the ground ten times. Rava said: In hard ground. Rav Kahana said: But (only for) a knife that is not serrated. Similarly, it was also taught: A knife in good condition that is not serrated—one sticks it in the ground ten times. Rav Huna the son of Rav Yehoshua said: (Only) to eat cold foods with it, as in the case when Rav Yehudah and Bati bar Tovi were sitting in front of King Shapur (and) an *etrog*[67] was brought before them. (King Shapur) cut off (a slice of the *etrog*) and ate it. He cut off (another slice) and gave it to Bati bar Tovi. (King Shapur then) stuck the knife into the ground ten times, cut off (a slice) and gave it to Rav Yehudah. Bati bar Tovi said to (King Shapur): And is that man [i.e., Bati bar Tovi] not a Jew? (King Shapur) said (to Bati bar Tovi): Regarding this master, I am certain of his (nature), but regarding this master, I am uncertain of his (nature). Others say thus—(King Shapur) said to (Bati bar Tovi): Remember what you did last night!

The mishnah at the beginning of this passage teaches that one must "polish" a gentile knife in order to cleanse it. After this law is cited, several Babylonian Amoraim add a list of preconditions for an alternative method of purification—that is, sticking the knife into the ground ten times. This second measure for purifying a gentile knife, by sticking it into the ground, also appears in the anonymous layer of the Yerushalmi Talmud's discussion of this same mishnah: "A knife should be stuck in the ground three times, and that is enough," a statement followed by Rav Yehudah's clarification that this applies only in the case of a small knife.[68] Before the Shapur narrative begins in *b. 'Abod. Zar.* 76b, the three Babylonian Amoraim (Rav Huna, Rava, and Rav Kahana) debate the practice of cleansing a gentile knife in the ground, and successively ratchet up its governing terms: ten times, hard ground, not serrated, in good condition (baraita), and cold food. All these short apodictic statements stand in contrast with the aggadah about Shapur that Rav Huna the son of Yehoshua explicitly cites ("as in the case when") as an illustration of two of the five conditions cited earlier on the subject: Shapur sticks the knife into the ground ten times, and Shapur is cutting *etrog*, cold food.

The Shapur narrative in *b. 'Abod. Zar.* 76b is an example of how the rabbis employ the Persian other to negotiate issues of self-identity as they relate to rabbinic power and authority in Sasanian Babylonia. At stake in this narrative are the boundaries of Babylonian rabbinic identity as delimited by legal practices outlined in the Bavli. As Richard Kalmin has shown,[69] this passage is concerned with the dichotomy of rabbis versus non-rabbis, invoking here the trio of powerful men (king, rabbi, influential ex-slave) as test cases for the practice of the specifically Babylonian rabbinic law on how to purify gentile knives. As expected, in the end of this polemical narrative, only Rav Yehudah is deemed worthy of the rabbinic practice. According to the story, Shapur, who is from the start knowledgeable about Jewish dietary laws, ends up deciding the Jewish identity of his two guests, determining that only the rabbi warrants a ritually cleansed utensil, whereas Bati and the king himself are not obligated. For the authors of this aggadah, empowering Shapur with such a consequential decision helped to ease the tension of their boundary making, thereby allowing them to create their group identity through an interplay of individuals outside their social context.

One of the latent messages that this narrative implies is that the Babylonian rabbis sought to base their identity on something beyond a Jew's self-definition or willingness to practice rabbinic law as in the case of the non-rabbi the half-slave Bati. Instead, this text reveals that the rabbis conceived of Babylonian rabbinic identity as also being shaped by how others, including a Persian imperial king, categorize and understand a Jew's actions. In other words, Bati is not solely in control of his Jewish identity, since it takes others to define him as a Jew in order for him to be within the group's boundaries. As a symbol of authority, Shapur decides who is a part of the rabbinic class based on what he knows of their moral character ("Regarding this master I am certain of his [nature]"). The moral of this story is that a man should not act like Bati and be enticed by Persian sexual habits, according to the second tradition, lest the Persians define him more like them and less like the rabbis. In this narrative, therefore, the Persian king becomes the defender of rabbinic practices against the threat of gentile (and specifically Persian) promiscuity or dietary corruption. The rabbis utilize Shapur's external otherness as a means of casting aspersions on one of their internal non-rabbinic others.

CONCLUSION

This chapter has explored the Sasanian context of sage-Shapur dialogues, with the goal of unraveling how Shapur I became a symbolizing authority among the rabbis and Persian elite over the course of many centuries. This feature of Sasanian religious culture presumably also extends to Christians, Manichaeans, Gnostics, and other organized religious groups that resided in or around Mesopotamia in late antiquity. Each of these groups had an evolving ideological stake in how it described past Persian kings in the literature that it produced. In the three Talmudic texts examined in this chapter, for instance, the rabbis invoke Shapur I as a figure of authority in order to highlight Babylonian rabbinic claims to power. When seen from within a Persian context, the Talmud's images of Shapur I, though not exhibiting signs of direct textual parallels with Middle Persian sources, nevertheless resonate well within the wider Persian imperial and Zoroastrian priestly constructs of the second Sasanian king that promoted his reputation as a ruler who succeeded in managing an era of radical change in the social order. During and after Shapur I's reign, the Persian monarch thus became a literary figure who superficially represented the ubiquitous changes to the structures of society in early Sasanian Iran in relation to which later Jewish sages and Zoroastrian priests continued to define their own authority.

5

Rabbis and Zoroastrian Priests in Judicial Settings

As Jacob Neusner observed nearly half a century ago, the Babylonian rabbis and Zoroastrian priests functioned in comparable capacities in Jewish and Persian societies in late antiquity.[1] Both groups operated as judges, scholars, magicians, dream interpreters, and storytellers, among other real and imagined roles. In these positions, the rabbis and Zoroastrian priests were players in intersecting structures of Mesopotamian society. Living in proximity to each other near the administrative heart of the empire, the rabbis and priests were two of the numerous groups that sought authority in a network of social and intellectual settings. In the realms of law and magic in particular, the rabbis and priests competed for political and epistemic forms of authority.[2] With respect to political authority, there was a clear imbalance between the rabbis and the Zoroastrian priesthood in light of the latter group's standing as imperial administrators. Yet like the Zoroastrian priests, the rabbis held judicial offices and titles on a local scale. Moreover, the rabbis and priests also shared in common their maintenance of expertise in scripture and, in some cases, magic, with the goal of enhancing their reputations among coreligionists and outsiders as possessors of legitimate and efficacious knowledge.

What are we to make of these similarities and differences between the rabbis and the Persian priests? Unlike Neusner, who inaccurately attributes the shared qualities to the impact of Hellenism,[3] in this chapter I concentrate on the role of the Sasanian context in the ties between the rabbis and the priests.[4] For the rabbis of Babylonia, the Zoroastrian priests were a threat to the boundaries of rabbinic identity and authority, not only because they were simultaneously "like us" and "not like us" but also because they possessed the imperial power to claim to "be us."[5] In grappling with their closeness to the priests in function but distance from them in beliefs, practices, and imperial power, the rabbis in the end were forced to contend with their own identity. Talmudic literature's engagement with Persia situates rabbinic identity and culture within the context of Persian imperial authority. One of the ways that the rabbis responded to the priests was by depicting them negatively and generically as others.

TALMUDIC PORTRAYALS OF ZOROASTRIAN PRIESTS: THE PHILOLOGICAL BACKGROUND

The Talmud describes the Zoroastrian priests negatively as sorcerers, grave robbers, or persecuting administrators offended by Jewish burial and fire practices. On several occasions the Talmud compares the Persian priests to rabbinic scholars and Jewish judges. Some Talmudic and Syriac texts mention the names of particular Zoroastrian priests, including one in the Talmud named Parwah.[6] The Bavli calls Zoroastrian priests one of two titles (with variants): either אמגושא, "magian," or חברא, a metonym for a Zoroastrian priest, literally a "charmer."[7] There is a greater hostility in the Talmud's attitudes toward the latter group. The word *amgûšā* appears to come from the Old Persian nominative form *maguš*, "magian,"[8] whence also come the cognates in Syriac and Greek, which the Greeks used derogatorily to mean "magician" as early as the fifth century B.C.E. Iranian philologists debate whether the Old Persian word is related to Avestan *mogu-*, which may mean "(member of a) tribe," "priestly caste," or "(the one in charge of the ceremony of exchanging) gifts [or: "riches"]."[9] Whatever the case, *amgûšā* is attested both in Jewish Babylonian Aramaic and in Syriac texts as an unambiguous reference to the Zoroastrian priesthood.[10] It is noteworthy that the Jews do not adopt any of the Middle Persian titles (e.g., *mog* or *mowbed*)[11] but rather preserve a more ancient rendering. This suggests that the term has origins before or outside of the Persian context of Amoraic Babylonia, perhaps through the intermediary of Official Aramaic. The association that the Talmud makes between the *amgûšā* and sorcery also betrays Hellenistic influences,[12] making the Greek context relevant as well. It is, however, hard to know the precise history of the terminology since the Aramaic word for magian priest does not appear in any meaningful way in other works of ancient Jewish literature prior to the Babylonian Talmud, save for two Elephantine papyri from the fifth century B.C.E.[13]

The second appellation that the Talmud uses in reference to the Zoroastrian priests is חברי or חברים. The precise history of these words, and why they are used as a title for Zoroastrian priests, is not straightforward. The root is Semitic, not Persian.[14] The Talmud juxtaposes them with the Persians, and, in texts that I analyze in this chapter, depicts them as performing Zoroastrian practices such as disinterring the dead out of concern for the pollution of the earth caused by corpses. As for the connection between the *ḥabarei* and the *amgûšā*, the Talmud does not make this explicit, but what connects them is each term's association with the Persians or magic.[15] Rashi's commentaries, which lack historical specificity, suggest that the *ḥabarei* were a people who descended from or resided near the Persians, but who were more destructive and forceful than they were.[16] These explanations have partly guided academic interpretations. In contemporary scholarship, Isaiah Gafni's equation of the *ḥabarei* with the Zoroastrian scholar-priests (called *hērbeds*), though philologically uncorroborated,[17] is conceivable to the extent that the scholastic strand of Talmudic Judaism exhibits more similarities with this type of priest than it does with the Sasanian *mowbeds*.

The Soncino Hebrew-English edition of the Babylonian Talmud edited by Isidore Epstein translates *ḥabarei* "Guebers,"[18] a derogatory term for Zoroastrians residing in Persia or India, or "Parsees." The term "Guebers" appears in a diverse literary and cultural field, including Early Modern European writings on travel, history, and religion. It is of interest that Voltaire's essay "Jews" (1756) places side by side the Guebers and the Jews in an account of dispersed peoples, as does James Bassett's Christian missionary travelogue *Persia, the Land of the Imams* (1890).[19] The word "Gueber" appears to come from New Persian *gabr* ("Zoroastrian, magus, infidel"),[20] first attested in early Persian writings from the tenth century C.E., including Ferdowsi's *Šāhnāme*, as well as in early Arabic literature.[21] Linguists have traced the etymology of *gabr* to three possible ends:[22] either *gabr* is a corrupted form or even mispronunciation of Arabic *kāfer*, "infidel";[23] or *gabr* is related to the Pahlavi heterogram for a Zoroastrian priest (*mog-mard*), spelled mwg-GBRA, with the second term a symbol corresponding to Aramaic *gabrā*, "man";[24] or else *gabr* stems from the Semitic root *ḤBR*, as attested in the Bavli. Not surprisingly, linguists are divided on this word's origins across disciplinary lines: whereas scholars of Islam have tended toward the first explanation, Iranists have preferred the second or the third.[25] Problematically in the study of Iranian religions, attempts at etymologizing ambiguous words implicitly co-opt traditions into one's field. In light of this, scholars should be cautious in advancing historical claims on the basis of opinions in regard to the meanings of debated words. A comparison of the entries for *gabr* in the *Encyclopedia of Islam* (by the scholar of Islam Alessandro Bausani) and *Encyclopaedia Iranica* (by the Iranist Mansour Shaki) exemplifies this problem. Bausani argues that *gabr* is a corrupted form of Arabic *kāfer*, a proposition that rests upon the plausible determination that tenth-century Persians exchanged Arabic *k* for Persian *g*, perhaps because of mispronunciation.[26] This proposition is also historically reasonable, since the tenth century C.E., when *gabr* appears, was a time when Arabic was already flourishing as a religious, administrative, and literary language and began to penetrate into New Persian lexicography. In contrast to Bausani, the Iranist Mansour Shaki states that New Persian *gabr* derives, "in all likelihood, from Aramaic" *gabrā*, which means "man" or "husband." Citing a relatively obscure secondary source, Shaki explains that *gabrā* "was used to indicate the free peasants in the region of Mesopotamia."[27] In the relevant *Encyclopaedia Iranica* entry, Shaki concludes that it is "likely that *gabr*, used already in Sasanian times in reference to a section of Zoroastrian community in Mesopotamia, had been employed by the converted Persians in the Islamic period to indicate their Zoroastrian compatriots, a practice that later spread throughout the country."[28] For Shaki, the term's origins are thus Sasanian Persian. There are, however, flaws with Shaki's thesis, as well as with the third explanation above, that *gabr* is related to the Semitic root *ḤBR*. Both explanations rest upon unfounded presuppositions regarding Aramaic-Iranian interchanges. The argument that *gabr* is somehow related to Middle Persian *mog-mard*, "magian," which is transliterated mwg-GBRA, incorrectly assumes not only that Middle Persian or New Persian authors comprehended the denotation or connotation of the Aramaic noun behind Middle Persian's heterographic signs but also that they would then go on to adopt this term to designate a Zoroastrian priest.[29] It is worth remembering that the Aramaic word *gabrā* by itself has no specific connections to Zoroastrians. Moreover, there is no proof that Middle Persian script's Aramaic heterograms served as a medium for linguistic exchanges between Aramaic and Iranian speakers or scribes. In fact, Middle Persian scribes themselves did not understand the meanings of the frozen Aramaic words.[30] The third explanation for the term *gabr* argues, dubiously in my view, that the Semitic root *ḤBR* was borrowed into New Persian, perhaps through the intermediary of Middle Persian. But in evaluating this analysis, one must consider its implications—namely, given the fact that *ḤBR* designates a Zoroastrian priest only in the Bavli, and in no other Aramaic texts of Sasanian Persia, this proposition seems to imply that the Persian authors knew the rabbinic usage. This conclusion, however, attributes to the Persian writers too great an awareness of the Bavli's rhetoric. Even though there exists evidence for Iranian words' entering Arabic through the intermediary of Aramaic,[31] there are few Aramaic loanwords attested in Middle Persian or New Persian texts.[32] In the end, these claims of Irano-Semitic linguistic interchanges, which are debated, are susceptible to scholars' tendencies toward harmonization and co-option.

To come back full circle to the Talmud: one should not dismiss the Soncino translators' error in utilizing the derogatory term "Gueber" as merely a problem of translation or identification. That mistranslation, which was influenced by the linguistic confusion surrounding the incorrect etymological connection between Semitic *ḤBR* and New Persian *gabr*, represents a larger interpretive problem in modern scholarship on the Talmud in its Persian setting. The mistranslation "Guebers" (or "Parsees") misconstrues the rabbis' original meaning into a derogatory modern appellation—an error that distances us from the original subtleties of the rabbis' usage of the carefully chosen metonym in a late antique context. From the time of the Geonim until today, these types of misunderstandings, which surface innocently because of the commentators' collective unfamiliarity with and distance from pre-Islamic Persia, have muted the Iranian influences on the Bavli where they exist.

Rather than embed ourselves in an etymological debate over whether *gabr* comes from *ḤBR* (which it does not), we should focus our energy on researching further what the latter term may have meant to Aramaic-speaking inhabitants in Sasanian Mesopotamia. The Semitic root *ḤBR* has a complicated history, and in late antique Judaism generally denotes either "(scholarly) colleague, companion, friend, neighbor," or "sorcery." It is possible that these two meanings originate from different roots, but it is not difficult to see their correspondence. *ḤBR*'s core meaning is "to unite, to connect," as reflected in both these definitions: that is, a companion is someone with whom one is personally connected, and a sorcerer connects words (through recitation) or ties (magic knots).[33] Both meanings are attested in the Hebrew Bible, Palestinian rabbinic literature, the Bavli, and the Jewish Aramaic bowls.[34] Although scholars typically assume that the Bavli's use of this term with reference to the Zoroastrian priests is derived from the second meaning of the root ("sorcery"), it is, I believe, also true that the term's first meaning ("colleague") was a part of its polemical thrust in Sasanian Mesopotamia.[35]

THE HISTORICAL CONTEXT: QUESTIONS AND SOURCES

This chapter's subsequent emphasis on the historical context of the rabbinic-priestly interface raises fundamental questions about Jewish society's ties to the Sasanian world. For example, were Babylonian Jewish society and the rabbis therein in any way a subsystem of a Sasanian administrative superstructure run by the Zoroastrian priests? Was the social stratification in Sasanian sacerdotalism between the administrative *mowbeds* and the ritual scholar-priests (*hērbeds*), including the latter's techniques of training disciples (*hāwišts*), in any way mirrored in the social stratification or authority structures of the Babylonian rabbis in Jewish society? And last, were there any historical developments in the Sasanian judicial and cultural institutions, especially the courts and priestly-scholar schools called *hērbedestāns*, that were paralleled by similar developments in the rabbinic legal system or other comparable institutions, such as the study circles or academies, that partially served as Jewish courts?

Even though admittedly it is challenging to answer these questions with nuance given the limits of the Talmudic evidence, there are primary and secondary resources in Iranian studies that Talmudists can use as starting points to advance our understanding of Jewish society's ties to the Sasanian world. In terms of secondary literature, there is a trove of social and political histories about ancient Iran that, among other details, delineate the policies of the empire toward non-Zoroastrians. There also exists a substantial collection of diverse literary and material sources that emanate from a Zoroastrian priestly milieu in the late Sasanian and early Islamic periods. The primary sources that are firsthand testimonies of Zoroastrian priestly culture include, for example, numerous works from the Pahlavi corpus, typically composed by the priests themselves, including the *Hērbedestān* and *Nērangestān*, two Zand-Avestan study manuals for scholar-priests that are representative of Zoroastrian scholastic culture in the late Sasanian and early Islamic eras. These books offer scholars a rare glimpse into the priestly rituals, study habits, and social laws of scholar-priests in those periods. Along with these works, the seventh-century Sasanian legal compilation *Mādayān ī Hazār Dādestān* provides information on the roles of the various types of Zoroastrian priests in official Sasanian courts. In addition to these literary sources, one can access relevant historical information about the role of Zoroastrian priests in society from archaeological remains such as the imperial inscriptions of the high priest Kirder, administrative seals, numismatics, and the remains of fire temples. Although all these literary and material sources only rarely mention the Jews or Judaism, they collectively add much-needed nuance to our understanding of the interfaces between societies and cultures in late antique Mesopotamia, where the rabbis and Zoroastrian priests resided.

ZOROASTRIAN PRIESTS AS JUDGES AND ADMINISTRATORS

One disparity in sociocultural status between the Jewish sages and the Zoroastrian priests known in Middle Persian as *mowbeds* is the ability of the latter group to impose governmental policies in Sasanian territories as a hierarchical class of imperial administrators of both secular and religious institutions.[36] The Zoroastrian priesthood, composed of numerous types of priests, functioned as the main institutional administrators of the Sasanian Empire and was a major instrument of its ideological system. Scholarship on the precise relationship between the monarchy and the priesthood remains a desideratum, with the question often incorrectly framed according to the *Letter of Tansar*'s famous but late statement that "church and state were born of the one womb, joined together and never to be sundered."[37] As Philippe Gignoux has correctly emphasized, Pahlavi and New Persian portrayals of the harmonious ties between Sasanian church and state are early Islamic retrojections of a mythical past, and not historical fact.[38] Gignoux writes that "the sacred alliance between kingship and religion is but a literary theme which developed mainly after the Sasanian period and, I would add, under Islamic influence."[39] The late antique reality was more complicated than our late literature indicates.

Beginning under Shapur I or soon thereafter,[40] Sasanian *mowbeds* acted in all sorts of administrative and ritual capacities related to the clergy, including the supervision of fire temples, purification rites, property, temple treasuries, life-cycle events, courts of law, the military, and dream interpretation.[41] The *mowbeds*' styling on seals as "Protector of the Poor and Judge" hints at their role in defending the poor through charity and perhaps also in court trials.[42] According to the seventh-century *Mādayān ī Hazār Dādestān, mowbeds* were also in charge of overseeing the appeals of defendants, verifying the validity of seals, and appointing trustees or guardians (*stūrs*). The *Mādayān ī Hazār Dādestān* mentions in passing the existence of a manual entitled "The Book Regarding the Duties of the *Mowbeds*,"[43] thus suggesting that there were specific tasks assigned to these figures. In all, the Sasanian *mowbeds* were first and foremost administrative priests, performing a dual function related to their ancient Near Eastern heritage. Albert de Jong has noted that in the Elamite Persepolis tablets the magians are ritual specialists who oversaw the transfer of goods and not necessarily religious practices.[44] In the Sasanian period, these priests were endowed with institutional authority in part because their ranking atop the scriptural social hierarchy was the estate of the "priests," *āθrauuan-*, an Avestan term that came to be used in late antiquity (MP *āsrō*) to designate any member of the priestly class.[45] As attested in the *Mādayān ī Hazār Dādestān,* the *rad* (sometimes translated "spiritual chief") and *mowbeds* were active in the legal system alongside the "judge," or *dādwar,* a word attested in early Sasanian inscriptions and in the Bavli.[46] A few centuries earlier, perhaps in the fourth or fifth century, the government developed a hierarchy separating *mogs* and *dādwars*, who acted on the district level, from *mowbeds*, who were provincial. The judges acted on a district level, alongside *mogs*, under the auspices of a provincial *mowbed.*[47] If the rabbis qua judges can be compared to any class of Persian administrative priest, it would probably be the lower-level *mogs*, who worked on a local or district level. In addition to the district level, the provincial division of the empire sustained its ability to maintain stable governance throughout its territories.[48] Many of these posts are known to have existed only in the late Sasanian period. The *Mādayān ī Hazār Dādestān* dates the use of seals by *mowbeds* and *āmārgars* to the reign of Kawad son of Peroz (488–96, 498–531 C.E) and those by judges under his son who succeeded him, Khusrow I (531–79 C.E).[49] In an excellent synthesis of the application of seals in Persian law,[50] Maria Macuch explains that there were three categories of seals—private, personal, and anonymous administrative. Private seals were used for civil law, deeds and contracts, bills of sale, and court transcripts. Courts often probed the validity of these private seals, which were not necessarily owned by state officials. Personal seals, each inscribed with the function, title, and name of its owner, were those of the highest officials in the empire. As Macuch delineates, seals of *mowbeds* and *dādwars*, with their names and locales written on them, were administrative seals that were employed in criminal and civil cases. The *mog*, a title found on plenty of Sasanian seals, was a lower-level priest who functioned on a district level and likely oversaw economic transactions.[51] An example of a seal for a magian in Weh-Ardashir reads: "Mogvēh of Pērōz-Šābuhr; Weh-Ardaxšīr," with the partly identifiable name, "mage [mgw] son of Gušnasp."[52] In this hierarchy of jurisdictions, each type of priest or judge handled a different category of cases and crimes, these being divided into moral crimes, which were tried before a *rad* and required ordeals as repentance, and civil or criminal crimes adjudicated in official courts.[53]

The Sasanians inaugurated the post of chief priest (*mowbedān mowbed*) in the fourth or fifth century.[54] This post is challenging to date and reconstruct, given the absence of seals and a reliance upon Syriac literature. The *Mādayān ī Hazār Dādestān*, by contrast, provides a good deal of information about this post. A central position, it had final say over administrative policies and any legal case brought before it, and it was not subject to verification or doubt.[55] The *Mādayān ī Hazār Dādestān* stresses that this high priest's judicial rulings are considered more valid than ordeals.[56] This high priest was also responsible for producing the record of investigation (MP *pursišn-nāmag*) in capital cases and for establishing fire temples.[57] These social functions of the chief priest in the Sasanian period were altered after the loss of imperial authority in the middle of the seventh century. The post-Sasanian Zoroastrian priesthood mythologized the *mowbedān mowbed* by retrojecting it into Avestan history—for example, the *Bundahišn* declares that Zarathustra's oldest son, Isadvāstar, "was *āsrō* and *mowbedān mowbed*,"[58] and the *Pahlavi Rivāyat Accompanying the Dādestān ī Dēnīg* says that Sōšyans, the Savior, will become the high priest.[59] In the *Kārnāmag ī Ardaxšēr ī Pābagān*, the high priest saves Shapur and is the king's main confidant. Pahlavi sources also identify several important *mowbedān mowbeds*, such as the fourth-century priest Ādurbād son of Mahrspandān, to whom are attributed *andarz* texts as well the Ten Counsels to Yima against Dahāg, which polemicize against the Jews in *Dēnkard* Book 3,[60] though it is unlikely that this passage in the *Dēnkard* dates to the fourth century.

In addition to the *mowbeds*, there also existed scholar-priests (MP *hērbed*, Av. *aēθrapaiti-*),[61] who headed priestly-scholar schools (*hērbedestāns*).[62] *Hērbeds* were Eastern Iranian scholar-priests whose main contribution to Sasanian Zoroastrian sacerdotalism was the transmission of religious knowledge, especially as specialists in Avestan. Similar to Jewish sages, the Zoroastrian scholar-priests transmitted Zand-Avestan traditions and trained disciples (MP *hāwišt*, Av. *hāuuišta-*) in scripture, law, ritual, prayer, theology, and other pious subjects. In later Pahlavi sources, the *hērbed* is typically portrayed as studying and reciting Avestan. The third book of the *Dēnkard* contains a passage describing *hērbeds* deliberating with Jews over the Zoroastrian practice of next-of-kin marriage, according to the title given by de Menasce: "Sur l'altercation [*drāyišn*] d'un Juif avec un erpat qu'il interroge sur la cause et la raison de la pratique du *xvētōdas;* avec la réponse de l'erpat."[63] Although this title is suggestive of actual disputations between Jews and *hērbeds*, it is imprudent to try to build historical conclusions on such a small sample size. Nevertheless, shelving the question of whether the Babylonian rabbis were willing and able to converse with Zoroastrian priests about topics of importance, it is manifest that the rabbis exhibit greater similarity with the *hērbeds* than with the administrative class of priests. Such similarity, of course, need not be construed as affinity, a term that suggests social ties; paradoxically, it may have been the *mowbeds* and other Sasanian officials with whom the Jews would have had more contact. In the Parthian era, the scholar-priests (*hērbeds*) were actually the dominant priestly class, whereas, as Mary Boyce writes, "'magpat' or 'magbad' (as it appears in Parthian) may have been used mainly for the chief priest of a fire temple."[64] With the rise of the Persian Sasanian dynasty, the *hērbeds* were superseded by the *mowbeds* and exerted less administrative authority. In the Sasanian era, *hērbeds* functioned locally, where they may have worked in agriculture or through the generosity of sponsors. This does not mean that there were not *hērbeds* in positions of power; on the contrary, various key figures in Zoroastrian history, including Kirder and Tansar, carried this title. The post of the *hērbedān hērbed,* mirroring the *mowbedān mowbed,* is a later Sasanian invention, which, if it existed at all, may have originated with the grand vizier (MP *wuzurg-framādār*) Mihr-Narseh, whose oldest son, Zurwāndād, was called by this title in the first half of the fifth century.[65]

The social and institutional ties between the administrative *mowbeds* and scholar-priest *hērbeds* is poorly understood.[66] There were functional differences between them that sprang from each group's independent history in the ancient Near East. Though debated, some historians argue that the *hērbeds* taught the Avesta to the Magi, who converted to Zoroastrianism in the Achaemenid era or later.[67] The early Sasanians integrated the Old Persian and Avestan strands of the sacerdotal traditions. Both *mowbeds* and *hērbeds* are accounted for in the appointment of the third-century high priest Kirder as the official *hērbed, mowbed,* and *Ohrmazd-mowbed.*[68] It is unknown whether the consolidation of these priestly titles is related to Kirder's claims in his inscriptions, composed in the time of Wahram II (274–93 C.E.),[69] of having persecuted non-Zoroastrians, including Jews, Manichaeans, and heretics.[70] Late antique Iran syncretized the Eastern Iranian Avestan scholar-priest (*hērbed*), often mentioned alongside his disciple (*hāwišt*) and many other ritual priests,[71] with the Medo-Persian tradition of priests who played a central administrative and ritual role in Achaemenid society, as seen in the Persepolis Fortification Tablets,[72] and who also subsequently came to inherit a disparaged status in ancient Greece and Rome as magicians.[73] In Greek and Latin literature written in the name of Zoroaster and the Magi, often called Zoroastrian pseudepigrapha, these Persian personages became the figurehead for astrology and magic, giving rise to the notion of *les mages hellénisés* made famous by Joseph Bidez and Franz Cumont but since debunked.[74] In the history of ancient Iranian sacerdotalism, the late antique era thus stands as a synthetic phase in a millennium-long process of various interchanges between Persian and Eastern Iranian (Avestan) systems, and Greco-Roman and Persian traditions.

The Sasanian Empire promoted its imperial hegemony by integrating Avestan ideals into the Persian social fabric. In one description of the history of priestly power in the Indo-European tradition that aptly describes the Sasanian Zoroastrian priesthood, Bruce Lincoln writes:[75]

> The class of priests was effectively the ideological apparatus of society. As such, the priests propagated myths—the mode of ideology most characteristic of the preindustrial world—that encoded the dominant, normative view of reality, cosmic as well as social. . . . Priests viewed themselves as discovering, articulating, and transmitting the most sacred and profound of all truths, in which were revealed nothing less than the fundamental structures of reality—cosmic as well as social. Their self-image must not be mistaken for objective reality, however, nor can we take their truth-claims at face value. However much these priests felt themselves to be concerned with sacred and eternal truths, their actual concern was a set of ideas and norms peculiar to a certain society and period of history, which enabled that society—among other things—to organize and replicate itself along hierarchic and exploitative lines. And the norms and ideas they propagated granted the priests a position of great power and privilege. Here was a classic symbiosis of ideological and socio-material factors, in which the privileged position of priests permitted them to formulate and disseminate a brilliantly persuasive ideology, while that ideology—among its other effects—chartered and legitimated the privileged position of priests.

The Zoroastrian priesthood promoted ideologies and myths in order to maintain its legal authority and social status over other groups. Zoroastrian scriptural practices helped to legitimize Sasanian institutions. With this broad merger of sacerdotal culture and political power, the Zand-Avesta became a component of Sasanian social ideology, and as centuries passed, the priesthood became increasingly invested in the institutionalization of its Avestan-based authority as priests (*āsrō*). This notion is illustrated in several excerpts from the Pahlavi Zand to *Yašt* 1:12, which records Ahura Mazda's first-person list of names:[76]

> [Avestan] āθrauua nąma ahmi āθrauuatəma nąma ahmi
>
> I am by name Priest. I am by name the Most Priestly . . .
>
> [Pahlavi] āsrō nām ham āsrōtom nām ham az abārīg yazdān ay pad hamāg abestāg ēn kū āsrōnīh xwāstārīh bawēd az ēn gyāg paydāg.
>
> I am by name Priest, I am by name the Best Priest among the other divinities—that is to say, in the whole Avesta the desire of priestly office is manifest from this passage.

This text's exegetical expansion to its translation of *Yašt* 1:12 demonstrates the ideological connection that its authors make between the office of the priestly class and Ahura Mazda's self-declaration as Highest Priest (*āsrōtom*). In this and a plethora of other Middle Persian literary texts, the Zoroastrian clergy manufactures an ideology of priestly power related to its position in society. Pahlavi texts, for instance, emphasize the priests' connection to foundational deities and figures, especially Ohrmazd and Zardušt.[77] In Middle Persian literature, the Zoroastrian priests attribute to themselves cosmic and temporal authority. The politicization of the Avestan strand of the Zoroastrian priesthood had ramifications for the government apparatus and the priesthood itself, including Sasanian policies toward non-Zoroastrian groups.

SASANIAN POLICIES AND JEWISH LEGAL AUTONOMY

As a general policy, the Sasanian Empire did not micromanage the local legal systems of non-Zoroastrian communities, presumably including Jewish ones. Neither did the Sasanians institute a single or structured policy toward Jews or Christians.[78] According to the *Mādayān ī Hazār Dādestān*, the Sasanians appear most concerned with non-Zoroastrians in cases regarding slaves, marriage, and conversion.[79] As János Jany has elucidated, the Sasanian legal system encouraged disputes to be handled on a local level without imperial intervention, usually by "extra legal means, e.g. negotiations between the heads of the families involved."[80] If this argument is true and applicable to the Jewish communities, then the Babylonian Jews were able to set up a local court system in order to deal with legal situations that the Sasanians did not want or were unable to adjudicate in an official capacity. The historian Richard Frye summarizes well a general consensus among Iranists that the "Christians and especially the Jews had their own courts to deal with disputes between co-religionists, and presumably when Zoroastrians were involved the state courts and Iranian laws took precedence."[81] Thus, the existence of citizens who functioned in their communities as local arbitrators for cases involving non-Zoroastrians was a feature of Sasanian governance. The Talmudic evidence, for its part, suggests that this system opened up an executive space in which the rabbis, public experts, judges, and exilarch could operate. The legal autonomy of non-Zoroastrian communities was, however, only partial, as it transpired within the empire's mechanisms of control. This tactic of governance is reminiscent of a similar policy used by the Achaemenids, the Sasanians' Persian forebears—a fact that displays the continuity of ancient political traditions from the region of Fārs.

Although non-Zoroastrian communities governed themselves according to their laws in certain aspects of communal life, they were nevertheless subject to imperial courts run by Persian judges in specific situations. For instance, as Frye stated (above), the state apparatus took precedence in legal cases involving a non-Zoroastrian and Zoroastrian.[82] *Mowbed*s were involved in the adjudication of criminal cases involving heretics and non-Zoroastrians.[83] In some realms of life wherein differing identities intersected, including marriage and divorce, Jewish and Persian courts imposed on each other.[84] The Iranist Maria Macuch explains aspects of interaction in litigation as follows: "Foreigners (*an-ēr*) and infidels (*ag-dēn*) were accepted as 'subjects of law' when they had concluded a contract with a Zoroastrian or were involved in litigation with an Iranian citizen, but were not conceded the same rights as Zoroastrian Iranians in the field of family law and succession."[85] Elsewhere, Macuch cites a passage from the *Dēnkard* that describes litigation between Iranians and non-Iranians: "On the litigation of an Iranian against a non-Iranian (and) against non-Iranians; of a non-Iranian against an Iranian; of a slave against a citizen regarding an object of property."[86] The date of this passage is obscure, but it is possible that it originates from the late Sasanian period. Macuch argues that based on this text, "non-Iranians were accepted as legal persons, i.e. as plaintiffs and defendants, in court when dealing with Iranians. The evidence also points to the fact that legal transactions with non-Iranians took place."[87] When non-Zoroastrian inhabitants violated imperial will or Zoroastrian sensibilities of fire worship or burial rites, it was the administrative priests who implemented justice and reestablished the rule of law. Syriac sources in particular attest the responsibility of the administrative priests, judges, and *rad*s in executing Christians or Zoroastrian converts to Christianity.[88]

What was the legal status of the Babylonian Jews in the Sasanian Empire? The Sasanian government categorized citizens according to various dichotomies of identity: as a slave or a free person, a noble or a peasant, and an Iranian or a non-Iranian. Macuch delineates how the Sasanian Empire's classification of citizens and noncitizens resulted in a hierarchy of legal statuses in the court system:[89]

> Being a "subject of the King" (*šāhān šāh bandag*), an Iranian (*ēr*) and a Zoroastrian (*weh-dēn*) were almost synonymous. A person who converted from Zoroastrianism to another religion became not only an "infidel" (*ag-dēn*), but also an *an-ēr*, a "non-Iranian." It is often not clear, whether foreigners in the literal sense of the word are meant by the term *an-ēr* or also persons confessing another religion. . . . However, in either case the *an-ēr* was not—or no longer—regarded legally as an Iranian citizen.

Macuch later describes, based on a reading of a text from *Dēnkard* Book 8, that in the hierarchy of legal statuses those "persons without full legal capacity were *not* treated in the same manner."[90] There were different legal processes and judgments for Iranians as opposed to non-Iranians, with advantages for Iranian Zoroastrians—for example, the right to establish a substitute succession or enforce property inheritances.[91] Macuch goes on to distinguish "three kinds of litigation involving persons with limited legal capacity in civil cases," namely:[92]

1. litigation involving an Iranian who puts forward a claim as plaintiff against a non-Iranian or several non-Iranians as defendants;
2. litigation involving a non-Iranian as plaintiff against an Iranian as defendant;
3. claim of a slave, who—as the non-Iranian is not a citizen—against a citizen of the realm (*mard ī šahr*).

This outline of litigation implies that an Iranian could sue a non-Iranian in the Sasanian courts, or vice versa. At the end of the same article, Macuch offers a schematization of legal constructions of identity, the fourth of which reads as follows:[93]

> Persons with limited legal capacity, accepted under certain conditions in practice (e.g. in litigation) as "subjects of law", when dealing with Iranian citizens:
> (a) infidels (*ag-dēn*);
> (b) foreigners (*an-ēr*).

What can Macuch's research tell us about the legal status of Jews in the Sasanian courts? Unfortunately, with so few overt references to Jews in Sasanian legal literature, one is forced to try to extrapolate the definition of a Jew within the empire's system of legal constructions of identity. Were Jews considered men of evil religion (*agdēn*), non-Iranians (*anēr*), or both? Iranists debate what these two terms, *agdēn* and *anēr*, meant over the course of the Sasanian period. Pahlavi literature uses the designation *agdēn* in reference to Jews, Christians, and Muslims.[94] The term *anēr* is more complicated, as it carries simultaneous political, ethnic, and religious connotations. In the *Hērbedestān* the word is used as an exegetical gloss for demon worshippers, and it appears only twice in the *Mādayān ī Hazār Dādestān*.[95] It is, unfortunately, still unclear at present whether the Sasanians considered Babylonian Jews who had resided within the border since the beginning of the empire, or people of mixed marriages as seen in the Aramaic bowls, Iranians or non-Iranians[96]—though I would conjecture that in the late Sasanian period a Jew may have in fact been considered an Iranian man of evil religion: in Middle Persian, **mard ī ēr ī agdēn*.[97]

RABBINIC JUDICIAL AUTHORITY IN A SASANIAN CONTEXT

Over the past several decades scholars of late antique Judaism have debated the question to what extent the rabbis possessed judicial authority in Palestine and Babylonia. Earlier historians, as for example Gedalyahu Alon, often assumed that rabbinic texts reflect the laws and practices of the Jewish masses in late antiquity. Alon's Zionistic worldview affected how he described the rabbis as authoritative figures in late antique Jewish society.[98] Shaye Cohen and Seth Schwartz, among others, have critiqued this perspective as too normative and an exaggeration of rabbinic power in Palestine; to the contrary, they argue, the rabbis and patriarchs were marginal, insular figures in Roman Palestine, including in judicial settings with respect to the Roman Empire. In an important essay entitled "The Rabbi in Second-Century Jewish Society," Cohen writes:[99]

> The rabbis were not the sole leaders of Jewry. . . . Their institutions were oriented not to the masses but to the select few. Their judicial authority extended only to a few circumscribed topics. The rabbis were but a small part of Jewish society, an insular

> group which produced an insular literature. . . . There was great tension between rabbinic ideology and social reality.

According to this viewpoint, the Palestinian rabbis were a marginal group in Jewish society whose judicial authority was delimited by the Roman Empire. In several articles, Cohen and Schwartz individually demonstrate that one of the few tools of enforcement held by the Palestinian Tannaim and Amoraim was the power to excommunicate or banish a Jew from the community for committing one of around twenty-four sins.[100] Broadly conceived, rabbinic judicial authority in Palestine was dependent upon the communal acceptance of the judges' reputation for impartiality, personal charisma, and legal proficiency—and simultaneously tied to the Roman imperial context.

But was this also the state of affairs in Jewish Babylonia? And if so, what can we learn about the position of the Babylonian rabbi in judicial life by contextualizing it in Sasanian Iran and, more specifically, vis-à-vis the position of the Zoroastrian priests in Persian jurisprudence as described above?

In comparison with the status of lay leaders in Palestine, the Babylonian Amoraim were more influential in their communities on a local level. According to the Talmud, certain locales, especially Sura and Nehardea, were known for their courts of law. Specific authorities were experts in certain areas of law, such as the first-generation Amora Qarna, the judge of the Diaspora, whose specialization may have been the laws of damages.[101] As for how this relates to the Sasanian context, Richard Kalmin has demonstrated in several studies that there is a correspondence between the decentralizing of the Babylonian rabbis and the decentralized system of the Sasanians, concluding that "the feudal character of the Persian government during the Parthian and Sasanian periods very likely accounts in part for the extremely decentralized character of the rabbinic 'movement' in Babylonia."[102] Richard Hidary, in a monograph on legal pluralism in the Bavli, builds on Kalmin's earlier conclusions and summarizes well the role of the rabbis in Babylonian Jewish society as opposed to those in Palestine:[103]

> These findings overlap those of Richard Kalmin, who has similarly shown that the rabbis in Babylonia were decentralized and had only occasional contact with one another while rabbis in Palestine were better organized and sometimes cooperated in joint ventures. . . . The rabbis of Palestine . . . were not recognized as local authorities in their respective cities.

Hidary argues that even though the Palestinian rabbis were more organized than their Babylonian counterparts, the Babylonians were more authoritative as local leaders in Jewish society. The author continues:

> In Babylonia, on the other hand, the rabbi was the official and recognized administrator for all such matters. . . . The recognition of the rabbi as administrator in

> Babylonian communities goes hand in hand with the recognition of the rabbi as the halakhic authority in all matters. Babylonian society often looked to the rabbi as their leader and administrator in many areas. This resulted in local Babylonian communities centered around a particular rabbinic figure in each region. . . . In sum, the rabbi as local authority was more institutionalized in Babylonia than in Palestine. Pluralism for local practice was built into the Babylonian social and political framework in a way that it was not in Palestine.

For Hidary, the Babylonian rabbis were official directors of legal matters on a local scale. In comparison with the Roman context, the Persian government's encouragement for citizens to resolve legal cases through heads of families may be one cause of the Babylonian rabbis' increased authority among Jews on the communal level.[104]

In a book entitled *School, Court, Public Administration: Judaism and Its Institutions in Talmudic Babylonia*, Jacob Neusner also tackled the question of how much legal authority the rabbis had over litigation and rituals. Among other areas of life, Neusner argues that the rabbis had control over laws of marriage and divorce, family affairs, inheritances and estates, property crimes, and debt collection. He explains:[105]

> Our survey of cases . . . can leave no doubt whatever of the nature of rabbinic jurisdiction. However ambiguous the role of the rabbis in deciding points of religious observance, when a litigation involving exchanges of property, torts and damages, court-enforced documents, and the like came up, it was the rabbis, and they alone, who decided it for Babylonian Jewry. . . . They were hired to decide just these cases, and the exilarch himself was expected by the Sasanian government to preside over an orderly and stable Jewish administration.

Neusner claims that the rabbis had power in the realm of litigating disputes over property and damages. Although I disagree with some of Neusner's conclusions, I believe that his method of targeting court cases and the Sasanian context has the potential to yield valuable insights into the areas of law over which the rabbis presided. In studies of rabbinic legal authority, it is vital to utilize Middle Persian resources for understanding the ramifications for Jewish history of how the Sasanian Empire applied its legal system.

The Jewish court system in Babylonia was ad hoc and probably functioned in both harmony and tension with study circles and the exilarchate.[106] In a thorough study of this subject, Shalom Albeck argues that "the power of the permanent appointed judges has no foundation in Halakhah, and the principal laws of judges and the basis of their power are not applied only to them, but are given to everyone in Israel and are common to all the people of the nation equally."[107] As this quote suggests, the communal acceptance of judges was central to the judicial system. Unlike the top-down imperial authority of Persian administrators, the localized nature of the Jewish judicial system was dictated by an amalgamation of different parties—for instance, Torah scholars who researched the law, Jewish judges who heard and issued rulings on cases, and the exilarch, who granted authorization to public experts and perhaps used his privileged status with the Sasanians in order to influence the implementation of judicial rulings. How these different groups related to one another is currently poorly understood, but as Geoffrey Herman has spelled out, it seems to be the case that the office of the exilarch exerted greater sway over the courts than it did over the rabbinic academies.[108]

As one would expect, scholars interested in Jewish legal practices face the task of defining how and why discrete Bavli sugyot reflect historical realities.[109] Certain positions in the Bavli are influenced by the Mishnah or by fictionalized accounts, making it difficult for scholars to know when the Bavli's descriptions of jurisprudential procedures—such as the testing of witnesses, recording practices, the liability of judges—are records of actual legal practices done by the Jewish masses. In the hope of circumventing such limitations, scholars have devised ways of extracting documentary or archival texts, especially several hundred court cases, that more accurately reflect the Jewish system. Eliezer Segal contends that some of these cases were initially recorded in archives and later redacted into the Bavli.[110] Additionally, passages on court procedure and official posts can be compared with information found in the *Mādayān ī Hazār Dādestān*, which is a collection of court cases.[111]

Supplementing our literary sources, there are also around two dozen Sasanian Jewish seals that offer a small window into Jewish administrative practices from an archaeological perspective.[112] The precise owners and meaning of these seals are elusive, and it is unknown whether they were in any way authorized by the Sasanians.[113] They do, however, participate in the Sasanian glyptic tradition. The identification of seals as Jewish is typically based on Jewish imagery or the names of the owners being written in Hebrew. Judith Lerner has summarized the status of Jewish iconography in the seals as follows:[114]

> Except for the *lulav* (sprouting branches or a palm frond) and *ethrog* (citron), unique symbols of Judaism that appear on a number of seals, glyptic imagery is shared by Jews with others. Otherwise, there is no "Jewish" iconography and no "Jewish" style, and we can only be sure that a seal is "Jewish" by the name of its owner, written in Hebrew. Seals engraved with the Sacrifice of Isaac or Daniel in the Lions' Den are not indicative of Jewish ownership, as these subjects were also popular among Christians. . . . Other motifs on seals bearing Jewish names—male portrait heads or various animals—are widespread within the Sasanian glyptic repertory and were used by members of other minority religious groups in the Sasanian Empire—Christians, Mandaeans, Mazdakites, Manichaeans—as well as, of course, by the dominant religious group, the Zoroastrians.

The Jews and other minorities in Sasanian Iran worked from a shared stock of glyptic imagery that they shared with Zoroastrians. Rika Gyselen has called attention to a Sasanian glyptic inscribed with a Pahlavi legend and the image of a *lulav* and an *ethrog*.[115] Not unlike the Jewish Aramaic bowls, some seals identify Jews who happen to have quite common names that correspond with figures known from the Talmud, most notably one inscribed with the name Huna bar Nathan.[116] Shaul Shaked has proposed that this seal may indeed be connected with the Talmudic sage of the same name: "There seems to be no strong reason . . . to deny that it may indeed be a seal of the Talmud sage Huna bar Natan."[117] If this is true, then it corroborates the view that the rabbis were administrators of transactions. Geoffrey Herman has raised questions about this identification and scholars' attempts to interpret the seal's symbolism as part of the office of the exilarch. Herman, who concludes that Huna bar Nathan was probably not an exilarch, explains that these names were quite common in the Sasanian period and that the symbolism on the seals suggests a priestly context.[118] Regardless of whether this particular seal in fact belonged to the Talmud's Huna bar Nathan, which is an intriguing possibility, it is reasonable to believe that overall these seals were utilized in some official capacity by a Jew in a leadership position. On this point, Shaked hypothesizes "that people who felt the need to use the Hebrew script on seals were mostly 'official' Jews, who held some office or position of leadership within the Jewish community."[119] In a different interpretation, Lerner has reasoned that the owners of the seals may have been Jewish merchants.[120] In all, the limited Jewish iconography that does exist is firmly rooted in the Sasanian glyptic tradition.

The Babylonian Talmud includes several passages that demonstrate what intricate knowledge of official documents the rabbis possessed. One of these texts (*b. B. Meṣiʿa* 73b), on the poll tax, has two loanwords, one that is broadly related to Middle Persian *muhr*, "seal," and that in the Bavli means "document," and the other related to Iranian **sapat*, "box, basket, chest." The relevant line, based on manuscript Hamburg 165, reads: "Thus Rav Sheshet said: The document of these people is placed in the king's chest [מוהרקיהו דהני בספטא דמלכא מנח]."[121] This tradition reports that those people who paid the poll tax have a document attesting the payment located in the king's chest. The existence of a central Sasanian archive is implied by the evidence of the seals, as Rika Gyselen has explicated:[122]

> It seems that the archive was constituted during the last years of Khusrō I's reign and the first years of Ohrmazd IV's, that is, in the years 570 to 580. The location of the archive is quite uncertain. We can, however, postulate that the place which received messages and/or merchandise originating in all parts of the empire was a central "office" of the military, financial and civil administration. It remains to be seen what the "central" administration in question was. It may be suggested as a hypothesis that we are dealing with the "royal" treasury, which may not have been permanently headquartered in the imperial capital at Ctesiphon but rather have been "itinerant", accompanying the ruler as he moved from place to place.

Although the Talmud uses Iranian loanwords in reference to a royal treasury, Rav Sheshet's tradition about a king's depository of tax documents is probably not a direct allusion to the imperial archive that Gyselen describes above. Nevertheless, this short text provides another piece of evidence that demonstrates that some rabbis were cognizant of Sasanian administrative practices. The Iranian term for "document" appears also in the Talmudic phrase מוהרקי ואבורגאני, found in *b. 'Erub.* 62a, where it means "valid documents." Maria Macuch has analyzed this passage in comparison with the *Mādayān ī Hazār Dādestān,* maintaining that the phrase refers to "documents bearing the seals of officials" and, in the context of rabbinic judicial authority over civil and other noncapital crimes, that "Jewish officials were authorized to validate documents with their seals."[123]

PUBLIC EXPERTS IN JEWISH BABYLONIA

In general, the Bavli describes Jewish courts functioning in various capacities, such as overseeing certificates of *ḥalîṣā,* examining the statements of witnesses, and issuing deeds of divorce.[124] The Talmud also records different judicial positions such as the distinguished man (*mûplā*), lay judges (*hedîyôṭ*), court judges (*dayyān*), and the public expert (*mûmḥe*).[125] Let us now turn our attention to this final title, the public expert. In Jewish Babylonia, a public expert (מומחה) was a recognized individual who made legal rulings on certain types of cases.[126] According to the Talmud, a public expert had the authority for the annulment of vows, the lifting of bans, *ḥalîṣā* (the rite marking a man's refusal to marry his brother's childless widow), the permission of slaughter in the law of firstlings, and perhaps other types of situations. If these texts reflect social realities, the public experts appear to have overseen the release of social burdens such as vows, bans, and ritual marriage, especially in circumstances where a single official might be preferable. For instance, *b. Ned.* 77a and *b. B. Bat.* 120b–121a discuss the public expert in the context of the annulment of vows. The former text cites Rav Yosef's position that it is a single public expert who can absolve the annulment of vows on the Sabbath, since the gathering of three laymen may be mistaken for the formation of a court. Also treating the topic of vows, *b. B. Bat.* 120b–121a quotes two traditions from Rav Ḥisda in the name of R. Yoḥanan that correlate Numbers 30:2's reference to "the heads of the tribes" with the public expert. In addition, *b. Ned.* 8a–9a and *b. Yebam.* 25b mention the role of the public expert in the lifting of bans and the practice of *ḥalîṣā*. Another key text on the public expert is *b. Bek.* 25b, where Rava asserts that public experts permit the slaughtering of firstlings. This final sugya questions whether the permission of the expert is indeed necessary, an inquiry that appears multiple times in the relevant texts. The tenor of these passages implies that the position of the public expert was debated and not fully institutionalized. In spite of any controversy, the position was held in high esteem, as seen in *b. Roš Haš.* 25b's designation of Moses as the most universally recognized public expert in Israel. The Geonim, building on the Talmud's description, define a *mûmḥe* as someone instructed in Mishnah and Talmud with the capacity for rational thinking and reputed among members in the community as a just and experienced adjudicator.[127] Public experts appear not to have required ordination[128] and, crucially, were entitled to a special dispensation that other judges were not afforded: they were not held liable for judicial mistakes.[129] However, this dispensation may have been contingent upon receiving exilarchate authorization to make legal judgments, as seen in perhaps the best source on the public expert, *b. Sanh.* 4b–5a.

This lengthy sugya, which I have broken down into smaller units, debates whence a public expert was endowed with authority to act as a judge: Was an expert's authority derived from the recognition of the litigants and the community at large? Or perhaps from the exilarch, the Tannaim, the Sasanians, or God? The Talmud here deliberates these very questions regarding the legitimacy of the expert's judicial authority:[130]

> The rabbis taught in a baraita: Monetary cases are adjudicated before three (judges), but if he was a public expert [*mûmḥe*] he may even judge alone.
>
> Rav Naḥman said: One such as myself may judge monetary cases alone; and so said R. Ḥiyya: such as myself may judge monetary cases alone.
>
> They raised the question: one such as myself, for I have acquired learning by tradition and studied by logical deduction, and I have received authority from the exilarchate, but if one has not received authority—his judgments do not hold; or perhaps (it means that) even though one has not received authority his judgments hold?

This passage starts with a Tannaitic tradition reported by the rabbis stating that a single public expert can judge monetary cases in lieu of three judges. Building on this, Rav Naḥman and R. Ḥiyya declare in the first person that they are examples of rabbis who judge monetary cases alone.[131] Merging their two voices, the text then explains the three qualities that have endowed them with the authority to act as public experts in matters of money—acquiring learning by tradition, studying by logical deduction, and receiving authorization from the exilarch. This last prerequisite is, however, challenged: Does one really need the authority of the exilarch? The answer hinges on the question of an expert's financial liability for judicial errors. On this topic, the text continues by telling a story about Mar Zutra the son of Rav Naḥman coming before Rav Yosef after making a judicial error:[132]

> Come and hear! Mar Zutra the son of Rav Naḥman ruled and erred. He came before Rav Yosef. (Rav Yosef) said to him: If they accepted you upon themselves, do not pay; but if not, go and pay! Hear from this that his judgments hold; and even if he has not received authority from the exilarchate, hear from this!
>
> Rav said: Whosoever desires to act as judge, and if he is found in error, to be exempt (from liability for his error) and not pay; he should receive authority from

the exilarchate. And so said Shmuel: he should receive authority from the exilarchate.

Rav Yosef responds to Mar Zutra's judicial error by declaring that the judgments of a public expert who did not receive exilarchal authorization are in fact valid. Thus, in the case of judicial error an expert is not liable to pay so long as the litigants accepted him as judge. For Rav Yosef, then, it is the noncompulsory acceptance by the Jewish community of the public expert as a fair judge that indemnifies the judge in the event of judicial error.[133] But Rav Yosef's communal view is contradicted by the earlier figures of Rav and Shmuel, who agree that a public expert benefits from the authorization of the exilarchate. Unfortunately, there exists no Persian evidence to corroborate the claim that the institution of the exilarch had formalized ties to the Sasanian regime, which could prove that a channel of authority ran from the monarchy to the exilarch to the rabbis qua public experts. On this topic, Geoffrey Herman has concluded that the exilarch's "status as leader of the Jewish community, one close to the throne, with access to power must have given the Exilarch de facto influence on a par with certain nobles."[134] This privileged status allowed the head of the Exile to influence the Jewish legal system.

In the final section of *b. Sanh.* 5a, the Talmud digresses into a discussion of the validity of authority between the rabbinic centers in Babylonia and Palestine. This sugya then ends with Rava b. Rav Huna maintaining that he received his authorization to act as a public expert not from the exilarch but rather from his predecessors, a chain of authority going back to Rabbi. The rest of the passage reads:[135]

> (The position) is self-evident from here [i.e., Babylonia] to here, and from there [i.e., Palestine] to there. And from here to there, too, the authority [i.e., of the exilarch] is beneficial, since "here" is "scepter" and "there" is "staff," as it is written, "the scepter shall not depart from Judah, nor the staff from between his loins" (Gen. 49:10). "The scepter shall not depart from Judah"—these are the exilarchs in Babylonia who oppress Israel with a scepter; "nor the staff from between his loins"—these are the descendants of Hillel, who teach Torah in public.
>
> What is the rule concerning from there to here? Come and hear! Rava b. Rav Huna judged a case and was found in error. He came before Rav. (Rav) said to him: If they accepted you upon themselves—you do not pay; but if not—go and pay! But behold, Rava b. Rav Huna received authority! Conclude from here that from there to here the authority does not benefit: conclude from here.
>
> Is it not beneficial? But behold, when Rava b. Rav Huna would squabble with the exilarchal affiliates he would say: I did not receive authority from you! I received authority from my honorable father; and my honorable father from Rav, and Rav from R. Ḥiyya, and R. Ḥiyya from Rabbi! He was merely berating them. Now if the authority had no benefit, why did Rava b. Rav Huna acquire the authority? It was beneficial for Rava b. Rav Huna to acquire the authority from Rabbi for the towns close to the borders.

As in the Mar Zutra–Rav Yosef encounter, in this text Rava b. Rav Huna makes a judicial error and then comes before Rav, who like Rav Yosef advises him that if the parties agreed to his authority, then he need not pay restitution. After clarifying that Rava b. Rav Huna did have the exilarch's approval, the sugya describes the sage in conflict with the exilarch, declaring that his authority comes from a long line of sages before him, from Rabbi to R. Ḥiyya to Rav to his father, Rav Huna, and finally to him. In the end, this entire text in *b. Sanh.* 4b-5a delineates three points of view regarding whence a public expert derived the authority to judge monetary cases, as well as the exemption from liability—from the exilarch, from the parties involved, or from one's rabbinic forefathers. These rabbinic debates regarding how a rabbi derives the mandate to judge illustrate a lack of cohesion or institutionalization of the Jewish legal system. Without imperial backing or an enforceable hierarchy, the rabbinic class was stretched to fulfill the dual role of judges and scholars, a division of labor that the Sasanians, by contrast, were organized and equipped to handle by virtue of the dual heritage of administrative *mowbeds* and scholar-priest *hērbeds*. The Sasanians' policies of promoting the resolution of legal conflicts on a communal level offer an illuminating historical background for understanding why the Babylonian rabbis debated the function and indemnification of the public expert in Jewish society.

ANXIETIES OF ENFORCEMENT

The authority to punish criminals, including in cases of capital crimes, is at the center of questions of rabbinic judicial power.[136] Several Talmudic stories express anxiety over rabbinic judicial authority in cases of corporal or capital punishment. One typical narrative trope for these tales depicts a rabbi punishing another Jew and being caught by the imperial government for wielding authority, before then being saved from punishment and in fact receiving authority from them to carry out the punishment.[137] The relationship between rabbinic judicial authority and the Sasanian Empire is discussed, for example, in a story about R. Shila in *b. Ber.* 58a, translated in full below. In this tale, R. Shila punishes a Jew for having sex with a gentile, an act of authority that the imperial government initially considers an affront before then endowing him with the mandate to judge. Although the manuscripts contextualize the story in Rome, censors changed the standard printed editions to a Persian rather than Roman context. This substitution of Persia for Rome is also found in other rabbinic texts.[138] Ephraim Urbach remarks on this phenomenon in *b. Sanh.* 97b, where one Marcus Marinus Brixianus censored the edition published in Basel (1578–81) by replacing references to Rome with Babylon or, in this case, Persia.[139] By changing the text, the medieval censors bastardized the original rabbinic engagements with Persia, leading subsequent readers to misinterpret them on the basis of incorrect evidence. The printed editions of *b. Ber.* 58a remove references to Caesar (cf. the Munich, Florence, and Oxford manuscripts) and inject two Iranian loanwords—"authority" (הרמנא; cf. Parthian **hramān*)[140] and "messenger" (פריסתקא; cf. MP *frēstag*).[141] A third loanword, "club" (קולפא; cf. NP *kūpāl*),[142] which is also attested in Mandaic and Syriac, appears in all the witnesses, suggesting a Babylonian cultural context for this narrative about Rome. If this is true, then it is possible that the Babylonian rabbis, as represented in the manuscripts, were latently expressing their attitude toward Persian authorities through the creation of stories about Rome. The intended historical setting of this story is still somewhat vague, as is its protagonist, R. Shila, who is probably a first-generation Amora in Nehardea.[143] In an analysis of this text, Jacob Neusner disagreed, promoting a more positive perspective on the historicity of this source. Neusner concludes:[144]

> This story poses no significant historical difficulties, but, on the contrary, reveals accurate knowledge of Persian legal terminology (firman, frestak); the exchange with the government agent rings true; and the account conforms to the fact that R. Shila did exert considerable authority among the Jews in the early part of Sasanian rule. That the new regime supervised the activities of Jewish courts is beyond question.

Based on the testimony of R. Sherira Gaon, who calls R. Shila *rêš sîdrā*, Neusner believes that he may have been a "judge by appointment of the exilarch" and in charge of the administration of justice. In my view, this story is more about the anxiety that the rabbis felt with respect to judicial authority than it is a reflection of real historical events. Here is the story as it appears in the Vilna edition:[145]

> R. Shila lashed a man who had sex with an Egyptian [or: "gentile"].[146]
> (The man) went and defamed (R. Shila) at the palace.[147]
> He said: There is a certain man among the Jews who judges without the king's authority [הרמנא].
> He sent a messenger [פריסתקא] to him.
> When he came they asked him: Why did you lash that man?
> He said: For he had sex with a female ass.[148]
> They said to him: Do you have witnesses?
> He said: Yes.
> Elijah came in the form of a man and testified.
> They said to (R. Shila): If it is so, he should be killed.
> He said: Since we were exiled from our land, we do not have authority [רשותא] to kill. Do to him what you want.
> As they were reviewing the case, R. Shila said: "Yours, Lord, are greatness, might" (1 Chr. 29:11).
> They said to him: What are you saying?
> He said to them: This is what I am saying, Blessed is the Merciful, who brings the kingdom of the earth in the form of kingdom of the heavens, and he has given to you authority [שולטנא] and merciful ones of law.

They said: He is eager for the love of the kingdom.

They gave him a staff [קולפא].

They said to him: Judge!

When (R. Shila) left, the (man whom he had lashed) said to him: The Merciful One makes a miracle happen in (Elijah's) lying like this.

(R. Shila) said: Miscreant, are they not called donkeys, as it is written: "whose members were like those of asses" (Ezek. 23:20)?

(R. Shila) saw that the (man) was going to inform them that he called them donkeys.

He said: This man is a *rodef*, and the Torah said if someone comes to murder you, kill him first.

(R. Shila) hit him with the staff and killed him.

This story begins with R. Shila lashing a Jew for having sexual intercourse with a gentile. The punished man seeks revenge against R. Shila by declaring to the (presumably) Persian monarchy that the sage is acting as judge without the king's authority. Inquiring into the claim, the palace sends a messenger to follow up with R. Shila regarding why he lashed the man. R. Shila lies and states that the crime was bestiality (rather than sex with a non-Jew). Elijah appears as a miraculous witness and the palace declares the man should die. Showing deference for their authority, R. Shila says that the Jews do not have the authority to execute such criminals, and that they should take charge. As the officials consider his words, the rabbi begins to pray with the hope that he has saved himself, which they overhear and ask about. The officials declare that R. Shila is a friend of the kingdom and give him a staff (or "iron staff"),[149] a symbol of authority and strength, and tell him to judge. After encountering the man whom he had punished, who threatens to inform the palace that the rabbi called them donkeys, R. Shila strikes him with the staff, killing him. The story thus comes full circle—whereas at the beginning, R. Shila gets into trouble with the palace for lashing a sexual deviant, at the end he uses the authority granted to him by the palace to kill the man who sinned and threatened his life.

RABBINIC ATTITUDES TOWARD JEWISH AND SASANIAN COURTS OF LAW

There are several Talmudic passages that express a negative and hostile attitude toward both Jewish and Sasanian courts of law. To be sure, some Babylonian sages were wary of their role as judges in their local communities. For instance, in *b. Ketub.* 105b, the Talmud delineates how Jewish judges should avoid conflicting interests and corrupt behavior such as bribes. The text describes Rava reflecting on his love/hate relationship with the people in Maḥoza over whom he acted as a judge: "Rava said: At first I thought that all the people of Maḥoza liked me. When

I was a judge, I thought that some hated me and others liked me. When I saw that one who is guilty today gains tomorrow, I said that if I am liked they all like me, and if I am hated they all hate me."[150] Rava's tradition speaks of the resentment that litigants may hold against a Jewish judge who has ruled against them. The rabbis express conflicting feelings and opinions regarding their role as judges in the community.

The Talmud contains two related sugyot that negatively portray Jewish and Persian judges.[151] Both these texts rail against corrupt judges and government officials. The tradition that connects these two passages is attributed to Rav Pappa and stems from Isaiah 1:25 and Zephaniah 3:15. This Midrashic text takes its cue from Isaiah 1:25, which is an eighth-century B.C.E prophetic objection to the corruption of the dominant classes.[152] Here is *b. Sanh.* 98a:

[A] R. Ḥanina said: The son of David will not come until a small fish, wanted for someone ill, will not be found, as it is said: "Then I will let their waters settle, and make their rivers flow like oil" (Ezek. 32:14), and after that it is written: "On that day I will cause a horn to sprout for the House of Israel" (Ezek. 29:21).

[B] R. Ḥama b. Ḥanina said: The son of David will not come until the debased government is removed from Israel, as it is said: "He will trim away the twigs with pruning hooks" (Isa. 18:5), and after that it is written: "In that time, tribute shall be brought to the Lord of Hosts from a people far and remote" (Isa. 18:7).

[C] Zeiri said in the name of R. Ḥanina: The son of David will not come until the proud are removed from Israel, as it is said: "For then I will remove the proud and exultant within you, and you will be haughty no more on My sacred mount"(Zeph. 3:11), and [then] it is written: "But I will leave within you a poor, humble folk, and they shall find refuge in the name of the Lord" (Zeph. 3:12).

[D] R. Simlai said in the name of R. Eleazar the son of R. Simon: The son of David will not come until all judges and officials[153] are removed from Israel, as it is said: "I will turn My hand against you, and smelt out your dross as with lye, and remove all your tin" (Isa. 1:25), [and then it is written]: "I will restore your judges like the first, and your counselors as of yore" (Isa. 1:26).

[E] Ulla said: Jerusalem will not be saved except through charity, as it is written: "Zion shall be saved in the judgment; her repentant ones, in the retribution" (Isa. 1:27).

[F] Rav Pappa said: If the haughty cease to exist, the magians [אמגושי] will cease to exist. If the judges cease to exist, the court-appointed officers [גזירפטי] will cease to exist. If the haughty cease to exist, the magians

> [אמגושי] will cease to exist, as it is written: "I will turn My hand against you, and smelt out your dross as with lye, and remove all your tin" (Isa. 1:25). If the judges cease to exist, the court-appointed officers [גזירפטי] will cease to exist, as it is written: "The Lord has annulled the judgment against you; He has swept away your foes" (Zeph. 3:15).

In this sugya the Talmud discusses what Israel needs to do to induce the arrival of the Messiah. It repeats the phrase "the son of David will not come until" four times in lines A–D before citing ties between a single biblical text's verses. In line D, R. Simlai says in the name of R. Eleazar that the judges and officials (*šoftîm, šotrîm;* cf. Deut. 16:18) must be destroyed or removed in order for the Messiah to come. The tradition cites Isaiah 1:25–26, a biblical text that plays on the words "tin" and "judge" and describes the Lord's actions against a sinful Israel. God hopes to renew the nation's institutions and revitalize Jerusalem as a city of righteousness. Similarly, the text from Zephaniah 3:12 in line C chronicles Israel's restoration when the Lord "takes away their judgments," and after the Israelites' lips are purified so that they are no longer "arrogant" or "haughty." The theme of arrogance is a common leitmotif in the Talmudic portrayals of Persians, as we saw in chapter 3 of this book. The biblical texts on Israel's restoration underpin the rabbis' wishes of bringing about the messianic era through national renewal in their own time. Rav Pappa's statement in line F conjoins the fate of the haughty with the fate of Zoroastrian priests, and the fate of the judges with the fate of the *gĕzîrpatei.* Linguists have debated whether the term *gĕzîrpatei* is a hybrid of Semitic *gāzîr,* "officer," or Iranian *wizīr* (cf. MP *wizīr,* "judgment") with the Middle Iranian **pati* (cf. the MP suffix, *-bed,* "master").[154] It means something like "court-appointed officers" and also appears in *b. Taʿan.* 20a in Rav Judah's interpretation of Malachi 11:9: "'Therefore have I also made you contemptible and base before all the people' (Mal. 11:9). Rav Judah said: Blessing—of you no overseers of rivers nor officers shall be appointed." As Rav Pappa's tradition in line F articulates, the Talmud associates corrupt Jewish judges with the Persian administrative class.

Rav Pappa's tradition is also in *b. Šabb.* 139a. This parallel text opens with a lengthy baraita about the causes of Jewish hardship. The passage states that the Divine Presence is affected by judicial corruption and will not come until such corruption is eradicated. The difference between *b. Sanh.* 98a and our text here is that the former examines the messianic consequences of the judicial officials' actions, whereas the latter discusses the Divine Presence. The text reads:[155]

> [A] It was taught in a baraita that R. Jose b. Elisha said: If you see a generation upon which many evils come, go examine the judges of Israel, for there is no punishment that comes to the world except as a result of the judges of Israel, as it is said: "Hear this, you rulers of the House of Jacob, you chiefs of the House of Israel, who detest justice

and make crooked all that is straight, who build Zion with crime, and Jerusalem with iniquity! Her rulers judge for gifts, her priests give rulings for a fee, and her prophets divine for pay; yet they rely upon the Lord, [etc.]" (Mic. 3:9–11). They are wicked, but they place their trust in Him who decreed, and the world came into existence. Therefore the Holy One, blessed be He, will bring three punishments upon them answering to the three sins that they develop, as it is said: "Assuredly, because of you Zion shall be plowed as a field, and Jerusalem shall become a heap of ruins, and the Temple Mount a shrine in the woods" (Mic. 3:12).

[B] And the Holy One, blessed be He, will not cause His Divine Presence to rest upon Israel until the evil judges and officers are removed from Israel, as it is said: "I will turn My hand against you, and smelt out your dross as with lye, and remove all your tin. I will restore your judges like the first, and your counselors as of yore" (Isa. 1:25–26).

[C] Ulla said: Jerusalem will not be saved except through charity, as it is written: "Zion shall be saved in the judgment; her repentant ones, in the retribution" (Isa. 1:27).

[D] Rav Pappa said: If the haughty cease to exist, the magians [אמגושי] will cease to exist. If the judges cease to exist, the court-appointed officers [גזירפטי] will cease to exist. If the haughty cease to exist, the magians [אמגושי] will cease to exist, as it is written: "I will turn My hand against you, and smelt out your dross as with lye, and remove all your tin" (Isa. 1:25). If the judges cease to exist, the court-appointed officers [גזירפטי] will cease to exist, as it is written: "The Lord has annulled the judgment against you; He has swept away your foes" (Zeph. 3:15).

[E] R. Melai said in the name of R. Eleazar son of R. Simon: What is meant by the verse "The Lord has broken the staff of the wicked, the rod of the tyrants" (Isa. 14:5)?

[F] "The Lord has broken the staff of the wicked" refers to the judges who become a stick for their sheriffs; "the rod of tyrants" refers to the scholars in the families of the judges. Mar Zutra said: This refers to the scholars who teach the general laws to ignorant judges.

[G] R. Eleazar b. Melai said in the name of Resh Lakish: What is meant by the verse "For your hands are defiled with crime, and your fingers with iniquity; you speak falsehood, your tongue utters treachery" (Isa. 59:3)?

[H] "For your hands are defiled with crime" refers to the judges; "and your fingers with iniquity" refers to the court scribes; "you speak falsehood" refers to the advocates of the judges; "your tongue utters treachery" refers to the litigants.

This passage about the bringing of the Divine Presence to Israel pleads for the elimination of the haughty and the magians, and then the judges and the *gĕzîrpatei*. Rav Pappa's tradition has causality worked into it—if the Jews get rid of their own corruption, then the Persians' corruption will follow suit. Beginning in line E, the sugya gives a Midrashic exegesis on Isaiah 14:5 and 59:3 to critique forms of corruption. One of the first attacks, given by Mar Zutra, is against "the scholars in the families of the judges": those who teach ignorant judges the laws of the public. The rabbinic scholars are portrayed here as being a part of the problem. In lines G and H, the social commentary connects the powerfully accusatory verses from Isaiah 59:3 ("your hands are defiled with crime") with judges, advocates, court scribes, and litigants. This passage's attitude toward the Jewish and Persian judicial systems is one of suspicion and negativity.

RECORDS OF INVESTIGATION AND BRIBES

Sasanian Mesopotamia was home to both Jewish and Sasanian courts of law that prosecuted internal others for turning to or espousing rival claims to epistemic authority. The Persian courts sometimes used physical violence to punish crimes. For example, according to the Sasanian-Zoroastrian legal system, apostasy, rebellion, heresy, and sorcery were crimes worthy of death (MP *margarzān*) adjudicated by the Sasanian courts of law.[156] Sasanian courts used less strict forms of punishment for sorcery as well. For instance, the following passage in the *Mādayān ī Hazār Dādestān* illustrates that sorcerers in the late Sasanian period were punished monetarily:[157]

> That which has been said: All the property of a sorcerer [*jādūg*] shall go to the *rad* when it is reliably established that he is a sorcerer. But when he has destroyed [a man's property], (then it goes) to (the man) to whom he brought destruction. And if testimony is given concerning (the sorcerer), but it is not clear against whom in particular he perpetrated the crime [*wināh*], then (the property) is seized for the witnesses. Heresy [*zandīgīh*] is treated as sorcery.

This passage stipulates that the property of a convicted sorcerer should be confiscated and given to either the Sasanian *rad* or the individual who was harmed by the sorcerer's actions. If no victim can be identified, the witnesses may be awarded the penalties, a feature of the law that rewards citizens for coming forward to report the crime of magic. The end of the passage equates sorcery with *zandīg*, a term that means "heretic" or "Manichaean." According to the *Mādayān ī Hazār Dādestān*, the Sasanian judicial procedure in capital cases required a "record of investigation" (MP *pursišn-nāmag*), a technical term that appears in the Bavli. Maria Macuch argues that the rabbis' use of this term corroborates their high level of knowledge of Sasanian law:[158]

> The context in which this technical term is used in the Talmud is remarkable, since it demonstrates beyond doubt that Sasanian law was not only known to the rabbis, but that they were well acquainted with the details of court proceedings and used Iranian legal terminology with full knowledge of its implications.

As Macuch explains, in Sasanian law a record of investigation was "a very one-sided document in which mainly charges against the accused were recorded."[159] The document included testimony about the defendant's bad reputation from members of the community.[160] In a lengthy passage on this document, the *Mādayān ī Hazār Dādestān* states that this type of trial record was necessary for capital crimes, including *yazdān dušmenīh* (enmity toward the gods), *xwadāy dušmenīh* (enmity toward the lord), and *ahlomōgīh* (heresy).[161] This document appears to have been part of a memorandum (*ayādgār*) that was sealed by the *mowbedān mowbed,* in this case Weh-Shapur.[162] In another passage, the *Mādayān ī Hazār Dādestān* records the judicial procedure for composing a record of investigation declared by the *rads* and *kār-framāns* of Ardashir-Xwarrah in the reign of Khusrow son of Kawad.[163]

The Sasanian legal term *pursišn-nāmag* appears in *b. Giṭ.* 28b where it is often translated "protocol of investigation." In this sugya, Rav Yosef and Abaye discuss the differences between a capital case tried in a Jewish court as opposed to one in a gentile court. Presumably a Sasanian court is meant here. This text is another in which the rabbis express a negative attitude toward imperial law. The passage from *b. Giṭ.* 28b reads:[164]

> Rav Yosef said: They taught (that this applies) only to (someone executed) by a Jewish court. But in the nations of the world, as soon as the judgment has been decided for capital punishment, they execute him immediately. Abaye said to him: The courts of the nations of the world also take bribes. (Rav Yosef) said to him: When do they take (the bribes)? Before the protocol of investigation is signed. They do not take (them) after the protocol of investigation is signed.

Rav Yosef clarifies that the mishnah cited just before our passage is the law in cases when the accused is tried in a Jewish court, not a gentile one. Jewish courts accept the testimony of defense witnesses up until the moment of execution, and thus a condemnation to death does not necessarily end in execution. Rav Yosef says that the ruling does not apply to capital cases in gentile courts, since they do not accept witnesses at a late stage and instead rush to execution. Abaye contests Rav Yosef's position by adding that gentile (Persian) courts accept bribes, to which Rav Yosef responds that they do so before but not after the protocol of investigation is signed.

The motif of taking bribes also appears in a text about the Zoroastrian priests' "coming to Babylonia" (*b. Yebam.* 63b). In this passage, the Talmud portrays the Persian priests as corrupt. Scholars such as Moshe Beer and E. S. Rosenthal have cited these passages in studies on Sasanian oppression of Jews, especially in the third century during the era of the high priest Kirder, whose inscriptions pronounce the persecution of Jews, Christians, and other groups.[165] These types of interpretive connections between Talmudic texts and selective Sasanian sources are, however, problematic in several ways. This well-known passage has been treated in detail by Richard Kalmin, who thoroughly revised the opinion of earlier generations of scholarship on the text's chronology and historical context:[166]

> "I . . . shall vex (Israel) with a nation of fools" (Deut. 32:21). . .
>
> R. Yoḥanan said: These are the *ḥabarîm.*
>
> They said to R. Yoḥanan: The *ḥabarei* have come to Babylonia.
>
> He bent over and fell.
>
> They said to (R. Yoḥanan): They accept bribes.
>
> He sat up straight.
>
> They decreed about three (things) because of three (things). They decreed about meat because of (the priestly) gifts; they decreed about bathhouses because of (ritual) immersion; they disinter the dead because they rejoice on the day of their festivals (as it is said):
>
> "The hand of God will strike you and your fathers" (1 Sam. 12:15).
>
> Rabbah bar Shmuel said: This is the disinterring of the dead, as the master said—On account of the sin of the living the dead are disinterred.

This narrative is about divine punishment: God uses the priests as a tool for punishing the Jews. The Talmud connects the Zoroastrian priests with Deuteronomy 32:21, a verse about God's punishment of the Israelites for their covenantal contraventions. As Kalmin shows, the priests' three decrees against the Jews—meat, bathhouses, and burial—are "Persian responses to Jewish practices that violate Persian ritual law, and that offend Persian sensitivities because they violate basic Zoroastrian principles."[167] Unraveling the ties between the text's various strata, Kalmin's analysis demonstrates that[168]

> the third punishment/transgression pair, was added some time after or contemporary with the mid-fourth-century Amora Rabbah bar Shmuel, since it bases itself on his statement. Greater precision than this, unfortunately, as well as the provenance of the rest of the statement, is at present beyond our grasp.

Kalmin's detailed literary analysis complicates the historian's task of chronological precision, since (as the author adds) "any time during the Sasanian period could have provided such a context" for the three prohibitions listed. It is, indeed, difficult to chronologically align intricate Talmudic texts with specific events in Sasanian history. In a related story,[169] *b. Giṭ.* 16b–17a mentions the coming of the *ḥabarei* to Babylonia and the Jews' affront to Zoroastrian tenets. The offense here involves the use of a lamp as a potential source of conflict with Zoroastrians, who revere fire. A Persian priest removes a lamp from the presence of the rabbis, prompting Rabbah bar bar Ḥanah to lament life in Babylonia as opposed to in Rome. The

Talmud concludes by clarifying that it was the arrival of the *ḥabarei* in Babylonia that had negative consequences.

THE PARALLEL HISTORICAL CONTEXT OF THE RABBIS AND ZOROASTRIAN PRIESTS AS JUDGES

Although the rabbis and the Zoroastrian priests functioned as scholars and judges in intersecting societies, there was a political imbalance between the legal authority held by the two groups: the Zoroastrian priests oversaw imperial courts of law, to which the Jews and other minorities were ultimately subject in serious crimes or cases involving Zoroastrian Iranians. In Sasanian Babylonia Jewish legal autonomy on a communal level existed with the assent of the empire, which endorsed the resolution of intracommunal legal cases on a local scale without its intervention. There were thus arenas of life—such as perhaps marriage, debts, rituals, and vows—in which Jewish judges were likely active. But enforcement against serious crimes that necessitated physical punishment caused the rabbis anxiety, since it challenged the authority of the empire. Over the course of the Sasanian era the Persian court system became increasingly institutionalized. As we saw, the seals of judges and other administrators came into full use in the sixth century, within roughly the same general time frame as the editors of *b. Sanh.* 5a probed the limits and benefits of a public expert's exilarchate authorization to adjudicate cases. Whereas the rabbis essentially worked in a dual capacity as both Mishnah scholars and judges, turning their study circles and academies into courts, the Zoroastrian priests, by contrast, were divided between administrative priests such as *mowbeds*, who ran the official courts, and scholar-priest *hērbeds*, who were in charge of scriptural study. In Jewish society there were fewer opportunities for differentiation. One can conjecture, based on the historical picture, that the rabbis had a greater cultural affinity with the Zoroastrian scholar-priests than with the Sasanian *mowbeds*. Yet this does not mean that the role of the rabbis as judges was separate from the administrative priests. On the contrary: the Talmudic debate over the authority and indemnification of the public expert vis-à-vis the exilarch serves as an apt example of how the Sasanian Empire's structures of authority and policies toward non-Persians impacted upon the Jewish judicial system. According to some rabbinic opinions, the public expert's authority was, as Rav Yosef's tradition in *b. Sanh.* 4b–5a implies, based on communal acceptance of his reputation as an impartial judge, without the intervention of any institution. Jewish courts and public experts were probably to some degree assimilated to the empire's promotion of localized arbitration in cases involving non-Zoroastrians. In the end, the Talmud's own deliberations over whether legal authority is derived from the public, from earlier rabbis, or from the noble exilarchs reveal a complicated, multilayered Sasanian social background to Jewish law.

6

Rabbis, Sorcerers, and Priests

In Sasanian Mesopotamia, magic was linked to an anxiety of contact with others. In the Talmud and Middle Persian literature, the casting of outsiders as harmful sorcerers was a polemical device of alterity used to label dangers to group identity and claims to authority. The rabbis and Zoroastrian priests constructed terms of otherness, such as heretic, apostate, or sorcerer, that designated their peers liable to punishment. Law courts and magical exchanges were two social arenas wherein this phenomenon manifested itself. One difference between the rabbis and Zoroastrian priests, on the one hand, and the Jewish Aramaic sorcerers on the other, was their stance toward those considered others: whereas the rabbis and priests expressed an obsessive awareness of insider-outsider boundaries that they tried to control through the creation of laws and narratives promoting social separation from internal and external others in daily interactions such as food and sex,[1] by contrast the popular sorcerers, working without the impositions of institutions, contributed to the amalgamation of ethnic, linguistic, and religious identities.

The Babylonian rabbis were challenged by the presence of competing systems of sacred knowledge and rituals that could hold sway over Jews. As Joshua Levinson makes clear in a study of contest narratives between rabbis and magicians, the Babylonian Talmud presents magic as a "threatening Other" and "a type of anti-culture"[2] posing a danger to rabbinic authority and identity:[3]

> Rabbis and magicians are a powerful pair, and because they both manipulate unearthly powers for various ends, one could say that they compete over the means of production of sacred power and prestige. . . . Since the magician was a type of rabbinic doppelgänger, he constituted a serious challenge to rabbinic authority and identity, and no one was more aware of this challenge than the rabbis themselves.

Rabbis and magicians contended with each other's claims of sacred knowledge, as well as over the social power that such claims imparted. This mission for status is at the heart of the self-aggrandizing discourses, so prevalent in the literature from our period, that assert internal authority while downplaying external traditions.[4]

The Talmud portrays the Zoroastrian priests as sorcerers as a way of constructing group identity through an us/them dialectic. In what follows I wish to explore such images in light of the Sasanian context, not the Hellenistic one, especially by comparing the Talmud with the Jewish Aramaic bowls. The Hellenistic context, and its trope of magians as magicians, must have played some role in the formulation of the Babylonian rabbis' representations of Zoroastrian priests as sorcerers, perhaps through the intermediary of the Palestinian rabbis or Second Temple sources who similarly depict the magi as sorcerers.[5] These sources do not, however, explain the role of Persian culture on the Babylonian Talmudic texts. In addition to examining the origins of the Talmudic depictions of the Zoroastrian priests as sorcerers, it is crucial to examine the Talmud's portrayals in light of the fact that these priests were historical figures in Babylonia. The evidence supports contextualizing these images in a Persianized setting. In the first place, it is worth noting that the image of Zoroastrian priests as magicians or miracle workers appears not only in the Greek tradition but also in the Iranian national epic.[6] For their part, Palestinian rabbinic texts do not reference the Persian priests, nor do they equate them with sorcery. The Jerusalem Talmud and *Ecclesiastes Rabbah* both include passages about the Babylonian sage Shmuel that depict Persians (but not Persian priests) giving death curses,[7] but these sources unfortunately do not offer much help by way of determining the provenance of the rabbis' association of Persian priests with magic. It is the Bavli, by contrast, which contains references to the *amgûšā*, which is from Old Persian, and the *ḥabarei*, with the latter term's allusion to Persians extant only in Babylonia. Moreover, the Babylonian Talmud contains stories about Persian priests that are of Babylonian provenance, notably *b. Mo'ed Qaṭ.* 18a, which describes Pharaoh in the time of Moses as an *amgûšā* before citing Exodus 7:15 ("As he is coming out to the water"). As Abraham Goldberg has noted, this story is a Babylonian folktale.[8] This context is confirmed by the presence of the Iranian loanword פרמשתק[9] in reference to Pharaoh's penis, which was one cubit and a finger-length in size. In a similar text, the *Targum Pseudo-Jonathan* on Exodus 7:15 reads: "Behold, (Pharaoh) goes out to observe the divinations at the water like an *amgûšā*." The date and provenance of this text, as well as its ties to *b. Mo'ed Qaṭ.* 18a, are debated.[10] In the end, the totality of the evidence points to the relevancy of the Persian context for an analysis of the Talmudic portrayals of the Zoroastrian priests as sorcerers.

In a well-known text in *b. Šabb.* 74b–75a the two Babylonian Amoraim Rav and Shmuel debate whether magianism (*amgûštā*) is to be considered blasphemy or sorcery, two terms with distinctive implications in Sasanian Mesopotamia, as I discuss below. What stimulates *b. Šabb.* 74b–75a's debate regarding the definition of magianism is its need to explain the meaning of an anterior tradition, attributed to Rav Zutra bar Ṭoviyah, who records a statement of Rav that prohibits one from "learning one thing from the magian [*ha-māgôš*]," a crime punishable by death. This restriction illustrates the sages' desire for separation from the types of knowledge held by the Zoroastrian priests, although the editors of this passage conclude that learning sorcery is needed in order to understand it. The passage, beginning with *m. Šabb.* 7:2, reads as follows:[11]

> [*M. Šabb.* 7:2] "Tearing in order to sew." Rabbah[12] and R. Zeira both said: For when there was a curtain upon which a worm fell, they would rend it and sew it. Rav Zutra bar Ṭoviyah[13] said that Rav said: One who pulls the thread of a stitch on the Sabbath is liable to a sin offering. And one who learns one thing[14] from the magian [המגוש] is liable to death.[15] And (if) one knows how to calculate seasons and constellations, and he does not calculate (them), (then) it is forbidden to relate (rulings) from him.
>
> Magianism [אמגושתא].[16] Rav and Shmuel: One said sorceries [חרשי]; one said blasphemies [גדופי].[17] It can be concluded that Rav is the one who says blasphemies, for Rav Zutra bar Ṭoviyah said that Rav said: One who learns one thing from the magian is liable to death. For[18] if you think (that it means) sorceries, surely it is written: "You shall not learn to do" (Deut. 18:9), but you may learn in order to understand and instruct. It can be concluded.

The opening citation is an entry in the mishnah's list of the thirty-nine labors prohibited on the Sabbath. The mishnah's ruling against "tearing in order to sew," which is liable to a sin offering, directs the sages' digression into two other crimes and punishments, including "learning one thing from the magian," which here Rav declares a capital crime. Rav's tradition, as reported by Rav Zutra bar Ṭoviyah, cites a rare form of the title of the Persian priest, using the Hebrew definite article, "the magian" (*ha-māgôš*), which the editors connect to the Aramaic noun *amgûštā*, "magianism."[19] This change transforms the Persian priests into an abstract legal concept that needs to be defined: What is it about learning from the magian that makes magianism such a serious crime? To answer this question, the text brings in a debate between Rav and Shmuel wherein one sage defines magianism as sorcery and the other as blasphemy. The tradition does not clarify which sage declared which opinion. In resolving this ambiguity, the passage concludes that it was Rav who defined magianism as blasphemy, since Rav stated that one who learns from the magian incurs the death penalty. This identification of Rav's definition is correct, because learning and teaching sorcery is permitted, despite Deuteronomy 18:9's prohibition against performing magical acts.[20] The attitude toward gaining and teaching magical knowledge is in the end lenient.

Deuteronomy 18:9–12 is a common biblical stimulus for the Talmud's portrayals of the Zoroastrian priests. It prohibits Israelites from performing the foreign magic of gentile nations, especially the Canaanites.[21] The Deuteronomic text lists the "illicit ritual professions" as follows:

> When you enter the land that the Lord your God is giving you, you shall not learn to do the abhorrent practices of those nations. Let no one be found among you who consigns his son or daughter to the fire, or who is an augur, a soothsayer, a diviner, a magician [מכשף], one who does sorcery [חבר חבר], or who consults ghosts or familiar spirits, or one who inquires of the dead. For anyone who does such things is abhorrent to the Lord, and it is because of these abhorrent things that the Lord your God is dispossessing them before you.

In its critique of foreign nations, this passage's catalogue of illicit magical trades became the basis of the late antique rabbis' polemical use of sorcery as a reaction against threatening others, including the Zoroastrian priests. The root of the phrase *ḥōvēr ḥāver,* "sorcery," is related to the root of *ḥabarei,* the title for Zoroastrian priests in the Bavli. Additionally, the case of the status of the magician (*měkašēf*), which appears in the Mishnah, helps to illustrate the rabbinic definition of magic. The Misnah differentiates between someone who performs actual magical acts, a sin punished by stoning, and someone who merely creates illusions, which is exempt.[22] The following passage from the Mishnah (*m. Sanh.* 7:11) gives an example of this distinction:

> The magician. One who does a (magical) act, and not one who deceives the eyes. R. Akiva says in the name of R. Yehoshua: If two were collecting cucumbers (by using magic), one collector may be exempt, and one collector may be culpable: the one who did the act is culpable, and the one who deceives the eyes is exempt.

R. Akiva here explains the difference between magical acts and illusions with a story about two men gathering cucumbers: the man who actually performed the act is guilty, but the illusionist is not. In relation to this passage in the Mishnah, a baraita in *b. Sanh.* 68a provides a lengthier version, describing how R. Akiva learned to grow cucumbers by magic. The narrative context of the tale is the excommunication of R. Eliezer, known also from the Oven of Aknai legend in *b. B. Meṣiʿa* 59a–b. In the baraita, R. Akiva visits the excommunicated R. Eliezer, who is on his deathbed, on Sabbath eve and begins to ask him questions. The embittered R. Eliezer, still under the ban, rebukes his colleague by saying that he will die a cruel death, before soliloquizing how all his knowledge has gone to waste because of the ban. R. Eliezer explains that he learned many laws regarding the magical act of planting cucumbers, demonstrating his ability to do so with a single word in front of an interested R. Akiva as the two of them were walking down the road one day. Toward the end of the story, after the funeral of R. Eliezer, the Talmud explains that R. Akiva actually did not understand the magic of growing cucumbers based on his educational experience with R. Eliezer but rather learned it from

R. Yehoshua. The Gemara then concludes with an explanation of R. Eliezer's magical act in light of both *m. Sanh.* 7:11 and Deuteronomy 18, recapitulating the claim that it is permissible to learn magic in order to understand it:[23]

> How could (R. Eliezer) act thus [i.e., cause cucumbers to grow using magic]? Surely, we have learned: one who does the (magical) act is liable? For teaching, it is different. For it is said: "You shall not learn to do" (Deut. 18:9). [You may not learn in order to do],[24] but you may learn in order to understand and instruct.

This Talmudic passage justifies R. Eliezer's magical demonstration by claiming that he did it for the sake of teaching and learning. This example echoes the call in *b. Šabb.* 74b–75a that magic is permitted knowledge; instead of turning a blind eye toward it, the Bavli wants to control it by understanding it. Magic as a type of knowledge was at the heart of the contestations between various groups in Sasanian Mesopotamia.[25]

CONTEXTUAL RESEARCH ON THE BAVLI: THE CASE STUDY OF MAGIC

What more can we learn about *b. Šabb.* 75a and magic in Jewish Babylonia more generally by contextualizing them in light of non-Talmudic cultures in Sasanian Mesopotamia? In other words, how does a consideration of the Sasanian context of *b. Šabb.* 75a change our understanding of Rav's prohibition against learning one thing from a Zoroastrian priest, the Rav-Shmuel debate regarding the definition of an *amgûštā* as sorcery or blasphemy, or the editors' leniency toward learning and teaching magic?

Popular magic was an aspect of everyday life for the inhabitants of Sasanian Mesopotamia and a nexus between different languages, ethnicities, and religions.[26] Among Jews, Mandaeans, Zoroastrians, and Manichaeans,[27] magical practices and beliefs formed one sphere of intercultural interaction and social competition in which individuals of diverse religions and ethnicities encountered one another in their common quest to battle illnesses and demons, curse foes, or promote success in business and family. That social contact between groups occurred in this aspect of life is substantiated by a large selection of material relics, including bowls, amulets, magical seals, and even a handful of human skulls with Aramaic inscriptions.[28] The names on the bowls are unique testimonials to the lives of families in Mesopotamia. The ubiquity of magic in this period is exemplified by the following apotropaic incantation, which protects its Persian client Farrokdad and his home from the sorceries of various ethnic groups, as well as those by men or women made in the "seventy languages," which is a motif that also appears in rabbinic texts about the seventy nations who descended from Noah (see Genesis 10). Notably, this bowl uses the same word for "sorcery" that *b. Šabb.* 74b–75a does, applying it to various ethnic groups:[29]

> And let there cease from this dwelling and threshold of this Farrokdad the son of Zebinta, and of Qamoi the daughter of Zaraq, Aramean sorcery, Jewish sorcery, Arab sorcery, Persian sorcery [חרשין פרסאין], Indian sorcery, Greek sorcery, Roman sorcery—sorcery that is made in the seventy languages either by woman or by man.

This bowl text intentionally names all the potential sources of sorcery against its client, in part demonstrating the popularity of beliefs in magic in Sasanian Mesopotamia. In an important article on this topic, Shaul Shaked insists that "one can speak of a broad common denominator in the field of popular religious beliefs, around which members of different communities could be united, and which made it possible for them to turn to magic specialists outside their own community."[30] Popular magic was a social setting wherein late ancient peoples crossed over identity boundaries—or, more precisely, our modern conceptions of those ancient boundaries that, in the case of late antique Babylonian Judaism, we typically base on internal Talmudic definitions. In tension with the insularity of our literature, the study of Sasanian religious identities, especially in the realm of magic, would benefit from cultivating polythetic classifications of Iranian religions.[31] The bowls can assist us in this endeavor.

SYNCRETISM IN THE ARAMAIC BOWLS

Jewish sorcerers wrote incantations for clients with Semitic, Iranian, or mixed names. Drawing from a common stock of deities, evil spirits, and recipes, the sorcerers designed spells that were at once formulaic and yet personalized: each client had different needs—some may have wanted to protect against eye diseases; others, to send death curses upon their neighbors. In addition to the many Jewish elements in the bowls, some incantations also utilize pagan, gnostic, or Christian sources.[32] It is noteworthy that there are few Iranian linguistic or demonological influences on the Jewish bowls, especially given the fact that Zoroastrian sources contain a plethora of narratives about antagonistic demons and sorcerers who were believed to threaten Zarathustra and wreak havoc on the world.[33] It is, then, the rabbinic movement that exhibits greater Iranization than the syncretistic Jewish sorcerers do. Even ostensible Iranian influences on the bowls, such as Bagdāna, sometimes called the king of demons, do not necessarily reflect genuine borrowings.[34] Thus, magic in late antique Mesopotamia was predominantly an Aramaic phenomenon, with a strong Jewish component.[35]

Sorcerers shared recipes with one another, oral and perhaps written, across Aramaic dialects, as demonstrated by extant duplicate incantations in different languages.[36] For example, Jews and Mandaeans influenced each other in the realm of magic. The residential vicinity of these groups has been confirmed by excavations in Nippur, as Erica Hunter has explained:[37]

> Recent archaeological evidence has shed further light onto the Aramaic-speaking communities of Sasanid Mesopotamia. Excavations at Nippur of Area WG—adjoining the Jewish settlement dug a century earlier and from which Montgomery published his forty specimens—revealed in the seventh-century Level III five down-turned incantation bowls. These were randomly buried in a courtyard which also featured an oven. Three of the specimens were written in Aramaic and two in Mandaic, the latter pair being for brothers. . . . The placement of the Aramaic and Mandaic incantation bowls strongly suggests that two families, one possibly Jewish and the other Mandaean, shared adjacent domestic quarters.

In light of the fact that Jews and Mandaeans lived in close quarters, it is not surprising that Mandaic incantations affected Jewish ones, sometimes serving as their *Vorlagen,* and even absorbed Targumic and Merkavah traditions.[38] Mandaean sources express a complicated engagement with Judaism, one that was simultaneously hostile yet receptive.[39] The Jewish-Mandaic interface thus encapsulates one of the questions that scholars in this field need to address—namely, to what extent are borrowings or shared common elements polemically motivated? In other words, is the syncretism of the magical bowls a mask for exclusion of others? Or is it an attempt at harmonization and inclusion? Or both? Many of the incantations not only follow the conventions of one official religion but also invent or invert the names of deities and adversaries in other traditions. Examples of this latter phenomenon in Jewish and Mandaic spells include invocations of Bagdāna the king of demons, Adonai the chief of the evil spirits, and El-Shaddai the sorcerer (אל שדאי חברא).[40] What are the implications of such discourses for understanding the type of Judaism represented in the bowls and in the Talmud?

Experts regarding the bowls often describe them as being popular and syncretistic.[41] Both these terms require clarification and are often maligned as euphemisms for marginal or inferior groups.[42] If by "syncretism" we mean simply the mingling of identity boundaries, then it is true that we can fairly characterize the bowls as such.[43] But such a simple definition does not go far enough in clarifying the causes, motivations, and outcomes of these processes of mixture. Part of what is at stake here is understanding to what extent the Jewish incantations were composed with a pro-Jewish bias and, if they were, whether this complicates their current categorization among experts as syncretistic and popular. In a discussion of syncretism in the history of religions, Robert Baird explains that the term "is to be reserved for cases where two conflicting ideas or practices are brought together and are retained without the benefit of consistency. Syncretism occurs only when the result is not a harmonious unity."[44] In this definition, syncretism applies in cases wherein contrary ideas are amalgamated into a system that lacks unity. This quotation raises a pertinent question regarding the syncretism of the bowls—that is, whether the outcome of a given incantation promotes the reconciliation of conflicting ideas or, alternatively, the primacy of one idea over another. The study of syncretism engages a politics of synthesis, in which the role of antisyncretists cannot be overlooked. As Rosalind Shaw and Charles Stewart explain in the introduction to an edited volume on syncretism in religious studies, antisyncretism often occurs in light of discourses of authenticity:[45]

> If we recast the study of syncretism as the politics of religious synthesis, one of the first issues which needs to be confronted is what we have termed 'anti-syncretism': the antagonism to religious synthesis shown by agents concerned with the defence of religious boundaries. Anti-syncretism is frequently bound up with the construction of 'authenticity', which is in turn often linked to notions of 'purity'.

In light of this dichotomy between syncretism and antisyncretism, one wonders: Was Sasanian Mesopotamia composed of interrelated groups that sought to defend their self-defined boundaries versus those that sought to break those boundaries down? Were the Babylonian Amoraim, Stammaim, or even Geonim in any way antisyncretists interested in the promotion of rabbinic culture as authentic? In order to engage these questions in their full complexity, scholars interested in Sasanian Mesopotamia must first analyze the relationship between the various manifestations of Judaism found in the Bavli and the bowls, as well as, so far as is possible, the social context of the rabbis and Jewish sorcerers.

The question of harmony and reconciliation in the bowls is complicated by the multiplicity of identities involved in any exchange between sorcerers, clients, and both human and supernatural adversaries. It is unknown, for instance, how and to what extent the sorcerers, the clients, or both dictated the bowls' contents, language, or script. Religious affiliations are also largely indeterminable. In a detailed examination of depictions of Jesus in the bowls and the Bavli, Markham J. Geller has pointed to the uncertainty in identifying the religion of either the sorcerers or their clients:[46]

> First, it is often impossible to determine the religion of the clients in the magic bowls. . . . As for the religion of the magician who inscribes the bowl, this too is difficult to determine. The nature of magic is so syncretistic that pagan magicians use Jewish or Christian formulae, and Jewish-Christian magicians invoke pagan gods. One Mandaic bowl, for instance, refers to the Rabbinic *geṭ* (divorce writ), while Greek papyri mention *Iao Sabaoth,* and Aramaic bowls invoke Hermes, or a host of pagan deities. It is specious, therefore, to assume that such invocations will determine the religion of the magician; it is more reasonable to assume that a magician will invoke whatever authority will aid his incantation. Hence, it is possible that Jesus could be invoked even by a Jewish magician, as did the seven sons of Sceva.

Sorcerers' expressions of identifiable religious traditions emanated from a common Mesopotamian heritage that dictated what tradition would be appropriate for a specific need of the client. Thus, the sorcerer's religion—if such a term is even apt—was professionalized and purpose-driven for someone else's gain. Even if much of the evidence points to the sorcerer's being in charge of the spell, it is not impossible that a client's worldview influenced a sorcerer's selection of a recipe. Given that some bowls include specific details about a client's life, there must have been considerable communication between sorcerer and client in order for the practitioner to gather the names of both the clients and the enemies and to learn about the specific needs of the family. Adding another complication to the question of communication, it appears to be the case that spells were not always composed in languages or scripts understood by the clients, as is evidenced by short instructions on some bowls that tell the client where to place the object in his or her home. For instance, in one case the directions to place the ritual object at "the great door" (MP *dar ī wuzurg*) are written in Pahlavi, presumably the language of the client, and not in the language of the incantation.[47] A second label—the client's name, which, as Shaked notes, the sorcerer may have written in order to recall for whom the bowl was being produced—contains in the language of the incantation, save for the first name, Busa, the following name: Busa "son of Gušnai, Marqonta, Barukh, Zardoi, Yanti." According to Shaked, what all this indicates is that "at least this particular writer could write more than one script, and that the division of languages shows that the clients were familiar with a different language and script than the main language of the practitioner."[48] The implications of this conclusion are revealing, since it shows how clients did not even need to be able to read or understand the incantation in order for them to trust practitioners' skills. In a sense, for magicians and clients alike, language was more a medium of healing than of intercommunal communication. The practitioners were medical healers, whose words, like a placebo, were presupposed. The bowl's contents may not have been any type of religious declaration of faith by the client, who knowingly turned to an outsider practitioner.

The fact that the archaeological relics include the names of clients offers tantalizing insight into the family structures and daily struggles of real people in antiquity. There were clearly Irano-Semitic families, but the religious and ethnic backgrounds of these people are hard to determine based on the onomastic data alone.[49] As we know from the Bavli, bowls, and Dura-Europos synagogue, Sasanian Jews had Iranian names, even ones with imperial or perhaps Zoroastrian connotations. For example, the Bavli records Jews named Bahrām (the name of five Sasanian monarchs) or Xudāī (literally "Lord").[50] Despite these challenges, the evidence documents intermarriages between different religious groups. One bowl in Manichaean script, which has around a dozen crosses inscribed on it, belongs to a family of Christian converts with ties to other faiths: the family patriarch has a Zoroastrian name (Dadbeh son of Asmandukh), and one of the sons has a Christian (or perhaps Jewish) name (Abraham). This family owned both a Christian bowl in Manichaean script and a Syriac bowl with rabbinic themes that are paralleled in an extant Jewish Aramaic bowl. Shaul Shaked describes the identification of the family as follows:[51]

> The head of the family for whom this bowl was made is Dadbeh son of Asmandukh, an acceptable Persian name, with a Zoroastrian connotation: "Having the good law," son of "Daughter of the sky." The same client is also the owner of a Jewish Aramaic bowl, where the names of his wife and their children are also given. Among the names of the children in this family it is interesting to find the name Abraham. One may speculate that this was a Zoroastrian family that converted to Christianity, hence the Zoroastrian names of the parents and the biblical name of one of the children. Of the two bowls made for them in the Manichaean script, one is at any rate explicitly Christian. Another bowl made for them is a Syriac version of a text with Jewish contents, based as it is on the Jewish divorce formula and the figure of Rabbi Joshua bar Perahia. The same divorce text is also extant in a bowl in Jewish Aramaic. The situation described here shows that a family could turn to various practitioners who used formulae in different languages and scripts, and who seem to have belonged to different religious groups.

The identities of such mixed families defy easy categorization, and it is impossible to know whether clients from such mixed families were inclined to seek out syncretistic forms of religiosity as a result of their composite makeup.

Although the lion's share of the published bowls to date are intended to protect clients from demons and illness, there are also incantations that were created with the intent to harm a client's personal foes. Other spells are countercharms, which were intended to reverse an enemy's curses and send them back whence they came.[52] One recently published countercharm contains a list of around thirty names of people living in one town, perhaps Yazd,[53] from whom its two male clients (Amitiel son of Mahlapta and Elishebakh son of Shumuni) sought protection. It represents an example of local intercommunal friction and the dialectic between beliefs about the supernatural and the construction of society and culture. As the editor of the bowl, Dan Levene, spells out, the text contains "a simile based on the story" in Daniel 3:23–38 that "is employed as part of a magical formula to affect the annulment of curses, and is followed by a long list of the names of people whose curses this amulet was meant to bind."[54] In the biblical story, Nebuchadnezzar throws Hannaniah, Mishael, and Azariah into a furnace only to witness the miraculous survival of the men, whose hair does not even get singed. The incantation below analogizes the three men of Daniel 3 with the two clients—just as the angels delivered the former from the furnace, so too may the clients be delivered from the curses of their enemies:[55]

> May the earth admonish/(*cover*) the town. Sakrel, Qatiel Yehuel Yahel come forward (?). By your name Michael the great angel and Mishael the angel of fire. Just as you delivered Hannaniah Mishael and Azariah into the midst of the burning furnace and the fire did not touch them at all, so too may curses and affliction and knocks may not afflict the house of Amitiel son of Mahlapta and may not afflict the dwelling of Elishebakh son of Shumuni. And may there not afflict, not the curse of Jewish and

> not the curse of pagans and not a curse of the mother-in-law and the daughter-in-law, and not the curse of neighbors and adversaries, not the curse of distant or near relatives.
>
> And may these curses go out and flee to *fallow fields and to white clefts*, and you the dead receive them.
>
> Being handed over is the curse of Aba daughter of Asharkum. Being handed over is the curse of Mirdukh daughter of Abakh . . . [the text continues with a list of around thirty other names].

After the allusion to the Daniel story, the spell enumerates several classes of unnamed groups whose curses it forces away, including Jews, pagans, neighbors, in-laws, and distant relatives. The range of protection granted is intentionally large, and yet it also covers familial categories, resolving the problems of the near other. After these curses, the sorcerer then lists dozens of antagonists, who carry both Iranian and Semitic names, individually by name. One name in the list is Abraham bar Lili, a man with a biblical first name and Iranian last name; another is Yazdan-afrid, a name with Zoroastrian overtones. This bowl invokes the biblical story as a positive force in its agenda of dispute resolution, occurring partly in the realm of the supernatural, between the clients and their many antagonists.

As we have seen, the sorcerers of our Aramaic bowls served patrons of different and mixed backgrounds and drew from a common stock of magical recipes that they shared with others in their profession. However, these features of the bowls do not necessarily preclude the possibility that certain sorcerers were partial toward a specific religious system or community. Many of the incantations express this attachment through their choice of deities or scriptural texts, especially in their opening and closing formulas. As Tapani Harviainen has pointed out, the bowls[56]

> vary with respect to their initial phrases. *It is not only the alphabet and script, but also the opening formulae which keep the different groups of Eastern Arameans apart. . . .* The magicians knew how they had to commence the bowl texts in order to remain in the realm of their particular religious and social groups.

As this thesis points out, the formal and stylistic features of the spells helped the sorcerers to create the necessary effect for the bowl's intended purpose, message, and audience. Harviainen thus suggests that the sorcerers were intentional in creating incantations for their religious groups. Similarly, Erica Hunter proposes that the audiences of the bowls also influenced the extent to which incantation texts adhered to particular religious traditions. Agreeing with the thesis that incantation texts were differentiated by the use of specific terms, she writes that:[57]

> Incantation texts were adapted by their 'audiences', with internal tailoring to meet the cultural profiles of the communities in which they circulated. Syncretism is the outstanding feature of incantation texts, but each group, Jewish, pagan, gnostic and Christian, demarcated itself by its own distinctive terminology.

The syncretistic or non-Jewish elements in Jewish bowls for Jewish clients were reworked to match the desires of Jewish audiences. Typifying this phenomenon, one recently published Jewish bowl, edited by Dan Levene and Gideon Bohak, reworks an extensive list of pagan deities to match its Jewish context. The editors explain:[58]

> Such a long list of "pagan" deities in a Jewish incantation bowl certainly is unexpected. That our bowl was produced by a Jewish scribe is clear not only from the script and language, but also from the divine and angelic names it uses and the inclusion of a few Hebrew phrases and biblical idioms. . . . Moreover, as this kind of list of local "pagan" deities has Babylonian antecedents, it seems quite likely that the Jewish scribe who produced this bowl had access to a "pagan" list of deities and decided to incorporate it in his own incantation.

In magical contexts, Jews co-opted pagan lists of deities because they were deemed efficacious.

In summing up these questions about the bowls, Shaul Shaked has described the melting pot of magic in Sasanian Mesopotamia as follows:[59]

> As a rule, and unless proven wrong, it seems to me a sound working hypothesis to accept the premise that the writer of a bowl used his own cultural background for the composition of the bowl text. The cultural background naturally includes also the various syncretistic elements that were freely exchanged between the different groups within the common cultural composite of Sasanian Mesopotamian society. To borrow the phrase used for linguistic purposes by Harviainen, one may speak of a cultural koiné, in which themes and ideas, and sometimes even whole textual passages, were taken over by each group of practitioners in Mesopotamia from the neighbouring communities. The writers of Syriac often borrowed heavily from the Jewish practitioners, and to a lesser extent this was also done by Mandaeans. Jews occasionally introduced Mandaean phrases into their texts (this is, for example, the case of Montgomery 1913, Bowl 4), and all three communities made extensive use of the elements of the common popular culture, which included some popular Zoroastrianism as well as late Mesopotamian paganism. The result seems like a syncretistic melting-pot.

As explained here, the sorcerers created spells for people of diverse backgrounds and worked simultaneously within both a demarcated religious framework (e.g., Jewish, Christian, Mandaean) and a common cultural reservoir. What this paradoxical situation leads to, according to Shaked, is that even within the syncretism and common heritage of Mesopotamian magic there still existed the building up of boundaries according to Jewish, Mandaean, or Christian contexts:[60]

> Certain rules can nevertheless be observed, which appear to mark the borderline between the different communities. References to specific Mandaean deities and notions occur as a rule only in Mandaean bowls (e.g., the notion of Life, the 'uthras,

> the planets). Jewish references, such as quotations from the Hebrew Bible in the original language, the use of biblical antecedents, the reference to certain Talmudic sages, such as Hanina ben Dosa and Joshua bar Perahia, quotations from Hekhalot literature, the insertion of Hebrew words and forms, and other elements, occur as a rule only in the Jewish bowls.

Shaked attributes the content of the bowls to the cultural background of the sorcerers and emphasizes the dialectic between borrowing and syncretism on the one hand and the desire, on the other, to follow certain rules that were differentiated according to official religious systems.

RABBIS AND JEWISH SORCERERS

What are the ramifications of this Aramaic cultural koiné for our understanding of the Bavli's engagement with sorcery, the supernatural, and the body? Although there is cultural intersection between the rabbis and the sorcerers with respect to such topics as illnesses and demons,[61] the precise social ties between Babylonian rabbis and Jewish sorcerers are poorly understood. Was it a hostile relationship, or lenient? Did one group have sway over the other? Did they operate in overlapping, or separate, social spheres?[62]

One approach toward answering these questions is to examine the power dynamics between the groups as we currently understand them. Is it, one may wonder, fair to dichotomize the rabbis and sorcerers according to a model that assumes the rabbis were an elite group of Torah scholars, whereas the sorcerers represent the religion of the masses? As folklore theorists such as Dina Stein have elucidated, this dichotomy is problematic insofar as it deems magic to be nonhegemonic, or the culture of the ignorant folk, who are responsible for allowing non-Jewish influences to permeate rabbinic Judaism.[63] Rather than dichotomize the rabbis and the Jewish sorcerers, it behooves comparativists to explore how the rabbis and sorcerers shared the same social circles and cultural spaces. Not only do many of the Jewish bowls invoke certain rabbinic figures as authorities, and halakhic concepts such as divorce deeds and vows, but there is also evidence that some rabbis may have turned to bowl magicians, as seen in a recently published spell against a lilith composed for a client named Rav Mesharshiya b. Qaqay.[64]

The Aramaic sorcerers were free agents, not bound by internal institutions or hierarchical authorities. In a paper on female sorcerers, Rebecca Lesses describes how these sorcerers were free to use shared formulas that served the specific needs of their clients:[65]

> No ruling authority, as far as we know, determined what the formulas should be, and there was no process of editing or redaction of the formulas in a final form, as we can tell from comparing the same formula used on different bowls. . . . The practitioner

made use of a set of previously known formulas and put them together according to the needs of the client. There was scope for the creativity of the practitioner, both in the formulas chosen and in the way they were put together, but the texts were not the unique spontaneous creations of each practitioner.

Working independently, the sorcerers creatively put together series of established spells that would fulfill the needs of the client. Yet despite this lack of internal institutionalization, it is an open question whether the Aramaic sorcerers of our bowls were subject to the Jewish and Zoroastrian courts of law that I discussed in chapter 5. Ruling authorities in Sasanian Mesopotamia distanced themselves and their followers from outsiders through the use of legal constructions of identity that labeled others as such. Examples of terms of otherness include "heretic," "apostate," and "sorcerer."[66] As part of these groups' rhetoric of insularity, these categories, often derived from scripture, are intentionally imprecise in order to allow for multiple identifications and fluidity over time. In an article on the definition of magic in rabbinic literature, Philip Alexander has summarized well the posture of the ruling classes toward magic, which they used as a form of social control through the criminalization of knowledge or practices:[67]

The attitude of the ruling classes towards magic was at best ambivalent, but usually negative. Magic was almost by definition 'forbidden', and in legal texts it is included in lists of forbidden things. 'Magic' tended to function sociologically as a category of disapproval and control, deployed to marginalize and even criminalize certain activities that were not acceptable to the religious and political elites.

The relationship between the religious elite and the magicians may have been partly adversarial. The Jewish sorcerers transmitted traditions that contradict rabbinic law. This is the case with Bowl M102's "elaboration of part of the first of the eighteen benedictions which includes the glorification of God with the three epithets האל הגדול הגבור והנורא (Deut. 10:17 and Nehemiah 9:32)," expansions that rabbinic Halakhah repudiates.[68] As Gideon Bohak explains, "the rabbis were well aware of the magical activities taking place all around them, both among non-Jews and among Jews."[69] Still, it is not clear that the Bavli's laws against sorcery specifically target the sorcerers who produced the extant bowls,[70] nor is it proven that the Jewish courts were able or willing to punish illicit magicians.

One of the challenges of researching our current topic is how the Talmud and Middle Persian sources refer to others using general terms. In other words, who are the heretics, apostates, and sorcerers in the Bavli and Zoroastrian literature? A classic example of this phenomenon is rabbinic literature's elusive figure of the heretic (*mînā'*).[71] Past studies of the heretic illustrate the stakes involved in analyzing ambiguous identities as evidence of identity formation: on a text-by-text basis, scholars conclude that "heretic" refers to Jewish-Christians, gnostics, Sadducees, and even Zoroastrians.[72] In a sense, however, these scholarly identifications ignore the fact that the rabbis used such ambiguity as a strategy of distancing themselves from others nearby.[73] Scholars face a similar challenge in understanding Zoroastrian texts' use of terms such as "sorcerer" (*jādūg*), "infidel" (*agdēn*), and "non-Iranian" (*anēr*).[74] Whether these terms were applied to Jews, Christians, and Muslims is difficult to prove, although it appears that *agdēn* was used for this purpose. Some terms of otherness are clever or polemical titles, such as *ḥabarei,* or the Middle Persian term for a Manichaean, *zandīg,* literally "distorter of the Zand."[75]

With respect to the attitude of the sorcerers toward elites, one can conjecture that the sorcerers' syncretistic tendencies were in some way a response to the official religions. In an important article on the syncretism of the bowls, Harviainen astutely comments on the goal of the popular magicians to "fill in the gaps" in the supernatural world that the official religions left untreated:[76]

> The official religion (Judaism, Christianity, Mandaeism, Islam) has not been considered sufficiently effective to protect a human being against secret adversaries. There are gaps in the security system, and the gaps should be closed. As a consequence, all aggressive forces must always be mentioned by name and then they can be sealed, counter-sealed, uprooted, and expelled. *Horror vacui,* the avoidance of empty space, is a leading principle of popular magic. To be on the safe side, it is also profitable to pay attention to foreign cults, demons, and deities.

The popular sorcerers of Sasanian Mesopotamia offered remedies to clients against all the demons and evil spirits that could harm them, and not just the ones from their own traditions of which they were aware. Evil spirits did not discriminate. In fact, it may have been the very externality of the supernatural evils from outside a particular belief system—from the shadows, so to speak—that added to their harmful potency. In this equation, the rhetoric of insularity espoused by the rabbis and Persian priests could not offer solutions, since their metonymic system of labeling others as sorcerers or heretics, although convenient for legal proceedings and boundary making, was too generic to treat specifically named spirits. In filling in this gap, the sorcerers availed themselves of specialized symbolic and medical knowledge, using their prestige as capital to subvert the social classifications that the ruling legal authorities may have imposed (or wanted to impose) on them or on others like them. In Sasanian Persia, the Jewish and Persian scholastic elite and judicial officials sought to control social classifications and promote separation between insiders and outsiders, including heretics and sorcerers. To the extent that each of these groups was willing and able to control dissidence, they can be characterized as striving toward some semblance of orthodoxy.[77] The sorcerers, however, offered another option, in the realm of the supernatural, catering to a different worldview of the society that they shared with the elite and their clients: that is, the sorcerers, by using syncretistic incantations, restructured the official or authoritative discourses of the scholastic and judicial elites, with the effect being the creation of alternative or borderline identities. Sasanian Persia was culturally and intellectually heterogeneous, and the formation of culture was dictated by a desire for social differentiation that could be symbolically articulated (e.g., by portraying one's others in stories) or enforced through legal authority in courts of law. It is the social context, albeit so evasive to reconstruct, that helps us explain why the rabbis and Persian priests espoused a rhetoric of insularity in a heterodox environment, striving for an orthodoxy that did not crystallize until the establishment of Islam.[78]

The cultural nexus between the Talmud and many of the Jewish Aramaic bowls is unambiguous. For instance, the Jewish Aramaic bowls contain numerous rabbinic elements, including citations from or echoes of the Hebrew Bible, liturgical texts, the Mishnah, and Merkavah literature.[79] Typically, these sources are used as positive words to combat evils and heal clients. In an article on the appearance of *m. Šebu.* 4:13 in a bowl for a Persian-named man Abandad, Dan Levene has explained the meaning of this overlap in law and the supernatural:[80]

> In D3 we find a quotation from mShevu. 4:13 that is used as a name of power in this magical text the presence of which is remarkable even purely on account of the fact that mishnaic texts are incredibly rare in magic bowl texts. The fact that the section of Mishna that we have here concerns the binding nature of particular invocations of names within the context of judicial oaths makes it even more significant, as the names mentioned therein are the same as those found in the magical literature of the bowls, amulets and recipe books of late antiquity. . . . This particular ruling on the nature of oaths in mShevu. 4:13 is of interest to us here as it crosses the boundaries of human context of legal proceedings, extending terrestrial jurisprudence to the world of the supernatural.

As noted here, the Jewish bowls rarely cite Mishnaic texts. This bowl does so in the context of judicial oaths. Indeed, the most prominent component in the bowls' engagement with rabbinic Judaism is in the realm of oaths, bans, and divorce writs. In contrast to the few passages from the Mishnah that are found in the bowls, there are numerous citations from the Hebrew Bible. The ties between scripture and magical incantations were fluid, as is seen in one bowl from Nippur composed solely of a collection of Masoretic and Targumic citations of Ezekiel 21:21–23 and Jeremiah 2:1–3.[81] In addition, references to biblical figures, such as the Patriarchs and Solomon, are common in the bowls, as are invocations of the deities YHWH (and variations), El-Shaddai, the Divine Presence, the Torah, Israel, and even the Sanhedrin. Dan Levene has recently made available one bowl that is a midrash on Moses not found elsewhere. One obvious junction between the bowls and the Bavli is the former's summoning of two wonder-working Tannaim, the Galilean rabbi Ḥanina ben Dosa and the teacher of Jesus Rabbi Joshua b. Peraḥia, as authoritative figures who combat the demons.[82] Shaked has noted the title "rabbi" on some spells—including two names not found elsewhere in rabbinic literature (Rav Aḥma son of Aḥat, who is a client, and Rav Maḥlafa son of Khwardukh) and two that are (Rav Yosef Šeda and Rav Aḥa bar Rav Huna).[83] Although many of these names were common in Jewish Babylonia, it is not impossible that this last personage, who is mentioned in passing on the bowl as the landlord of a property next to the client, is the fourth-century rabbi quoted around a dozen times in the Bavli. In addition to rabbinic names in the bowls, the spells' deployment of halakhic terms such as divorce deeds[84] and bans as a way of separating clients from evil supernatural beings reveals an overlapping set of discourses between the rabbis and sorcerers.

Let us now analyze one bowl that includes many of these features. Given its length, I have divided it up into three sections:[85]

> By your name I act, great holy one. By the name of Rabbi Joshua bar Peraḥia. Liliths, male and female lilith, the grabber and the snatcher: the three of you, and the four of you, and the five of you. You are stripped naked [and] are not clothed, your hair is dishevelled and cast behind your back. It was heard concerning you, that your father's name is Palḥas and your mother is [the lilith Pa]l[ḥadad]. Go out from the house and from the body and from the dwelling of Mat-Yišu daughter of Bat-Sahde.

This spell is intended to ward off the liliths from the house and bodies of two clients, Mat-Yišu daughter of Bat-Sahde and her husband, Drakhtaq. The woman's first and family names are Christian in origin, meaning "Maidservant of Jesus" (Mat-Yišu) and "daughter of the Martyrs" (Bat-Sahde), respectively.[86] The bowl's opening dedications ("by your name") appeals first to the great holy one and then to R. Joshua b. Peraḥia. After the dedication, the spell describes the liliths as naked and disheveled. As Shaul Shaked has explained, these depictions are meant to humiliate and expose the liliths in order to control them.[87] The same bowl continues:

> It was heard concerning you that one sent against you with the ban that Rabbi Joshua bar Peraḥia sent against you. . . . A deed of divorce has descended to us from across heaven, and there was found written in it neither your name nor your remembrance. By the name of Palsa Pelisa (who) gives to you your deeds of divorce and your (writs of) release, your deeds of divorce and your (writs of) release, that is you, the grabber, by the ban (that) Rabbi Joshua bar Peraḥia (sent) against you. And thus Rabbi Joshua bar Peraḥia said to us: A de[ed of divorce has come] to us from across the sea, and there was found written in it, that your father's name is Palḥas and your mother is the lilith Palḥadad. . . . Listen and go out from Mat-Yišu daughter of Bat-Sahde and from Drakhtaq, her husband. And do not appear to her, neither by night nor [by day---] You are bound by the bond of Asriel and sealed by the signet-ring of El Shaddai and by the signet-ring of Rabbi Joshua bar Peraḥia [---]

In the spell, R. Joshua b. Peraḥia reports to the demons that a divorce deed "has come to us from the across the sea" (other bowls read "from heaven"), with the lilith's father's name, Palḥas,[88] written in it. The rabbi, who also has a signet ring to seal the documents, initiates the divorce between the clients and the lilith. The bowl continues:

> I beswear you by the Light of Abraham, by [the Ro]ck of Isaac, by Shaddai of Jacob, by Yah-is-My-Name of Jacob, by Yah-is-My-Name [---] you, you, Lili, and any name that you have, [that] you shall take from Mat-Yišu daughter of Bat-Sahde your deed of divorce and [your] deed of r[e]le[ase and your letter of dismissal and] yo[ur document of] divorce [according to the law of --- Isra]el, the daughters of Moses and Israel.

At the end of the incantation, after appealing to the "Light of Abraham, Rock of Isaac, and Shaddai of Jacob," the spell declares that the documented separation is binding "according to the law of Israel, the daughters of Moses and Israel." In all respects, except for the Christian implications of the client's name, this bowl contains biblical and rabbinic components alongside liliths.

Other rabbis also appear in the corpus of the bowls. The following bowl, for instance, includes invocations made in the name of Rav Agzar bar Dibšata and Rav Yosef Šeda. This bowl, composed for a man named Abudimme son of Daday, has an image of a feline-woman crossbreed with long hair and a curved body.[89] After naming the bowl's purpose of protecting the client's family and property, the bowl declares a series of bans (*šamtā*) that wards off the demons. Part of this incantation reads:[90]

> And may you be under the ban of Rabbi Joshua bar Peraḥia. And may you be under the ban by the name of Ashmedai, the king of demons. And may you be under the ban by the name of Rav Agzar bar Dibšata. And may you be under the ban by the name of Ram Šad, the king of demons. And may you be under the ban of Rav Yosef Šeda. And may you be under the ban of all demons and dark ones that are in Babylonia.

In the context of a ban, Rabbi Joshua bar Peraḥia is juxtaposed with supernatural figures, including Ashmedai and the demons of Babylonia. This bowl's reference to Rav Yosef Šeda is paralleled in the Bavli. In a passage on the magic of pairs, *b. Pesaḥ.* 110a, the Babylonian Talmud records that Rav Yosef, a Babylonian Amora with ties to Persia and demonological knowledge, encountered a demon named Yosef who reported that Ashmedai the king of demons was appointed over all pairs.[91]

ḤRŠ IN THE ARAMAIC BOWLS

The question of the linguistic affinities between Talmudic Aramaic, Standard Literary Babylonian Aramaic, and the Aramaic dialects of the bowls[92] has far-reaching methodological and historical implications for the question of to what extent the scholarly activity of comparing Aramaic sources is or is not a reconstruction of literary or oral records from communities in social contact. Are the Jewish Aramaic corpora of the Bavli and the bowls composed in dialects whose similarities imply that there existed communication between groups? And does this logic extend also to Syriac, Mandaic, and even Pahlavi?

In an influential essay published in 1974, Jonas Greenfield showed "that the phrase רטין מגושא," which means "the magian mumbles" in *b. Soṭah* 22a, "had its roots in the linguistic usage of the day in the Sassanian empire."[93] Greenfield's article points to the *Targum Onqelos* on Deuteronomy 18:11's association of *ḥōvēr ḥāver* with the verb *raṭan*. Just before this, the *Targum* to Deuteronomy 18:10 translates *mĕkašēf* as *ḤRŠ*,[94] "sorcery," the same term that *b. Šabb.* 75a used in its debate on magianism. This word, rare in the Bavli, also appears in one of the few passages in which the Talmud discusses magic bowls. The Talmud here uses one of the common designations for a bowl that the bowls themselves use.[95] The passage from *b. B. Meṣiʿa* 29b reads: "R. Yoḥanan said: Better a bowl used by sorcerers [כסא דחרשין] than a bowl used by exorcists."[96] The editors of *b. Šabb.* 75a, it may be recalled, concluded that it was permitted to learn sorcery in order to understand and instruct. Is this allowance specifically referencing the learning of bowl magic? This short reference offers this intimation, though one would hope for more proof. We can, however, expand our lens to analyze the meaning of *ḤRŠ* in the Aramaic bowls, where it appears ubiquitously, often in the phrase "evil sorcery" as a harmful spirit. For example, in a bowl that Christa Müller-Kessler and Theodore Kwasman identify as one of the rare examples of a spell written in Talmudic Aramaic, a female client named Gušnazdukht daughter of Aḥat takes on the persona of the demons and, speaking directly to the evil sorcerers, invites them into her flooded home to eat what she eats.[97] The bowl, which is not particularly Jewish in content, mentions the Babylonian deities Bablita and Borsippa and displays parallel lines with Mandaic incantations. Other bowls that introduce the *ḥaršei* are countercharms that clients ordered to combat the spells that their neighbors or relatives had commanded against them (e.g., "This is a countercharm to overturn sorceries").[98] In these and other instances, the *ḥaršei* appear in the Aramaic bowls, including Syriac ones,[99] as the evil spirits who must be combatted. The term *ḥaršei* is one example of the intersecting terminologies between the Aramaic incantations and the Talmud, or, put in larger terms, between a form of Judaism rooted in a syncretistic, common Aramaic heritage of magic as opposed to one that was oriented inwardly toward rabbinic scholasticism.

THE BAVLI AND THE BOWLS

Scholars interested in Babylonian Judaism should compare the Bavli and the bowls in order to understand better the spectrum of identities of Jews living in Sasanian

Mesopotamia. The bowls give us insight into these mixtures of identities in several ways. For instance, the names on the bowls demonstrate that there were intermarried families who may or may not have subscribed to the official religions. Moreover, the bowls' syncretism and shared elements, including with Mandaic and Syriac magical texts, illustrate the intellectual and social interactions between actual families and sorcerers. The fact that the bowls are archaeological relics with named clients provides scholars with evidence of what was happening on the ground, in contrast to the rabbinic sources, which are hard to analyze sociologically. As I described in this chapter, it appears that the cultural context of the sorcerers determined an incantation's contents and that the clients sometimes did not understand the language in which their spell was composed. To the extent that the clients of the bowls, the sorcerers, and the rabbis all turned to the Hebrew Bible as well as to certain figures such as R. Joshua b. Peraḥia as authoritative discourses, these intersecting groups may have had some sense of shared identity with one another. With the Sasanian historical record being so heterogeneous, the study of Babylonian Judaism should consider evidence external to the Talmud, such as the bowls and Persian sources. These second-order sources problematize rabbinic normativity from both historical and academic trajectories.

Conclusion

Rabbis, Sorcerers, Kings, and Priests in Sasanian Iran

The Babylonian rabbis who produced perhaps the most important corpus in the Jewish sacred canon resided in a complex society that was governed by the Persian elite and populated with a mix of ethnicities, languages, and religions. Despite its self-presentation as an internal hermeneutical work created within the walls of the rabbinic academies, the Talmud constructs rabbinic identity and structures of authority in relation to non-Jewish groups, including average Persians, the Persian monarchy, and the Zoroastrian priests. The Babylonian rabbis were deeply influenced by their non-Jewish surroundings, particularly the Persian imperial world. Zoroastrianism as a religion in the Sasanian period, especially as artificially articulated in the late Pahlavi sources, was less prominent of an influence on rabbinic law. In what follows, I would like to summarize some of the main arguments of this book regarding the interdisciplinary merger of Jewish and Iranian studies, the portrayals of the Persians in the Talmud, and the impact of Persian culture on the Jews of Babylonia.

CONTEXT AND COMPARISON

Researching the Babylonian Talmud in its Sasanian context is a necessary and worthwhile project that promotes a much-needed counterpoint to studies of the Talmud that emphasize hermeneutics over history. Sources external to the Talmud, notably Middle Persian texts and artifacts, as well as the Jewish Aramaic bowls, offer Talmudists insight into the broader sociohistorical context in which the rabbis were operating, how they interacted with the Persian government and priests, and their intersections with popular sorcerers. Studying the Talmud in its historical context need not imply comparing Talmudic texts with Persian ones, or even trying to ascertain the historicity lurking beneath Halakhah and Aggadah. Rather, the process of contextualization means availing oneself of non-Talmudic and non-Jewish data as a way of seeing beyond the insular worldview that the rabbis present. What did the cultural horizon outside the rabbinic academies look like, and how did it shape what the rabbis discussed in them? This question clearly matters. Contextual studies of the Talmud should respect the internal nature of the sources insofar as they need not force textual juxtapositions that lead to historical claims; instead, these studies should probe the reasons for rabbinic insularity in the historical setting of Sasanian Persia as illuminated by research in Iranology. Indeed, the field of Talmudic studies has much to gain by incorporating into its academic repertoire Iranology's methods, data, and arguments, in addition to its primary sources. Until recently, Talmudic history has been based on reading and interpreting Talmudic texts as evidence for Jewish history. But our scholarly methods of historical inquiry cannot stop there—we must exert ourselves to incorporate all relevant information at our disposal. This type of historical education enriches textual research in important ways, but only if it is taken seriously as its own topic of inquiry and not used merely to explain hermeneutical disjunctions. In my opinion, in-depth studies of the Babylonian rabbis' historical realities—such as the heterogeneity of religions, peoples, and languages that they encountered in Sasanian Mesopotamia, and the presence and power of the Persian Empire—give scholars today a more accurate understanding of rabbinic culture and society. In sum, research on the Sasanian context of the Talmud elucidates aspects of Jewish history that would otherwise be irrecoverable. In this book, I hope to have demonstrated at least two benefits of stressing the Sasanian sociohistorical context of the rabbis and the Talmud:

1. Attention paid to the sociohistorical context of the Talmud helps to avoid the common pitfalls of comparative inquiry that are common in the phenomenological tradition—namely, the emphasis (or overemphasis) on similarities, textual juxtapositions, or taxonomic parallels. By cultivating a nuanced view of Sasanian history, scholars of late antique Babylonian Jewry can delimit areas of similarity, difference, and intersection between the rabbis and other groups that they can then target with purpose. In chapters 5 and 6 in this book, I singled out courts of law and magic as two social contexts in which the rabbis intersected with other groups, such as Zoroastrian priests and popular sorcerers, in part because both these social contexts have historically valuable archaeological resources extant (e.g., seals and bowls). Contrary to the views of scholars who remain skeptical of the value of the evidentiary record of Sasanian Persia, there is an abundance of relevant materials that assist in the study of Babylonian Jewry, including but not limited to the Middle Persian literary corpus, Sasanian inscriptions and seals, and

the Jewish, Christian, and Mandaean magical spells. True, many of these sources do not directly address or discuss Jews, and less so the rabbis. But what they do offer is a way forward to comprehend in a sophisticated manner the impact of the broader Sasanian government on non-Persian groups, as well as insight into the mixture of its citizenry that the Talmud describes so evasively. By incorporating second-order resources from the Sasanian context into studies of Talmud, Talmudists can problematize some of their presuppositions and arguments regarding the role of the non-Jewish world on the formation of Babylonian rabbinic authority and identity.

2. A history-first approach toward Talmudic texts transcends the problematic quest for extracting ur-traditions or historical kernels from Halakhah and Aggadah, since it uses non-Jewish history as a way of setting up literary readings. By emphasizing Sasanian history as much as the Tosafistic view, Talmudists can research cultural phenomena contemporaneous with the Amoraim proper. This comparative viewpoint opens up new avenues of contextual interpretation of the Talmud, such as the meaning of its symbols, the possibility of communication between speakers of different Aramaic dialects (or between Aramaic and Middle Iranian), or the role of courts of law. Crucially, the sociohistorical setting of the rabbis helps scholars delineate how the rabbis' positions in both Jewish and Sasanian societies as authoritative or marginal figures affects their ideologies toward non-rabbinic others, including toward the Persians.

Unfortunately, the comparison of Talmudic and Middle Persian sources is plagued with problems. Textual comparativists bear the burden of proof of showing how their textual parallels imply or act as evidence of intercommunal activity, especially when texts do not explicitly engage one another or are produced centuries apart. When comparing the Talmud to other resources from Sasanian Iran, scholars must stress both similarities and differences between the texts' contents, dates, contexts of production, transmission, and reception, and other factors. As I argued in chapter 2, there are numerous divergences between the Talmud and Middle Persian works that hamper our ability to draw direct parallels between them. Many Pahlavi works were produced in the ninth and tenth centuries C.E., and thus after the formation of the Talmud, thereby rendering textual comparisons between these two corpora chronologically challenged. The ruptures and changes that took place in the Zoroastrian priesthood as a result of the Islamic conquests are in my opinion decisive factors in the study of Pahlavi literature, since these late sources do not offer much help by way of researching what the religion we call Zoroastrianism actually was in late antiquity. Despite certain pitfalls, the Middle Persian corpus is also ripe with literature that is of high value to Talmudists, such as *The Book of a Thousand Judgements* and specific works of Zand, as well as valuable material evidence, including Sasanian seals and imperial inscriptions, that helps to complete the picture. Scholars have access to a wide selection of Middle Persian literary and archaeological relics that can assist historians in explicating the political and cultural ties between the rabbis and the Persian monarchy and Zoroastrian priesthood.

TALMUDIC PORTRAYALS OF PERSIANS

The portrayals of Persians in rabbinic literature range in topic from fashion and food, to festivals and imperial law, to magic and scripture. Rabbinic literature typically refers to the Persians as either an ethnoclass or as the Achaemenid, Parthian, or Sasanian Empire. Coupled with the images of kings and priests, the Talmud's explicit engagement with Persia is thus more imperial than it is theological. The fact that the rabbis, *mowbeds*, and *hērbeds* did not participate in the interpretation of the same scriptures, and spoke different languages, reduced the possibilities for and tensions around theological discussions. This is, in part, why there is so little Zoroastrianism present in the Jewish Aramaic bowls—the Iranian-Aramaic divide was not always easily eclipsed. For their part, the Babylonian rabbis depict the Persians as imperial and ethnic others descended from the biblical Noah and on par with the Romans in imperial stature. As is typical of their engagement with other others, the Babylonian rabbis invoke Persians as contrastive others in order to clarify their own group identity and limits of authority, including vis-à-vis the Persian Empire. The rabbis internally debate whether Jewish law should accommodate Persian customs (e.g., meat dishes with bread), Persian language (e.g., in divorce documents), or fashion (e.g., the Persian ornamental belt—not the *kustīg*). The rabbis are uninterested in ethnography, though they do present the Persians in ethnic or cultural terms (e.g., dress, food, and sex), embedded with negative and positive biases. Thus, perhaps a bit paradoxically, the Babylonian Talmud's portrayals of Persians further the rabbis' goal of rhetorical and social insularity within Mesopotamian heterogeneity: that is to say, the rabbis used the portrayals of Persians to emphasize their own ethnic and political differences with them, in part by creating signals for Persian otherness as a way of maintaining their identity relative to the presence of other groups. As we saw in chapter 3, some of the common leitmotifs that the rabbis use as signals of Persian otherness include riding horses, eating *ṭabhĕqei* and other Persian foods, and the quality of pride. The Talmud also invokes Iranian loanwords intentionally as a way of identifying Persians as others.

The Iranian loanwords in the Talmud and other Aramaic dialects of Sasanian Iran are evidence of interactions between Iranian and Aramaic speakers over the course of many centuries of contact. The presence of the loanwords does not, however, necessarily indicate that Aramaic and Persian speakers could communicate orally. Although the number of loanwords in the Babylonian Talmud is less than the number of Greek and Latin loanwords in Palestinian rabbinic literature, the evidence nevertheless proves linguistic penetration, especially in the realm of everyday fashion and food. Whether such transferences of words in these realms is a result of the proverbial marketplace encounters between Jews and Persians is hard to substantiate, but clearly the entrance of Iranian words into Aramaic for everyday goods suggests that such social contexts were ones in which words, and the people who spoke them, came into contact.

TALMUDIC PORTRAYALS OF SASANIAN KINGS

For the Babylonian sages, the Sasanian kings Shapur I, Shapur II, and Yazdegird were symbols of the Persian Empire's authority. The rabbis use these figures in their stories and legal discussions in order to discuss how they thought about their own authority relative to the Persian Empire. The Talmudic portrayals of the Sasanian kings are imaginary dialogues and encounters in which Babylonian sages discuss such issues as the Torah's principles for burial and the coming of the Messiah. On multiple occasions the Persian kings are portrayed as knowing Torah or practicing Jewish law. Other common motifs in the Talmudic texts about the Persian kings are those of money and charity. Finally, the stories of the encounters between the rabbis and the mother of Shapur II, Ifra Hormiz, are part of a larger trend in late antique sources that portrays the Jews as having access to the Persian monarchy and especially the queen. The purpose of these stories is to praise rabbinic knowledge in light of the tests of the monarchy.

When studied as a test case, the Talmud's images of Shapur I do not exhibit signs of direct textual parallels with Middle Persian sources, but they resonate well within the wider Persian imperial and Zoroastrian priestly constructs of the second Sasanian king, which promoted his reputation as a ruler who succeeded in managing an era of radical change in the social order. During and after Shapur I's reign, the Persian monarch became a literary figure who represented the ubiquitous changes to the structures of society in early Sasanian Iran, in relation to which later Jewish sages and Zoroastrian priests continued to define their own authority. Each of these groups had an evolving ideological stake in how it described past Persian kings in the traditions it produced after the reign of that monarch. In addition, Sasanian propaganda and historiographical discourses, attested in state inscriptions as well as Middle Persian literary narratives, played a role in shaping how the rabbis depicted these monarchs. In constructing stories about the rabbis' dialogues and encounters with the Persian monarchs, as well as with Ifra Hormiz, the Talmud uses them as contrastive others in order to explore questions of rabbinic identity and authority.

TALMUDIC PORTRAYALS OF ZOROASTRIAN PRIESTS

The Zoroastrian priests and Babylonian rabbis had different levels of political authority. As part of a hierarchical network of imperial institutions, the *mowbeds* and *mogs* functioned in all sorts of capacities throughout the empire, including on the local level, notably as administrators and judges. The rabbis, by contrast, were part of a localized system of governance that depended on a sage's reputation and communal acceptance as a fair and impartial judge—which, if anything, resembles the status of a *mog*. The judicial structures in Jewish Babylonia are broadly related to the Sasanian Empire's policies of endorsing the adjudication of cases not involving Persian Zoroastrians on a local, communal level. The position of the public expert (*mûmḥe*) demonstrates the intertwined structures of authority of judges in Jewish Babylonia in that it involved exilarchic authorization as insurance against being held liable for judicial errors. According to *b. Sanh.* 4b–5a, public experts were able to make legal rulings based on the communal acceptance of their legal erudition and through exilarchic authorization. As such, the public experts serve as a useful test case for investigating the question of Jewish legal autonomy in the Persian Empire. It seems to be the case that the Jewish courts had sway over debts, marriages, and rituals, among other aspects of life. However, the Jewish courts functioned alongside the Sasanian courts that were being run by *dādwar*s, *mowbed*s, and other Persian Zoroastrian figures. The Jews were presumably subject to these courts in cases that involved Zoroastrians. Several Talmudic texts illustrate the rabbis' anxiety over the right to punish sinners for sex or other crimes. As is to be seen in the Talmudic texts' negative attitude toward Persian courts of law, the rabbis were acutely aware of the limits of their power to enforce judicial rulings. The structures of legal authority of the Zoroastrian priesthood and the rabbinic movement interfaced, a historical backdrop against which we can better understand the Talmud's images of Persian priests as administrators.

The social or intellectual interactions between religious groups in Sasanian Mesopotamia led each of them to fabricate an ideological stance toward the encroachment of others on their structures of authority and identity boundaries. Sasanian Mesopotamia was a culturally competitive environment wherein various religious groups sought authority over internal and external others through social practices and intellectual activity. Polemical and apologetic discourses were one means by which these religious groups gained power. For instance, some groups constructed ideologies of religious syncretism whereby certain aspects of other faiths were tactically embraced, a phenomenon exemplified in the rise of Manichaeism and the popular sorcerers. Other religious groups, such as the rabbis, responded differently to their surroundings and manufactured exclusivistic ideologies that thrived on a purposeful silencing of others and a denial of outside influences. The question in Irano-Talmudica of how much context is enough, and how much context is too much, relies on our knowledge of the historical situation of the authors who produced the literature that we have at our disposal. As internally driven exegetical sources, the Talmud and Middle Persian texts are insider expressions of each group's reflections on social contexts through the lens of received traditions, yet oddly they do not typically represent the existence of those social contexts. If at least some of the laws in the Talmud were indeed practiced by the Jews of Babylonia, then the rabbinic quest for orthodoxy via the practice and prestige of Torah study in the midst of Mesopotamian heterodoxy was in part a quest for localized legal authority. In the end, the Bavli's isolationist rhetoric does not result from the rabbis' lack of awareness of the outside world, but to the contrary rabbinic identity constructed its insularity in a world replete with other groups that were likewise building boundaries of identity through the use of logotherapy, generic metonyms, and the enforcement of law. For the rabbis, part of their response to the heterogeneity of Sasanian Babylonia was to promote themselves as different from surrounding cultures and peoples, and in many ways to resist assimilation.

RABBIS AND SORCERERS

The Babylonian rabbis, Persian authorities, and Aramaic Jewish magicians held divergent ideologies toward others: the rabbis and Persian priests constructed boundaries between themselves, their followers, and outsiders in various measures, including through the use of metonymical legal rubrics such as "sorcerer," "heretic," or "apostate" that were potentially enforceable in courts of law over which the elite presided. By contrast, the popular magicians who produced the corpus of Aramaic bowls espoused syncretistic forms of cultural expression that broke down the very ethnic, linguistic, and religious boundaries that the rabbis and priests built. Yet this is not to say that the dichotomy did not break down, since we find many rabbinic motifs in the incantation texts, including the divorce deed, oaths, and bans, all of which imply an appropriation of legal discourse for the purposes of warding off the supernatural demons. By analyzing both the similarities and differences between the Bavli and the bowls, scholars of late antique Babylonian Judaism have an opportunity to problematize the boundaries of identity that are expressed in the rabbinic corpus, and thus, by extension, the way that we today define and research rabbinic culture. When studied alongside the Talmud, the Jewish Aramaic bowls are the most valuable resources for delineating the spectrum of Jewish identities in late antique Persia.

THE TALMUD AS EVIDENCE FOR THE STUDY OF SASANIAN HISTORY

What does the Babylonian Talmud offer historians of Sasanian Persia? To begin with, the Talmud is a rich case study, in the form of a vast corpus, of the legal discussions of a non-Zoroastrian population living within the Sasanian Empire. As such, the Talmud is a corpus that broadly reflects the practices and thoughts of a nonimperial group that adjudicated legal cases on a local level and that discussed the Persians as others in their oral traditions. Although often lacking historicity, the Talmudic portrayals of the imperial government contain attitudes and perceptions about Persia that shed light on the Jewish experience in the empire. What is more important, the Talmud offers a wealth of information that historians of Sasanian Persia can add to their repertoire of data—including intriguing details about administrative geography, such as the existence of an *ōstāndār* in Kashkar; the earliest witnesses of Iranian words, in the form of loanwords, that either are completely unattested in Middle Persian or are known only from later ninth-century forms; or information on Sasanian taxation. These are just some examples of information in the Talmud that scholars of Sasanian Iran may find useful. For Iranian linguists, the Middle Iranian words in the Talmud are a trove of unique data regarding the transmission of Iranian into Aramaic from the Achaemenid through the early Islamic period. Finally, in seeking out the mutual fruition between Jewish and Iranian studies, Iranists have much to gain by adopting and integrating into their discipline Talmudic studies' source-critical approaches toward exegetical works.

NOTES

In addition to the abbreviations listed at the beginning of this book, the following abbreviated titles of Aramaic dictionaries and Middle Persian works appear throughout these notes:

AWN	F. Vahman, *Ardā Wirāz Nāmag: The Iranian "Divina Commedia"* (London: Curzon Press, 1986)
Bund.	B. T. Anklesaria, *Zand-Ākāsīh: Iranian or Greater Bundahišn—Transliteration and Translation in English* (Bombay: Rahnumae Mazdayasnan Sabha, 1956)
Dēnk.	*Dēnkard*
Dēnk. III	J. de Menasce, *Le troisième livre du Dēnkart* (Paris: Klincksieck, 1973)
Dēnk. V	J. Amouzgar and A. Tafazzoli, *Le cinquième livre du Dēnkard* (Paris: Association pour l'Avancement des Études Iraniennes, 2000)
Dēnk. VI	S. Shaked, *The Wisdom of the Sasanian Sages: Dēnkard VI* (Boulder: Westview Press, 1979)
Dēnk. VII	M. Molé, *La légende de Zoroastre selon les textes pehlevis* (Paris: Klincksieck, 1967)
Dēnk. IX	Y. Vevaina, "Studies in Zoroastrian Exegesis and Hermeneutics, with a Critical Edition of the *Sūdgar Nask* of *Dēnkard* Book 9" (Ph.D. dissertation, Harvard University, 2007)
DīD	M. Jaafari-Dehaghi, *Dādestān ī Dēnīg*, part 1, *Transcription, Translation, and Commentary* (Paris: Association pour l'Avancement des Études Iraniennes, 1998)
DJBA	M. Sokoloff, *A Dictionary of Jewish Babylonian Aramaic of the Talmudic and Geonic Periods* (Ramat-Gan: Bar Ilan University Press, 2002)
DJPA	M. Sokoloff, *A Dictionary of Jewish Palestinian Aramaic of the Byzantine Period* (Ramat-Gan: Bar-Ilan University Press, 1990)

FīP	B. Utas, *Frahang ī Pahlavīk: Edited, with Transliteration, Transcription, and Commentary from the Posthumous Papers of Henrik Samuel Nyberg* (Wiesbaden: Harrassowitz, 1988)
Giz. Abāliš	H. F. Chacha, *Gajastak Abâlish* (Bombay: The Trustees of the Parsi Punchayet Funds and Properties, 1936)
Hērb.	F. Kotwal and P. Kreyenbroek, with James R. Russell, *The Hērbedestān and Nērangestān,* volume 1 (Paris: Association pour l'Avancement des Études Iraniennes, 1992)
Kārn.	F. Grenet, *La geste d'Ardashir fils de Pâbag: Kārnāmag ī Ardaxšēr ī Pābagān* (Die: Éditions A Die, 2003)
MHD	A. Perikhanian, *Mādayān ī Hazār Dādestān: The Book of a Thousand Judgements, a Sasanian Law-Book* (Costa Mesa: Mazda Publishers, 1997)
Nērang.	F. Kotwal and P. Kreyenbroek, with James R. Russell, *The Hērbedestān and Nērangestān,* volumes 2–4 (Paris: Association pour l'Avancement des Études Iraniennes, 1995–2002)
Pahl. Vīdēv.	M. Moazami, *Wrestling with the Demons of the Pahlavi Widēwdād: Transcription, Translation, and Commentary* (Leiden: Brill, 2014)
PRDīD	A. V. Williams, *The Pahlavi Rivāyat Accompanying the Dādestān ī Dēnīg,* 2 vols. (Copenhagen: Munksgaard, 1990)
Pursišnīhā	K. M. Jamaspasa and H. Humbach, *Pursišnīhā: A Zoroastrian Catechism,* part 1, *Text, Translation, Notes* (Wiesbaden: Harrassowitz, 1971)
ŠīĒr.	T. Daryaee, *Šahrestānīhā ī Ērānšahr: A Middle Persian Text on Late Antique Geography, Epic, and History* (Costa Mesa: Mazda Publishers, 2002)
ŠnŠ	J. Tavadia, *Šāyast-nē-šāyast: A Pahlavi Text on Religious Customs* (Hamburg: De Gruyter, 1930)
Zādsp.	P. Gignoux and A. Tafazzoli, *Anthologie de Zādspram: Édition critique du texte pehlevi, traduit et commenté* (Paris: Association pour l'Avancement des Études Iraniennes, 1993)
ZWY	C. Cereti, *The Zand ī Wahman Yasn: A Zoroastrian Apocalypse* (Rome: Istituto Italiano per il Medio ed Estremo Oriente, 1995)

INTRODUCTION

1. See the overviews in Yaakov Elman, "Middle Persian Culture and Babylonian Sages: Accommodation and Resistance in the Shaping of Rabbinic Legal Tradition," in *The Cambridge Companion to the Talmud and Rabbinic Literature,* ed. Charlotte Elisheva Fonrobert and Martin S. Jaffee (Cambridge: Cambridge University Press, 2007), 165–97, and "Talmud ii: Rabbinic Literature and Middle Persian texts," *Encyclopaedia Iranica,* online ed., 2010: www.iranica.com/articles/talmud-ii. For a collection of essays that demonstrates the diverse methods used in the field, see Carol Bakhos and M. Rahim Shayegan, eds., *The Talmud in Its Iranian Context* (Tübingen: Mohr Siebeck, 2010).

2. Shai Secunda, *The Iranian Talmud: Reading the Bavli in Its Sasanian Context* (Philadelphia: University of Pennsylvania Press, 2013).

3. See the two important works from the early 1980s on the Iranian context of the Talmud by E. S. Rosenthal, "For the Talmudic Dictionary—Talmudica Iranica," in *Irano-Judaica: Studies Relating to Jewish Contacts with Persian Culture throughout the Ages*, ed. Shaul Shaked (Jerusalem: Ben-Zvi Institute, 1982), 38–134 (Hebrew); and Daniel Sperber, "On the Unfortunate Adventures of Rav Kahana: A Passage of Saboraic Polemic from Sasanian Persia," in *Irano-Judaica*, 83–100.

4. See the volumes on the Greco-Roman cultural context of the Jerusalem Talmud edited by Peter Schäfer, *The Yerushalmi Talmud and Graeco-Roman Culture*, vols. 1 and 3 (Tübingen: Mohr Siebeck, 1998 and 2002); and by Peter Schäfer and Catherine Hezser, *The Yerushalmi Talmud and Graeco-Roman Culture*, vol. 2 (Tübingen: Mohr Siebeck, 1999). For an example of a work of classical Midrash interpreted in a Hellenized Roman and Byzantine context, see Burton L. Visotzky, *Golden Bells and Pomegranates: Studies in Midrash Leviticus Rabbah* (Tübingen: Mohr Siebeck, 2003).

5. See Seth Schwartz, *Imperialism and Jewish Society, 200 B.C.E. to 640 C.E.* (Princeton: Princeton University Press, 2001), 1 n. 1 ("I have omitted all discussion of the Jews in the Parthian and Sassanian empires, due to the nearly complete absence of information outside the Babylonian Talmud"), and "The Political Geography of Rabbinic Texts," in *The Cambridge Companion to the Talmud and Rabbinic Literature*, ed. Charlotte Elisheva Fonrobert and Martin S. Jaffee (Cambridge: Cambridge University Press, 2007), 75–96, esp. 89, arguing that the bowls do not help all that much "to fill out the picture of Jewish life in Mesopotamia" and that Sasanian history "is itself very poorly attested." See also the comparable assessment regarding a lack of external sources for Talmudic history in Christine Hayes, *Between the Babylonian and Palestinian Talmuds: Accounting for Halakhic Difference in Selected Sugyot from Tractate Avodah Zarah* (New York: Oxford University Press, 1997), 23. The present book clearly disagrees with such skeptical positions toward the field of Sasanian studies and the value of the Aramaic bowl spells. For my contrary view on the availability and value of these sources, see "The Middle Persian Corpus" and "The Material Remains of Sasanian Persia" in chapter 2 below.

6. For more on the incongruities between the two fields, see chapter 2 below and the negative appraisal by Geoffrey Herman, "Persia in Light of the Babylonian Talmud—Echoes of Contemporary Society and Politics: *hargbed* and *bidaxš*," in *The Talmud in Its Iranian Context*, ed. Carol Bakhos and M. Rahim Shayegan (Tübingen: Mohr Siebeck, 2010), 58–82, esp. 58–60: the Talmud's "potential for the study of the Sasanian history has not, however, been fully realized, both due to the compartmentalization of scholarship, and due to the fact that much of the relevant scholarship appears only in Hebrew. It is, of course, obvious that such a situation is to the detriment of all, but the gap which exists between the Iranologists and the Talmudists appears, unfortunately, to be widening."

7. The total number of references to Persians of course depends upon which sources one counts as falling under that category. Moreover, this number would increase were one to include allusions to unnamed kings (or other titles) that can be understood as references to Persians. For a full list of the Talmudic texts on Persians, see chapters 3 through 6 of this book.

8. For an overview and representative bibliography on the study of others in rabbinic literature, see Carol Bakhos, *Ishmael on the Border: Rabbinic Portrayals of the First Arab* (Albany: State University of New York Press, 2006); Richard Kalmin, *The Sage in Jewish Society of Late Antiquity* (New York: Routledge, 1999), esp. 27–50 on the portrayals of

interactions between rabbis and non-rabbis in rabbinic literature; Christine Hayes, "The 'Other' in Rabbinic Literature," in *The Cambridge Companion to the Talmud and Rabbinic Literature*, ed. Charlotte Elisheva Fonrobert and Martin S. Jaffee (Cambridge: Cambridge University Press, 2007), 243–69, and *Gentile Impurities and Jewish Identities: Intermarriage and Conversion from the Bible to the Talmud* (New York: Oxford University Press, 2002); William Scott Green, "Otherness Within: Towards a Theory of Difference in Rabbinic Judaism," in *"To See Ourselves as Others See Us": Christians, Jews, "Others" in Late Antiquity*, ed. Jacob Neusner and Ernest S. Frerichs (Chico: Scholars Press, 1985), 49–69; Gary Porton, *Goyim: Gentiles and Israelites in the Mishnah-Tosefta* (Atlanta: Scholars Press, 1988); Sacha Stern, *Jewish Identity in Early Rabbinic Writings* (New York: Brill, 1994); Jenny R. Labendz, *Socratic Torah: Non-Jews in Rabbinic Intellectual Culture* (New York: Oxford University Press, 2013); Eduard Iricinschi and Holger M. Zellentin, "Making Selves and Marking Others: Identity and Late Antique Heresiologies," in *Heresy and Identity in Late Antiquity*, ed. Eduard Iricinschi and Holger M. Zellentin (Tübingen: Mohr Siebeck, 2008), 1–27.

9. See the similar statement in Adam H. Becker, "The Comparative Study of 'Scholasticism' in Late Antique Mesopotamia: Rabbis and East Syrians," *Association for Jewish Studies Review* 34 (2010): 91–113, esp. 112.

10. See ibid. 113.

11. For more on comparative religion as social history, see the concept of the sociology of knowledge, which emphasizes the ties between thinkers and their social worlds, as discussed in Eric J. Sharpe, *Comparative Religion: A History*, 2nd ed. (La Salle: Open Court Publishing, 1986), 309–10; Timothy Fitzgerald, *The Ideology of Religious Studies* (New York: Oxford University Press, 2000), 71, arguing about the study of religion that "the social, understood as the values of a particular group and their institutionalization in a specific context, including the way power is organized and legitimated, has to be the actual locus of nontheological interpretation." Fitzgerald adds that scholars of religion are in reality researching institutions, authority, and identity (227). See also Jonathan Z. Smith, *Imagining Religion: From Babylon to Jonestown* (Chicago: University of Chicago Press, 1982), 29, who seeks "the integration of a complex notion of pattern and system with an equally complex notion of history."

1. THE SOURCES AND METHODS OF TALMUDIC AND IRANIAN STUDIES

1. On the study of rabbinic stories in various contexts, see Jeffrey L. Rubenstein, *Talmudic Stories: Narrative Art, Composition, and Culture* (Baltimore: The Johns Hopkins University Press, 1999), 11–15.

2. There are various points of view on this issue, many of which argue for a balanced approach to questions of exegesis versus history; on the study of Midrash, see Steven D. Fraade, *From Tradition to Commentary: Torah and Its Interpretation in the Midrash Sifre to Deuteronomy* (Albany: State University of New York Press, 1991), esp. 14–15; on the Bavli, see the cultural poetics of Daniel Boyarin, *Carnal Israel: Reading Sex in Talmudic Culture* (Berkeley and Los Angeles: University of California Press, 1993), esp. 12–18, for a discussion of New Historicism, and "Hellenism in Jewish Babylonia," in *The Cambridge Companion to the Talmud and Rabbinic Literature*, ed. Charlotte Elisheva Fonrobert and Martin S. Jaffee (Cambridge: Cambridge University Press, 2007), 336-63, esp. 343, where, responding to the work of Hayes, he summarizes his position thus: "I am exploring here a third option, one

that deconstructs the very opposition between 'external' and 'internal' approaches, namely, positing that precisely the textual, exegetical/hermeneutical, dialectical, redactorial factors are themselves bound up with complex historical, cultural interactions between the rabbis, respectively, of Palestine and Mesopotamia and the other communities in which they were embedded." For an article that is critical of New Historicists, see Burton L. Visotzky, "Review Article: Leaning Literary, Reading Rabbinics," *Prooftexts: A Journal of Jewish Literary History* 28 (2008): 85–99, esp. 90–93, on how they "consciously blur the boundaries between history and literature" and "produce a new literary product, descriptive of the era under examination" (quoted from pp. 90 and 93, respectively).

3. See Richard Kalmin, *Jewish Babylonia between Persia and Roman Palestine* (New York: Oxford University Press, 2006), 10–17 and 121; Geoffrey Herman, *A Prince without a Kingdom: The Exilarch in the Sasanian Era* (Tübingen: Mohr Siebeck: 2012), 16–20. For other research in this vein, see below.

4. On how the findings that come from the implementation of Stammaitic theory have not been applied to the history of the Talmudic period, see Adiel Schremer, "Stammaitic Historiography," in *Creation and Composition: The Contribution of the Bavli Redactors (Stammaim) to the Aggada*, ed. Jeffrey L. Rubenstein (Tübingen: Mohr Siebeck, 2005), 219–36, esp. 219–20.

5. See David Goodblatt, "Towards the Rehabilitation of Talmudic History," in *History of Judaism: The Next Ten Years*, ed. Baruch M. Bokser (Chico: Scholars Press, 1980), 31–44, esp. 36–38.

6. For historiographical overviews on the formation of the Bavli, see Richard Kalmin, "The Formation and Character of the Babylonian Talmud," in *The Cambridge History of Judaism*, vol. 4, *The Late Roman–Rabbinic Period*, ed. Steven T. Katz (New York: Cambridge University Press, 2006), 840–76. On Aggadah, see Jeffrey L. Rubenstein, "Criteria of Stammaitic Intervention in Aggada," in *Creation and Composition: The Contribution of the Bavli Redactors (Stammaim) to the Aggada*, ed. Jeffrey L. Rubenstein (Tübingen: Mohr Siebeck, 2005), 417–40.

7. For the problem of attributions, see, for instance, William Scott Green, "What's in a Name? The Problematic of Rabbinic 'Biography,'" in *Approaches to Ancient Judaism: Theory and Practice*, ed. William Scott Green (Missoula: Scholars Press, 1978), 77–96.

8. For a review of theories of Talmudic authorship, see Moulie Vidas, *Tradition and the Formation of the Talmud* (Princeton: Princeton University Press, 2014), esp. 3–13, 23–26, and 45–50.

9. See Shamma Friedman, "On the Historical Aggada in the Babylonian Talmud," in *Saul Lieberman Memorial Volume*, ed. Shamma Friedman (New York: Jewish Theological Seminary, 1993), 119–63 (Hebrew); David Weiss Halivni, *Sources and Traditions: A Source-Critical Commentary on the Talmud Tractate Baba Bathra* (Jerusalem: Magnes Press, 2007), 1–148 (Hebrew), and the English version, "Aspects of the Formation of the Talmud," in *Creation and Composition: The Contribution of the Bavli Redactors (Stammaim) to the Aggada*, ed. and trans. Jeffrey L. Rubenstein (Tübingen: Mohr Siebeck, 2005), 339–60; and *Midrash, Mishnah, and Gemara: The Jewish Predilection for Justified Law* (Cambridge, Mass.: Harvard University Press, 1986).

10. See Jeffrey L. Rubenstein, "Translator's Introduction," in David Weiss Halivni, *The Formation of the Babylonian Talmud* (New York: Oxford University Press, 2013), xvii–xxx, esp. xxix.

11. On Halivni's changes to the dating of the Talmudic editors, see ibid. xxvii–xxviii.

12. Schremer, "Stammaitic Historiography," 220–22.

13. Yaacov Sussmann, "Returning to Yerushalmi Nezikin," *Talmudic Studies* 1 (1990): 55–134, esp. 109–10 (Hebrew; Engl. trans. Schremer, "Stammaitic Historiography," 221).

14. Vidas, *Tradition,* 45. For another essay that challenges the lateness of anonymous layers, see also Robert Brody, "The Anonymous Talmud and the Words of the Amoraim," in *Iggud: Selected Essays in Jewish Studies,* vol. 1, *The Bible and Its World, Rabbinic Literature and Jewish Thought,* ed. Baruch J. Schwartz, Aharon Shemesh, Abraham Melamed (Jerusalem: World Union of Jewish Studies, 2008), 213–32.

15. Vidas, *Tradition,* 45.

16. See Isaiah Gafni, "Rethinking Talmudic History: The Challenge of Literary and Redaction Criticism," *Jewish History* 25 (2011): 355–75, esp. 358.

17. By way of example, see Friedman, "On the Historical Aggada," esp. 122; Jonah Fraenkel, "The Study of Aggadic Literature: A View into the Future," *Jewish Studies* 30 (1990): 21–30, esp. 25 (Hebrew). For more on these authors' positions on history, see Geoffrey Herman, *Prince,* 17–18 nn. 87–88; Isaiah Gafni, "The Modern Study of Rabbinics and Historical Questions: The Tale of the Text," in *The New Testament and Rabbinic Literature,* ed. Reimund Bieringer, Florentino García Martínez, Didier Pollefeyt, Peter J. Tomson (Boston: Brill, 2010), 43–61, esp. 49 and 52.

18. Fraenkel, "Study," 25 (trans. Gafni, "Modern Study," 49).

19. See, e.g., Jonah Fraenkel, "Time and Its Role in the Aggadic Story," in *Binah: Jewish Intellectual History in the Middle Ages,* vol. 2, ed. Joseph Dan (Westport: Praeger, 1989), 31–56.

20. For a survey of the implications of Jonah Fraenkel's research for historians, see Hillel Newman, "Closing the Circle: Yonah Fraenkel, the Talmudic Story, and Rabbinic History," in *How Should Rabbinic Literature Be Read in the Modern World?* ed. Matthew Kraus (Piscataway: Gorgias Press, 2006), 105–13, esp. 112.

21. For synthetic histories of Babylonian Jewry, see Isaiah Gafni, *The Jews of Babylonia in the Talmudic Era: A Social and Cultural History* (Jerusalem: Merkaz Zalman Shazar, 1990; Hebrew), and "The Political, Social, and Economic History of Babylonian Jewry, 224–628 CE," in *The Cambridge History of Judaism,* vol. 4, *The Late Roman–Rabbinic Period,* ed. Steven T. Katz (New York: Cambridge University Press, 2006), 792–820; David Goodblatt, "The Jews in Babylonia, 66–c. 235 CE," ibid. 82–92; Kalmin, *Jewish Babylonia;* Jacob Neusner, *A History of the Jews in Babylonia,* 5 vols. (Leiden: Brill, 1965–70); Geo Widengren, "The Status of the Jews in the Sassanian Empire," *Iranica Antiqua* 1 (1961): 117–62.

22. Scholarship on Babylonian rabbinic social history is scarce when compared with the plethora available on the Jews of Roman Palestine; for representative examples of the former, see Julius Newman, *The Agricultural Life of the Jews in Babylonia between the years 200 C.E. and 500 C.E.* (London: Oxford University Press, 1932); David Goodblatt, *Rabbinic Instruction in Sasanian Babylonia* (Leiden: Brill, 1975); Moshe Beer, *The Babylonian Amoraim: Aspects of Economic Life* (Ramat Gan: Bar-Ilan University Press, 1974; Hebrew), and *The Babylonian Exilarchate in the Arsacid and Sasanian Periods* (Tel Aviv: Devir, 1976; Hebrew); Aharon Oppenheimer, with Benjamin Isaac and Michael Lecker, *Babylonia Judaica in the Talmudic Period* (Wiesbaden: Reichert, 1983); Jacob Neusner, *School, Court, Public Administration: Judaism and Its Institutions in Talmudic Babylonia* (Atlanta: Scholars

Press, 1987); Isaiah Gafni, "Synagogues in Babylonia in the Talmudic Period," in *Ancient Synagogues: Historical Analysis and Archaeological Discovery,* vol. 1, ed. Dan Urman and Paul V. M. Flesher (Leiden: Brill, 1998), 221–31; Kalmin, *Jewish Babylonia;* Geoffrey Herman, *Prince.*

23. For more on the question of how rabbinic texts can and cannot be used as sources for social history, see Richard Kalmin, "Midrash and Social History," in *Current Trends in the Study of Midrash,* ed. Carol Bakhos (Leiden: Brill, 2006), 133–59, and "Rabbinic Literature of Late Antiquity as a Source for Historical Study," in *Judaism in Late Antiquity,* vol. 2, ed. Jacob Neusner and Alan J. Avery-Peck (Leiden: Brill, 1999), 187–99, and the other articles in ibid. 123–230.

24. See Geoffrey Herman, *Prince;* and Richard Kalmin's recently published monograph *Migrating Tales: The Talmud's Narratives and Their Historical Context* (Berkeley and Los Angeles: University of California Press, 2014).

25. Neusner, *History.* For more on the problems of past historical models in the field, see the surveys by Seth Schwartz, "Historiography on the Jews in the Talmudic Period," in *The Oxford Handbook for Jewish Studies,* ed. Martin Goodman, Jeremy Cohen, and David Sorkin (Oxford: Oxford University Press, 2002), 79–114, esp. 109–10, and "The Political Geography of Rabbinic Texts," 75–96, esp. 80–87, on the question of rabbinic leadership, with critiques of Alon, Goodenough, Lieberman, and Neusner.

26. Gafni, *Jews.* See also the same author's summary of Babylonian rabbinic culture in "Babylonian Rabbinic Culture," in *Cultures of the Jews,* vol. 1, *Mediterranean Origins,* ed. David Biale (New York: Schocken Books, 2002), 223–66.

27. Gafni, "Rethinking," 355. See also the review in Gafni, "Modern Study."

28. Joseph Heinemann, *Aggadah and Its Development* (Jerusalem: Keter, 1974; Hebrew).

29. Joseph Heinemann, "The Nature of the Aggadah," in *Midrash and Literature,* ed. Geoffrey H. Hartman and Sanford Budick (New Haven: Yale University Press, 1986), 41–55, esp. 42.

30. See Moshe Herr, "The Conception of History among the Sages," in *Proceedings of the Sixth World Congress of Jewish Studies, Jerusalem, August 13–19, 1973,* vol. C, div. C (Jerusalem: World Union of Jewish Studies, 1977), 129–42 (Hebrew); Isaiah Gafni, "Rabbinic Historiography and Representations of the Past," in *The Cambridge Companion to the Talmud and Rabbinic Literature,* ed. Charlotte Elisheva Fonrobert and Martin S. Jaffee (Cambridge: Cambridge University Press, 2007), 295–312.

31. See Goodblatt, "Towards the Rehabilitation," 31, who defines Talmudic history as "the Talmud as history, i.e., attempting to write history on the basis of Talmudic or rabbinic sources." Responding to Neusner's criticism of Talmudic history that our sources do not record what life was actually like in the time of its composers, Goodblatt (p. 33) explains: "In sum, whatever the intent of its creators, rabbinic literature is full of information about what was going on in the time in which it came into being." Goodblatt's article reflects on the major trends in the field in the early 1980s—for example, what he calls "debiographization" (p. 35)—and highlights the value of social and economic research (e.g., by Moshe Beer).

32. See the comparable statement by Gafni, "Modern Study," 60–61.

33. Christine Hayes, *Between the Babylonian and Palestinian Talmuds: Accounting for Halakhic Difference in Selected Sugyot from Tractate Avodah Zarah* (New York: Oxford University Press, 1997), 8.

34. Ibid.

35. Ibid.

36. Ibid. 171–79. The author concludes (p. 178), based on the differences between the Talmud and earlier rabbinic sources: "Here we may draw historical conclusions with some confidence, for here there is an explicit reversal of a previous prohibition—a reversal that is attributed to the circumstances of life under Persian rule. Thus, whatever Persian-Jewish relations in the early amoraic period might have been . . . it seems that by the late amoraic period (early fifth century) the Babylonian rabbis felt secure enough to cooperate with the regime in the supply of weapons-grade material. Historians of Babylonian Jewry describe the talmudic period in Babylonia in a manner that supports this claim. According to Gafni, the Sassanian period, beginning in the third century, was already a time of increasing alliance and loyalty toward the government (1975: 18-19)."

37. Ibid. 6.

38. Ibid. 5–6.

39. For the similarities and differences between Hayes's notion of exegetical irregularities and Halivni's notion of forced interpretations, see ibid. 201–2 n. 57.

40. See Rubenstein, "Translator's Introduction," xx–xxi.

41. Halivni, *Formation,* 42.

42. Ibid.

43. David Weiss Halivni, *The Book and the Sword: A Life of Learning in the Shadow of Destruction* (New York: Farrar, Straus, and Giroux, 1996), 137. In his autobiography, Halivni postulates that the reason that he probably does not venture outside of the Jewish tradition and do comparison is because it gives him a sense of security, whereas leaving it evokes harrowing memories of his experiences in the Holocaust (p. 139).

44. For critiques of the notion of ur-texts from various angles, see Talya Fishman, *Becoming the People of the Talmud: Oral Torah as Written Tradition in Medieval Jewish Cultures* (Philadelphia: University of Pennsylvania Press, 2011), 5: "Not all variants in medieval manuscripts of the same text are products of scribal error. Indeed, the very impulse to search for a correct *ur*-text is often misguided." Compare the debate on this topic between Peter Schäfer, "Research into Rabbinic Literature: An Attempt to Define the Status Quaestionis," *Journal of Jewish Studies* 37 (1986): 139–52 (esp. 151–52, emphasizing the variations in manuscripts and expressing skepticism over the existence of ur-texts), and the response by Chaim Milikowsky, "The Status Quaestionis of Research in Rabbinic Literature," *Journal of Jewish Studies* 39 (1988): 201–11, esp. 201–2, 206, and 208–9. The question of a text's purported original meaning in history is also related to the difference between *pešaṭ* and *deraš,* of which the former would contain greater historical value; on this topic, see Stephen Garfinkel, "Applied *Peshat:* Historical-Critical Method and Religious Meaning," *Journal of the Ancient Near Eastern Society* 22 (1993): 19–28, esp. 21–22.

45. See chapter 2 below for more on this trend in comparative inquiries. For one take here, see Luther H. Martin, "Comparison," in *Guide to the Study of Religion,* ed. Willi Braun and Russell T. McCutcheon (New York: Cassell, 2000), 45–56, esp. 51: "On the other hand, attempts have been made to explain religious similarities by historical contact. According to this 'syncretistic' view, some aspects of an originally autonomous religious tradition were influenced by or became blended with (or were corrupted by) those of one or more others as the consequence of cultural contact, whether through conquest, through commerce or

through the centrifugal tendencies of political development. Theories of diffusion and contact both assume some view of an original religiosity from which the various historical religions either diverged or converged. Such genealogical views based upon origination are unhelpful, however, since such origins are finally unavailable to historical or anthropological research and, consequently, tend simply to be retrojections of contemporary imaginings."

46. See Jeffrey L. Rubenstein, *The Culture of the Babylonian Talmud* (Baltimore: The Johns Hopkins University Press, 2003), 145–46, on how the Tosafists continue the work of the editors and harmonize and make consistent the Bavli. On the similarities and differences between approaches toward the Talmud from late antiquity until today, see Gerald J. Blidstein, "Method in the Study of Talmud," *Journal of the American Academy of Religion* 39 (1971): 186–92, esp. 188–91, regarding the tendencies among Tosafists and modern Yeshivot to harmonize differing opinions and avoid sociohistorical analysis. In this section I wish to suggest not that there are straightforward continuities or correlations between the Geonim, Tosafists, and contemporary Yeshivot but rather that they all share in common certain philosophies of reading Talmud that converge or diverge with academic studies.

47. Michael Rosensweig, "The Study of the Talmud in Contemporary Yeshivot," in *Printing the Talmud: From Bomberg to Schottenstein,* ed. Sharon Liberman Mintz and Gabriel M. Goldstein (New York: Yeshiva University Museum, 2005), 111–20, esp. 113.

48. Fishman, *Becoming,* 2–3.

49. For an example of research on Talmudic reasoning, see Leib Moscovitz, *Talmudic Reasoning: From Casuistics to Conceptualization* (Tübingen: Mohr Siebeck, 2002), esp. 11 nn. 38–41 on how the study of legal conceptualization is found in medieval writings, modern Lithuanian Yeshivot, and the thought of Soloveitchik. Reading the Bavli as an ideal concept was common among nineteenth-century Talmudists; for a description of Haym Soloveitchik's view of Halakhah as an "ideal structure" that can be implemented in one's life, and how the Brisker method turned the Bavli into conceptualized abstractions, see Marc B. Shapiro, "Talmud Study in the Modern Era: From *Wissenschaft* and Brisk to *Daf Yomi,*" in *Printing the Talmud: From Bomberg to Schottenstein,* ed. Sharon Liberman Mintz and Gabriel M. Goldstein (New York: Yeshiva University Museum, 2005), 103–10, esp. 107–8, and "The Brisker Method Reconsidered: Review Essay," *Tradition* 31 (1997): 78-102.

50. Fishman, *Becoming,* 3 (with bibliographic information on p. 232 nn. 8 and 9).

51. For a description of the Talmud's status as a living work, see Lawrence H. Schiffman, "Medium and Message: The Talmud as a Transmitter of Jewish Culture," in *Printing the Talmud: From Bomberg to Schottenstein,* ed. Sharon Liberman Mintz and Gabriel M. Goldstein (New York: Yeshiva University Museum, 2005), 163–67, esp. 166: "So the Talmud is not just a book to study. It is an approach to life, in which inquiry and debate transform the mundane into the holy. . . . How do you describe a living organism as if it is an artifact or series of artifacts?"

52. Although there are some flaws with the analogy, it is nevertheless instructive to ponder the ramifications on Talmudic scholarship of the history of the Talmud's unique canonical status as a normative work in light of Jonathan Z. Smith's insights into the negative effects of Christianity's claims regarding the uniqueness of the Christ-event on historical scholarship on early Christianity. See Jonathan Z. Smith, *Drudgery Divine: On the Comparison of Early Christianities and the Religions of Late Antiquity* (Chicago: University of Chicago Press, 1990), 38–43. For a description of Smith's contributions to exposing the

problems of certain scholarly presuppositions, see Aditya Behl, "Pages from the Book of Religions: Comparing Self and Other in Mughal India," in *Notes from a Maṇḍala: Essays in the History of Indian Religions in Honor of Wendy Doniger,* ed. Laurie L. Patton and David L. Haberman (Newark: University of Delaware Press, 2010), 113–49, esp. 120: "Smith's analyses have been exemplary in demonstrating the ways in which illicit assumptions—such as of a pristine originary religion later corrupted, or the 'true' inner meaning of a doctrinal position—have been imported into the arguments of scholars claiming historical objectivity."

53. Robert Brody, *The Geonim of Babylonia and the Shaping of Medieval Jewish Culture* (New Haven: Yale University Press, 1998), 161-62. For more on the status of the Talmud in the Geonic period, see also Fishman, *Becoming,* 1–10.

54. On the Geonim, see ibid. 10.

55. See Ra'anan S. Boustan, Oren Kosansky, and Marina Rustow, eds., "Introduction," in *Jewish Studies at the Crossroads of Anthropology and History: Authority, Diaspora, Tradition* (Philadelphia: University of Pennsylvania Press, 2011), 1.

56. Ibid. 2. See also Bruce Lincoln, "Theses on Method," *Method and Theory in the Study of Religion* 8 (1996): 225–27, esp. 227: "When one permits those whom one studies to define the terms in which they will be understood, suspends one's interest in the temporal and contingent, or fails to distinguish between 'truths', 'truth-claims', and 'regimes of truth', one has ceased to function as historian or scholar."

57. See Gavin Flood, "Reflections on Tradition and Inquiry in the Study of Religions," *Journal of the American Academy of Religion* 74 (2006): 47–58, esp. 54.

58. For an influential work on social theory that emphasizes the notion of authorial agency within specific social contexts, see Pierre Bourdieu, *The Field of Cultural Production: Essays on Art and Literature,* ed. Randal Johnson (New York: Columbia University Press, 1993), esp. 29-73. See also the discussion of textualists, who separate texts from their authors and authors' worlds, by Quentin Skinner, described in Robert Segal, "How Historical Is the History of Religions?" *Method and Theory in the Study of Religion* 1 (1989): 2–17. For an argument for textualism in the study of the Talmud in Iran, see Shai Secunda, *The Iranian Talmud: Reading the Bavli in Its Sasanian Context* (Philadelphia: University of Pennsylvania Press, 2013), 127–33.

59. See Jonathan Z. Smith, *Imagining Religion: From Babylon to Jonestown* (Chicago: University of Chicago Press, 1982), 24, where the author, quoting Franz Boas, argues that comparisons are best done within the logic of space and time.

60. On Fraenkel's inattention to sociocultural contexts of rabbinic narratives, see Rubenstein, *Talmudic Stories,* 12; on Halivni's lack of engagement with the Persian context, see also Rubenstein, "Translator's Introduction," xxix.

61. See André Levy and Alex Weingrod, eds., "Introduction," in *Homelands and Diasporas: Holy Lands and Other Places* (Stanford: Stanford University Press, 2005), 5, on how currently "'diasporas' are enthusiastically embraced as arenas for the creative melding of cultures and the formation of new 'hybridic,' mixed identities. To be part of a diaspora is, presumably, to be 'on the cutting edge' of new cultural and other formations."

62. For a historical overview of the various peoples and religious communities in Sasanian Mesopotamia, as well as their social contacts with one another, see Michael Morony, *Iraq after the Muslim Conquest* (Princeton: Princeton University Press, 1984), 169–506; Theodor Nöldeke, *Geschichte der Perser und Araber zur Zeit der Sasaniden: Aus der arabischen*

Chronik des Tabari (Leiden: Brill, 1879); Shaul Shaked, "Religion in the Late Sasanian Period: Eran, Aneran, and Other Religious Designations," in *The Sasanian Era,* vol. 3 of *The Idea of Iran,* ed. Vesta Sarkhosh Curtis and Sarah Stewart (New York: I.B. Tauris, 2008), 103–17; Touraj Daryaee, *Sasanian Persia: The Rise and Fall of an Empire* (New York: I.B. Tauris, 2009), 69–97; Yaakov Elman, "Middle Persian Culture and Babylonian Sages: Accommodation and Resistance in the Shaping of Rabbinic Legal Tradition," in *The Cambridge Companion to the Talmud and Rabbinic Literature,* ed. Charlotte Elisheva Fonrobert and Martin S. Jaffee (Cambridge: Cambridge University Press, 2007), 165–97; and, from the perspective of art history, Prudence O. Harper, *In Search of a Cultural Identity: Monuments and Artifacts of the Sasanian Near East, 3rd to 7th Century A.D.* (New York: Bibliotheca Persica, 2006), 57–96 and 163–81. See also the statement of Parvaneh Pourshariati, *Decline and Fall of the Sasanian Empire: The Sasanian-Parthian Confederacy and the Arab Conquest of Iran* (New York: I.B. Tauris, 2008), 323, on how Iranists are in agreement regarding the diversity of Sasanian religions: "And so in the post-Avestan period, the Iranian religious landscape came to be dominated by a bewildering array of religious beliefs and practices. This is a primary dimension of the post-Avestan religious landscape about which there is little disagreement in the scholarly community." On the evidence for heterogeneity from settlement patterns, see St John Simpson, "Mesopotamia in the Sasanian Period: Settlement Patterns, Arts and Crafts," in *Mesopotamia and Iran in the Parthian and Sasanian Periods: Rejection and Revival c. 238 BC–AD 642—Proceedings of a Seminar in Memory of Vladimir G. Lukonin,* ed. John Curtis (London: British Museum Press, 2000), 57–66.

63. See Kalmin, *Jewish Babylonia,* 3–10.

64. See Yaakov Elman, "Why Is There No Zoroastrian Central Temple? A Thought Experiment," in *The Temple of Jerusalem: From Moses to the Messiah—In Honor of Professor Louis H. Feldman,* ed. Steven Fine (Boston: Brill, 2011), 151–70, esp. 158–59.

65. See Geoffrey Herman, *Prince,* 22, with references in n. 4. See also Aharon Oppenheimer and Michael Lecker, "The Genealogical Boundaries of Jewish Babylonia," in Aharon Oppenheimer, *Between Rome and Babylon: Studies in Jewish Leadership and Society,* ed. Nili Oppenheimer (Tübingen: Mohr Siebeck: 2005), 339–55, esp. 340, on "the correspondence of the genealogical boundaries of Babylonia with regional boundaries within the Sasanian empire."

66. See, for example, Philippe Gignoux, "Titres et fonctions religieuses sasanides d'après les sources syriaques hagiographiques," *Acta Antiqua Academiae Scientiarum Hungaricae* 28 (1983): 191–203, esp. 197-201, on Syriac sources that attest the presence of a *mowbed* and *rad* in the region.

67. See Rika Gyselen, *La géographie administrative de l'empire sassanide: Les témoignages sigillographiques* (Leuven: Peeters, 1989), 15-18, 39, and 61–62.

68. Geoffrey Herman, *Prince,* 27. On the ties between the territorial administration of the Christian church and the Sasanian state, see Gyselen, *Géographie,* 78.

69. For maps of Sasanian Babylonia, see Michael Avi-Yonah, with the assistance of Shmuel Safrai, *Carta's Atlas of the Period of the Second Temple, the Mishnah, and the Talmud* (Jerusalem: Carta, 1966; Hebrew), maps 153–57 on pages 98–100.

70. For images of the royal palace at Ctesiphon, see Roman Ghirshman, *Persian Art: The Parthian and Sassanian Dynasties, 249 B.C.–A.D. 651,* trans. Stuart Gilbert and James Emmons (New York: Golden Press, 1962), figs. 172 and 173 on p. 136.

71. For more on the flourishing of Ctesiphon as a major urban center in the Sasanian era, see Robert McCormick Adams, *Land behind Baghdad: A History of Settlement on the Diyala Plains* (Chicago: University of Chicago Press, 1965), 70–74.

72. For more on Maḥoza, see Ben-Zion Eshel, *Jewish Settlements in Babylonia during Talmudic Times: Talmudic Onomasticon, Including Geographical Locations, Historical Notes, and Indices of Place-Names* (Jerusalem: Magnes Press, 1979), 141–44 (Hebrew); Oppenheimer, with Isaac and Lecker, *Babylonia Judaica*, 179–235, with map on page 233; J.M. Fiey, "Topographie chrétienne de Mahozé," *L'Orient Syrien* 12 (1967): 397–420.

73. See Yaakov Elman, "The Socioeconomics of Babylonian Heresy," *Jewish Law Association Studies* 17 (2007): 80–127, "Talmud, ii: Rabbinic Literature and Middle Persian Texts," *Encyclopaedia Iranica*, online ed., 2010: www.iranica.com/articles/talmud-ii, and "Middle Persian Culture."

74. On the ties of the exilarch to Maḥoza, including its market, see Geoffrey Herman, *Prince*, 11, 156–58, 173–76.

75. The contextual study of the Babylonian Talmud, especially in light of Christianity, has a complicated historiography that I do not claim to have exhausted here, in part because my book focuses on the understudied topic of its Iranian setting. On the Bavli and Christianity, see, for instance, Michal Bar-Asher Siegal, *Early Christian Monastic Literature and the Babylonian Talmud* (New York: Cambridge University Press, 2013); Geoffrey Herman, *Prince*, 14–15, 123–32; Reuven Kiperwasser and Serge Ruzer, "Zoroastrian Proselytes in Rabbinic and Syriac Christian Narratives: Orality-Related Markers of Cultural Identity," *History of Religions* 51 (2012): 197–218; Adam H. Becker, "The Comparative Study of 'Scholasticism' in Late Antique Mesopotamia: Rabbis and East Syrians," *Association for Jewish Studies Review* 34 (2010): 91–113; Peter Schäfer, *Jesus in the Talmud* (Princeton: Princeton University Press, 2007); Daniel Boyarin, *Dying for God: Martyrdom and the Making of Christianity and Judaism* (Stanford: Stanford University Press, 1999).

2. COMPARING SASANIAN RELIGIONS

1. The tension between scholars' constructs of sameness and difference is well known in the history of religions; see, for example, Wendy Doniger, "Minimyths and Maximyths and Political Points of View," in *Myth and Method*, ed. Laurie L. Patton and Wendy Doniger (Charlottesville: University Press of Virginia, 1996), 109–27, esp. 109, synopsizing the trend as follows: "The tension between sameness and difference has become a crucial issue for the self-definitions of postmodernism. . . . For postmodernism, sameness is the devil, difference the angel."

2. Jonathan Z. Smith, *Drudgery Divine: On the Comparison of Early Christianities and the Religions of Late Antiquity* (Chicago: University of Chicago Press, 1990), 42.

3. For a discussion of the concept of literary influences, see Ihab H. Hassan, "The Problem of Influence in Literary History: Notes towards a Definition," *The Journal of Aesthetics and Art Criticism* 14 (1955): 66–76, esp. 67, where he emphasizes causality in defining influence, which is "any relationship, running the gamut of incidence to causality, with a somewhat expansive range of intermediate correlations." For a treatment of the concept of influence as it pertains to Jewish studies, see Michael L. Satlow, "Beyond Influence: Toward a New Historiographic Paradigm," in *Jewish Literatures and Cultures: Context and Intertext*, ed.

Yaron Eliav and Anita Norich (Providence: Brown University Press, 2008), 37–53. On influences in the study of the Talmud in Iran, see Shai Secunda, *The Iranian Talmud: Reading the Bavli in Its Sasanian Context* (Philadelphia: University of Pennsylvania Press, 2013), 111–16.

4. Albert de Jong, "Zoroastrian Religious Polemics and Their Contexts: Interconfessional Relations in the Sasanian Empire," in *Religious Polemics in Context: Papers Presented to the Second International Conference of the Leiden Institute for the Study of Religions (LISOR), Held at Leiden 27–28 April 2000*, ed. T.L. Hettema and A. van der Kooij (Assen: Royal van Gorcum, 2004), 48–63, esp. 58.

5. Secunda, *Iranian Talmud*, 131.

6. At stake here is the problem of under what circumstances and to what extent scholars should suspend a religious group's internal perspective; for one take, see Russell T. McCutcheon, "'It's a Lie. There's no Truth in It! It's a Sin!': On the Limits of the Humanistic Study of Religion and the Costs of Saving Others from Themselves," *Journal of the American Academy of Religion* 74 (2006): 720–50, esp. 730.

7. For an early discussion of the idea of parallelomania as it applies to ancient Jewish and Christian texts, see Samuel Sandmel, "Parallelomania," *Journal of Biblical Literature* 81 (1962): 1–13, esp. 1: "We might for our purposes define parallelomania as that extravagance among scholars which first overdoes the supposed similarity in passages and then proceeds to describe source and derivation as if implying literary connection flowing in an inevitable or predetermined direction."

8. William E. Paden, "Elements of a New Comparativism," in *A Magic Still Dwells: Comparative Religion in the Postmodern Age*, ed. Kimberley C. Patton and Benjamin C. Ray (Berkeley and Los Angeles: University of California Press, 2000), 182–92, esp. 183.

9. See Carl Olson, *The Allure of Decadent Thinking: Religious Studies and the Challenge of Postmodernism* (New York: Oxford University Press, 2013), 82–83: "By creative hermeneutics, Eliade means more than a method of interpretation, because it is also 'a spiritual technique that possessed the ability of modifying the quality of existence itself.' Thus, hermeneutics, a never-completed task, is creative in a dual sense: It is creative for the particular interpreter by enriching his or her mind and life, and it is creative because it reveals values unavailable in ordinary experience. This type of awareness is liberating for Eliade. Besides its potential ontological implications for the individual interpreter, the study of unfamiliar religions more than broadens one's horizon of understanding because one encounters representatives of foreign cultures, which results in culturally stimulating the interpreter." On the humanistic value of history of religions, see Mircea Eliade, *The Quest: History and Meaning in Religion* (Chicago: University of Chicago Press, 1969), 1–11.

10. For an overview of the criticisms of Eliade's work specifically, see Bryan S. Rennie, *Reconstructing Eliade: Making Sense of Religion* (Albany: State University of New York Press, 1996), 119–212. See also ibid. 89–108 on Eliade's notion of history. For critiques of Eliade's notion of history, see Robert D. Baird, *Category Formation and the History of Religions* (Paris: Mouton, 1971), 153; Guilford Dudley, "Mircea Eliade as the 'Anti-Historian' of Religions," *Journal of the American Academy of Religion* 44 (1976): 345–59; Douglas Allen, "Eliade and History," *Journal of Religion* 68 (1988): 545–65, esp. 547–49; Ivan Strenski, *Thinking about Religion: An Historical Introduction to Theories of Religion* (Malden: Blackwell Publishing, 2006), 311–13; Jonathan Z. Smith, "The Eternal Deferral," in *Hermeneutics, Politics, and the History of Religions: The Contested Legacies of Joachim Wach and Mircea*

Eliade, ed. Christian K. Wedemeyer and Wendy Doniger (New York: Oxford University Press, 2010), 215–37, esp. 237. To be fair, Eliade discusses the relationship between phenomenology and history on numerous occasions; for a representative statement, see Mircea Eliade, *Patterns in Comparative Religion,* trans. Rosemary Sheed (New York: Sheed and Ward, 1958), 2, on how "each category of evidence (myths, rites, gods, superstitions, and so on) is really equally important to us if we are to understand the religious phenomenon. And this understanding will always come about in relation to history. Every hierophany we look at is also an historical fact. Every manifestation of the sacred takes place in some historical situation." See also Eliade, *Quest,* 9.

11. Timothy Fitzgerald, *The Ideology of Religious Studies* (New York: Oxford University Press, 2000), 3–32.

12. See David Gordon White, "The Scholar as Mythographer: Comparative Indo-European Myth and Postmodern Concerns," in *A Magic Still Dwells: Comparative Religion in the Postmodern Age,* ed. Kimberley C. Patton and Benjamin C. Ray (Berkeley and Los Angeles: University of California Press, 2000), 47–54, esp. 50–51.

13. On comparison disguised as genealogy, see Smith, *Drudgery,* 51.

14. On this issue, see Peter Donovan, "Neutrality in Religious Studies," in *The Insider/Outsider Problem in the Study of Religion: A Reader,* ed. Russell T. McCutcheon (New York: Cassell, 1999), 235–47. For more on the ramifications of a scholar's personal perspective in research, see Fitzgerald, *Ideology,* 37, describing Joachim Wach's hermeneutics, "whereby he fully acknowledged that the interpreter of 'other religions' relies on an intuitive understanding of religions deriving from his own natural religious disposition. Doing the comparative study of religion thus becomes an explicitly theological enterprise, bringing to light and giving expression to the forms of religious experience and making judgements about its spiritual value for the human being."

15. For an overview of various stances regarding the proper balance between similarities and differences, see Mark C. Taylor, "Introduction," in *Critical Terms for Religious Studies,* ed. Mark C. Taylor (Chicago: University of Chicago Press, 1988), 1–19, esp. 6–8 and 14–15 on Smith and Doniger. But compare the critical assessment of Taylor by Robert Segal, "All Generalizations Are Bad: Postmodernism on Theories," *Journal of the American Academy of Religion* 74 (2006): 157–71, esp. 164–65.

16. Jonathan Z. Smith, *Imagining Religion: From Babylon to Jonestown* (Chicago: University of Chicago Press, 1982), 35 on how patterns are simple to construct, whereas "the 'how' and the 'why' and, above all, the 'so what' remain most refractory."

17. Ibid. 21 (author's italics).

18. See Jonathan Z. Smith, "The 'End' of Comparison: Redescription and Rectification," in *A Magic Still Dwells: Comparative Religion in the Postmodern Age,* ed. Kimberley C. Patton and Benjamin C. Ray (Berkeley and Los Angeles: University of California Press, 2000), 237–41, esp. 237.

19. Smith, *Imagining,* 23, defines the encyclopedic method as the "topical arrangement of cross-cultural material culled, most usually, from reading. The data are seldom either explicitly compared or explained. They simply cohabit within some category, inviting comparison by their coexistence, but providing no clues as to how this comparison might be undertaken. The encyclopaedic mode consists of contextless lists held together by mere surface associations in which the overwhelming sense is that of the exotic."

20. Ibid. 22.

21. Smith, *Drudgery*, 52.

22. Ibid. 47: "It is as if the only choices the comparativist has are to assert either identity or uniqueness, and that the only possibilities for utilizing comparisons are to make assertions regarding dependence. In such an enterprise, it would appear, dissimilarity is assumed to be the norm; similarities are to be explained as either the result of the 'psychic unity' of humankind, or the result of 'borrowing.'"

23. Ibid. 143.

24. Compare the statement by Fitzgerald, *Ideology*, 22, regarding how confusion over what the study of religion is can lead to "cognitive imperialism," which is "an attempt to remake the world according to one's own dominant ideological categories, not merely to understand but to force compliance."

25. Luther H. Martin, "Comparison," in *Guide to the Study of Religion*, ed. Willi Braun and Russell T. McCutcheon (New York: Cassell, 2000), 45–56, esp. 52.

26. Smith, *Drudgery* 53. The question of to what extent scholars who research comparative exegesis are engaging questions of interreligious dialogue is valid here; see David Tracy, "Western Hermeneutics and Interreligious Dialogue" in *Interreligious Hermeneutics*, ed. Catherine Cornille and Christopher Conway (Eugene: Cascade Books, 2010), 1–43, esp. 9.

27. For more on the relationship between comparative inquiry and discourses of power, see, e.g., Wendy Doniger, "Post-modern and -colonial -structural Comparisons," in *A Magic Still Dwells: Comparative Religion in the Postmodern Age*, ed. Kimberley C. Patton and Benjamin C. Ray (Berkeley and Los Angeles: University of California Press, 2000), 63–74, esp. 67: "Comparison has long been an imperial enterprise. We need to know this, so that we can stop doing it the way they did it and start doing it the way we do it. . . . In pursuing the multivocal, multicultural agenda, we must face the implications of the fact that we use other peoples' stories for our purposes. The political problem inheres in the asymmetry of power between the appropriating culture and the appropriated. Thus, if Europe has dominated India, it is deemed wrong for a European to make use of an Indian text. But it seems to me that there are very different ways of using other peoples' texts, some of them fairly innocuous, and that the usual alternative . . . can be even worse: ignoring it or scorning it."

28. See, e.g., Fitzgerald, *Ideology*, 8.

29. Guy G. Stroumsa, *A New Science: The Discovery of Religion in the Age of Reason* (Cambridge, Mass.: Harvard University Press, 2010), 106. And see ibid. 101–13.

30. Ibid. 112.

31. Jacques Duchesne-Guillemin, *The Western Response to Zoroaster* (Oxford: Clarendon Press, 1958), 10–11.

32. Stroumsa, *New Science*, 112.

33. Ibid.

34. By way of example, see Robert C. Zaehner, *At Sundry Times: An Essay in the Comparison of Religions* (London: Faber and Faber, 1958), 141–44, regarding the purported parallels of the dualistic motifs of light and darkness attested in the Dead Sea Scrolls and Gathas. As with Hyde, these studies, which argue for Iranian-Jewish interchanges, often center on the dichotomy of Judaism's monotheism versus Zoroastrianism's dualism; see, e.g., George William Carter, *Zoroastrianism and Judaism* (New York: AMS Press, 1918), 51–54; and Ugo Bianchi, *The History of Religions* (Leiden: Brill, 1975), 148, who finds the

hypothesis of Jewish origins to the monotheism of the Gathas "attractive, if not convincing." Anachronism abounds in some of these works. Additionally, it is noteworthy that the idea of Semitic-Iranian fusion has captured the imagination of nonspecialists, who use it for polemical purposes; see, for instance, Edmond Bordeaux Székely, *The Essene Teachings of Zarathustra* (Cartago: International Biogenic Society, 1973), 22: "The ten commandments of Moses are represented in Zoroastrianism by this famous sentence from the *Avestas:* 'Good thoughts, good words, good deeds.'"

35. The series entitled *Irano-Judaica: Studies Relating to Jewish Contacts with Persian Culture throughout the Ages,* edited by Shaul Shaked and Amnon Netzer, is an example of research that avoids the common pitfalls that existed in Irano-Judaica.

36. Many Pahlavi manuscripts contain damaged pages and errors of transmission, on which see the example elucidated in Alberto Cantera, "Lost in Transmission: The Case of the Pahlavi-Vīdēvdād manuscripts," *Bulletin of the School of Oriental and African Studies* 73 (2010): 179–205. In some cases the authors, editors, or scribes of Pahlavi works did not understand the nuances of the language, which was already in decline circa the eighth and ninth centuries C.E.; on this, see the introduction in Mahmoud Jaafari-Dehaghi, *Dādestān ī Dēnīg,* part 1, *Transcription, Translation, and Commentary* (Paris: Association pour l'Avancement des Études Iraniennes, 1998), 25, on how "the art of composing original texts in Pahlavi had become somewhat artificial by the ninth century," resulting in this text's abstruse style.

37. See Carlo G. Cereti, "Primary Sources for the History of Inner and Outer Iran in the Sasanian Period (Third–Seventh Centuries)," *Archivum Eurasiae Medii Aevi* 9 (1997): 17–71, esp. 19.

38. For example, see the project aimed at providing a critical edition of the *Pahlavi Vīdēvdād* led by Alberto Cantera: ada.usal.es/videvdad/project.htm; the watershed analysis of the Zand by Cantera, *Studien zur Pahlavi-Übersetzung des Avesta* (Wiesbaden: Harrassowitz, 2004); the Middle Persian dictionary in preparation by Shaul Shaked, discussed in Shaked, "Towards a Middle Persian Dictionary," in *Iran: Questions et connaissances—Actes du IVe Congrès européen des études iraniennes, organisé par la Societas Iranologica Europaea, Paris, 6–10 septembre 1999,* vol. 1, *La période ancienne,* ed. Philip Huyse (Paris: Association pour l'Avancement des Études Iraniennes, 2002), 121–34.

39. See Carlo G. Cereti, "On the Date of the Zand ī Wahman Yasn," in *K.R. Cama Oriental Institute, Second International Congress Proceedings,* ed. H. J .M. Desai and H. N. Modi (Bombay: K.R. Cama Institute, 1996), 243–58; Judith Josephson, *The Pahlavi Translation Technique as Illustrated by the Hōm Yašt* (Uppsala: Uppsala Universitetsbibliotek, 1997).

40. For a comparative analysis of the Zand, the Quran, and oral Torah, see Shaul Shaked, *Dualism in Transformation: Varieties of Religion in Sasanian Iran* (London: School of Oriental and African Studies, 1994), 115-19.

41. For more on orality in the Bavli and Middle Persian texts, see Shai Secunda, "The Sasanian '*Stam*': Orality and the Composition of Babylonian Rabbinic and Zoroastrian Legal Literature," in *The Talmud in Its Iranian Context,* ed. Carol Bakhos and M. Rahim Shayegan (Tübingen: Mohr Siebeck, 2010), 140–60.

42. For more on these figures, see Cantera, *Studien,* 207–20, who dates many of them to the fifth century; Yaakov Elman, "Toward an Intellectual History of Sasanian Law: An Intergenerational Dispute in *Hērbedestān* 9 and Its Rabbinic and Roman Parallels," in *The Talmud in Its Iranian Context,* ed. Carol Bakhos and M. Rahim Shayegan (Tübingen: Mohr Siebeck, 2010),

21–57, esp. 24, where he dates Sōšāns and Gōgušnasp to circa 375–450 C.E. and Abarag and Mēdōmāh to circa 450–550 C.E., concluding that "the careers of these sages make them contemporaries with the last generations of the Babylonian amoraim, while the redactors of the Zand would then be contemporaries of the anonymous redactors of the Babylonian Talmud." See also Shai Secunda, "On the Age of the Zoroastrian Sages of the Zand," *Iranica Antiqua* 47 (2012): 317–49, who draws from numerous Middle Persian works and concludes (346): "Based on this study, it seems plausible that nearly every Zoroastrian commentator of significance lived in some proximity to the sixth-century."

43. For an analysis of the oral and textual transmission of Zoroastrian literature, see Prods Oktor Skjærvø, "The Importance of Orality for the Study of Old Iranian Literature and Myth," *Nāme-ye Irān-e Bāstān: The International Journal of Ancient Iranian Studies* 5 (2005–6): 1–23.

44. For an alternative point of view that sees the Zand as similar to the Bavli, see Secunda, *Iranian Talmud,* 24: "More generally speaking, much of the excitement that has energized the renewed interest in the Bavli's Iranian context stems from the almost tangibly rabbinic 'feel' of the discursive Zand."

45. On intertextuality in Middle Persian, see Yuhan Sohrab-Dinshaw Vevaina, "Relentless Allusion: Intertextuality and the Reading of Zoroastrian Interpretive Literature," in *The Talmud in Its Iranian Context,* ed. Carol Bakhos and M. Rahim Shayegan (Tübingen: Mohr Siebeck, 2010), 206–32, and "Studies in Zoroastrian Exegesis and Hermeneutics, with a Critical Edition of the *Sūdgar Nask* of *Dēnkard* Book 9" (Ph.D. dissertation, Harvard University, 2007), 101: "The texts like the *Sūdgar Nask* are 'intertextual' because their meanings are derived from their relationships with other texts (cotexts) in the Zoroastrian religious corpus." The author adds (105) that the "*Sūdgar Nask* derives its exegetical trajectories and literary structure from its relationship with other texts," such as the *Mēnōg ī Xrad, Ardā Wirāz Nāmag,* and *Pahlavi Vīdēvdād.*

46. The application of source-critical methods to Middle Persian technical terms can yield important new insights; see, for instance, Prods Oktor Skjærvø, "On the Terminology and Style of the Pahlavi Scholastic Literature," in *The Talmud in Its Iranian Context,* ed. Carol Bakhos and M. Rahim Shayegan (Tübingen: Mohr Siebeck, 2010), 178–205.

47. Unless indicated otherwise, the dates in this section of the book are based on the conclusions of two up-to-date summaries of Middle Persian literature by leading scholars in the field: Maria Macuch, "Pahlavi Literature," in *The Literature of Pre-Islamic Iran,* ed. Ronald E. Emmerick and Maria Macuch (New York: I. B. Tauris, 2009), 116–96; and Carlo G. Cereti, "Middle Persian Literature, i: Pahlavi Literature," *Encyclopaedia Iranica,* online ed., 2009: www.iranica.com/articles/middle-persian-literature-1-pahlavi.

48. See the critical editions of the *Mādayān ī Hazār Dādestān* by Anahit Perikhanian, *Mādayān ī Hazār Dādestān: The Book of a Thousand Judgements, a Sasanian Law-Book* (Costa Mesa: Mazda Publishers, 1997); Maria Macuch, *Das sasanidische Rechtsbuch "Mātakdān ī hazār dātistān,"* part 2 (Wiesbaden: Deutsche Morgenländische Gesellschaft, Kommissionsverlag F. Steiner, 1981). See further Macuch, "Pahlavi Literature," 188, who writes that this legal work "was compiled sometime during or after the reign of Xosrau II (590–628)."

49. See William W. Malandra and Pallan Ichaporia, *The Pahlavi Yasna of the Gāthās and Yasna Haptaŋhāiti* (Wiesbaden: Reichert, 2013); Bamanji Nusserwanji Dhabhar, *Translation of Zand-i Khūrtak Avistāk* (Bombay: K. R. Cama Oriental Institute, 1963).

50. See Dan D. Y. Shapira, "Studies in Zoroastrian Exegesis: *Zand*" (Ph.D. dissertation, Hebrew University of Jerusalem, 1998), xxxi–xxxii.

51. Macuch, "Pahlavi Literature," 129, dates this text to after 528 C.E. See the new edition by Mahnaz Moazami, *Wrestling with the Demons of the Pahlavi Widēwdād: Transcription, Translation, and Commentary* (Leiden: Brill, 2014), esp. 7–8, where the editor dates the text to the Sasanian era with some additions in the early Islamic period. For an older critical edition, see Behramgore Tahmuras Anklesaria, *Pahlavi Vendidâd (Zand-î Jvîṭ-dêv-dâṭ): Transliteration and Translation in English* (Bombay: K. R. Cama Oriental Institute, 1949). For one article that fruitfully compares this work's concept of pollution with the Bavli, see Yaakov Elman, "The Other in the Mirror: Iranians and Jews View One Another—Questions of Identity, Conversion, and Exogamy in the Fifth-Century Iranian Empire (Part One)," in Carol Altman Bromberg, Nicholas Sims-Williams, and Ursula Sims-Williams, eds., *Iranian and Zoroastrian Studies in Honor of Prods Oktor Skjærvø, Bulletin of the Asia Institute* 19 (2009): 15–25.

52. See Götz König, "Der Pahlavi-Text *Zand ī Fragard ī Juddēvdād*," in *Ancient and Middle Iranian Studies: Proceedings of the 6th European Conference of Iranian Studies, Held in Vienna, 18–22 September 2007*, ed. Maria Macuch, Dieter Weber, and Desmond Durkin-Meisterernst (Wiesbaden: Harrassowitz, 2010), 115–32. For a dating to the sixth century, see also Yaakov Elman and Mahnaz Moazami, "*Zand ī Fragard ī Jud-dēw-dād*," *Encyclopaedia Iranica*, online ed., 2014: www.iranicaonline.org/articles/zand-fragard-jud-dew-dad.

53. See Shai Secunda, "*Dashtana—'Ki Derekh Nashim Li'*: A Study of the Babylonian Rabbinic Laws of Menstruation in Relation to Corresponding Zoroastrian Texts" (Ph.D. dissertation, Yeshiva University, 2007).

54. See the editions by Firoze M. Kotwal and Philip G. Kreyenbroek, with contributions by James R. Russell, *The Hērbedestān and Nērangestān*, 4 vols. (Paris: Association pour l'Avancement des Études Iraniennes, 1992–2009). Macuch, "Pahlavi Literature," 129, dates the completion of these works to "some time after the reform of the calendar by Yazdegird III in 632 CE." For a reading of this text in an Islamic context, see Jamsheed K. Choksy, *Conflict and Cooperation: Zoroastrian Subalterns and Muslim Elites in Medieval Iranian Society* (New York: Columbia University Press, 1997), 90. On this later dating, see Philip G. Kreyenbroek, "Review: J. K. Choksy, *Conflict and Cooperation: Zoroastrian Subalterns and Muslim Elites in Medieval Iranian Society* (New York: Columbia University Press, 1997)," *Indo-Iranian Journal* 42 (1999): 387–92, esp. 388–89, who notes that the work actually does not explicitly refer to Muslims but rather only to Christians.

55. For more on the date of the Zand-Avesta, see Macuch, "Pahlavi Literature," 124–26, who hypothesizes, based on the totality of the evidence, that its writing down came to prominence in the early third century C.E., with later updates by Khusrow I. Most of the evidence for early datings of a written Zand, however, stem from later literary sources or short references to connotative words such as *nask*, as explained in Prods Oktor Skjærvø, "'Kirdir's Vision': Translation and Analysis," *Archäologische Mitteilungen aus Iran* 16 (1983): 269–306, esp. 290.

56. Cantera, *Studien*, 235–36; and see also the evaluation of some of Cantera's propositions by Prods Oktor Skjærvø, "Review: Cantera, Alberto. *Studien zur Pahlavi-Übersetzung des Avesta*," "Cantera, *Pahlavi-Übersetzung des Avesta*," *Kratylos* 53 (2008): 1–20.

57. For a critical edition, see Jehangir C. Tavadia, *Šāyast-nē-šāyast: A Pahlavi Text on Religious Customs* (Hamburg: De Gruyter, 1930); Macuch, "Pahlavi Literature," 146, and

Cereti, "Middle Persian Literature," agree that the lack of reference to Islam indicates that this work was probably brought together in the late Sasanian era.

58. See Frantz Grenet, *La geste d'Ardashir fils de Pâbag: Kārnāmag ī Ardaxšēr ī Pābagān* (Die: Éditions A Die, 2003). The exact date of the *Kārnāmag*'s composition is not entirely clear, as a result of the book's having undergone several stages of redaction, the last taking place perhaps as late as the ninth century. For more on the difficulties of dating this text, see Grenet's comments on the manuscripts and changing linguistic characteristics, ibid. 26. See also the discussion in Macuch, "Pahlavi Literature," 178–79.

59. See Geoffrey Herman, "Ahasuerus, the Former Stable-Master of Belshazzar, and the Wicked Alexander of Macedon: Two Parallels between the Babylonian Talmud and Persian Sources," *Association for Jewish Studies Review* 29 (2005): 283–97, esp. 288–93; Jeffrey L. Rubenstein, "Astrology and the Head of the Academy," in *Shoshannat Yaakov: Jewish and Iranian Studies in Honor of Yaakov Elman*, ed. Shai Secunda and Steven Fine (Boston: Brill, 2012), 301–21, esp. 315–16.

60. For an overview, see Macuch, "Pahlavi Literature," 160–72.

61. This piece of *andarz* literature is attributed to this famous sage from the time of Khusrow I, but its exact date of composition is unknown; see Macuch, "Pahlavi Literature," 165–66.

62. This work is sometimes called *The Book of the Counsels of Zoroaster* (*Pand-Nāmag ī Zardušt*). For the text and translation, see J. C. Tarapore, *Pahlavi Andarz-Nāmak, Containing Chītak Andarz ī Pōryōtkaêshān; or, The Selected Admonitions of the Pōryōtkaêshān and Five Other Andarz Texts* (Bombay: The Trustees of the Parsee Punchayet Funds and Properties, 1933); Maneck Fardunji Kanga, *Čītak Handarž i Pōryōtkēšān: A Pahlavi Text Edited, Transcribed, and Translated into English, with Introduction and a Critical Glossary, and with a Foreword by Professor H. W. Bailey* (Bombay: M. F. Kanga, 1960).

63. According to Cereti, "Middle Persian Literature," the language of this text can perhaps be dated to the late Sasanian period. Macuch, "Pahlavi Literature," 169, agrees that it was "most probably written in the Sasanian period, during the reign of Xosrau I, but contains much older material." See Tehmuras Dinshaw Anklesaria, *Dânâk-u Mainyô-i Khard: Pahlavi, Pazand, and Sanskrit Texts* (Bombay: The Fort Printing Press, 1913), which does not have a translation; the Persian glossary by Ahmad Tafazzoli, *Vāža-nāma-ye mīnū-ye ḵarad* (Tehran: Iranian Culture Foundation, 1969); and the English translation, E. W. West, *The Book of the Mainyo-i-Khard: The Pazand and Sanskrit Texts (in Roman Characters) as Arranged by Neriosengh Dhaval in the Fifteenth Century, with an English Translation, a Glossary of the Pazand Text, Containing the Sanskrit, Persian and Pahlavi Equivalents, a Sketch of Pazand Grammar, and an Introduction* (Stuttgart: Grüninger, 1871).

64. This epic poem shows traces of a Parthian rendering, but its precise compositional history is unclear; see Macuch, "Pahlavi Literature," 177, and the edition by Davoud Monchi-Zadeh, *Die Geschichte Zarēr's* (Uppsala: Almqvist and Wiksell International, 1981).

65. Macuch, "Pahlavi Literature," 156–57, who states that it is an Islamic-era work but that it contains earlier traditions that may have been brought together in the sixth century. The only complete version of this work is in Pāzand, with some Pahlavi fragments also extant; see the edition by Giuseppe Messina, *Libro apocalittico persiano Ayātkār i Žāmāspīk* (Rome: Pontificio Istituto Biblico, 1939). See also Harold W. Bailey, "To the Zamasp-Namak,

I," *Bulletin of the School of Oriental Studies* 6 (1930): 55–85, and "To the Zamasp-Namak, II," *Bulletin of the School of Oriental Studies* 6 (1931): 581–600.

66. On the conversion of Wištāsp, see *Dēnk. VII* chapter 4.63–7.38 (Marijan Molé, *La légende de Zoroastre selon les textes pehlevis* [Paris: Klincksieck, 1967], 52–79).

67. On the debates over the date of this work, see Macuch, "Pahlavi Literature," 154–55; Cereti, "On the Date," 252, argues that it is made up of content from both the late Sasanian and the early Islamic era, and that Iranian apocalyptic traditions generally date from the seventh to the eighth century.

68. Macuch, "Pahlavi Literature," 159–60, argues that this work contains older content that was redacted in the post-Sasanian era. For two editions of this text, see Philippe Gignoux, *Le livre d'Ardā Vīrāz: Translittération, transcription et traduction du texte pehlevi* (Paris: Éditions Recherche sur les Civilisations, 1984) and Fereydun Vahman, *Ardā Wirāz Nāmag: The Iranian "Divina Commedia"* (London: Curzon Press, 1986).

69. Macuch, "Pahlavi literature," 138: "It is impossible to date the first compilation of the *Bundahišn* (which may well have been undertaken in late Sasanian times), since the text has gone through different redactions down to the last important one in the second half of the ninth century (the final redaction is even dated according to the year 1178 given in the text itself to the 12th century)."

70. On the *Letter of Tansar*, attributed to the high priest Tansar during the reign of Ardashir, see Macuch, "Pahlavi Literature," 181–82. What is attested of this work today is a thirteenth-century Persian translation of the mid-eighth century Zoroastrian convert to Islam ibn al-Muqaffa's Arabic translation of the original Middle Persian text. For an English translation with extensive introduction, see Mary Boyce, *The Letter of Tansar* (Rome: Istituto Italiano per il Medio ed Estremo Oriente, 1968), esp. 2–8.

71. On political treatises, see Macuch, "Pahlavi Literature," 181–83. On the *Testament of Ardashir*, see Mario Grignaschi, "Quelques spécimens de la littérature sassanide conservés dans les bibliothèques d'Istanbul," *Journal Asiatique* 254 (1966): 1–142.

72. On the *Xwadāy-Nāmag*, see Macuch, "Pahlavi Literature," 173–77; Shapur Shahbazi, "On the *Xwadāy-Nāmag*," in *Papers in Honor of Professor Ehsan Yarshater* (Leiden: Brill, 1990), 208–29, esp. 213–15 on its various datings, including its compilation in the era of Khusrow I. For more on the Iranian national tradition, see Ehsan Yarshater, "Iranian National History," in *The Cambridge History of Iran*, vol. 3.1, *The Seleucid, Parthian, and Sasanian Periods*, ed. Ehsan Yarshater (Cambridge: Cambridge University Press, 1983), 359–480.

73. Macuch, "Pahlavi Literature," 174.

74. On the decline of the Zoroastrian priesthood and rise of Islam in Iran, see Aptin Khanbaghi, "De-Zoroastrianization and Islamization: The Two Phases of Iran's Religious Transition, 747–837 CE," *Comparative Studies of South Asia, Africa, and the Middle East* 29 (2009): 201–12, esp. 206, who argues that the de-Zoroastrianization of Iran occurred in the eighth century, whereas the ninth century saw its Islamization. Elite Persian culture and language remained influential in the early Islamic Empire as well. On this topic, see Hugh Kennedy, "Survival of Iranianness," in *The Rise of Islam*, vol. 4 of *The Idea of Iran*, ed. Vesta Sarkhosh Curtis and Sarah Stewart (New York: I. B. Tauris, 2009), 13–29.

75. See Philip G. Kreyenbroek, "The Zoroastrian Priesthood after the Fall of the Sasanian Empire," in *Transition Periods in Iranian History: Actes du Symposium de Fribourg-en-Brisgau, 22–24 Mai 1985* (Paris: Association pour l'Avancement des Études Iraniennes, 1987),

151–66, esp. 153–54 and 165–66. For more on the status of priests in the post-Sasanian period, see also Kreyenbroek, "The *Dādestān ī Dēnīg* on Priests," *Indo-Iranian Journal* 30 (1987): 185–208, esp. 196–97 on the economic tension between *hērbeds* and *hāwišts* as a result of the latter's status as practitioners in the early Islamic context, thus demonstrating yet another example of how post-Sasanian sources do not accurately represent the Sasanian priesthood.

76. Kreyenbroek, "Zoroastrian Priesthood," 153.

77. See also Albert de Jong, "The Contribution of the Magi," in *Birth of the Persian Empire,* vol. 1 of *The Idea of Iran,* ed. Vesta Sarkhosh Curtis and Sarah Stewart (New York: I.B. Tauris, 2005), 85–99, esp. 92, on how Pahlavi sources rarely use the title *mog,* which is ubiquitously attested in Sasanian seals.

78. Kreyenbroek, "Zoroastrian Priesthood," 160.

79. Ibid. 165.

80. For one recent study that compares the rabbis and Persian priests using the post-Sasanian Pahlavi books the *Dādestān ī Dēnīg* and the *Zand ī Wahman Yasn* as sources for understanding recitation practices, see Moulie Vidas, *Tradition and the Formation of the Talmud* (Princeton: Princeton University Press, 2014), 150–66.

81. On this work, see Jean de Menasce, *Le troisième livre du Dēnkart, traduit du pehlevi* (Paris: Klincksieck, 1973).

82. The translation into French forty years ago by de Menasce, *Troisième livre,* is still the best resource; see also Shaul Shaked, "Zoroastrian Polemics against Jews in the Sasanian and Early Islamic Period," in *Irano-Judaica II: Studies Relating to Jewish Contacts with Persian Culture throughout the Ages,* ed. Shaul Shaked and Amnon Netzer (Jerusalem: Ben-Zvi Institute, 1990), 85–104.

83. See Touraj Daryaee, "Apocalypse Now: Zoroastrian Reflections on the Early Islamic Centuries," *Medieval Encounters* 4 (1998): 188–202, with numerous examples of primary sources translated therein. On the Arabs in Middle Persian texts, see *ZWY* chapters 4.59, 6.10, and 9.10 (Carlo G. Cereti, *The Zand ī Wahman Yasn: A Zoroastrian Apocalypse* [Rome: Istituto Italiano per il Medio ed Estremo Oriente, 1995], 157, 161, and 167); *Dēnk. III* chapters 176, 308, and 420 (de Menasce, *Troisième livre,* 185, 297, and 380); *Dēnk. VII* chapters 1.34 and 8.47 (Molé, *Légende,* 10–11 and 88–89); *Zādsp.* chapter 3.13 (Philippe Gignoux and Ahmad Tafazzoli, *Anthologie de Zādspram* [Paris: Association pour l'Avancement des Études Iraniennes, 1993], 42–43); *Ayādgār ī Jāmāspīg* chapter 16.2 (Messina, *Libro,* 66 and 112); *Bund.* chapters 0.2, 14.38, 31.37, 33.1–22, 36.0, and 36.9 (Behramgore Tahmuras Anklesaria, *Zand-Ākāsīh: Iranian or Greater Bundahišn* [Bombay: Rahnumae Mazdayasnan Sabha, 1956], 2–3, 134–35, 268–69, 272–79, and 304–7). For a transcription of these passages in the *Bundahišn,* see Fazlollah Pakzad, *Bundahišn—Zoroastriche Kosmogonie und Kosmologie,* vol. 1, *Kritische Edition* (Tehran: Centre for the Great Islamic Encyclopaedia, 2005), 2, 193, 357, 362–67, 410, and 414. See also Khanbaghi, "De-Zoroastrianization," 211, citing a telling line from the *Dēnkard:* "The state of affairs now evident is indicative of how Iranian rule has come to an end in the country of Iran."

84. This is *Bund.* chapter 33.21–22 (Behramgore Tahmuras Anklesaria, *Zand-Ākāsīh: Iranian or Greater Bundahišn* [Bombay: Rahnumae Mazdayasnan Sabha, 1956], 276–79), a later addition to the work, translated by Daryaee, "Apocalypse Now," 192.

85. This Islamicized work was composed in the ninth century, though it may contain some older materials; see Cereti, "Middle Persian Literature." Macuch, "Pahlavi Literature,"

149–50, dates the composition of the *Škand Gumānīg Wizār* to the ninth century at the hands of Mardānfarrox son of Ohrmazddād. For the French translation, see Jean de Menasce, *Une apologétique mazdéenne du IXe siècle: Škand-gumānīk vičār, la solution décisive des doutes* (Fribourg: Librairie de l'Université, 1945).

86. See Jacob Neusner, "A Zoroastrian Critique of Judaism (Škand Gumanik Vičar, Chapters Thirteen and Fourteen: A New Translation and Exposition)," *Journal of the American Oriental Society* 83 (1963): 283–94.

87. Macuch, "Pahlavi Literature," 150.

88. De Jong, "Zoroastrian Religious Polemics and Their Contexts," 60–61.

89. See Yuhan Sohrab-Dinshaw Vevaina, "Miscegenation, 'Mixture,' and 'Mixed Iron': The Hermeneutics, Historiography, and Cultural Poesis of the 'Four Ages' in Zoroastrianism," in *Revelation, Literature, and Community in Late Antiquity*, ed. Philippa Townsend and Moulie Vidas (Tübingen: Mohr Siebeck, 2011), 237–69, esp. 245.

90. On the *Rivāyat ī Ēmēd ī Ašawahištān*, including its usefulness in the study of Sasanian laws of marriage and inheritance, see Macuch, "Pahlavi Literature," 145. For a critical edition, see Nezhat Safa-Isfehani, *Rivāyat-i Hēmīt-i Ašawahištān: Edition, Transcription and Translation—A Study in Zoroastrian Law* (Cambridge, Mass.: Harvard University Press, 1980). See also other *Rivāyats*, including Behramgore Tahmuras Anklesaria, *The Pahlavi Rivāyat of Āturfarnbag and Farnbag-Srōš*, part 1, *Text and Transcription* (Bombay: Cama Athornan Institute, 1969); Bamanji Nusserwanji Dhabhar, *The Persian Rivayats of Hormazyar Framarz and Others* (Bombay: K. R. Cama Oriental Institute, 1932). See also the unique work that is part of this genre, Kaikhusroo M. Jamaspasa and Helmut Humbach, eds., *Pursišnīhā: A Zoroastrian Catechism*, part 1, *Text, Translation, Notes* (Wiesbaden: Harrassowitz, 1971). As Macuch, "Pahlavi Literature," 148–49, states, this latter book is a post-Sasanian work that is focused on preserving Zoroastrianism against the threat of conversion in an early Islamic environment.

91. See the flawed attempt to compare the Bavli with the *Rivāyats* by Jacob Neusner, *Judaism and Zoroastrianism at the Dusk of Late Antiquity: How Two Ancient Faiths Wrote Down Their Great Traditions* (Atlanta: Scholars Press, 1993), 53–86.

92. For more on these two figures, see Macuch, "Pahlavi Literature," 131. Scholars are not in full agreement on the identification of these two men, on which see Jaleh Amouzgar and Ahmad Tafazzoli, *Le cinquième livre du Dēnkard* (Paris: Association pour l'Avancement des Études Iraniennes, 2000), 15–17.

93. See Homi F. Chacha, *Gajastak Abâlish* (Bombay: The Trustees of the Parsi Punchayet Funds and Properties, 1936). For a comparison of this source with the Bavli, see Secunda, *Iranian Talmud*, 129–31.

94. According to Mary Boyce, *Zoroastrians: Their Religious Beliefs and Practices* (Boston: Routledge, 1979), 153, Ādurfarnbag ī Farroxzādān's successor and son Zardušt may have converted to Islam during the reign of Mutawakkil circa the middle of the ninth century. This demonstrates the personal impact that Islam had on the Pahlavi authors.

95. On these figures, see Macuch, "Pahlavi Literature," 141–45; the introduction to the *Dādestān ī Dēnīg* (*DīD* 23–24); and the introduction to the *Zādspram* (*Zādsp.* 21).

96. See the conservative view in *DīD* 24: this work "belongs to a group of Pahlavi texts which appear almost wholly Sasanian in its content and references," and was likely "written several years before 881 A.D." The *Dādestān ī Dēnīg* is accompanied by a separate, tenth-

century work by an anonymous author referred to as the *Pahlavi Rivāyat Accompanying the Dādestān ī Dēnīg*, on which see the two volumes by A. V. Williams, *The Pahlavi Rivāyat Accompanying the Dādestān ī Dēnīg*, part 1, *Transliteration, Transcription and Glossary* (Copenhagen: Munksgaard, 1990), and *The Pahlavi Rivāyat Accompanying the Dādestān ī Dēnīg*, part 2, *Translation, Commentary and Pahlavi Text* (Copenhagen: Munksgaard, 1990).

97. See Bamanji Nusserwanji Dhabhar, *The Epistles of Mânûshchîhar* (Bombay: The Trustees of the Parsee Panchayat Funds and Properties, 1912). The writings of Manūščihr represent a clear rupture from previous works in the Middle Persian tradition.

98. See the critical edition by Philippe Gignoux and Ahmad Tafazzoli, *Anthologie de Zādspram* (Paris: Association pour l'Avancement des Études Iraniennes, 1993). Macuch, "Pahlavi Literature," 139, dates it to around 880 C.E.

99. For the argument that the diversity of Sasanian Zoroastrian beliefs and schools of thought on such topics as eschatology or the powers of man is not reflected in the Pahlavi books of the ninth and tenth centuries, see Shaked, *Dualism*, 32, 57, 93–98. See also Pourshariati, *Decline*, 338, on the difficulties of using foreign or Middle Persian sources for researching Zoroastrian religion in the Sasanian period. The question of sectarianism in late antique Zoroastrianism is complicated and debated, in part because of the errant attempts by past scholars to characterize Zurvanism as a Zoroastrian sect. On this now-defunct theory, see Robert C. Zaehner, *Zurvan: A Zoroastrian Dilemma* (Oxford: Clarendon Press, 1955), and the refutation of Zurvanism as a "scholarly invention which lacks historical substance," by Shaul Shaked, "The Myth of Zurvan: Cosmogony and Eschatology," in *Messiah and Christos: Studies in the Jewish Origins of Christianity, Presented to David Flusser on the Occasion of His Seventy-Fifth Birthday*, ed. I. Gruenwald, S. Shaked, and G. G. Stroumsa (Tübingen: Mohr Siebeck, 1992), 219–40, esp. 228. For a key essay on the issue of sectarianism, see Marijan Molé, "Le problème des sectes zoroastriennes dans les livres pehlevis," *Oriens* 13–14 (1960–61): 1–28.

100. On the heretics Zarduštagan and Mazdak, both of whom according to later sources had ties to the Zoroastrian priesthood, see Patricia Crone, "Kavād's Heresy and Mazdak's Revolt," *Iran* 29 (1991): 21–42, including the references in 37 n. 72.

101. For more on Zoroastrian polytheism, see the ninth- or tenth-century Middle Persian text containing thirty prayers for the deities who watch over the days of the month, edited by Enrico G. Raffaelli, *The Sīh-rōzag in Zoroastrianism: A Textual and Historico-Religious Analysis* (New York: Routledge, 2014). On the importance of the worship of Mihr and Anahita, and the limits of using Pahlavi sources for their study, see Shaked, *Dualism*, 91-98.

102. Ibid. 93.

103. Ibid. 14–15 on cosmogony and eschatology, and 97. Shaked argues for three types of religious expression in the Sasanian era—namely, elite, popular (magic), and common. On the elite versus popular dichotomy, see below, chapter 6.

104. Cereti, "Primary Sources," 18.

105. The date of the invention of the script and writing down of the Avesta has long been debated, though there is a consensus that it occurred in the Sasanian era, probably sometime between the fourth and the sixth century. Earlier scholars (Henning and Hoffman) dated it to the fourth, and still others (Bailey and Boyce) to the fifth or sixth century. On this topic, see the summary in Michael Stausberg, "The Invention of a Canon: The Case of Zoroastrianism," in *Canonization and Decanonization: Papers Presented to the International*

Conference of the Leiden Institute for the Study of Religions (LISOR), Held at Leiden 9–10 January 1997, ed. A. van der Kooij and K. van der Toorn (Leiden: Brill, 1998), 257–78, esp. 262 and n. 14 for the literature.

106. See Mary Boyce, *Zoroastrianism: Its Antiquity and Constant Vigour* (Costa Mesa: Mazda Publishers, 1992); Boyce, "On the Orthodoxy of Sasanian Zoroastrianism," *Bulletin of the School of Oriental and African Studies* 59 (1996): 11–28. But see the convincing critiques of notions of Zoroastrian conservatism and orthodoxy by Albert de Jong, *Traditions of the Magi: Zoroastrianism in Greek and Latin Literature* (Leiden: Brill, 1997), 53–57 and 67. To be fair, Boyce sometimes does acknowledge the impact of the author's own time period on the compositions; see, e.g., Boyce, *Zoroastrians*, 155.

107. Macuch, "Pahlavi Literature," 120–21.

108. On these sources, see below. Resources include the magical seals of Sasanian Iran presented in Rika Gyselen, *Sceaux magiques en Iran sassanide* (Paris: Association pour l'Avancement des Études Iraniennes, 1995); Sasanian coins that have iconographic representations of fire temples and priestly attendants, on which see Robert Göbl, *Sasanian Numismatics* (Würzburg: Braunschweig, Klinkhardt, and Biermann, 1971), 17–19; remains of Sasanian Zoroastrian fire temples, as seen in Klaus Schippmann, *Die iranischen Feuerheiligtümer* (New York: De Gruyter, 1971); and Sasanian stamp seals that have images of Zoroastrian priests and fire altars, as cited in Christopher J. Brunner, *Sasanian Stamp Seals in the Metropolitan Museum of Art* (New York: The Metropolitan Museum of Art, 1978), 10 and 65.

109. On the hierarchy of Sasanian sources, see Philippe Gignoux, "Problèmes de distinction et de priorité des sources," in *Prolegomena to the Sources on the History of Pre-Islamic Central Asia*, ed. János Harmatta (Budapest: Akadémiai Kiadó, 1979), 137–41, and "Pour une nouvelle histoire de l'Iran sasanide," in *Middle Iranian Studies: Proceedings of the International Symposium Organized by the Katholieke Universiteit Leuven from the 17th to the 20th of May 1982*, ed. Wojciech Skalmowski and Alois Van Tongerloo (Leuven: Peeters, 1984), 253–62; Rika Gyselen, "Primary Sources and Historiography on the Sasanian Empire," *Studia Iranica* 38 (2009): 163–90; Cereti, "Primary Sources."

110. For examples of studies in Sasanian social or political history, see Richard N. Frye, "The Political History of Iran under the Sasanians," in *The Cambridge History of Iran*, vol. 3.1, *The Seleucid, Parthian, and Sasanian Periods*, 116–80; Ahmad Tafazzoli, *Sasanian Society* (New York: Bibliotheca Persica Press, 2000); and on the administrative structure of the empire as reconstructed from material sources, see Gyselen, *Géographie*.

111. See Rika Gyselen, *Sasanian Seals and Sealings in the A. Saeedi Collection* (Leuven: Peeters, 2007), 8. For a study of the Iranian word for "seal" or "document" (cf. MP *muhr*, "seal") as it appears in the Talmud, see *DJBA* 646 and the study by Maria Macuch, "Iranian Legal Terminology in the Babylonian Talmud in Light of Sasanian Jurisprudence," in *Irano-Judaica IV: Studies Relating to Jewish Contacts with Persian Culture throughout the Ages*, ed. Shaul Shaked and Amnon Netzer (Jerusalem: Ben-Zvi Institute, 1999), 91–101, esp. the conclusions on 96–97.

112. Guitty Azarpay, with Catherine Demos, Edward Gans, Lydia Gans, Wolfgang Heimpel, Anne Draffkorn Kilmer, Sanjyot Mehendale, and Jeanette Zerneke, "Sasanian Seals from the Collection of the Late Edward Gans, at the University of California, Berkeley," online: www.ecai.org/sasanianweb/docs/sasanianseals.html, 20.

113. For an overview of Sasanian glyptics, see Cereti, "Primary Sources," 44–50. For more on the Sasanian seals and bullae used among Sasanian officials in the late sixth century, including those presumably stored in a central imperial archive or royal treasury either housed in Ctesiphon or itinerant, see Gyselen, *Sasanian Seals and Sealings*, 12–14. On magian seals, see also Gyselen, "Les sceaux des mages de l'Iran sassanide," in *Au carrefour des religions: Mélanges offerts à Philippe Gignoux*, ed. Rika Gyselen (Bures-sur-Yvette: Groupe pour l'Étude de la Civilisation du Moyen-Orient, 1995), 121–50.

114. Based on the *Mādayān ī Hazār Dādestān* and the glyptics, Gyselen, *Géographie*, 3, dates the offices of the *mowbed* and *āmārgar* to Kawad I (488–96 and 498–531) and the *dādwar* to Khusrow I.

115. Azarpay, "Sasanian Seals," 29.

116. The Aramaic incantation bowls dating circa the fourth through seventh centuries C.E. have been critically edited in several recent volumes by Shaul Shaked, James Nathan Ford, and Siam Bhayro with contributions from Matthew Morgenstern and Naama Vilozny, eds., *Aramaic Bowl Spells: Jewish Babylonian Aramaic Bowls* (Boston: Brill, 2013), and see 1–8 for the provenance and dating of this collection; and Dan Levene, *Jewish Aramaic Curse Texts from Late-Antique Mesopotamia: "May These Curses Go Out and Flee"* (Boston: Brill, 2013). Shaked notes in *Aramaic Bowl Spells*, xv, that these are part of nine volumes that will be published, including Mandaic, Syriac, and Pahlavi spells. Previous volumes include James Montgomery, *Aramaic Incantation Texts from Nippur* (Philadelphia: University Museum, 1913); Joseph Naveh and Shaul Shaked, *Amulets and Magic Bowls: Aramaic Incantations of Late Antiquity*, 3rd ed. (Jerusalem: Magnes Press, 1998); Dan Levene, *A Corpus of Magic Bowls: Incantation Texts in Jewish Aramaic from Late Antiquity* (New York: Kegan Paul, 2003). For an overview of the value of the bowls to the study of ancient Jewish magic, see Gideon Bohak, *Ancient Jewish Magic: A History* (New York: Cambridge University Press, 2008), 183–93.

117. See Dan Levene and Gideon Bohak, "A Babylonian Jewish Aramaic Incantation Bowl with a List of Deities and Toponyms," *Jewish Studies Quarterly* 19 (2012): 56–72, esp. 65–67.

118. For an incantation on prosperity in business, see Dan Levene and Siam Bhayro, "'Bring to the Gates . . . upon a Good Smell and upon Good Fragrances': An Aramaic Incantation Bowl for Success in Business," *Archiv für Orientforschung* 51 (2005–6): 242–46.

119. Shaul Shaked, "Notes on the Pahlavi Amulet and Sasanian Courts of Law," *Bulletin of the Asia Institute* 7 (1993): 165–72, esp. 165.

120. For an early statement on the potential for comparison between the bowls and Bavli, see Julian Obermann, "Two Magic Bowls: New Incantation Texts from Mesopotamia," *The American Journal of Semitic Languages and Literatures* 57 (1940): 1–31, esp. 29: "Indeed a corpus of all extant incantation texts from Mesopotamia—an urgent scientific desideratum in itself—is likely to yield aid of first magnitude to the critical study of the Talmud." See also the discussion of the antiarchaeological slant of "Talmudic history" in an article by Jacob Neusner and Jonathan Z. Smith, "Archaeology and Babylonian Jewry," in *Near Eastern Archaeology in the Twentieth Century: Essays in Honor of Nelson Glueck*, ed. James A. Sanders (Garden City: Doubleday, 1970), 331–47.

121. According to Shaked, *Aramaic Bowl Spells*, xiii (preface), the Schøyen collection includes 654 Aramaic bowls and jugs from around the fifth to the seventh or the eighth century. See also Bohak, *Ancient Jewish Magic*, 183, on how there have been only several

hundred bowls published out of more than 1,500 in existence. Shaked's new project will add to this number.

122. See Secunda, *Iranian Talmud,* 7, 27–28, and (discussing Elman) 114.

123. On various occasions Secunda acknowledges the differences between the texts but eschews them in favor of discussing similarities; see, for instance, Secunda, *Iranian Talmud,* 63, where he analyzes the Talmudic texts on the *bei abeidan* vis-à-vis a *Dēnkard* passage that may stem from the late Sasanian era: "But regardless of the differences, there seem to be enough similarities to offer a final, admittedly speculative claim: in a place that Jews referred to as a *bei abeidan,* Sasanian authorities gathered scrolls and people of various extractions in order to explore, discuss, and dispute their learned traditions in an effort to 'recover' the sacred Zoroastrian tradition."

124. Ibid. 111.

125. Ibid. 50.

126. Ibid. 33.

127. Ibid.

128. Ibid. 131.

129. Ibid. 127.

130. Ibid. 42-43 and 50-63.

131. Ibid. 42–45.

132. Ibid. 50.

133. Ibid. 132.

3. RABBINIC PORTRAYALS OF PERSIANS AS OTHERS

1. On the word טבהקי, "meat dish," see *DJBA* 492, and cf. NP *tabāha,* "stewed meat," in Francis Joseph Steingass, *A Comprehensive Persian-English Dictionary* (London: Routledge, 1892), 278. The loanword is repeated a second time consecutively in MS Vatican 109 and MS Oxford Opp. Add. fol. 23. On the etymology of this word, see Shaul Shaked, "Between Iranian and Aramaic: Iranian Words Concerning Food in Jewish Babylonian Aramaic, with Some Notes on the Aramaic Heterograms in Iranian," in *Irano-Judaica V: Studies Relating to Jewish Contacts with Persian Culture throughout the Ages,* ed. Shaul Shaked and Amnon Netzer (Jerusalem: Ben-Zvi Institute, 2003), 120–37, esp. 124–25 on how it is perhaps related to "poor; ruined" (MP *tabāh*) and, by extension, "spoiling by heat." The author also notes that it is a plural form (124 n. 19).

2. *B. 'Erub.* 29b (MS Vatican 109).

3. Although MS Vatican 109 (which is the principal witness according to *DJBA* 55) reads "Rava," it is the only witness that does so. I have therefore translated this name according to the majority reading, "Rabbah." These names are often confused, as explained in Shamma Friedman, "The Orthography of the Names Rabbah and Rava in the Babylonian Talmud," *Sinai* 110 (1992): 140–64 (Hebrew).

4. The printed editions read והתנן, whereas MS Vatican 109 and MS Munich 95 read either והא תניא or והתניא.

5. The verse from Exodus 12:9, which describes the Israelites' preparations for the Exodus, reads: "Do not eat any of it raw [נא], or cooked in any way with water, but roasted—head, legs, and entrails—over the fire."

6. See *DJBA* 77, and Shaked, "Between Iranian and Aramaic," 124.

7. On these words, which appear multiple times in the Talmud, see *DJBA* 91 and 586.

8. See *b. Qidd.* 33a, where Abaye stands up as soon as he sees the ears of Rav Yosef's donkey in the distance.

9. See the similar phrase in *b. 'Erub.* 28a, in reference to Babylonia ("Is Babylonia the majority of the world?"), applied to the question regarding the use of green grain in an *eruv*.

10. For overviews of this field's historiography, see Yaakov Elman, "'Up to the Ears' in Horses' Necks (B.M. 108a): On Sasanian Agricultural Policy and Private 'Eminent Domain,'" *Jewish Studies: An Internet Journal* 3 (2004): 95–149, esp. 95–101; Geoffrey Herman, "Ahasuerus, the Former Stable-Master of Belshazzar, and the Wicked Alexander of Macedon: Two Parallels between the Babylonian Talmud and Persian Sources," *Association for Jewish Studies Review* 29 (2005): 283–97, esp. 283–88; Shai Secunda, *The Iranian Talmud: Reading the Bavli in Its Sasanian Context* (Philadelphia: University of Pennsylvania Press, 2013), 10–14.

11. For examples, see Alexander Kohut, *Ueber die jüdische Angelologie und Daemonologie in ihrer Abhängigkeit vom Parsismus* (Leipzig: Brockhaus, 1866), and "Parsic and Jewish Legends of the First Man," *Jewish Quarterly Review* 3 (1891): 231–50.

12. Isidor Scheftelowitz, *Die altpersische Religion und das Judentum: Unterschiede, Übereinstimmungen und gegenseitige Beeinflussungen* (Giessen: Verlag von Alfred Töpelmann, 1920). Although the book does point to some differences between the two religions, it is, as is typical, mostly concerned with purported similarities between them.

13. Zsigmond Telegdi, "Essai sur la phonétique des emprunts iraniens en araméen talmudique," *Journal Asiatique* 226 (1935): 177–256. For other research in this area, see my discussion of the loanwords below. Earlier philological research should also be noted here, including Paul de Lagarde, *Gesammelte Abhandlungen* (Leipzig: Brockhaus, 1866); Joseph Perles, *Etymologische Studien zur Kunde der rabbinischen Sprache und Alterthümer* (Breslau: Schletter, 1871); Jacob Levy, *Wörterbuch über die Talmudim und Midraschim*, 4 vols., 2nd ed., ed. Lazarus Goldschmidt (Berlin, Harz, 1924), and *Neuhebräisches und chaldäisches Wörterbuch über die Talmudim und Midraschim*, 4 vols. (Leipzig: Brockhaus, 1876–89).

14. On Schorr, see Ezra Spicehandler, "Joshua Heschel Schorr—The Mature Years," *Hebrew Union College Annual* 40–41 (1969–70): 503–28, esp. 521, and "Dina de Magista and Bei Dawar: Notes on Gentile Courts in Talmudic Babylonia," *Hebrew Union College Annual* 26 (1955): 333–54; Daniel Sperber, "Bab Nahara," *Iranica Antiqua* 8 (1968): 70–73; E.S. Rosenthal, "For the Talmudic Dictionary—Talmudica Iranica," in *Irano-Judaica: Studies Relating to Jewish Contacts with Persian Culture throughout the Ages*, ed. Shaul Shaked (Jerusalem: Ben-Zvi Institute, 1982), 38–134 (Hebrew). For the extensive publications of Shaul Shaked, see the bibliography to this book.

15. Louis Ginzberg, *Introductory Essay: The Palestinian Talmud* (New York: The Jewish Theological Seminary of America, 1941), xxxii.

16. See Shaul Shaked, "Iranian Influence on Judaism: First Century B.C.E. to Second Century C.E.," in *The Cambridge History of Judaism*, vol. 1, *Introduction; The Persian Period*, ed. W.D. Davies and Louis Finkelstein (New York: Cambridge University Press, 1984), 308–25; David Winston, "The Iranian Component in the Bible, Apocrypha, and Qumran: A Review of the Evidence," *History of Religions* 5 (1966): 183–216.

17. Sperber, "Bab Nahara," 70.

18. See this book's conclusion for more on how the Talmud is a source of information for Iranists.

19. Jacob Neusner, "How Much Iranian in Jewish Babylonia?" *Journal of the American Oriental Society* 92 (1975): 184–90, esp. 190.

20. Jacob Neusner, "Talmud, Persian Elements in," *Encyclopaedia Iranica*, online ed., 2005: www.iranicaonline.org/articles/talmud-persian-elements-in-2.

21. See Jacob Neusner, *Judaism and Zoroastrianism at the Dusk of Late Antiquity: How Two Ancient Faiths Wrote Down Their Great Traditions* (Atlanta: Scholars Press, 1993), and "A Zoroastrian Critique of Judaism (Škand Gumanik Vičar, Chapters Thirteen and Fourteen: A New Translation and Exposition)," *Journal of the American Oriental Society* 83 (1963): 283–94. To be fair, in the former publication (pp. 75–76), Neusner does raise some interesting comparative points about the differences between the collective voice of the sages in the Bavli vis-à-vis the authorial voice of the *Rivāyats*. Similarly, although the latter publication's analysis of the *Škand Gumānīg Wizār* assumes too much knowledge of rabbinic and biblical stories on the part of the *Škand*'s author, Neusner's formal exposition of this excerpt has some commendable points.

22. For a comparable assessment of the influence of Jacob Neusner's skepticism on the study of the Iranian context of the Talmud, see Secunda, *Iranian Talmud*, 152 n. 32.

23. See Yaakov Elman, "Acculturation to Elite Persian Norms and Modes of Thought in the Babylonian Jewish Community of Late Antiquity," in *Neti'ot le-David: Jubilee Volume for David Weiss Halivni*, ed. Ephraim B. Halivni, Zvi A. Steinfeld, and Yaakov Elman (Jerusalem: Orhot, 2004), 31–56.

24. Elman, "'Up to the Ears,'" 101.

25. See Elman, "Middle Persian Culture and Babylonian Sages: Accommodation and Resistance in the Shaping of Rabbinic Legal Tradition," in *The Cambridge Companion to the Talmud and Rabbinic Literature*, ed. Charlotte Elisheva Fonrobert and Martin S. Jaffee (Cambridge: Cambridge University Press, 2007), 165–97, esp. 166. For another take on how otherness and differences imply closeness as opposed to distance, see William Scott Green, "Otherness Within: Towards a Theory of Difference in Rabbinic Judaism," in *"To See Ourselves as Others See Us": Christians, Jews, "Others" in Late Antiquity*, ed. Jacob Neusner and Ernest S. Frerichs (Chico: Scholars Press, 1985), 49–69, esp. 50.

26. An exception would be Yaakov Elman, "Marriage and Marital Property in Rabbinic and Sasanian Law," in *Rabbinic Law in Its Roman and Near Eastern Context*, ed. Catherine Hezser (Tübingen: Mohr Siebeck, 2003), 227–76, esp. 259–76 on how the black plague and demographic crisis affected the legal status of women.

27. See Shai Secunda, "Talmudic Text and Iranian Context: On the Development of Two Talmudic Narratives," *Association for Jewish Studies Review* 33 (2009): 45–69; Yishai Kiel, "Selected Topics in Laws of Ritual Defilement: Between the Babylonian Talmud and Pahlavi Literature" (Ph.D. dissertation, Hebrew University of Jerusalem, 2011; Hebrew).

28. See Elman, "Middle Persian Culture," on the idea of acculturation between Jews and Persians.

29. Rosalind Shaw and Charles Stewart, "Introduction: Problematizing Syncretism," in *Syncretism/Anti-Syncretism: The Politics of Religious Synthesis*, ed. Rosalind Shaw and Charles Stewart (New York: Routledge, 1994), 1–24, esp. 6.

30. Yaakov Elman, "The Babylonian Talmud in Its Historical Context," in *Printing the Talmud: From Bomberg to Schottenstein,* ed. Sharon Liberman Mintz and Gabriel M. Goldstein (New York: Yeshiva University Museum, 2005), 19–27, esp. 27.

31. See Maria Macuch, "An Iranian Legal Term in the Babylonian Talmud and in Sasanian Jurisprudence: *dastwar(īh),*" in *Irano-Judaica VI: Studies Relating to Jewish Contacts with Persian Culture throughout the Ages,* ed. Shaul Shaked and Amnon Netzer (Jerusalem: Ben-Zvi Institute, 2008), 126–38, esp. 136, on *b. Qidd.* 60b and *b. ʿArak.* 28a: "I take these two passages as further proof that the rabbis were well acquainted with Sasanian legal terminology and that they employed it with full knowledge of its juridical implications and its technical meaning."

32. For more on Iranian-Jewish names, see Tal Ilan, with Kerstin Hünefeld, *Lexicon of Jewish Names in Late Antiquity,* part 4, *The Eastern Diaspora, 330 BCE–650 CE* (Tübingen: Mohr Siebeck, 2011), 163–256.

33. On the Persian background of the Rav Kahana story, see Daniel Sperber, "On the Unfortunate Adventures of Rav Kahana: A Passage of Saboraic Polemic from Sasanian Persia," in *Irano-Judaica: Studies Relating to Jewish Contacts with Persian Culture throughout the Ages,* ed. Shaul Shaked (Jerusalem: Ben-Zvi Institute, 1982), 83–100; Geoffrey Herman, "The Story of Rav Kahana (BT Baba Qamma 117a–b) in Light of Armeno-Persian Sources," in *Irano-Judaica VI,* ed. Shaked and Netzer (Jerusalem: Ben-Zvi Institute, 2008), 53–68. On Rabbah bar bar Ḥanah, see Reuven Kiperwasser, "Rabba bar bar Channa's Voyages," *Jerusalem Studies in Hebrew Literature* 22 (2008): 215–42 (Hebrew). For other relevant studies by this author, see Reuven Kiperwasser and Dan D. Y. Shapira, "Irano-Talmudica I: The Three-Legged Ass and *Ridyā* in B. Taʿanith—Some Observations about Mythic Hydrology in the Babylonian Talmud and in Ancient Iran," *Association for Jewish Studies Review* 32 (2008): 101–16, and "Irano-Talmudica II: Leviathan, Behemoth, and the 'Domestication' of Iranian Mythological Creatures in Eschatological Narratives of the Babylonian Talmud," in *Shoshannat Yaakov: Jewish and Iranian Studies in Honor of Yaakov Elman,* ed. Shai Secunda and Steven Fine (Boston: Brill, 2012), 203–35.

34. On the influence of Persian genres on Bavli narratives, see Geoffrey Herman, "'*One Day David Went Out for the Hunt of the Falconers*': Persian Themes in the Babylonian Talmud," in *Shoshannat Yaakov: Jewish and Iranian Studies in Honor of Yaakov Elman,* ed. Shai Secunda and Steven Fine (Boston: Brill, 2012), 111–36.

35. Isaiah Gafni, "How Babylonia Became 'Zion': Shifting Identities in Late Antiquity," in *Jewish Identities in Antiquity: Studies in Memory of Menahem Stern,* ed. Lee I. Levine and Daniel R. Schwartz (Tübingen: Mohr Siebeck, 2009), 333–48, esp. 342–48; Sperber, "On the Unfortunate Adventures of Rav Kahana," 97–99.

36. There are not many other portrayals of Persians in texts of obvious late antique Babylonian provenance. For examples of these works, the origins of some of which are still being debated, see the minor tractates of the Talmud in Abraham Cohen, ed., *The Minor Tractates of the Talmud,* 2 vols. (London: Soncino Press, 1966); the Targums, especially *Targum Onqelos,* which although having linguistic affinities with the Jewish Aramaic bowls from Mesopotamia appear to have arrived in Bavel from Palestine, as discussed in Philip S. Alexander, *The Targum of Lamentations: Translated, with a Critical Introduction, Apparatus, and Notes* (Collegeville: Liturgical Press, 2007), 12–13; and early Jewish mysticism, on which

see Ra'anan S. Boustan, Martha Himmelfarb, and Peter Schäfer, eds., *Hekhalot Literature in Context: Between Byzantium and Babylonia* (Tübingen: Mohr Siebeck, 2013). See also the portrayals of the Persian priests in *Tanna de-be Eliyahu*, another work whose date and provenance are debated. According to H. L. Strack and Günter Stemberger, *Introduction to the Talmud and Midrash*, 2nd ed. (Minneapolis: Fortress Press, 1996), 340–41, even though some scholars argue that it originated circa the third century in Babylonia, it likely dates to around the ninth century and may not even be Babylonian in origin. On this source, see William G. Braude and Israel J. Kapstein, *Tanna dĕḇe Eliyyahu: The Lore of the School of Elijah* (Philadelphia: Jewish Publication Society, 1981), 47–50, which has a first-person narrative of the protagonist walking through Ctesiphon when he gets nabbed by the authorities and sent to the king's house. A Persian priest then tells him that he will release him if he can answer why God created creeping creatures, an allusion to Zoroastrian *xrafstar* ("noxious creature"), to which the Jew offers a lengthy response regarding creation. The dialogue continues when the Persian priest questions whether Leviticus 6:6's reference to an always-burning altar fire suggests that fire is divine. See also ibid. 102–3 on the fusion of the figures of Nimrod, Abraham, and Zoroaster in a Hellenistic setting. On the figure of Zoroaster among Hellenistic Jews, see Mary Boyce and Frantz Grenet, *A History of Zoroastrianism*, vol. 3, *Zoroastrianism under Macedonian and Roman Rule* (New York: Brill, 1991), 436–40.

37. For two books on the Persians in rabbinic literature, see Jacob Neusner, *Persia and Rome in Classical Judaism* (Lanham: University Press of America, 2008), 75–144, and Samuel Krauss, *Persia and Rome in the Talmud and Midrashim* (Jerusalem: Mossad Harav Kook, 1948; Hebrew).

38. See *b. Ber.* 46b on מחוג, which is the Middle Persian loanword *māhwāg*, found in the tradition: "The Persians are different because they converse without gesture." For a detailed study of this source in its Sasanian context, see Geoffrey Herman, *A Prince without a Kingdom: The Exilarch in the Sasanian Era* (Tübingen: Mohr Siebeck, 2012), 245–57. According to *DJBA* 654, the term, which Sokoloff translates as "gesture," also appears in *b. Ḥag.* 5b in reference to Caesar: "Does a man who does not know how to communicate by gesture communicate by gesture before the king?"

39. The Talmud references the "law of the Persians" (דינא דפרסאי) in *b. B. Bat.* 173b (MS Escorial G-I-3) and *b. B. Qam.* 58b, and "Persian law" (דינא דפרסאה) in *b. Šebu.* 34b. Rav Naḥman is the tradent in the first two of these passages and in the third acts as a judge for a man disaffected by the decision of the exilarch, "who rules according to Persian law." For more on the MSS variants and Geonic interpretations that read this latter term as a reference to a species of palm, see Geoffrey Herman, *Prince*, 208–9 and n. 196. Another allusion to Persian law is *b. B. Meṣi'a* 28b ("we are not Persians who say that a lost object belongs to the king"). The word "Persian" is also used as an adjective, as in "Persian lances" (*b. Giṭ.* 70a), "Persian camel" (*b. B. Qam.* 55a), "Persian date palm" (*b. B. Qam.* 59a), and "Persian dates" (*b. Šabb.* 110b).

40. On this, see Moses Aberbach, "Did Alexander Yannai Negotiate an Alliance with the Parthians?" in *Biblical and Related Studies Presented to Samuel Iwry*, ed. Ann Kort and Scott Morschauser (Winona Lake: Eisenbrauns, 1985), 1–4. The sources in this legend cycle include a baraita in *y. Ber.* 7:2 (11b) and *y. Naz.* 5:5 (54b); *Genesis Rabbah* 91:3; and *Ecclesiastes Rabbah* 7.12.1. For more on the Hasmoneans in rabbinic literature, see Richard Kalmin, *The Sage in Jewish Society of Late Antiquity* (New York: Routledge, 1999), 61–67. For references

to Persians qua Parthians in Midrash, see *Song of Songs Rabbah* 8.9.3 and *Lamentations Rabbah* 1.13.41. The latter contains a play on words with Lamentations 1:13's verb *paras*, which appears in the phrase "to spread out a net," with the word "Persians." The verse reads, "If you see a Persian horse tied to a grave in Israel, look out for the footsteps of the Messiah."

41. See also Isaiah Gafni, "Babylonian Rabbinic Culture," in *Cultures of the Jews*, vol. 1, *Mediterranean Origins*, ed. David Biale (New York: Schocken Books, 2002), 223–66, esp. 258 n. 57: "It is interesting to note that the gentile is referred to in the PT as 'a Persian,' whereas in the BT simply as 'nokhri'—a gentile. It appears that the PT uses 'Persian' as a generic term for gentiles in Babylonia, whereas the BT reserves the use of 'Persian' to government or church officials."

42. Sacha Stern, *Jewish Identity in Early Rabbinic Writings* (New York: Brill, 1994), 6–7 n. 33.

43. Ibid. 14–15. Stern concludes from this that the rabbis therefore lacked "interest towards non-Jewish ethnic diversity."

44. See *b. 'Abod. Zar.* 2b, *b. Giṭ.* 16b–17a, *b. Yoma* 10a.

45. On this topic, see Touraj Daryaee, "National History or Keyanid History?: The Nature of Sasanid Zoroastrian Historiography," *Iranian Studies* 28 (1995): 121–41.

46. On portrayals of Ezra and Esther, see Kalmin, *Sage*, 15–18; on Ahasuerus, see Geoffrey Herman, "Ahasuerus"; on Cyrus, see Jason Sion Mokhtarian, "Rabbinic Depictions of the Achaemenid King Cyrus the Great: The *Babylonian Esther Midrash* (bMeg. 10b–17a) in Its Iranian Context," in *The Talmud in Its Iranian Context*, ed. Carol Bakhos and M. Rahim Shayegan (Tübingen: Mohr Siebeck, 2010), 112–39. The precise social channels by which stories about the past were exchanged are elusive. On the possibility of such exchanges at Dura-Europos, see Touraj Daryaee, "To Learn and to Remember from Others: Persians Visiting the Dura-Europos Synagogue," *Scripta Judaica Cracoviensia* 8 (2010): 29–37, esp. 33–34.

47. *B. Ber.* 8b (MS Oxford Opp. Add. fol. 23).

48. MS Oxford Opp. Add. fol. 23 (Yaakov) is the only witness that does not preface R. Akiva's tradition with תניא.

49. According to all the witnesses except MS Paris 671, which reads מפני.

50. According to the majority of the witnesses. MS Oxford Opp. Add. fol. 23 has a shortened form: "Rav Adda." There were two Babylonian Amoraim from the second and the fourth generation with this name.

51. Some MSS and the printed editions replace "sex" with דבר אחר.

52. MS Oxford Opp. Add. fol. 23 is the only witness with the introductory phrase "it is written" to Isaiah 13.

53. The verse continues: "to execute my Wrath; Behold, I have called My stalwarts, My proud exultant ones." As I discuss below, this verse is part of the Talmudic leitmotif of Persians as "haughty."

54. See Stern, *Jewish Identity*, 226 n. 175.

55. Biblical and Palestinian Rabbinic texts often juxtapose and confuse the Persians and Medes; see Mokhtarian, "Rabbinic Depictions," 112–14.

56. *B. Ketub.* 48a. On the comparison of sexuality in the Talmud and Middle Persian texts, see Yaakov Elman, "'He in His Cloak and She in Her Cloak': Conflicting Images of Sexuality in Sasanian Mesopotamia," in *Discussing Cultural Influences: Text, Context, and*

Non-Text in Rabbinic Judaism—Proceedings of a Conference on Rabbinic Judaism at Bucknell University, ed. Rivka Ulmer (Lanham: University Press of America, 2007), 129–64, including 140–41 and 145, where the author notes that there are no Middle Persian texts that discuss having sex with clothes on.

57. Elman, "Middle Persian Culture," 193, and "The World of the 'Sabboraim': Cultural Aspects of Post-Redactional Additions to the Bavli," in *Creation and Composition: The Contribution of the Bavli Redactors (Stammaim) to the Aggada,* ed. Jeffrey L. Rubenstein (Tübingen: Mohr Siebeck, 2005), 383–416, esp. 402 on Rav Yosef's associations with magic and the demon Ashmedai as evidence of the impact of Zoroastrian demonology on his traditions. The sage also appears in a tale in *b. B. Bat.* 8a about Ifra Hormizd, the mother of the Sasanian king, who sends Rav Yosef money for a good deed.

58. See *b. 'Abod. Zar.* 71a (= *b. Šabb.* 94a), רמות רוחא הוא דנקיטא להו; *b. Sanh.* 98a (= *b. Šabb.* 139a), יהירי; Zeph. 3:11, עליזי גאותך ולא תוספי לגבהה עוד; Isa. 13:3, עליזי גאותי; Eccl. 7:8, מגבה רוח.

59. On באזיאראן (< MIr. **bāzyārān*), see *DJBA* 182–83, and Telegdi, "Essai," 233–34. Cf. NP *bāzyār* in Steingass, *Comprehensive Persian-English Dictionary,* 146. Each MS has a different rendering: MS Oxford Opp. Add. fol. 23, which is the most accurate, reads סוסיא דבי זייארין. MS Munich 95, בי זירין. MS Bologna—Archivio di Stato Fr. ebr. 183, סוסיא דביזרן. Soncino Print Family, בי וייארן; and Vilna, בי וייאדן. Some differences between these renderings are the result of scribal confusion between the letters resh and dalet, or zayin and vav. Compare the narrative about King David in *b. Sanh.* 95a, which references שכר בזאי ("hunting of falconers"), related to MP **škār,* NP *šikār,* cited in *DJBA* 1146, and analyzed in Geoffrey Herman, "'*One Day,*'" 119–20. On related words, see also Geo Widengren, "Iran and Israel in Parthian Times with Special Regard to the Ethiopic *Book of Enoch,*" in *Religious Syncretism in Antiquity: Essays in Conversation with Geo Widengren,* ed. Birger A. Pearson (Missoula: Scholars Press, 1975), 85–129, esp. 96, on *naxčīr,* "hunting," found in the Dead Sea Scrolls; and Telegdi, "Essai," 248. Images of the Sasanian king's royal hunts and of Persian nobles on horseback are common in Sasanian artwork. See Edith Porada, *Art of Ancient Iran* (New York: Greystone Press, 1965), 207 (plate 57) for an image of hunting scenes from a relief on the iwan at Taq-i Bustan. Official Sasanian bullae, such as the personal seals of *spāhbeds,* contain the image of a military figure on horseback with armor and spear, as seen in Rika Gyselen, *Sasanian Seals and Sealings in the A. Saeedi Collection* (Leuven: Peeters, 2007), 248–77.

60. *B. Šabb.* 94a (MS Oxford Opp. Add. fol. 23). At the end, MS Vatican 108 adds בחלא, "in the sand."

61. MS Munich 95 omits this response.

62. Cf. the spelling of this sage's name in MS Munich 95 and MS Vatican 108.

63. This word appears in all the witnesses except for MS Oxford Opp. Add. fol. 23.

64. On פרדשכא or פרדכשא ("officer"), see *DJBA* 928, and the analysis in Geoffrey Herman, "Persia in Light of the Babylonian Talmud—Echoes of Contemporary Society and Politics: *hargbed* and *bidaxš,*" in *The Talmud in Its Iranian Context,* ed. Carol Bakhos and M. Rahim Shayegan (Tübingen: Mohr Siebeck, 2010), 58–82, esp. 75–81.

65. Ibid. 80–81.

66. On this text, see Marc Hirshman, *The Stabilization of Rabbinic Culture, 100 C.E.–350 C.E.: Texts on Education and Their Late Antique Context* (New York: Oxford University Press, 2009), 97–105. On page 101, Hirshman states that scholars disagree over whether *Ecclesiastes Rabbah* was affected by the Babylonian Talmud. See, however, the conclusion of Reuven Kiper-

wasser and Serge Ruzer, "To Convert a Persian and Teach Him the Holy Scriptures: A Zoroastrian Proselyte in Rabbinic and Syriac Christian Narratives," in *Jews, Christians and Zoroastrians: Religious Dynamics in a Sasanian Context*, ed. Geoffrey Herman (Piscataway: Gorgias Press, 2014), 101–38, esp. 96: "The redactor of *Kohelet Rabbah* seems to have been familiar enough with traditions brought to the Land of Israel by Babylonian tradents." For more on this text and its parallels in *Avot de-Rabbi Nathan* and *b. Šabb.* 31a, see Reuven Kiperwasser and Serge Ruzer, "Zoroastrian Proselytes in Rabbinic and Syriac Christian Narratives: Orality-Related Markers of Cultural Identity," *History of Religions* 51 (2012): 197–218, esp. 199–207.

67. Kiperwasser and Ruzer, "To Convert a Persian," 95 and 100.

68. *Ecclesiastes Rabbah* 7.8.1. The translation here is from Kiperwasser and Ruzer, "To Convert a Persian," 94–95, with minor changes.

69. Hirshman, *Stabilization*, 105.

70. See *DJPA* 449 for variations of "Persian" in the Jerusalem Talmud.

71. See *y. Ber.* 6:2 (10b) (Yaacov Sussmann, ed., *Talmud Yerushalmi: According to Ms. Or. 4720 [Scal. 3] of the Leiden University Library, with Restorations and Corrections* [Jerusalem: The Academy of the Hebrew Language, 2001], 52).

72. Hirshman, *Stabilization*, 102.

73. Another source from the Jerusalem Talmud on Persians that may be a reference to Persian Jews is *y. ʿErub.* 6:3 (23c) (Yaacov Sussmann, ed., *Talmud Yerushalmi: According to Ms. Or. 4720 [Scal. 3] of the Leiden University Library, with Restorations and Corrections* [Jerusalem: The Academy of the Hebrew Language, 2001], 479): "It happened that a Persian's wife rented out her courtyard without informing her husband. The case came before R. Shmuel and he declared it legal." Before this citation the passage mentions both Israel and gentiles. The fact that the case goes before the rabbi seems to me to suggest that the Persian (or at least the wife of the Persian) was a Jew.

74. *Y. Šabb.* 16:8 (15d) (Yaacov Sussmann, ed., *Talmud Yerushalmi: According to Ms. Or. 4720 [Scal. 3] of the Leiden University Library, with Restorations and Corrections* [Jerusalem: The Academy of the Hebrew Language, 2001], 440).

75. *B. Šabb.* 122b.

76. See *DJBA* 1177–78. Sokoloff derives this word from Middle Parthian.

77. *B. Taʿan.* 24a.

78. MS Jerusalem—Yad Harav Herzog 1: "Rav."

79. These two names vary in the MSS.

80. Printed eds.: קוסטא דחיקא, "poor district." Rashi's commentary explains it in terms of poverty as well. Cf. the more reliable witnesses—MS Munich 140, a Spanish MS of the thirteenth century, which reads קוסא רחיקא, "distant district," and the Yemenite MS Yad Harav Herzog 1, which shows some variance and does not contain the loanword but instead reads כפר רחוק, "distant village." The original context implied distance, not poverty, which may have been the reason for using the Middle Persian word for "district." MS Munich 95 glosses קוסטא with דוכתא.

81. According to the printed eds. and something similar in MS Jerusalem—Yad Harav Herzog 1. The other MSS exclude this.

82. See *DJBA* 385 and cf. NP *himyān*, "belt." The word appears elsewhere as well (e.g., *b. Šabb.* 10a). Another Iranian loanword for "belt" found in the Talmud is ורשכא, which appears to be related to Middle Persian **waršak*. See *DJBA* 396.

83. See *DJBA* 1026 and cf. MP *kamar,* "belt." For the Iranian etymology, see the literature cited in Geoffrey Herman, *Prince,* 79 n. 125, and 340 for a translation of the *Aruch Completum.* See also Geo Widengren, "Some Remarks on Riding Costume and Articles of Dress among Iranian Peoples in Antiquity," *Studia Ethnographica Upsaliensia* 11 (1956): 228–76, esp. 254 and 260, stating that the *kamar* in the Parthian era was used to hold up a tunic and is associated with the monarchy in Kirder's inscriptions. According to Widengren, "Iran," 96, "some Parthian names of articles of dress had been taken over, viz. *hemyān*, girdle, and *sarbāl* (*salvār*) is as natural as it is striking that the priestly girdle according to Josephus, *Antiquitates* III, VII 2 was known by this Parthian name." On Persian belts in the Bavli, see further Elman, "Middle Persian Culture," 181–82; Shaul Shaked, "'No Talking During a Meal': Zoroastrian Themes in the Babylonian Talmud," in *The Talmud in Its Iranian Context,* ed. Carol Bakhos and M. Rahim Shayegan (Tübingen: Mohr Siebeck, 2010), 161–77, esp. 165–71.

84. See esp. *Giz. Abāliš* chapter 7 (Homi F. Chacha, *Gajastak Abâlish* [Bombay: The Trustees of the Parsi Punchayet Funds and Properties, 1936], 23–25 and 45–46), and *Nērang.* chapters 67–69 (Firoze M. Kotwal and Philip G. Kreyenbroek, with James R. Russell, *The Hērbedestān and Nērangestān,* vol. 4 [Paris: Association pour l'Avancement des Études Iraniennes, 2009], 26–35); *ŠnŠ* chapter 4 (Jehangir C. Tavadia, *Šāyast-nē-šāyast: A Pahlavi Text on Religious Customs* [Hamburg: De Gruyter, 1930], 85–90). For an overview of the *kustīg* belt, see Michael Stausberg, "The Significance of the *kusti:* A History of Its Zoroastrian Interpretations," *East and West* 54 (2004): 9–29.

85. See Shaul Shaked, "Items of Dress and Other Objects in Common Use: Iranian Loanwords in Jewish Babylonian Aramaic," in *Irano-Judaica III: Studies Relating to Jewish Contacts with Persian Culture throughout the Ages,* ed. Shaul Shaked and Amnon Netzer (Jerusalem: Ben-Zvi Institute, 1994), 106–17, esp. 111. The word *kustīg* does appear in Syriac, according to Claudia A. Ciancaglini, *Iranian Loanwords in Syriac* (Wiesbaden: Reichert, 2008), 193.

86. See *DīD* chapter 38.31 (Mahmoud Jaafari-Dehaghi, *Dādestān ī Dēnīg,* part 1, *Transcription, Translation, and Commentary* [Paris: Association pour l'Avancement des Études Iraniennes, 1998], 164–65), which after discussing the *kustīg* mentions the wearing of the *kamar* by those who have no religious beliefs.

87. See below for more. In *b. Giṭ.* 14a–b, there are Iranian names and dress among early Babylonian figures. See Jacob Neusner, "Arda and Arta and Pyly Bryš," *Jewish Quarterly Review* 53 (1963): 298–305.

88. Shaked, "'No Talking,'" 171.

89. See Widengren, "Some Remarks," 260.

90. *B. Šabb.* 59b (MS Oxford Opp. Add. fol. 23). Cf. *Song of Songs Rabbah* 4.8.1 and *y. Šabb.* 6:1 (7d), which reads "Rav Huna permitted the wife of the exilarch to place a golden ornament on her *qpylyt*" (Geoffrey Herman, *Prince,* 237). The meaning of the final word is unknown. Marcus Jastrow, *Dictionary of the Targumim, Talmud Bavli, Talmud Yerushalmi, and Midrashic Literature* (New York: Judaica Treasury, 1971), 1401, defines it as "wig."

91. MS Vatican 108: "Rava."

92. MS Vatican 108: "Rami bar Abba."

93. Following MS Oxford Opp. Add. fol. 23. Cf. MS Munich 95: "in the name of Rav Sheshet." MS Vatican 109: "Mar Yehudah in the name of Rav Sheshet." The medieval Talmudic commentaries also disagree on this attribution.

94. The word רסוקא (other spellings: רסיקא [= MS Vatican 108], ריסוקא [= MS Oxford Opp. Add. fol. 23], ריסקא [= MS Munich 95]) is a different type of belt than the ones discussed above and may be another MP loanword. Shaked, "Items of Dress," 111, conjectures that it could be connected to MP *rasan*, "rope." The fact that this word appears alongside the other loanwords makes it more likely that it is in fact a MP word.

95. For a comparison of Jewish phylacteries and Zoroastrian belts, see Yishai Kiel, "Redesigning *Tzitzit* in the Babylonian Talmud in Light of Literary Depictions of the Zoroastrian *kustīg*," in *Shoshannat Yaakov: Jewish and Iranian Studies in Honor of Yaakov Elman*, ed. Shai Secunda and Steven Fine (Boston: Brill, 2012), 185–202.

96. This number is based on my count of Iranian loanwords listed in Sokoloff *DJBA*, using my best judgment with respect to questionable words that could or could not be included. The number is somewhat subjective, based on the parameters that I chose to place on the exercise. Some debatable loanwords that I included in this tally include, for instance, "poll tax" and "seal" (see *DJBA* 599 and 440). Examples of excluded loanwords are "sedan chair" and "large cup" (see *DJBA* 133–34 and 146). This number increases if one takes into account Iranian loanwords that appear exclusively in later Geonic sources (e.g., דוזד, "separate," from MP *jud az*, "separate from," as explained in *DJBA* 323), or in the Aramaic magical bowl spells (e.g., the word דנחיש, "demon," from a Middle Persian Manichaean word for "ailment," or the word מהרא, "spell," from MP **mahr*, "sacred word," on which see *DJBA* 344 and 645, respectively). I give other examples below. Other scholars have proffered higher totals than my tally of two hundred loanwords; see Secunda, *Iranian Talmud*, 168–69 n. 38, stating that Sokoloff's dictionary "counts approximately 340 Persian loanwords"; and Geoffrey Herman, *Prince*, 215 n. 29, on there being just over three hundred, citing an oral communication with Michael Sokoloff. As noted in Gafni, "Babylonian Rabbinic Culture," the study by Telegdi, "Essai," contains 130 loanwords.

97. See Gafni, "Babylonian Rabbinic Culture," 259 n. 66, on the fact that there are many fewer Iranian loanwords than the more than three thousand Latin and Greek ones in rabbinic literature as counted in Samuel Krauss, *Griechische und lateinische Lehnwörter im Talmud, Midrasch und Targum*, 2 vols. (Berlin: Calvary, 1898–99).

98. See Shaul Shaked, "Aramaic, iii: Iranian Loanwords in Middle Aramaic," *Encyclopaedia Iranica*, online ed., 1986: www.iranicaonline.org/articles/aramaic-#pt3.

99. On this word in the Talmud, see *DJBA* 945; in the book of Esther, see Henry S. Gehman, "Notes on the Persian Words in the Book of Esther," *Journal of Biblical Literature* 43 (1924), 321–28, esp. 325–26. For a list and discussion of the approximately twenty-two Persian loanwords found in biblical Hebrew, see Rick Wright, *Linguistic Evidence for the Pre-Exilic Date of the Yahwistic Source* (New York: T. and T. Clark International, 2005), 113–20.

100. On these two words, see *DJBA* 86 and 703.

101. For Iranian words in Syriac, see Ciancaglini, *Iranian Loanwords in Syriac* [henceforth *ILS*]. For examples of Iranian loanwords that appear in both the Talmud and Syriac, see, for instance: "cinnamon" (*DJBA* 353, *ILS* 158–59); "messenger" (*DJBA* 929, *ILS* 237–38); "artichoke" (*DJBA* 587, *ILS* 196); "gift, present" (*DJBA* 355, *ILS* 159); "bathtub" (*DJBA* 87, *ILS* 102).

102. See the list of words by category, *ILS* 41–42.

103. For a more positive assessment of the ability for speakers of Aramaic and Middle Persian to communicate with each other, see Secunda, *Iranian Talmud*, 38–39.

104. For another example, see *b. Tamid* 32b, where MS Oxford contains the loanword ארזניג, "important" (cf. MP *arzānīg*) in the sentence "They made me important," as opposed to MS Florence, which uses the common Semitic root in the sentence מיחשב חשיבנא, "I am important."

105. See *DJBA* 563 and *DJPA* 254. The second possible Iranian loanword is גושקרא.

106. On these two words, see *DJBA* 98–99 and 185.

107. Here are two examples of each—(1) for Iranian loanwords that appear in the Bavli, the bowls, and Geonic (or Karaite) sources, see זינא, "weapon" (cf. MP *zēn*, from Av. *zaēna-*; *DJBA* 410); and דותקא, "family" (MP *dūdag*, "family"; *DJBA* 323); (2) in both the Bavli and the bowls, see אידרונא, "an inner closed room" (MP *andarōn*, "inside"; *DJBA* 111); and הדמא, "limb, member" (MP *handām*, "limb, member"; *DJBA* 362–63); (3) in the bowls only, see זרגונא, "yellow" (MP *zargōn*, "golden"; *DJBA* 420); and גיתא, "inhabited world" (MP *gētīg*, "material world," a word with strong theological connotations; *DJBA* 284); (4) in Geonic sources only, see כואהישן, "request" (MP *xwāhišn*,"want, desire"; *DJBA* 555); and גראן,"expensive"(MP *garān*, "expensive"; *DJBA* 297). For an example of a bowl with two Iranian loanwords for "adversary" and "demon," see Dan Levene, *Curse or Blessing: What's in the Magic Bowl?* (Southampton: University of Southampton, 2002): www.southampton.ac.uk/vmba/documents/curse_or_blessing.pdf, 16–18.

108. On the number of words in the Bavli, see Yaakov Elman, "Orality and the Redaction of the Babylonian Talmud," *Oral Tradition* 14 (1999): 52–99, esp. 68–69.

109. Examples of Sasanian administrative terms or titles of office mentioned in the Bavli that I do not analyze in this book, each of which requires further philological explanation, include מרזבנא, "prefect," related to MP *marzbān*, "frontier commander, margrave," in *b. Meg.* 6b, in reference to Rome; פושתיבנא, "guard," related to MP *puštībān*, "bodyguard," in *b. Nid.* 25a; דסקרתא, "landed estate," with which compare MP *dastgird*, "estate," in *b. Meg.* 16a and, in reference to the exilarch, in *b. 'Erub.* 59a. For more information on these words, consult *DJBA* 705, 894, and 344–45, respectively. On words of everyday life, see esp. Shaked, "Items of Dress."

110. For examples, see דנקא, "a sixth of a denar" (*DJBA* 344), הנדזא, "measure" (*DJBA* 385), and קפיזא, "one-tenth griw" (*DJBA* 1032).

111. Shaked, "Aramaic, iii."

112. One exception might be the word פדמא, "mask" (*b. Šabb.* 66b), in Middle Persian *padām*, which is a ritual mask worn by Zoroastrian priests in order to protect fire from pollution. In the Bavli it is used in reference to the Mishnah.

113. See *DJBA* 801 on the word סייב or סיואה, which is related to MParth. *syāw*, "black," attested in *b. Nid.* 20a and the Aramaic bowls. The particle זי "now, then," with which compare NP *zī*, appears in imperatives, including in legal cases (*DJBA* 405: e.g., *b. Ketub.* 59a–b, "Now, tell me the case.") And on הם, "also," from MP *ham*, which appears frequently in Geonic texts, see the list of examples in *DJBA* 384–85. For the possible influence of MP *pad*, "to, at, on, by," on the Aramaic bowls, see Shaul Shaked, "Poetics of Spells: Language and Structure in Aramaic Incantations of Late Antiquity, 1: The Divorce Formula and Its Ramifications," in *Mesopotamian Magic: Textual, Historical, and Interpretative Perspectives*, ed. Tzvi Abusch and Karel van der Toorn (Groningen: Styx Publications, 1999), 173–95, esp. 181 n. 37. See also idem, "Notes on the Pahlavi Amulet and Sasanian Courts of Law," *Bulletin of the Asia Institute* 7 (1993): 165–72, esp. 168, proposing that the first word of the Talmudic phrase *bei dāwar* could be MP *pad*, which later becomes NP *be*.

114. For the two examples cited, see *DJBA* 86–87 and 385, respectively. For more on Iranian verbs in Jewish Babylonian Aramaic, see Shaked, "Aramaic, iii," explaining that "the strong linguistic impact of Iranian on Babylonian Aramaic appears most strikingly with the loanwords that were turned into Aramaic verbs: gnz 'to store;' bgn and pgn 'to cry for help;' bšqr 'to search, find out;' grb 'to seize,'" among others. See also idem, "Iranian Elements in Middle Aramaic: Some Particles and Verbs," in *Medioiranica: Proceedings of the International Colloquium Organized by the Katholieke Universiteit Leuven from the 21st to the 23rd of May 1990*, ed. Wojciech Skalmowski and Alois Van Tongerloo (Leuven: Uitgeverij Peeters and Departement Orientalistiek, 1993), 147–56.

115. On how Iranian loanwords indicate Babylonian reworkings of aggadot, see Marc Hirshman, "Aggadic Midrash," in *The Literature of the Sages*, part 2, *Midrash and Targum, Liturgy, Poetry, Mysticism, Contracts, Inscriptions, Ancient Science, and the Languages of Rabbinic Literature*, ed. Shmuel Safrai, Zeev Safrai, Joshua Schwartz, and Peter J. Tomson (Assen: Royal Van Gorcum and Fortress Press, 2006), 107–32, esp. 130–31: "Certainly the more one finds Persian loan words and manifestly Babylonian realia, one is on more solid ground in viewing the aggada as having undergone serious if not definitive reworking in Babylonia."

116. An important resource in this regard is Shelomo Morag and Yechiel Kara, *Babylonian Aramaic in Yemenite Tradition: The Noun* (Jerusalem: Magnes Press, 2002; Hebrew). On the unique value of the Yemenite MSS, see Michael Krupp, "Manuscripts of the Babylonian Talmud," in *The Literature of the Sages*, part 1, *Oral Tora, Halakha, Mishna, Tosefta, Talmud, External Tractates*, ed. Shmuel Safrai (Philadelphia: Fortress Press, 1987), 346–66, esp. 349–50, quoting Rosenthal's conclusion based on a study of tractate *Pesaḥim* that "the prototypes came from Babylonia and were of the time of the Geonim, being among the most genuine of the manuscripts of the Babylonian Talmud." One study of a Yemenite manuscript of tractate *Sanhedrin* shows how it conserves Persian loanwords relatively well; see the analysis of *b. Sanh.* 98a by Mordechai Sabato, *A Yemenite Manuscript of Tractate Sanhedrin and Its Place in the Text Tradition* (Jerusalem: Ben-Zvi Institute, 1998), 142–44 (Hebrew).

117. See *DJBA* 185, and the citation therein of the *Aruch*.

118. See *DJBA* 928.

119. *B. ʿAbod. Zar.* 71a (MS Paris 1337).

120. MS Oxford—Bodl. heb. c. 17 (2661) 58: ארמאי כתבי פרדשני.

121. This is the spelling of MS Paris 1337. On this word, see Telegdi, "Essai," 250–51. MS New York—JTS Rab. 15 and the printed editions: פרדישני. See also דשנא, "gift," from MP *dāšn*, which appears in *b. Sanh.* 94b alongside the longer form: "Is this gift deserving of this return gift?" (*DJBA* 355).

122. The printed editions, MS Oxford—Bodl. heb. c. 17 (2661) 58, and MS Munich 95 add "I say to you." This does not appear in MS Paris 1337 or MS New York—JTS Rab. 15.

123. Most of the evidence comes from later Pahlavi sources. See *Dēnk. VI* chapters 13–14 (Shaul Shaked, *The Wisdom of the Sasanian Sages: Dēnkard VI* [Boulder: Westview Press, 1970], 6–9) and the numerous other occurrences of this word in this work; *Dēnk. IX* chapters 2.20, 13.9 (Yuhan Sohrab-Dinshaw Vevaina, "Studies in Zoroastrian Exegesis and Hermeneutics, with a Critical Edition of the *Sūdgar Nask* of *Dēnkard* Book 9" [Ph.D. dissertation, Harvard University, 2007], 230–31, 268–70); *DīD* chapter 2.13 (Mahmoud

Jaafari-Dehaghi, *Dādestān ī Dēnīg*, part 1, *Transcription, Translation, and Commentary* [Paris: Association pour l'Avancement des Études Iraniennes, 1998], 46–47); *AWN* chapters 10:18–11:8 (Fereydun Vahman, *Ardā Wirāz Nāmag: The Iranian "Divina Commedia"* [London: Curzon Press, 1986], 94–97, 196).

124. Saul Lieberman, *Greek in Jewish Palestine* (New York: Jewish Theological Seminary, 1942), 6, and *Hellenism in Jewish Palestine* (New York: Jewish Theological Seminary, 1950), 3, where the author adds: "It is pertinent to inquire why the Rabbis employed the particular Greek word when an adequate Hebrew or Aramaic term was seemingly available. . . . If a common Greek word is employed by the Rabbis only very rarely, whereas they generally use its Aramaic equivalent, some reason must lie behind the rabbinic choice of a Greek term in a particular case."

125. For several examples of loanwords used in texts about Persians, see בהריק ("instead of"), from Iranian **vihrīk* (MP *guhrīg*), as explained in Shaul Shaked, "Iranian Elements in Middle Aramaic: Some Particles and Verbs," in *Medioiranica: Proceedings of the International Colloquium Organized by the Katholieke Universiteit Leuven from the 21st to the 23rd of May 1990*, ed. Wojciech Skalmowski and Alois Van Tongerloo (Leuven: Uitgeverij Peeters and Departement Orientalistiek, 1993), 150. This word is found in two Talmudic MSS in reference to Dubiel ("bear god"), a play on words related to the identification of the Persians as bears in Daniel 7:5 (see below). The relevant line is in *b. Yoma* 77a (MS New York—JTS Rab. 1623/2), which reads: "They brought Dubiel the angel of the Persians instead of (Gabriel)" (עיילוה לדוביאל איסרא דפרסאי בוהריקיה). MS Munich 95 reads similarly, except with the loanword written in corrupted form. The line appears differently in the other witnesses, sometimes without the loanword. Cf. MS New York—JTS Rab. 218: דוביאל שר פרס. MS London—BL Harl. 5508 (400) and MS Oxford Opp. Add. fol. 23 both read דוביאל שרא דפרסאי ואוקמוה בדוכתיה. This example demonstrates how Iranian loanwords appear in only some witnesses of a given sugya. A second example of a loanword used in a passage about Persians is in *b. B. Bat.* 55a, where the loanword דארישן, "possession" (< MP *dārišn*) appears in the line "possession (for ownership) for the Persians [דארישן דפרסאי] is forty years" (see MS Hamburg 165). This passage, about taxes, the law of the kingdom's being the law of the land, and the exilarch, is ripe for contextualization. Other witnesses, in lieu of the loanword, read ארעיה דפרסאי (MS Florence II-I-9) and ארישתא דפרסאי (MS Paris 1337). The concept of *dārišn* in Sasanian law "only denotes immediate possession, which can, but does not necessarily, include ownership" (see Maria Macuch, "Judicial and Legal Systems, iii: Sasanian Legal System," *Encyclopaedia Iranica*, online ed., 2012: www.iranicaonline.org/articles/judicial-and-legal-systems-iii-sasanian-legal-system), such as tenancy or stolen objects; for one example of how this law plays out in an imperial court of law, see *MHD* chapter 84.13–15 (Anahit Perikhanian, *Mādayān ī Hazār Dādestān: The Book of a Thousand Judgements, a Sasanian Law-Book* [Costa Mesa: Mazda Publishers, 1997], 198–99). Upon further inquiry, the Middle Persian texts could help illuminate a more refined understanding of the meaning of the word in the Bavli context. For a possible second loanword in *b. B. Bat.* 55a, consult *DJBA* 407, s.v. זיהררא, and for a treatment and translation of this source, see Geoffrey Herman, *Prince*, 203–4. Finally, there are also loanwords used in texts about Sasanian kings (*b. Sanh.* 98a and *b. B. Meṣiʿa* 119b; see below), about Persian falconry (*b. Šabb.* 94a, below), and in a dialogue between Ablat the Persian sage and Shmuel ("sweet wine," in *b. ʿAbod. Zar.* 30a). If one includes references to kings that are allusions to Persian monarchs

in this category of Iranian loanwords used in texts on Persians, then we have even more cases; see, for instance, *b. Ber.* 56a, which includes the loanwords פרדהגבנא, "guard" (MIr. **pāhrag-bān*); אפדנא, "mansion" (OP *apadāna*, "palace," a word already attested in Dan. 11:45); גנזורא, "treasury guard" (MP *ganjwar*, "treasurer"); שיראי, "silk garments" (MP *šērāi*, "silk"—on which see *FīP* chapter 4.11 [B. Utas, *Frahang ī Pahlavīk: Edited, with Transliteration, Transcription, and Commentary from the Posthumous Papers of Henrik Samuel Nyberg* [Wiesbaden: Harrassowitz, 1988], 66]); ריש טרזיא, "the head of the embroiderers" (NP *tarrāzgar*, "embroiderer"). Although it is admittedly not totally clear that this source is about the Persians, the fact that many of its protagonists are Babylonian sages is suggestive of this context. Finally, it is worth noting here that there are also Iranian loanwords used in texts about the Romans; see, for instance, *b. Giṭ.* 57a, which contains the words אושפיזא, "inn" (MP *aspinj*), תגא, "crown" (cf. MP *tāg*), and גושפנקא, "signet ring" (cf. MP *angustbān*, "finger guard"); and *b. Sanh.* 109a, which records ספטא, "box" (cf. NP *safad*, "wicker basket").

126. See the comparable assessment regarding the appearance of Greek and Latin loanwords in rabbinic literature by Amram D. Tropper, "Roman Contexts in Jewish Texts: On Diatagma and Prostagma in Rabbinic Literature," *Jewish Quarterly Review* 95 (2005): 207–27, esp. 207: "A loanword may have been employed in a text not merely for its meaning but for a specific image or association which it brought to mind. By means of a loanword from Greek or Latin, the author of a rabbinic text may have alluded to a specific setting or institution well known to his audience but unfamiliar to the modern reader. As a result, the historian today may hope to enhance our understanding of many rabbinic texts that use loanwords by interpreting these texts in the light of their loanwords' original contexts."

127. Geoffrey Herman, *Prince*, 215 n. 29.

128. The correct assumption that some Jews in Iran spoke Iranian dialects is supported by the reference in the Bavli to translation of the book of Esther into Elamite and Median (*b. Meg.* 18a, *b. Šabb.* 115a).

129. Gafni, "Babylonian Rabbinic Culture," 241, citing *b. ʿAbod. Zar.* 24b as an example.

130. Robert Brody, *The Geonim of Babylonia and the Shaping of Medieval Jewish Culture* (New Haven: Yale University Press, 1998), 140. And see also the tradition in R. Yehudai Gaon, *Sefer Halachot Pesuqot*, 130:13 to "Jews who know how to read the Persian script [כתבא פרסא]" (cited in *DJBA* 1040).

131. Other passages in the Talmud that address the meaning of Persian words include *b. Bek.* 60a, which refers to חד, "ten" (MP *dah*): "Rava said, 'The reason is because it so happens that in the Persian system of counting, they call ten חד [= דה].'" All the witnesses that I consulted reverse the letters, though surely MP *dah* is meant (see *DJBA* 323).

132. *B. ʿAbod. Zar.* 24b (MS New York—JTS Rab. 15).

133. MS Paris 1337: "Rav Adda."

134. Cf. MS Paris 1337, דסתנא; and MS Munich 95, דשתנא. This is from MP *daštān*, "menstruation." The word also appears in *b. Šabb.* 110a, which says that a woman approached by a snake should throw her hair and nails at it and exclaim, "I am menstruating." For a discussion of the polemical dimensions of *b. ʿAbod. Zar.* 24b, see Shai Secunda, "*Dashtana—'Ki Derekh Nashim Li'*: A Study of Babylonian Rabbinic Laws of Menstruation in Relation to Corresponding Zoroastrian Texts" (Ph.D. dissertation, Yeshiva University, 2007), 29–32, esp. 30–31: "From this perspective, it is possible that Rava and Rav Ashi were taking pains to show that what they deemed to be distinctively Jewish practices—the scribal art and the

menstrual laws—were actually ancient Jewish ones co-opted by the Persians. Rav Ashi tries to demonstrate that already in early biblical times, the Jewish matriarch Rachel observed the menstrual laws long before the Persians began their menstrual practices. And indeed, the Persian word for menstruation allegedly derives from Rachel's declaration. If this is a correct interpretation of Rav Ashi's statement, it may hint at rabbinic anxiety regarding the authenticity of Jewish menstrual practices in the face of an ancient and established Zoroastrian system."

135. See Elman, "'Up to the Ears,'" 131, offering the conclusion that Rav, Shmuel, and Rav Kahana could speak but not read Pahlavi.

136. For other texts on the Persian language, see *Esther Rabbah* 4:12, *b. Soṭah* 49b, and *b. B. Qam.* 83a.

137. *B. Giṭ.* 19b (MS Arras 889). See the parallel text in *b. Giṭ.* 11a.

138. See Jastrow, *Dictionary*, 1653.

139. It seems that this text is saying that Rav Pappa understood the language when it was read aloud to him, despite not knowing the script in which the document was composed, and that his process of verification was regarding the accuracy of their reading of the document. See Elman, "'Up to the Ears,'" 131 n. 101.

140. Barak S. Cohen, *The Legal Methodology of Late Nehardean Sages in Sasanian Babylonia* (Leiden: Brill, 2011), esp. 60, 64, 75, and 92 on how Ameimar sometimes disregards Tannaitic law, instead invoking reason and life's realities in his opinions.

141. See David Oppenheim, "Die Namen der persischen und babylonischen Feste im Talmud," *Monatsschrift für Geschichte und Wissenschaft des Judentums* 7 (1854): 347–52; Alexander Kohut, "Les fêtes persanes et babyloniennes dans les Talmuds de Babylon et de Jerusalem," *Revue des Études Juives* 24 (1892): 256–71; S. H. Taqizadeh, "The Iranian Festivals Adopted by the Christians and Condemned by the Jews," *Bulletin of the School of Oriental Studies* 10 (1940–42): 632–53, and "The Old Iranian Calendars Again," *Bulletin of the School of Oriental and African Studies* 14 (1952): 603–11; Baruch M. Bokser, "Talmudic Names of the Iranian Festivals," *Journal of the American Oriental Society* 95 (1975): 261–62; Secunda, *Iranian Talmud*, 188–89 n. 54.

142. Neusner, "How Much Iranian?" 185–86 (author's italics).

143. Shaked, "Iranian Elements," 147.

144. *B. ʿAbod. Zar.* 11b.

145. See the summary in Gafni, "Babylonian Rabbinic Culture," 242–43.

146. Taqizadeh, "Iranian Festivals," 637; Kohut, "Fêtes persanes," 260.

147. *Y. ʿAbod. Zar.* 1:3 (39c) (Yaacov Sussmann, ed., *Talmud Yerushalmi: According to Ms. Or. 4720 [Scal. 3] of the Leiden University Library, with Restorations and Corrections* [Jerusalem: The Academy of the Hebrew Language, 2001], 1377).

148. For more on this text and the *kustīg* belt, see Shaked, "'No Talking,'" 167–71, including his translation of *DīD* question 38; Shai Secunda, "Reading the Bavli in Iran," *Jewish Quarterly Review* 100 (2010): 310–42, and *Iranian Talmud*, 64–65. The symbolic meaning behind the ritual belt's division of the body between the spiritual upper body (the heart and brain) and lustful lower body (the stomach) has been described by Jivanji Jamshedji Modi, *The Religious Ceremonies and Customs of the Parsees* (Bombay: J. B. Karani's Sons, 1922), 188–90. In addition to the *Dādestān ī Dēnīg*, see also *Dēnk. V* chapter 24.16c (Jaleh Amouzgar and Ahmad Tafazzoli, *Le cinquième livre du Dēnkard* [Paris: Asso-

ciation pour l'Avancement des Études Iraniennes, 2000], 88–89): "The *kustīg* is a sign that indicates the border between the two, which is upon the body of man similar to the world, because that which is the upper half is superior, and that which is lower half [is worse]."

149. *B. Sanh.* 39a, according to MS Jerusalem—Yad Harav Herzog 1, but see notes below on the names Ohrmazd and Ahriman. Cf. a similar tradition found in *Deuteronomy Rabbah* 11:4: "Another explanation: What is the meaning of 'the man, God' (Deut. 33:1)? R. Abin said: His lower half is man (while) his upper half is of God."

150. According to MS Jerusalem—Yad Harav Herzog 1 and printed editions, הורמיז. MS Munich 95 and MS Florence II-I-9: הורמין.

151. MS Florence II-I-9, which is an early twelfth-century Ashkenazi manuscript (see Krupp, "Manuscripts," 352): אהרמין. This spelling, AHRMYN, appears to be a relatively accurate rendering of the Middle Persian word *Ahreman*. MS Jerusalem—Yad Harav Herzog 1 and the printed editions: אהורמיז.

152. The printed editions and MS Munich 95 add here, "If so."

153. Some of the manuscripts appear to have harmonized and thus confused these two names. Although the magian's reference here is clearly to the deity Ohrmazd. Rashi connects this name to a folkloric legend in *b. B. Bat.* 73a–b, where Hormiz is not the Zoroastrian deity but rather a demon who during a storm leaps around on the cupolas of Maḥoza, hopping from a horseman to two mules on two bridges of the Rognag River, all while pouring two cups of wine without spilling any. (This passage, it can be noted, also contains the Persian loanword for "cupola," on which see *DJBA* 160). Rashi, however, gets this wrong, as the commentator often does with respect to Persian elements in the Bavli. The name was in fact quite common in the Sasanian period, and it is found as a demon in both the Bavli and the bowls. Interestingly, the tale in *b. B. Bat.* 73a–b ends with (presumably) the (Persian) government's hearing about the incident of the demon and putting him to death. For more on the literary context of this story, see Eli Yassif, *The Hebrew Folktale: History, Genre, Meaning,* trans. Jacqueline S. Teitelbaum (Bloomington: Indiana University Press, 2009), 228–29.

154. See *Bund.* chapter 1.1–3 (Behramgore Tahmuras Anklesaria, *Zand-Ākāsīh: Iranian or Greater Bundahišn* [Bombay: Rahnumae Mazdayasnan Sabha, 1956], 4–5).

155. See Gafni, "Babylonian Rabbinic Culture," 229, on how the focus of exegetical passages like the ones discussed below "was not the Bible and a need for up-to-date knowledge of its geography but rather the self-image of the Jewish community of Babylonia in Late Antiquity."

156. See Gafni, "How Babylonia Became 'Zion.'"

157. See Aharon Oppenheimer, with Benjamin Isaac and Michael Lecker, *Babylonia Judaica in the Talmudic Period* (Wiesbaden: Reichert, 1983), 156–64, and the analysis in Aharon Oppenheimer, "Babylonian Synagogues with Historical Associations," in *Ancient Synagogues: Historical Analysis and Archaeological Discovery*, ed. Dan Urman and Paul V.M. Flesher (Leiden: Brill, 1995), 40–48.

158. On Mata Meḥasya, see Oppenheimer, with Isaac and Lecker, *Babylonia Judaica*, 421, and the primary sources *b. B. Bat.* 12b, *b. Meg.* 26a, and the debate in *b. Šabb.* 11a, which juxtaposes two traditions attributed to Rava bar Meḥasya in the name of Rav Ḥama bar Goria in Rav's name. In the first tradition, Rav states that "every city whose roofs are higher

than the synagogue will be destroyed," citing Ezra 9:9 as proof. After this, however, the editors, using two Persian words, clarify that these restrictions apply to "palaces" (קושקא, related to MP *kōšk*, "palaces," according to *DJBA* 1004) or "towers" (אברברי [MS Vatican 127] or אברואורי [MS Oxford Opp. Add. fol. 23]; cf. NP *barwāra*, "upper chamber," and *DJBA* 76–77). The second tradition offers a list of groups under which a Jew would not want to work, including "under a gentile but not under a *ḥabār*, under a *ḥabār* but not under the sages."

159. There are similarities and differences with this Bavli text and its Palestinian parallels. Compare *y. Meg.* 1:8 (71b), which refers to Asia, Adiabene, Germany, and Greece, which do not appear in the Bavli. This version, like the Bavli, contains the dispute between R. Simon and the rabbis regarding the identification of Tiras as Persia, yet without the resolution of Rav Yosef's baraita. See also *Genesis Rabbah* chapter 37, which interprets the sons of Japheth as references to Africa, Germania, Media, Macedonia, and Mysia. In this source R. Simon's interpretation of Tiras is the "Euphrates region," and it contains no reference to Persia. For more on the Table of Nations in rabbinic literature, see James M. Scott, *Paul and the Nations: The Old Testament and Jewish Background of Paul's Mission to the Nations, with Special Reference to the Destination of Galatians* (Tübingen: Mohr Siebeck, 1995), 51–54.

160. For more on Jewish settlements in Ctesiphon, see Ben-Zion Eshel, *Jewish Settlements in Babylonia during Talmudic Times: Talmudic Onomasticon, Including Geographical Locations, Historical Notes, and Indices of Place-Names* (Jerusalem: Magnes Press, 1979), 26–29 (Hebrew). On relevant Talmudic passages, see Oppenheimer, with Isaac and Lecker, *Babylonia Judaica*, 198–207. In Pahlavi, it is *tīsifōn;* see *ŠīĒr.* line 21 (T. Daryaee, *Šahrestānīhā ī Ērānšahr: A Middle Persian Text on Late Antique Geography, Epic, and History* [Costa Mesa: Mazda Publishers, 2002], 14).

161. Hamadan is also known as Ecbatana and was a main center of the Median Empire with continued prominence in the Sasanian era. On this city, see Adolphe Neubauer, *La géographie du Talmud* (Hildesheim: Olms, 1967), 375–76; and Oppenheimer, with Isaac and Lecker, *Babylonia Judaica*, 140–41 on Ernst Herzfeld's arguments regarding the tomb of Esther in this city.

162. Rav Yosef's demarcation between Inner and Outer Sakistan is unattested in Middle Persian. Sistan holds significance in the history of Zoroastrianism, on which see the short Middle Persian treatise called "The Wonders and Magnificence of Sistan" (which describes it as the region where the Zoroastrian tradition was remembered after the destruction by Alexander the Great), edited by Bo Utas, "The Pahlavi Treatise *Avdēh u Sahīkēh ī Sakistān;* or, 'Wonders and Magnificence of Sistan,'" in *From Hecataeus to Al-Huwarizmi: Bactrian, Pahlavi, Sogdian, Persian, Sanskrit, Syriac, Arabic, Chinese, Greek and Latin Sources for the History of Pre-Islamic Central Asia*, ed. J. Harmatta (Budapest: Akadémiai Kiadó, 1984), 259–67.

163. *B. Yoma* 9b–10a (MS Munich 6). Manuscript variants of place names are not recorded in the notes below.

164. MS London BL Harl. 5508 (400): "four hundred."

165. Oppenheimer, with Isaac and Lecker, *Babylonia Judaica*, 171–74, including his notes on the MSS on 171 n. 2 on the identification of this as Kashkar.

166. On Perat of Meishan, see ibid. 347–49, identifying this as a town on the lower Tigris in Mesene.

167. The tradition of identifying Tiras with Persia occurs again later in *b. Yoma* 10a, where the phrase "youngest of the flock" in Jeremiah 49:20, identified as a reference to Persia, is connected with the explanation of Tiras as Persia since Tiras is the last son mentioned (and thus youngest) in the line of Noah.

168. See Philip Wood, *The Chronicle of Seert: Christian Historical Imagination in Late Antique Iraq* (Oxford: Oxford University Press, 2013), 23; Geoffrey Herman, *Prince*, 25–26 on Arabic and other sources that mention the city as well as its Christian connections; Christelle Jullien, "Kaškar 'la sublime' et sa singulière prééminence sur le siège patriarcal de Séleucie-Ctésiphon," in *Proceedings of the Fifth Conference of the Societas Iranologica Europaea, Held in Ravenna, 6–11 October 2003*, vol. 1, *Ancient and Middle Iranian Studies*, ed. Antonio C. D. Panaino and Andrea Piras (Milan: Mimesis, 2006), 543–52.

169. See Oppenheimer, with Isaac and Lecker, *Babylonia Judaica*, 173.

170. For more on the meaning of *ōstān* as "royal domain," including in Armenian, see Mansour Shaki, "A Few Unrecognized Middle Persian Terms and Phrases," in *Middle Iranian Studies: Proceedings of the International Symposium Organized by the Katholieke Universiteit Leuven from the 17th to the 20th of May 1982*, ed. Wojciech Skalmowski and Alois Van Tongerloo (Leuven: Peeters, 1984), 95–102, esp. 97: "Each of the four provinces of Asurestān as well as some other provinces are referred to as *ōstān* in Sasanian times. In the Aram. Babylonian Talmud *'ystndr'* designates a provincial governor. The *MHD* describes the function of the *ōstāndār* in the following terms. . . . 'The *ōstāndār* is competent for restoring, laying taxes on, buying, accepting the price of, delivering, declaring (the destination of) property and (supervising) (its) going to the royal treasury.'" On this post's oversight over property finances directed at the royal treasury, see *MHD* chapter A27 (Anahit Perikhanian, *Mādayān ī Hazār Dādestān: The Book of a Thousand Judgements, a Sasanian Law-Book* [Costa Mesa: Mazda Publishers, 1997], 296–97). For a reference to a *dēwān ī ōstāndārīh* (or *ōstāndārišn*), see *MHD* chapter 65.9 (Perikhanian, *Mādayān*, 164–65).

171. *B. Giṭ.* 80b.

172. See *DJBA* 151–52.

173. MS Munich 95: "to Rava."

174. Oppenheimer, with Isaac and Lecker, *Babylonia Judaica*, 102–3.

175. *B. Sanh.* 109a (MS Jerusalem—Yad Harav Herzog 1).

176. As opposed to a valley, as Genesis 11:2 says.

177. The order of this list, as well as those in the subsequent lines, varies in the manuscripts.

178. MS Karlsruhe—Reuchlin 2: "Rav."

179. *B. Qidd.* 72a (MS Vatican 111). Rav Yosef's baraita is also in *b. Meg.* 11a and *b. 'Abod. Zar.* 2b. See also *b. Yoma* 77a's play on words between *doviel* and *dov* (and cf. *Leviticus Rabbah* 13:5), discussed already above.

180. The manuscripts differ slightly in the recording of this baraita. MS Munich 95 orders them eat and drink, restless, and grow hair, and excludes the description of them as shaggy. MS Oxford Opp. 248 (367) relates that "they eat like a bear, drink like a bear, are shaggy like a bear, and grow long hair like a bear."

181. The two principal witnesses (MS Vatican 111 and MS Munich 95) do not extend R. Ammi's tradition to include riding. Vilna and Venice Print add דרכיב "riding (a horse)," whereas MS Oxford Opp. 248 (367) reads "riding a camel." See the reference to a Persian camel in *b. B. Qam.* 55a.

182. Printed eds. and MS Munich 95: חבריין.

183. MS Munich 95 adds כך, "thus," after each response (e.g., "He said to him: Thus, they are like . . .").

184. Neubauer, *Géographie,* 374–75, remarking that these three provinces listed in R. Yoḥanan's statement were disputed between Rome and Persia.

185. Stern, *Jewish Identity,* 36–37.

186. *B. ʿAbod. Zar.* 2b. The translation is from Jeffrey L. Rubenstein, *Talmudic Stories: Narrative Art, Composition, and Culture* (Baltimore: The Johns Hopkins University Press, 1999), 215–19, with minor changes.

4. RABBIS AND SASANIAN KINGS IN DIALOGUE

1. The references in the Babylonian Talmud to Shapur I, Shapur II, and the latter's mother, Ifra Hormiz, include *b. ʿAbod. Zar.* 76b; *b. B. Bat.* 8a, 10b, 172b; *b. B. Meṣiʿa* 70b, 85a (= *b. Šabb.* 113b), 119a; *b. B. Qam.* 96b; *b. Ber.* 56a; *b. Ḥag.* 5b; *b. Ketub.* 60b–61a; *b. Moʿed Qaṭ.* 26a; *b. Ned.* 25a (= *b. Šebu.* 29b), 49b; *b. Nid.* 20b; *b. Pesaḥ.* 54a (= *b. B. Bat.* 115b); *b. Sanh.* 46b, 98a; *b. Šebu.* 6b; *b. Sukkah* 53a; *b. Taʿan.* 24b. The Jerusalem Talmud contains traditions regarding Shapur in *y. Ned.* 3:2 (37d) and in *y. Šebu.* 3:8 (34d), on Shapur's snake as seen in *b. Ned.* 25a. See the list provided in Gerd A. Wewers, "Israel zwischen den Mächten: Die rabbinischen Traditionen über König Schabhor," *Kairos* 22 (1980): 77–100, where the author categorizes which text is about which king. See also Alyssa Gray, "The Power Conferred by Distance from Power: Redaction and Meaning in b. A.Z. 10a–11a," in *Creation and Composition: The Contribution of the Bavli Redactors (Stammaim) to the Aggada,* ed. Jeffrey L. Rubenstein (Tübingen: Mohr Siebeck, 2005), 26–72, esp. 64–68.

2. For more on the generic use of proper names, see also Geoffrey Herman, "Ahasuerus, the Former Stable-Master of Belshazzar, and the Wicked Alexander of Macedon: Two Parallels between the Babylonian Talmud and Persian Sources," *Association for Jewish Studies Review* 29 (2005): 283–97, esp. 290–91 n. 39, where the author says that the authors use the name Shapur generically as meaning simply Persian king, similarly to how they use Caesar to mean the Romans.

3. On Ardawān, see *y. Peʾah* 1:1 (15d) and *b. ʿAbod. Zar.* 10b-11a. On Peroz, see *b. Ḥul.* 62b, which equates the king's name with the name of a homonymous type of bird. On later sources' allusions to this monarch's persecution of Jews, see Geo Widengren, "The Status of the Jews in the Sassanian Empire," *Iranica Antiqua* 1 (1961): 117–62, esp. 143. On Yazdegird, see *b. Ketub.* 61a–b and *b. Zebaḥ.* 19a. See also the ninth-century Middle Persian work entitled *Šahrestānīhā ī Ērānšahr* (Touraj Daryaee, *Šahrestānīhā ī Ērānšahr: A Middle Persian Text on Late Antique Geography, Epic, and History* [Costa Mesa: Mazda Publishers, 2002], 20) on Yazdegird's purported Jewish wife, and the studies by Widengren, "Status," 139–42, and Geoffrey Herman, *A Prince without a Kingdom: The Exilarch in the Sasanian Era* (Tübingen: Mohr Siebeck, 2012), 160–61.

4. For a classic book that deals with the relationship between memory, society, and authority, see Maurice Halbwachs, *The Collective Memory,* trans. Francis J. Ditter, Jr., and Vida Yazdi Ditte (New York: Harper and Row, 1980), and the helpful summary of Halbwachs by Patrick H. Hutton, *History as an Art of Memory* (Hanover: University Press of New England, 1993), 79: "For Halbwachs, therefore, the problem of memory is also one of

social power. What we remember depends on the contexts in which we find ourselves and the groups to which we happen to relate. The depth and shape of our collective memory reflect this configuration of social forces that vie for our attention."

5. For a discussion of this issue, see, e.g., Luc Herman and Bart Vervaeck, "Ideology," in *The Cambridge Companion to Narrative*, ed. David Herman (New York: Cambridge University Press, 2007), 217–30, esp. 218.

6. As noted by Georgina Hermann, "The Rock Reliefs of Sasanian Iran," in *Mesopotamia and Iran in the Parthian and Sasanian Periods: Rejection and Revival c. 238 BC–AD 642—Proceedings of a Seminar in Memory of Vladimir G. Lukonin*, ed. John Curtis (London: British Museum, 2000), 35–45, esp. 36: Sasanian rock reliefs, most of which are attested in the region of Fārs, began in the reign of the first monarch, Ardashir, who "initiated one of the most coherent and remarkable periods of rock relief art." This renaissance continued to flourish until the era of Shapur II (309–79 C.E.), when there began a rapid decline of such epigraphica.

7. For critical editions of Shapur I's inscriptions and rock reliefs, see the following: for the major inscription on the *Ka'ba-ye Zardušt* at Naqš-ī Rostam near Persepolis, consult Philip Huyse, *Die dreisprachige Inschrift Šābuhrs I. an der Ka'ba-i Zardušt (ŠKZ), Corpus Inscriptionum Iranicarum*, part 3, *Pahlavi Inscriptions*, vol. 1, *Royal Inscriptions, with Their Parthian and Greek Versions* (London: School of Oriental and African Studies, 1999); Michael Back, *Die sassanidischen Staatsinschriften: Studien zur Orthographie und Phonologie des Mittelpersischen der Inschriften zusammen mit einem etymologischen Index des mittelpersischen Wortgutes und einem Textcorpus der behandelten Inschriften* (Leiden: Brill, 1978).

8. For a general overview of the numismatic remains for Shapur I, see Robert Göbl, *Sasanian Numismatics* (Würzburg: Braunschweig, Klinkhardt, and Biermann, 1971), 43, 75–76, and coins 21–34, and "Šābuhr, König der Könige von Iran," *Quaderni Ticinesi di Numismatica e Antichità Classiche* 20 (1991): 239–45.

9. Middle Persian texts about Shapur I include passages in the *Kārnāmag ī Ardaxšēr ī Pābagān* and the *Dēnkard*, as well as the *Šahrestānīhā ī Ērānšahr* (Touraj Daryaee, *Šahrestānīhā ī Ērānšahr: A Middle Persian Text on Late Antique Geography, Epic, and History* [Costa Mesa: Mazda Publishers, 2002], 14–16 and 18–20) lines 13, 25, 43, 48, where the text describes the king's city building. In other Pahlavi texts that discuss the Sasanian kings in abbreviated list form, Shapur I is typically ignored; for two examples, see the long narrative about the destruction endured by Ērānšahr over the millennia, *Bund.* chapter 33.1–22 (Behramgore Tahmuras Anklesaria, *Zand-Ākāsīh: Iranian or Greater Bundahišn* [Bombay: Rahnumae Mazdayasnan Sabha, 1956], 272–79); and a discussion of the rite of ordeal in *Dēnk. V* chapter 22 (J. Amouzgar and A. Tafazzoli, *Le cinquième livre du Dēnkard* [Paris: Association pour l'Avancement des Études Iraniennes, 2000], 70–71).

10. For a general historical overview of the reign of Shapur I, see Touraj Daryaee, *Sasanian Persia: The Rise and Fall of an Empire* (New York: I. B. Tauris, 2009), 6–9, 13–15, 69–79; Arthur Christensen, *L'Iran sous les Sassanides*, 2nd ed. (Copenhagen: Munksgaard, 1944), 218–26; Richard N. Frye, "The Political History of Iran under the Sasanians," in *The Cambridge History of Iran*, vol. 3.1, *The Seleucid, Parthian, and Sasanian Periods*, ed. Ehsan Yarshater (Cambridge: Cambridge University Press, 1983), 118–27; Klaus Schippmann, *Grundzüge der Geschichte des sasanidischen Reiches* (Darmstadt: Wissenschaftliche

Buchgesellscahft, 1990), 19–26; Josef Wiesehöfer, *Ancient Persia from 550 B.C. to 650 A.D.*, trans. Azizeh Azodi (New York: I. B. Tauris, 1996), 160–75, 211–16.

11. The relationship between Shmuel and Shapur in the Talmud was the focus of several works by German scholars in the late nineteenth and the early twentieth century; see, for example, Jakob Horovitz, *Mar Samuel und Schabur I: Zur Erklärung der letzten Zeilen des Talmudtraktats Baba Mezia* (Breslau: Marcus, 1936); David Zvi Hoffman, *Mar Samuel, Rector der jüdischen Akademie zu Nehardea in Babylonien: Lebensbild eines talmudischen Weisen der ersten Hälfte des dritten Jahrhunderts, nach den Quellen dargestellt* (Leipzig: Leiner, 1873), 45–48; Siegmund Fessler, *Mar Samuel, der bedeutendste Amora* (Breslau: Frank, 1879). Cf. also Jacob Neusner, *A History of the Jews in Babylonia*, vol. 2, *The Early Sasanian Period* (Leiden: Brill, 1966), 64–72.

12. See Davoud Monchi-Zadeh, "Xusrōv i Kavātān ut Rētak: Pahlavi Text, Transcription and Translation," in *Monumentum Georg Morgenstierne*, vol. 2 (Leiden: Brill, 1982), 47–92, esp. 76–77.

13. For more on Shmuel's acculturation to Persian norms, see Yaakov Elman, "Middle Persian Culture and Babylonian Sages: Accommodation and Resistance in the Shaping of Rabbinic Legal Tradition," in *The Cambridge Companion to the Talmud and Rabbinic Literature*, ed. Charlotte Elisheva Fonrobert and Martin S. Jaffee (Cambridge: Cambridge University Press, 2007), 174.

14. *B. Sanh.* 98a. The dialogue follows MS Jerusalem—Yad Harav Herzog 1.

15. On this word, see *DJBA* 183, following MS Jerusalem—Yad Harav Herzog 1, which is the more accurate rendering. As Sokoloff notes, in all the witnesses the word סוסיא precedes the loanword as a gloss, thus causing a redundancy. Other manuscripts have ברקא, "lightning," on which cf. also *DJPA* 115, s.v. ברק, "riding an animal."

16. *B. Pesaḥ.* 54a, and cf. *b. B. Bat.* 115b. The MSS of this text vary, esp. with respect to the second tradition; e.g., MS Vatican 125 does not have the second reference to Rav Pappa and Rava, whereas MS Munich 95 reads "Rava said. . . . Rava."

17. The Talmud is here attempting to reconcile the contradiction between Genesis 26:20, where Anah is called Zibeon's brother, and Genesis 26:24, where he is called his son.

18. *B. B. Qam.* 96b. This excerpt appears amid a discussion regarding the penalties for robbery and, more specifically, in a case regarding stolen oxen.

19. *B. Sanh.* 46b.

20. Cf. *b. Ned.* 28a, *b. Giṭ.* 10b, *b. B. Qam.* 113a, *b. B. Bat.* 54b and 55a. For several treatments of this phrase, see Shmuel Shilo, *Dina De-Malkhuta Dina* (Jerusalem: Jerusalem Academic Press, 1974; Hebrew); Leopold Löw, "Dina de-Malekhuta Dina," *Ben Chananja* 5 (1862): 36–40; Jacob Neusner, *A History of the Jews in Babylonia*, vol. 3, *From Shapur I to Shapur II* (Leiden: Brill, 1968), 43–44.

21. Isaiah Gafni, "The Political, Social, and Economic History of Babylonian Jewry, 224-638 CE," in *The Cambridge History of Judaism*, vol. 4, *The Late Roman–Rabbinic Period*, ed. Steven T. Katz (New York: Cambridge University Press, 2006), 792–820, esp. 796.

22. For a discussion of Persian influences on the Talmud's civil law, see Yaakov Elman, "'Up to the Ears' in Horses' Necks (B.M. 108a): On Sasanian Agricultural Policy and Private 'Eminent Domain,'" *Jewish Studies: An Internet Journal* 3 (2004): 95–149.

23. See Richard Kalmin, *Jewish Babylonia between Persia and Roman Palestine* (New York: Oxford University Press, 2006), 122–29.

24. *Y. Pe'ah* 1:1 (15d) (Yaacov Sussmann, ed., *Talmud Yerushalmi: According to Ms. Or. 4720 [Scal. 3] of the Leiden University Library, with Restorations and Corrections* [Jerusalem: The Academy of the Hebrew Language, 2001], 82).

25. Cf. Proverbs 3:15. The reference here is to wisdom.

26. Gray, "Power," 60–61.

27. For a book that probes how ancient Jews used "the arts of cultural persistence," see Steven Weitzman, *Surviving Sacrilege: Cultural Persistence in Jewish Antiquity* (Cambridge, Mass.: Harvard University Press, 2005).

28. This is a debated issue in Sasanian history, on which see Shaul Shaked, "Religion in the Late Sasanian Period: Eran, Aneran, and Other Religious Designations," in *The Sasanian Era*, vol. 3 of *The Idea of Iran*, ed. Vesta Sarkhosh Curtis and Sarah Stewart (New York: I. B. Tauris, 2008), 103–17, where the author emphasizes the political motivations behind the early Sasanians' religious policies; and Philip G. Kreyenbroek, "How Pious was Shapur I? Religion, Church and Propaganda under the Early Sasanians," in *The Sasanian Era*, vol. 3 of *The Idea of Iran*, ed. Vesta Sarkhosh Curtis and Sarah Stewart (New York: I. B. Tauris, 2008), 7–16, where the author explores the king's religiosity. In Shapur's res gestae, the king discusses religious matters at length and characterizes the Sasanian throne as a divine calling. Ancient Iranists continue to debate the extent to which Zoroastrianism existed as an organized, single doctrine of belief and practice in this period. Shapur's relative openness toward other religions is attested in the rise of Mani, who had the king's permission to preach his message across the empire, and his Middle Persian book the *Šābuhragān* (literally, *Dedicated to Shapur*), on which see David Neil MacKenzie, "Mani's Šābuhragān, I," *Bulletin of the School of Oriental and African Studies* 42 (1979): 500–534, and "Mani's Šābuhragān, II," *Bulletin of the School of Oriental and African Studies* 43 (1980): 288–310; Manfred Hutter, *Manis kosmogonische Šābuhragān-Texte: Edition, Kommentar und literaturgeschichtliche Einordnung der manichäisch-mittelpersischen Handschriften M 98/99 I und M 7980–7984* (Wiesbaden: Harrassowitz, 1992). The general impression that Pahlavi sources give of Shapur's religiosity is of a believing Mazdayasnian who promoted the good religion and ordered the Avesta to be collected and reconstituted but who was at the same time open to the value of non-Mazdayasnian knowledge.

29. For more on the issue of taxation in Jewish Babylonia, see David Goodblatt, "The Poll Tax in Sasanian Babylonia," *Journal of the Economic and Social History of the Orient* 22 (1979): 233–95.

30. There is a vast literature on this important figure in early Sasanian history; see, for instance, Philippe Gignoux, *Les quatre inscriptions du mage Kirdīr: Textes et concordances* (Paris: Association pour l'Avancement des Études Iraniennes, 1991), esp. 69–70 for the reference to the persecution of Jews and other religious minorities in the inscriptions; Moshe Beer, "The Decrees of Kartir on the Babylonian Jews," *Tarbiz* 55 (1986): 525–39 (Hebrew); and "On Three Edicts against the Jews of Babylonia in the Third Century C.E.," in *Irano-Judaica: Studies Relating to Jewish Contacts with Persian Culture throughout the Ages*, ed. Shaul Shaked (Jerusalem: Ben-Zvi Institute, 1982), 25–37 (Hebrew); Kalmin, *Jewish Babylonia*, 124, 127–30, 136–38.

31. For more on the significance of this formative event in Iranian religious history, see Christelle Jullien, "La minorité chrétienne 'grecque' en terre d'Iran à l'époque sassanide," in *Chrétiens en terre d'Iran: Implantation et acculturation*, vol. 1, ed. Rika Gyselen (Paris:

Association pour l'Avancement des Études Iraniennes, 2006), 105–42; Kalmin, *Jewish Babylonia,* 5–8 and n. 39; and for Shapur's description of this event in his res gestae, see Back, *Sassanidischen Staatsinschriften,* 324–26, where the inscription records that the deportees from the Roman Empire (= *Anērān*) were settled in Persis, Parthia, Khuzestan, and Mesopotamia, among other provinces.

32. Transcription of Back, *Sassanidischen Staatsinschriften,* 284. For a detailed analysis of the two terms *Ērān* and *Anērān* and their significance for Sasanian royal ideology, see the monograph by Gherardo Gnoli, *The Idea of Iran: An Essay on Its Origin* (Rome: Istituto Italiano per il Medio ed Estremo Oriente, distributed by Brill [Leiden], 1989), esp. 129–74.

33. Shapur Shahbazi, "Shapur I," *Encyclopaedia Iranica,* online ed., 2002: www.iranica.com/articles/shapur-i.

34. *Kārn.* chapter 10 (F. Grenet, *La geste d'Ardashir fils de Pâbag: Kārnāmag ī Ardaxšēr ī Pābagān* [Die, 2003], 100–101).

35. *B. B. Meṣi'a* 118b–119a.

36. On this word, see *DJBA* 158. The spelling אפרין is attested in MS Munich 95 and MS Vatican 115. Cf. also MS Florence II-I-8, with two yods. Other witnesses, including the principal manuscript, Hamburg 165 (see *DJBA* 58), read אפריה. See R. N. N. Rabbinowicz, *Variae Lectiones in Mischnam et in Talmud Babylonicum,* vol. 13, *Baba Mezia* (Munich: Huber, 1883), 358.

37. The passage treated here comes from Book 4 of the *Dēnkard,* of which there exists no critical edition. *Dēnkard* Book 4 is a compilation of theological, philosophical, and historiographical passages and, as a result, has a particularly complex transmission history that Iranists have yet to untangle; see, e.g., the characterization by Philippe Gignoux, "Dēnkard," *Encyclopaedia Iranica,* online ed., 1994: www.iranicaonline.org/articles/denkard, where the author observes that "Book IV seems particularly incoherent in its organization." For another analysis of this text in comparison with the Bavli, see also Shai Secunda, *The Iranian Talmud: Reading the Bavli in Its Sasanian Context* (Philadelphia: University of Pennsylvania Press, 2013), 58–63.

38. When exactly the Avesta was dispersed, collected, and redacted is still debated, but there is emerging a general consensus (much of it based on the paleographic evidence of the Avestan script) that it was the Sasanians, with their so-called Sasanian archetype, who were the first to record the Avesta in written form. Linguistic evidence suggests that the Sasanians initially based the canon on varying oral traditions from different regions of Iran (especially Arachosia, Parthia, and Sogdia) during the Achaemenid and Arsacid eras, and then began to Westernize it according to their own Persian-Sasanian perspective. For more on this subject, see Almut Hintze, "The Avesta in the Parthian Period," in *Das Partherreich und seine Zeugnisse,* ed. J. Wiesehöfer (Stuttgart: Steiner, 1998), 147–62.

39. This passage in the *Dēnkard* poses many linguistic challenges to the translator, especially its complex syntax, challenging lexicon, and scribal corruptions; for a representative sample of conflicting translations and commentaries, see especially Shaul Shaked, *Dualism in Transformation: Varieties of Religion in Sasanian Iran* (London: School of Oriental and African Studies, 1994), 100–101, and esp. 103 n. 37, with further bibliographical references; Helmut Humbach, with Josef Elfenbein and Prods Oktor Skjærvø, *The Gāthās of Zarathustra and the Other Old Avestan Texts,* part 1, *Introduction: Text and Translation* (Heidelberg: Winter, 1991), 52–54; Mansour Shaki, "The Dēnkard Account of the History of the Zoroas-

trian Scriptures," *Archiv Orientální* 49 (1981): 114–25; Robert C. Zaehner, *Zurvan: A Zoroastrian Dilemma* (Oxford: Clarendon Press, 1955), 8 and 31–32. The primary text in Pahlavi of this narrative can be found in Dhanjishah Meherjibhai Madan, ed., *The Complete Text of the Pahlavi Dinkard,* 2 vols. (Bombay: Society for the Promotion of Researches into the Zoroastrian Religion, 1911), 412ff.; M. J. Dresden, ed., *Dēnkart: A Pahlavi Text* (Wiesbaden: Harrassowitz, 1966), 511; and see the version in Henrik Samuel Nyberg, *A Manual of Pahlavi,* vol. 1 (Wiesbaden: Harrassowitz, 1964), 108–9. The transcription and translation of the passage are my own, and in part based on what I deem to be the most convincing readings of these previous interpretations.

40. This is *ēwār,* "pillaging"; cf. *āvār* in Francis Joseph Steingass, *A Comprehensive Persian-English Dictionary* (London: Routledge, 1892), 117.

41. This is the word *ēk,* "one," and Shaki's rendering of it as **ēwar,* "certain, for sure" ("Dēnkard Account," 115 n. 4) is without grounds. Interestingly, the Bavli can be of use to Iranists in deciphering whether Shaki's reading is suitable in this context, since it contains the loanword *ēwar* in eight passages (*b. B. Bat.* 46a and 168a; *b. B. Meṣi'a* 8b; *b. B. Qam.* 117a; *b. Giṭ.* 56b, *b. Ḥul.* 59b; *b. Mo'ed Qaṭ.* 7b; *b. Šebu.* 10a). Although the Bavli's loanwords in no way represent definitive evidence of the semantic range of Pahlavi words, it is significant that the Bavli uses the loanword adverbially and in pseudodialogues between Talmudic figures. In the Bavli there is no connection between the word *ēwar* and the topic of choosing authoritative texts.

42. The phrase *frāz ō amāh* (literally, "up to us") is translated here as "restricted to us" because the adverb or preverb *frāz,* which typically expresses forward movement ("forth"), can also sometimes be used in a restrictive sense.

43. The word *frōd* is being used here to express deficiency; see, for instance, the Middle Persian word *frōdmānd,* which means "deficiency, shortcoming."

44. Cf. the translation of Shaki, "Dēnkard Account," 119: "(From now) on (only) those are true expositions which are based on the Mazdean religion, for now there is no lack of information and knowledge concerning them."

45. Ibid. 116 n. 6 reads *star-gōwišnīh* for *star-ōšmār,* "astrology."

46. Ibid. 116 n. 7, and Shaked, *Dualism,* 100 n. 6: *jahišn,* "accident." The script also plausibly reads *dahišn,* "creation."

47. Humbach, *Gāthās,* 54: **nērōgīh,* "strength," though Nyberg's manuscript reads *kirrōgīh.*

48. This word appears to be superfluous; Nyberg's manuscript reads: OLE, *ōy,* "he she, it."

49. Possible interpretations include *šāhīgān,* given by Shaki, "Dēnkard Account," 116, and David Neil MacKenzie, *A Concise Pahlavi Dictionary* (Oxford: Oxford University Press, 1971), 79; and *šabīgān,* given by Shaked, *Dualism,* 100 n. 3, where the author proposes the reading "the (royal) quarters."

50. Transliteration: *'lyst'n.* This disputed word has been interpreted in different ways. Both Humbach, *Gāthās,* 54, and Zaehner, *Zurvan,* 32, among other translators, understand the word as *(h)argestān,* meaning something like "academic disciplines; systems; school." Alternatively, Shaki, "Dēnkard Account," 116 n. 10, reconstructs this as **arist<agān,* meaning "unmixed principles," whereas Shaked, *Dualism,* 101 n. 9, interprets it as "provinces," from *arg,* "castle."

51. So translates Shaki, "Dēnkard Account," 119, with whom I concur. Other translators: "books taken from other (sources) than the (Zoroastrian) religion," or "writings deriving from the religion." The grammatical problems here are whether *dēn* refers specifically to Zoroastrianism, which it often does, or to religions more generally, and the meaning of the ambiposition *az* . . . *bē*. When the preposition *bē* is used in conjunction with another preposition (e.g., *bē* . . . *ēnyā*, *bē* . . . *tā*), which appears to be the case here in combination with *az* (though in reverse order), it most typically means "except" or other similar expressions of want (e.g., *bē az*, "without"); for other meanings, see also Henrik Samuel Nyberg, *A Manual of Pahlavi*, vol. 2 (Wiesbaden: Harrassowitz, 1974), 46–47.

52. Other translators have rendered this verb, *abāz handāxt*, as "added" (Zaehner, *Zurvan*, 8), "collated" (Shaki, "Dēnkard Account," 119), "collocated again" (Humbach, *Gāthās*, 54), or "caused to fit" (Shaked, *Dualism*, 101).

53. The word *ēstēnīdan* is a noun composed of the present stem of *ēstādan* (*ēst*-), "to stand; be; continue" with the causative addition -*ēn*, plus the infinitive ending, and means "establishment" or "perpetuation." Shaked, *Dualism*, 101, translates this word as "establishing."

54. Michael Stausberg, "The Invention of a Canon: The Case of Zoroastrianism," in *Canonization and Decanonization: Papers Presented to the International Conference of the Leiden Institute for the Study of Religions (LISOR), Held at Leiden 9–10 January 1997*, ed. A. van der Kooij and K. van der Toorn (Leiden: Brill, 1998), 257–78, esp. 264.

55. For studies on Greek influences on the Pahlavi corpus, see by way of example the encyclopedia entry by David Neil MacKenzie, "Bundahišn," *Encyclopaedia Iranica*, online edition, 1989: www.iranicaonline.org/articles/bundahisn-primal-creation, where MacKenzie states that the main author of the *Bundahišn* lived at the end of the Sasanian era and possessed encyclopedic knowledge of Avestan cosmology and the Greek sciences, including astronomy; and Philippe Gignoux, "Un témoin du syncrétisme mazdéen tardif: Le traité pehlevi des 'Sélections de'," in *Transition Periods in Iranian History: Actes du Symposium de Fribourg-en-Brisgau (22–24 Mai 1985)* (Paris: Association pour l'Avancement des Études Iraniennes, 1987), 59–72.

56. Shaki, "Dēnkard Account," 123 (cf. Madan, *Complete Text*, 428: 14–20).

57. Shaki, "Dēnkard Account," 120–21.

58. On this rabbinic dream book, see Philip S. Alexander, "Bavli Berakhot 55a–57b: The Talmudic Dreambook in Context," *Journal of Jewish Studies* 46 (1995): 230–48. For an article delineating the Persian context of Talmudic dream interpretation, see Richard Kalmin, "Talmudic Attitudes toward Dream Interpreters: Preliminary Thoughts on Their Iranian Cultural Context," in *The Talmud in its Iranian Context*, ed. Carol Bakhos and M. Rahim Shayegan (Tübingen: Mohr Siebeck, 2010), 83–99.

59. My translation of *b. Ber.* 55b–56a for the most part follows MS Oxford Opp. Add. fol. 23.

60. It is noteworthy that the motif of personally capturing the Roman emperor is common in Shapur I's Sasanian epigraphica, in which the Persian king is often depicted as having captured the Roman emperor; see, for instance, Back, *Sassanidischen Staatsinschriften*, 313–14.

61. David Winston, "The Iranian Component in the Bible, Apocrypha and Qumran: A Review of the Evidence," *History of Religions* 5 (1966): 183–216, esp. 186 n. 9.

62. See also Mark 10:24–25 and Luke 18:24–25.

63. Compare also *b. B. Meṣiʿa* 38b, where the aphorism is used in reference to the scholars of Pumbedita.

64. The translation is based on Jean de Menasce, *Une apologétique mazdéenne du IXe siècle: Škand-gumānīk vičār, la solution décisive des doutes* (Fribourg: Librairie de l'Université, 1945), 66–67, with some slight changes.

65. The information that Bati bar Tovi is a slave comes from tractate *Qiddushin,* and it is not necessarily the case that the transmitters of this narrative knew about that other reference.

66. *B. ʿAbod. Zar.* 76b.

67. According to *DJBA* 179–80, this word is Iranian (MIr. **ātrung;* cf. MP *wādrang*).

68. For a comparison of these Bavli and Yerushalmi passages, see David Brodsky, *A Bride without a Blessing: A Study in the Redaction and Content of Massekhet Kallah and Its Gemara* (Tübingen: Mohr Siebeck, 2006), 294–95. The Yerushalmi Talmud states that a small knife should be stuck in the ground three times but a large one should be heated up with sparks. The Tosefta (*t. ʿAbod. Zar.* 8:2) says that all knives should be heated up.

69. See Richard Kalmin, *The Sage in Jewish Society of Late Antiquity* (New York: Routledge, 1999), 52–53.

5. RABBIS AND ZOROASTRIAN PRIESTS IN JUDICIAL SETTINGS

1. See Jacob Neusner, "Rabbi and Magus in Third-Century Sasanian Babylonia," *History of Religions* 6 (1966): 169–78.

2. See Michael S. Berger, *Rabbinic Authority* (New York: Oxford University Press, 1998), 10–12 and 73–77. For an analogous breakdown of the concept of authority, see also Bruce Lincoln, *Authority: Construction and Corrosion* (Chicago: University of Chicago Press, 1994), 3–4. Scholars of rabbinic literature can utilize outside scholarship on authority to help conceptualize rabbinic authority in Babylonia; see, for example, Theodore L. Brown, *Imperfect Oracle: The Epistemic and Moral Authority of Science* (University Park: Pennsylvania University Press, 2009), 19–38, esp. 21–24, where the author fruitfully differentiates between rational-legal, traditional, charismatic, coercive, and moral types of authority.

3. Neusner, "Rabbi," 175.

4. See Kimberly B. Stratton, "Imagining Power: Magic, Miracle, and the Social Context of Rabbinic Self-Representation," *Journal of the American Academy of Religion* 73 (2005): 361–93, esp. 382–85, on differences between the Persian and Greek models of authority with respect to knowledge of magic and esoteric traditions.

5. See Jonathan Z. Smith, *Relating Religion: Essays in the Study of Religion* (Chicago: University of Chicago Press, 2004), 245. I have adopted the expressions in quotation marks, and the concept of situating, from Smith.

6. See *b. Yoma* 35a and *b. Ḥul.* 62b, on "Parwa the magian [אמגושא]." On this name, see Shai Secunda, "Parva—A Magus," in *Shoshannat Yaakov: Jewish and Iranian Studies in Honor of Yaakov Elman,* ed. Shai Secunda and Steven Fine (Leiden: Brill, 2012), 391–402. On the value of Syriac sources such as *Acts of the Persian Martyrs* for reconstructing the lives and positions of Sasanian *mowbeds* in the fourth and fifth centuries C.E., see Philippe Gignoux, "Éléments de prosopographie de quelques *mōbads* sasanides," *Journal Asiatique* 270 (1982): 257–69.

7. For references to the אמגושא and variants, see *b. B. Bat.* 58a; *b. Ḥul.* 62b; *b. Mo'ed Qaṭ.* 18a; *b. Šabb.* 75a; *b. Sanh.* 39a, 98a (= *b. Šabb.* 139a); *b. Soṭah* 21b–22a; *b. Yoma* 35a. In the Talmud the terms מגושתא (printed eds.) and אמגושתא (MS Munich 95 and MS Oxford Opp. Add. fol. 23) appear in *b. Šabb.* 75a. The rendering מגוש appears only in *b. Soṭah* 22a, as does, for the only time in a principal witness, מגושא (the latter word does appear elsewhere but not in a majority reading; see, e.g., MS Munich 95 of *b. Yoma* 35a). On the חברי and חברא, see *b. Yebam.* 63b, *b. Beṣah* 6a, *b. Šabb.* 45a, *b. Giṭ.* 16b–17a. The occurrences of חברים and חברין, which are understood as references to Zoroastrian priests based on Rashi and the commentaries, include *b. Qidd.* 72a, *b. Pesaḥ.* 113b, *b. Šabb.* 11a. There are additional attestations of these common words in the Talmud, though so far as I can tell none appears to contain evidence for being about Persians. For other pertinent texts, see the reference to the חברייא in *b. Sanh.* 65b: "Rava created a man and sent him to R. Zeira. R. Zeira spoke to him, but he did not answer. He said to him: You are a creation of the חברייא—return to your dust." This is the spelling in MS Florence II-I-9 and MS Jerusalem—Yad Harav Herzog 1. Scholars have interpreted this word, which appears elsewhere in the Talmud, differently; compare, for instance, the understanding of it as "pietist" in Moshe Idel, *Golem: Jewish Magical and Mystical Traditions on the Artificial Anthropoid* (Albany: State University of New York Press, 1990), 27–30, as opposed to as "magian" in *DJBA* 429. As Idel notes, it is true that other attestations of חברייא in rabbinic literature mean "colleagues" or "associates" (e.g., *b. Ḥag.* 25a, *b. Roš Haš.* 13b, and in Palestinian sources noted in *DJPA* 185–86), raising the prospect that scholars have associated this title with Persian priests because of the context of magic in *b. Sanh.* 65b. The Talmud also mentions the Zoroastrian priests indirectly by reference to a בי נורא, "Persian fire temple" in *b. Ned.* 62b (MS Vatican 110) and קאווקי ודמוניאקי, "braziers and bellows" (used in a fire temple), the latter term being Iranian (cf. MP *damēnag*), in *b. Sanh.* 74b (MS Jerusalem—Yad Harav Herzog 1).

8. See *DJBA*, 138. For the Old Persian form, see Roland Kent, *Old Persian: Grammar, Texts, Lexicon* (New Haven: American Oriental Society, 1959), 201. See also Pierfrancesco Callieri, "In the Land of the Magi: Demons and Magic in the Everyday Life of Pre-Islamic Iran," in *Démons et merveilles d'Orient*, ed. Rika Gyselen (Leuven: Peeters, 2001), 11–36, esp. 14 n. 32, who notes the "Greek plural form based on the Aramaic plural form aramaica *magūšaiā*," as well as the fact that there is "as yet no certainty about the formation of the Aramaic singular *magūšā*, which also seems to include in the root the Ancient Persian inflection of the nominative singular." Compare the opinion of Zsigmond Telegdi, "Essai sur la phonétique des emprunts iraniens en araméen talmudique," *Journal Asiatique* 226 (1935): 177–256, esp. 229, who hesitates to offer this proposal.

9. On this philological debate, see Albert de Jong, *Traditions of the Magi: Zoroastrianism in Greek and Latin Literature* (Leiden: Brill, 1997), 387; Émile Benveniste, *Les mages dans l'ancien Iran* (Paris: Maisonneuve, 1938), 11–17; Hanns-Peter Schmidt, "Gathic *maga* and Vedic *maghá*," in *K. R. Cama Oriental Institute, International Congress Proceedings* (Bombay: H. J. M. Desai and H. N. Modi, 1991), 220–39, esp. 222, where the author shows that the Pahlavi translators glossed the Avestan word with *abēzagīh* or *abēzag wehīh*, "pure goodness," a term used in reference to the priesthood, "based on the mistaken connection with the term *magu*."

10. Claudia A. Ciancaglini, *Iranian Loanwords in Syriac* (Wiesbaden: Reichert, 2008), 201–2, s.v. *mgušā* (and derivatives), meaning: "magic, the Magi, to worship according to

magian rites; to practice magic, to use enchantments." The author explains that "Syr. mgwš' is a loanword from OP into Off. Aramaic, then passed into Syriac."

11. Syriac, on the other hand, does have the form *mawhpāṭā,* related to the MP form *mowbed.* See Ciancaglini, ibid. 202–3.

12. See Geo Widengren, "The Status of the Jews in the Sassanian Empire," *Iranica Antiqua* 1 (1961): 117–62, esp. 159: "The meaning of 'sorcerers' given to the word properly denoting 'Magian' represents an interesting semantic development which we can follow in late-Hellenistic literature."

13. See Callieri, "In the Land of the Magi," 14 n. 32. The reference to the "Rav-Mag" in Jeremiah 39:13 does not appear to be a borrowing from Persian.

14. On this point, see Samuel Krauss, Bernhardo Geiger, Ludovico Ginzberg, Immanuele Löw, and Benjamino Murmelstein, eds., *Additamenta ad Librum Aruch Completum Alexandri Kohut* (Vienna: The Alexander Kohut Memorial Foundation, 1937), 178.

15. See *b. Qidd.* 72a and *b. Giṭ.* 16b–17a.

16. See, e.g., the explanations by Rashi in *b. Šabb.* 11a, s.v. *ḥabar,* and in *b. Qidd.* 72a, s.v. *ḥabarîn.* For the most part these explanations come from the Talmudic passages themselves.

17. Isaiah Gafni, "Babylonian Rabbinic Culture," in *Cultures of the Jews,* vol. 1, *Mediterranean Origins,* ed. David Biale (New York: Schocken Books, 2002), 223–66, esp. 256 n. 30; but the author provides no evidence for this connection.

18. See, for example, *b. Giṭ.* 16b–17a in *The Hebrew-English Edition of the Babylonian Talmud: Giṭṭin,* trans. Maurice Simon (London: Soncino Press, 1963). Cf. also *b. Šabb.* 11a and *b. Yebam.* 63b, where the translation is "Parsee." The editorial notes explain that the Persians are called *ḥabarîm* because they come from a place named Haber; but see the response by Jacob Neusner, *A History of the Jews in Babylonia,* vol. 1, *The Parthian Period* (Leiden: Brill, 1965), 160 n. 3. I have not been able to trace any information that supports the claim of Persian descent from this locale. For more on the word "Gueber," see also Theodor Nöldeke, *Geschichte der Perser und Araber zur Zeit der Sasaniden: Aus der arabischen Chronik des Tabari* (Leiden: Brill, 1879), 68–69 n. 1.

19. On the Voltaire essay, see Paul Mendes-Flohr and Jehuda Reinharz, eds., *The Jew in the Modern World: A Documentary History,* 3rd ed. (New York: Oxford University Press, 2011), 279–80. See also James Bassett, *Persia, the Land of the Imams: A Narrative of Travel and Residence, 1871–1885* (New York: Charles Scriber's Sons, 1886), 312–16. For a third example, see Vincent L. Milner, *Religious Denominations of the World: Comprising a General View of the Origin, History, and Condition of the Various Sects of Christians, the Jews, and Mahometans, as Well as the Pagan Forms of Religion Existing in the Different Countries of the Earth* (Philadelphia: Garretson, 1871), 452.

20. See Francis Joseph Steingass, *A Comprehensive Persian-English Dictionary* (London: Routledge, 1892), 1074. Cf. also the word *gāvr* (or perhaps *gāwur*), "infidel," ibid. 1101, which may be related.

21. Mansour Shaki, "Gabr," *Encyclopaedia Iranica,* online ed., 2000: www.iranicaonline.org/articles/gabr-.

22. See Alessandro Bausani, "Gabr," in *Encyclopedia of Islam,* 2nd ed., online: referenceworks.brillonline.com/entries/encyclopaedia-of-islam-2/gabr-SIM_2413.

23. See Bausani, "Gabr," and Shaki, "Gabr."

24. On the word *mog*, see the word list *FīP* chapter 13.2 (Bo Utas, *Frahang ī Pahlavīk: Edited, with Transliteration, Transcription, and Commentary from the Posthumous Papers of Henrik Samuel Nyberg* [Wiesbaden: Harrassowitz, 1988], 47 and 82; and Henrik Samuel Nyberg, *A Manual of Pahlavi*, vol. 2 (Wiesbaden: Harrassowitz, 1974), 122. See also A. V. Williams-Jackson, "The Religion of the Achaemenids," in *Indo-Iranian Studies: Being Commemorative Papers Contributed by European, American and Indian Scholars in Honour of Shams-Ul-Ullema Dastur Darab Peshotan Sanjana*, trans. D. Mackichan (New York: Routledge Library Editions, 1925 [reprint 2011]), 31–60, esp. 44–45.

25. Similarly, Modi, a Parsi scholar of the early twentieth century, argued for an Avestan origin of *gabr*, which means "blind" (cf. MP *kōr*); see Jivanji Jamshedji Modi, "An Avesta Amulet for Contracting Friendship," in *Anthropological Papers*, vol. 1 (Bombay: British India Press, 1911), 131–39.

26. For a plausible phonetic explanation of how "to a Persian ear the Arabic /k/ would have sounded more like a /g/ while the long /a/ would have sounded like the short closed /a/ in Persian," see Harry Stuart Neale, "Sufism, Godliness and Popular Islamic Storytelling in Farīd al-Dīn 'Aṭṭār's *Tadkiratu-l-'awliyā',*" (Ph.D. dissertation, University of California, Berkeley, 2007), 12–13 n. 39, citing a personal communication with Martin Schwartz (UC Berkeley, May 2, 2006). For more on the penetration of Arabic into Persian, see John R. Perry, "Lexical Areas and Semantic Fields of Arabic Loanwords in Persian and Beyond," in *Linguistic Convergence and Areal Diffusion: Case Studies from Iranian, Semitic, and Turkic*, ed. Éva Ágnes Csató, Bo Isaksson, and Carina Jahani (New York: RoutledgeCurzon, 2005), 97–110, esp. 99: "The bulk of the terms taken from Arabic reflect the spiritual and intellectual concerns of literate converts." The term *kāfer* could certainly be included in this category. Finally, note the counterargument of Shaki, "Gabr," who actually accepts that there is a semantic extension to Arabic, stating that "although *gabr* has been sometimes used to denote infidel (*kāfer*) by semantic extension . . . *kāfer* as a generic word could hardly refer to a specific revealed religion such as Zoroastrianism."

27. Shaki cites M. Shteyermanova, *Vsemirnaya Istoriya* (World History), vol. 2 (Moscow, 1955), 25.2.1. I have been unable to trace this reference. On the heterogram GBRA, see the word list *FīP* chapter 11.4 (Bo Utas, *Frahang ī Pahlavīk: Edited, with Transliteration, Transcription, and Commentary from the Posthumous Papers of Henrik Samuel Nyberg* [Wiesbaden: Harrassowitz, 1988], 46 and 78), which equates *gabrā*, "man," with *mard*, "man." This work does not have a separate entry for *mogmard*. See Maria Macuch, "Pahlavi Literature," in *The Literature of Pre-Islamic Iran*, ed. Ronald E. Emmerick and Maria Macuch (New York: I. B. Tauris, 2009), 116–96, esp. 122–23 on the unknown date of the earliest strata of the work, whose final editing took place in the post-Sasanian period.

28. Shaki, "Gabr."

29. According to Desmond Durkin-Meisterernst, "Huzwāreš," *Encyclopaedia Iranica*, online ed., 2004: www.iranicaonline.org/articles/huzwares: "The New Persian term Gabr (Zoroastrian) may have arisen 'as a contemptuous term for the people who wrote 'GBR'' instead of '*mard*'' (Sims-Williams, personal communication . . .), in which case it demonstrates a correct reading of the heterogram involved." I am not sure, however, that there is any way to corroborate this claim given the problems of our sources. Moreover, it is not clear to me why writing it this way would have been offensive.

30. This is generally agreed upon. See Durkin-Meisterernst, "Huzwāreš": "There is therefore no reason to believe that Sasanian scribes had any knowledge of Aramaic whatever, since they were not employed to work bilingually"; and see the comparable assessment by Prods Oktor Skjærvø, "Aramaic in Iran," *Aram* 7 (1995 [1998]): 283–318, esp. 313–15.

31. On Iranian words in Arabic, see Maarten Kossmann, "Borrowing," in *The Oxford Handbook of Arabic Linguistics,* ed. Jonathan Owens (New York: Oxford University Press, 2013), 349–68, esp. 350, quoting Nöldeke: "'[Persian words] were to the greatest degree, indeed to the very greatest degree, transmitted via Aramaic.'"

32. On the status of Aramaic loanwords in New Persian, see Bo Utas, "Verbal Ideograms in the *Frahang ī Pahlavik,*" in *Middle Iranian Studies: Proceedings of the International Symposium Organized by the Katholieke Universiteit Leuven from the 17th to the 20th of May 1982,* ed. Wojciech Skalmowski and Alois Van Tongerloo (Leuven: Peeters, 1984), 57–67, esp. 59, on the possibility that although there is an "astonishing scarcity of Aramaic loan-words in New Persian (i.e. of words that did not pass into Persian through Arabic)," it may be the case that some Aramaic words in the *Frahang ī Pahlavīk* are not heterograms but rather Aramaic loanwords into Middle Iranian. It is interesting that Utas here suggests that it is words of everyday life ("grain, fruits, drink and vegetables") with which this occurred, evidence that is in harmony with the ubiquity of Iranian loanwords of everyday life in the Bavli. There are around thirty Syriac words that appear in New Persian, according to Claudia A. Ciancaglini, "Iranian Loanwords in Syriac: Some Problems in Chronology and Cultural History," in *Middle Iranian Lexicography: Proceedings of the Conference Held in Rome, 9–11 April 2001* (Rome: Istituto Italiano per l'Africa e l'Oriente, 2005), 253–76, esp. 257. On Syriac words that entered New Persian directly or through Middle Persian, see also J. W. Weryho, "Syriac Influence on Islamic Iran," *Folia Orientalia* 13 (1971): 299–321, esp. 310–11, who rejects the connection between *gabr* and *gabrā,* instead arguing that it may come from a secondary sense of *gabrā* in Syriac meaning "slave." These Syriac sources may indeed contain further clues on the history of these words.

33. See Franz Rosenthal, *A History of Muslim Historiography* (Leiden: Brill, 1952), 10 n. 2, in a discussion of the Arabic cognate; and the entry in Wolf Leslau, *Comparative Dictionary of Geʿez (Classical Ethiopic)* (Wiesbaden: Harrassowitz, 1987), 257, who connects the meaning of magic with binding knots.

34. On this word, see *DJPA* 185–86 and *DJBA* 428–29. Both meanings are attested in the Bible; see Francis Brown, with S. R. Driver and Charles A. Briggs, *The Brown-Driver-Briggs Hebrew and English Lexicon: With an Appendix Containing the Biblical Aramaic* (Peabody: Hendrickson, 2001), 287–88. The charmer in Deuteronomy 18 is cognate with Akkadian *ubbūru,* "to bind magically," according to Brian B. Schmidt, "Canaanite Magic vs. Israelite Religion: Deuteronomy 18 and the Taxonomy of Taboo," in *Magic and Ritual in the Ancient World,* part 4, ed. Paul Allan Mirecki and Marvin W. Meyer (Leiden: Brill, 2002), 243–62, esp. 253.

35. The Bavli on several occasions compares the *ḥabarei* with the rabbinic scholars; see *b. Qidd.* 72a and *b. Pesaḥ.* 113b.

36. For more on the types and duties of the Sasanian priests in Iranian society, including the role of the *mowbeds* as administrators, see Touraj Daryaee, *Sasanian Persia: The Rise and Fall of an Empire* (New York: I. B. Tauris, 2009), 126–33; Arthur Christensen, *L'Iran sous*

les Sassanides, 2nd ed. (Copenhagen: Munksgaard, 1944), 116–22; Shaul Shaked, "Administrative Functions of Priests," in *Proceedings of the First European Conference of Iranian Studies*, part 1, ed. Gherardo Gnoli and Antonio Panaino (Rome: Istituto Italiano per il Medio ed Estremo Oriente, 1990), 261–73; Albert de Jong, "The Contribution of the Magi," in *Birth of the Persian Empire*, vol. 1 of *The Idea of Iran*, ed. Vesta Sarkhosh Curtis and Sarah Stewart (New York: I. B. Tauris, 2005), 85–99, esp. 92–93; Josef Wiesehöfer, *Ancient Persia from 550 B.C. to 650 A.D.*, trans. Azizeh Azodi (New York: I. B. Tauris, 1996), 183–91; James R. Russell, "The Sage in Ancient Iranian Literature," reprinted in *Armenian and Iranian Studies* (Cambridge, Mass.: Harvard University Press, 2004), 389–400; and the collection of articles on the subject by Philippe Gignoux, "Titres et fonctions religieuses sasanides d'après les sources syriaques hagiographiques," *Acta Antiqua Academiae Scientiarum Hungaricae* 28 (1983): 191–203; "Pour une esquisse des fonctions religieuses sous les Sasanides," *Jerusalem Studies in Arabic and Islam* 7 (1986): 93–108; "Une catégorie de mages à la fin de l'époque sasanide: Les *mogvēh*," *Jerusalem Studies in Arabic and Islam* 9 (1987): 19–23; and "Die religiöse Administration in sasanidischer Zeit: Ein Überblick," in *Kunst, Kultur und Geschichte der Achämenidenzeit und ihr Fortleben*, ed. Heidemarie Koch and David Neil MacKenzie (Berlin: Reimer, 1983), 253–66. For examples of glyptics that contain priestly administrative titles from various regions of the empire, see Rika Gyselen, *Sasanian Seals and Sealings in the A. Saeedi Collection* (Leuven: Peeters, 2007), 34–67 and 130–295; eadem, "Les sceaux des mages de l'Iran sassanide," in *Au carrefour des religions: Mélanges offerts à Philippe Gignoux*, ed. Rika Gyselen (Bures-sur-Yvette: Groupe pour l'Étude de la Civilisation du Moyen-Orient, 1995), 121–50; eadem, *La géographie administrative de l'empire sassanide: Les témoignages sigillographiques* (Leuven: Peeters, 1989), esp. 27–40.

37. Trans. Mary Boyce, *The Letter of Tansar* (Rome: Istituto Italiano per il Medio ed Estremo Oriente, 1968), 33–34. For more on the relationship between religion and politics, see Shaul Shaked, "Religion in the late Sasanian Period: Eran, Aneran, and Other Religious Designations," in *The Sasanian Era*, vol. 3 of *The Idea of Iran*, ed. Vesta Sarkhosh Curtis and Sarah Stewart (New York: I. B. Tauris, 2008), 103–17.

38. Philippe Gignoux, "Church-State Relations in the Sasanian Period," in *Monarchies and Socio-religious Traditions in the Ancient Near East: Papers Read at the 31st International Congress of Human Sciences in Asia and North Africa*, ed. HIH Prince Takahito Mikasa (Wiesbaden: Harrassowitz, 1984), 72–80, esp. 72–73.

39. Ibid. 80.

40. See Gyselen, *Géographie*, 30–31 on the complications of dating the origins of the *mowbed*.

41. On these roles, see the literature cited above. Material and literary evidence also suggests that Zoroastrian priests acted as generals and soldiers; see Marie Louise Chaumont, "Bōē," *Encyclopaedia Iranica*, online ed., 1989: www.iranica.com/articles/boe-gk, which cites a bulla from Qasr-e Abu Nasr, engraved with the name "Burzōy, the magian, son of Bōy," that may refer to a Sasanian general from the time of King Kawad. For information on the role of the priests in fire temples, see Jamsheed K. Choksy, "Reassessing the Material Contexts of Ritual Fires in Ancient Iran," *Iranica Antiqua* 42 (2007): 229–69. See also *MHD* chapter 95.16–96.3 (Anahit Perikhanian, *Mādayān ī Hazār Dādestān: The Book of a Thousand Judgements, a Sasanian Law-Book* [Costa Mesa: Mazda Publishers, 1997], 218–19), on the *mowbed*'s role in the perpetuation of holy fires, and *MHD* chapter A37.1–6 (Perikhanian,

Mādayān, 314–15) in ordering the replacement of idol temples with fire altars. Images of priests next to fire altars are also common on coins and seals. On the religious images on the seals, including priests and fire altars, see Rika Gyselen, "Note de glyptique sassanide: Quelques éléments d'iconographie religieuse," in *Contribution à l'histoire de l'Iran: Mélanges offerts à Jean Perrot,* ed. François Vallat (Paris: Éditions Recherche sur les Civilisations, 1990), 253–67, esp. the images on 267 (planche II). After the Islamic conquests, the titles and roles of priests in fire temples underwent changes; see, for instance, *FīP* chapter 13.5 (Bo Utas, ed., *Frahang ī Pahlavīk: Edited, with Transliteration, Transcription, and Commentary from the Posthumous Papers of Henrik Samuel Nyberg* [Wiesbaden: Harrassowitz, 1988], 47 and 82), where the *hērbed* and *dastwar* are listed under the entry for "A Master of Fires."

42. On the title "The Protector of the Poor and Judge," see Wiesehöfer, *Ancient Persia,* 187; Gyselen, *Géographie,* 31–33.

43. *MHD* chapter A26.11–16 (Anahit Perikhanian, *Mādayān ī Hazār Dādestān: The Book of a Thousand Judgements, a Sasanian Law-Book* [Costa Mesa: Mazda Publishers, 1997], 294–95).

44. On the purported Median origins of the Magi, a conclusion derived from Herodotus, see de Jong, "Contribution," 90–92.

45. The dominant position of the priestly class atop the threefold Avestan hierarchy of social classes is common to Indo-European cultures. See Prods Oktor Skjærvø, "Class System, i: In the Avesta," *Encyclopaedia Iranica,* online ed., 1991: www.iranica.com/articles/class-system-i; Mansour Shaki, "Class System, iii: In the Parthian and Sasanian Periods," *Encyclopaedia Iranica,* online ed., 1992: www.iranicaonline.org/articles/class-system-iii.

46. For more on בי דוואר (*b. B. Qam.* 114a, *b. ʿAbod. Zar.* 26a, *b. Giṭ.* 58b), related to MP *dādwar,* which is likely a reference to a Persian court, see Spicehandler, "Dina de Magista and Bei Dawar: Notes on Gentile Courts in Talmudic Babylonia," *Hebrew Union College Annual* 26 (1955): 333–54, esp. 340–44. For more on the literary context of this term, see also the present author's forthcoming article in the Harvard Theological Review on the topic of excommunication in Jewish Babylonia.

47. For a helpful list of administrative officials and their respective jurisdictions, see Negin Miri, *Sasanian Pārs: Historical Geography and Administrative Organization* (Costa Mesa: Mazda Publishers, 2012), 38–39.

48. For more on the administrative unit of the province in the Sasanian Empire, see Carlo G. Cereti, "Primary Sources for the History of Inner and Outer Iran in the Sasanian Period (Third-Seventh Centuries)," *Archivum Eurasiae Medii Aevi* 9 (1997): 17–71, esp. 49; Wiesehöfer, *Ancient Persia,* 186.

49. See *MHD* chapter 93.4–9 (Anahit Perikhanian, *Mādayān ī Hazār Dādestān: The Book of a Thousand Judgements, a Sasanian Law-Book* [Costa Mesa: Mazda Publishers, 1997], 214–15). See also Cereti, "Primary Sources," 48–50.

50. This section is a summary of the conclusions of Maria Macuch, "The Use of Seals in Sasanian Jurisprudence," in *Sceaux d'Orient et leur emploi,* ed. Rika Gyselen and Pierre Amiet (Leuven: Peeters, 1997), 79–87.

51. Daryaee, *Sasanian Persia,* 127–28.

52. This is MFT 47, cited in Philippe Gignoux and Rika Gyselen, eds., *Bulles et sceaux sassanides de diverses collections* (Paris: Association pour l'Avancement des Études Iraniennes, 1987), 41.

53. For an overview of the Sasanian legal system, see Maria Macuch, "Judicial and Legal Systems, iii: Sasanian Legal System," *Encyclopaedia Iranica*, online ed., 2012: www.iranicaonline.org/articles/judicial-and-legal-systems-iii-sasanian-legal-system."

54. Richard N. Frye, *The History of Ancient Iran* (Munich: Beck, 1984), 313, including n. 97, on the fact that *mowbedān mowbed* "is not found in the Syriac acts until the time of Mar Abha in the sixth century, but the office or an equivalent would seem to have existed earlier." For an analysis of the Syriac attestations to this position, as well as to the existence of a *mowbed* in charge of Bēt Aramāyē, see Gignoux, "Titres," 196–200. The author dates the position to the fifth or sixth century, arguing that Syriac sources are more accurate than Persian or Arabic sources in their dating of Sasanian positions. *Bund.* chapter 35.1 (Behramgore Tahmuras Anklesaria, *Zand-Ākāsīh: Iranian or Greater Bundahišn* [Bombay: Rahnumae Mazdayasnan Sabha, 1956], 302–3) dates this position to Shapur II, but this is likely a later, post-Sasanian retrojection.

55. *MHD* chapter A27.4–5 (Anahit Perikhanian, *Mādayān ī Hazār Dādestān: The Book of a Thousand Judgements, a Sasanian Law-Book* [Costa Mesa: Mazda Publishers, 1997], 294–95).

56. *MHD* chapter A28.5–7 (Perikhanian, *Mādayān*, 298–99).

57. On the role of the *mowbedān mowbed* in the production of the *pursišn-nāmag*, see *MHD* chapters A34.6–A35.3 (Perikhanian, *Mādayān*, 310–11). The *Mādayān ī Hazār Dādestān* also records that a *mowbedān mowbed* named Ādurpād ī Zartoštān, who circa the middle of the fifth century established a fire temple in his trust; see *MHD* chapter A36.3–12 (Perikhanian, *Mādayān*, 312–15).

58. *Bund.* chapter 35.56 (Behramgore Tahmuras Anklesaria, *Zand-Ākāsīh: Iranian or Greater Bundahišn* [Bombay: Rahnumae Mazdayasnan Sabha, 1956], 300–301).

59. *PRDīD* chapter 48.49 (A. V. Williams, *The Pahlavi Rivāyat Accompanying the Dādestān ī Dēnīg*, part 2, *Translation, Commentary and Pahlavi Text* [Copenhagen: Munksgaard, 1990], 83).

60. *Dēnk. III* chapter 288 (Jean de Menasce, *Le troisième livre du Dēnkart, traduit du pehlevi* [Paris: Klincksieck, 1973], 284–85). See Shaul Shaked, "Zoroastrian Polemics against Jews in the Sasanian and Early Islamic Period," in *Irano-Judaica II: Studies Relating to Jewish Contacts with Persian Culture throughout the Ages*, ed. Shaul Shaked and Amnon Netzer (Jerusalem: Ben-Zvi Institute, 1990), 85–104, esp. 93–94 and 102–3.

61. For research on the *hērbed*, see Marie Louise Chaumont, "Recherches sur le clergé zoroastrien: Le hērbad," *Revue de l'Histoire des Religions* 158 (1960): 55–80; Philip G. Kreyenbroek, "The Zoroastrian Priesthood after the Fall of the Sasanian Empire," in *Transition Periods in Iranian History: Actes du Symposium de Fribourg-en-Brisgau, 22–24 Mai 1985* (Paris: Association pour l'Avancement des Études Iraniennes, 1987), 151–66, esp. 152–53. For pertinent primary texts, see *Dēnk.* Book 8 chapter 27, on the profession of the *hērbed*, transcribed and translated in Chaumont, "Recherches," 69–70.

62. The *hērbedestān* appears to have been primarily a place of religious study for members of the priestly class, but one can assume that nonpriests attended as well, as argued by Firoze M. Kotwal and Philip G. Kreyenbroek, *The Hērbedestān and Nērangestān*, vol. 1 (Paris: Association pour l'Avancement des Études Iraniennes, 1992), 15–18. There is literary testimony that suggests that non-Zoroastrians or converts may have attended Zoroastrian *hērbedestāns*; see *Hērb.* chapter 12 (Kotwal and Kreyenbroek, *Hērbedestān and Nērangestān*,

vol. 1, 62–65), where in the context of a discussion of how long one is supposed to study in a *hērbedestān* the Middle Persian authors add commentaries to their verbatim translation of the Avesta regarding the case of a son of one in a state of mortal sin or the son of a non-Iranian (*pus-iz ī margarzān ud pus ī anēr*). This text includes a rare discussion of Christians in the Middle Persian corpus from the Sasanian period. Although exegetical, its lengthy comments suggest that it may reflect historical realia; but for an interpretation of these passages as indicative of exegesis and not history, see Shaked, "Religion," 108. See also *Hērb.* chapters 18–19 (Kotwal and Kreyenbroek, *Hērbedestān and Nērangestān*, vol. 1, 77–83), on learning from and teaching demon worshippers (glossed as *anērān*), as well as the reference to heretics (*ahlomōg*). For an analysis of *Hērb.* chapter 19 in relation to the Bavli, see Shai Secunda, "Studying with a Magus/Like Giving a Tongue to a Wolf," in *Iranian and Zoroastrian Studies in Honor of Prods Oktor Skjærvø*, ed. Carol Altman Bromberg, Nicholas Sims-Williams, and Ursula Sims-Williams, *Bulletin of the Asia Institute* 19 (2009): 151–57. For a parallel discussion regarding teaching to and learning from heretics the *mānsr*, Zand-Avesta, and judgments, see *Pursišnīhā* questions 6 and 7 (Kaikhusroo M. Jamaspasa and Helmut Humbach, eds., *Pursišnīhā: A Zoroastrian Catechism*, part 1, *Text, Translation, Notes* [Wiesbaden: Harrassowitz, 1971], 14–17).

63. See *Dēnk. III* chapter 80 (Jean de Menasce, *Le troisième livre du Dēnkart, traduit du pehlevi* [Paris: Klincksieck, 1973], 85–90).

64. See Mary Boyce, *Zoroastrians: Their Religious Beliefs and Practices* (Boston: Routledge, 1979), 97–98.

65. See Mansour Shaki, "A Few Unrecognized Middle Persian Terms and Phrases," in *Middle Iranian Studies: Proceedings of the International Symposium Organized by the Katholieke Universiteit Leuven from the 17th to the 20th of May 1982*, ed. Wojciech Skalmowski and Alois Van Tongerloo (Leuven: Peeters, 1984), 95–102, esp. 100. Much of our information about these figures comes from the Arabic writings of Ṭabarī.

66. For scholarship on this debated topic, see Kreyenbroek, "Zoroastrian Priesthood," 151–53; Stig Wikander, *Feuerpriester in Kleinasien und Iran* (Lund: Gleerup, 1946), 23–51. There is not a large selection of passages in Pahlavi literature that discuss the ties between these different types of priests; see, however, the stories in *Dēnk. VI* chapters D2–D5 (Shaul Shaked, *The Wisdom of the Sasanian Sages: Dēnkard VI* [Boulder: Westview Press, 1979], 176–83) about a *mowbedān mowbed* assessing the work of two *hērbed*s who are working the land and reciting the Zand-Avesta; the tale in *AWN* chapter 6 (Fereydun Vahman, *Ardā Wirāz Nāmag: The Iranian "Divina Commedia"* [London: Curzon Press, 1986], 86–87 and 193) that describes seven sisters, *hērbeds*, and *mowbeds* sitting with Wirāz and reciting Avesta; and Boyce, *Letter*, 61–62. These are all late sources and do not reflect the ties between these priests in the Sasanian period. For an earlier text that discusses the implications of the *drōn* for *mowbeds*, see *Nērang.* chapter 72.9 (Firoze M. Kotwal and Philip G. Kreyenbroek, *The Hērbedestān and Nērangestān*, vol. 4 [Paris: Association pour l'Avancement des Études Iraniennes, 2009], 38–39). See also the rare statement regarding trials according to the laws of the scholar-priest in *MHD* chapter 5.13.

67. For more on the debate of the origins of the magians and their purported conversion to Zoroastrianism, see the summary of the historiography in de Jong, *Traditions*, 388–91. The protohistory of the magians is bound up with the question of the Avesta's status in Persia, on which see de Jong, "Contribution," 89, who concludes that it is hard to know what the Avesta was in western Iran prior to the Sasanian era. On the "Persianization" of Avestan

sacred texts, and how eastern *aēθrapaitis* may have taught the western Magi to recite Avestan, see Philip G. Kreyenbroek, "The Zoroastrian Tradition from an Oralist's Point of View," in *K. R. Cama Oriental Institute, Second International Congress Proceedings*, ed. H.J.M. Desai and H.N. Modi (Bombay: K. R. Cama Oriental Institute, 1996), 231–37, esp. 224–25.

68. See Philippe Gignoux, *Les quatre inscriptions du mage Kirdīr: Textes et concordances* (Paris: Association pour l'Avancement des Études Iraniennes, 1991), 39 and 73. For the political background and significance of Kirder's appointment as *hērbed* by Ardashir, as *mowbed* and *hērbed* by Shapur I, and as *Ohrmazd-mowbed* by Ohrmazd I, see the discussion in Boyce, *Letter*, 8–10. There are a couple of seals with the title *Ohrmazd-mowbed*, published in Rika Gyselen, "Note de glyptique sassanide: Les cachets personnels de l'Ohrmazd-mogbed," in *Études irano-aryennes offertes à Gilbert Lazard* (Paris: Association pour l'Avancement des Études Iraniennes, 1989), 185–92.

69. On this date, see Philip Huyse, "Kerdīr and the First Sasanians," in *Proceedings of the Third European Conference of Iranian Studies, Held in Cambridge, 11–15 September 1995*, part 1, *Old and Middle Iranian Studies*, ed. Nicholas Sims-Williams (Wiesbaden: Reichert, 1998), 109–20, esp. 112.

70. See Gignoux, *Quatre inscriptions*, 69–71.

71. For one example of a text that mentions the other priests active in recitation and rituals (e.g., the *zōt, hāwanān, frabartār*, etc.), see *Nērang.* chapter 13.5 (Firoze M. Kotwal and Philip G. Kreyenbroek, *The Hērbedestān and Nērangestān*, vol. 2 [Paris: Association pour l'Avancement des Études Iraniennes, 1995], 86–87).

72. On the magians' administrative and ritual functions in the Achaemenid era, see the entries in Richard Treadwell Hallock, *Persepolis Fortification Tablets* (Chicago: University of Chicago Press, 1969), 723; and the discussion in Muhammed Dandamayev and V. A. Livshits, "Zattumēšu, a Magus in Babylonia," in *A Green Leaf: Papers in Honour of Professor Jes P. Asmussen* (Leiden: Brill, 1988), 457–59.

73. On the Greeks' conflation of the magians with magicians, see de Jong, *Traditions*, 387–88; Peter Kingsley, "Greeks, Shamans and Magi," *Studia Iranica* 23 (1994): 187–98, esp. 191–94; Roger Beck, "Thus Spake Not Zarathuštra: Zoroastrian Pseudepigrapha of the Greco-Roman World," in Mary Boyce and Frantz Grenet, with Roger Beck, *A History of Zoroastrianism*, vol. 3, *Zoroastrianism under Macedonian and Roman Rule* (Leiden: Brill, 1991), 491–565, esp. 511–21.

74. Joseph Bidez and Franz Cumont, *Les mages hellénisés: Zoroastre, Ostanès et Hystaspe d'après la tradition grecque*, 2 vols. (Paris: Société d'Éditions "Les Belles Lettres," 1938); and see the critical response regarding the invalidity of this thesis in de Jong, *Traditions*, 35–38, and Beck, "Thus Spake Not Zarathuštra," 492–93 and 564.

75. Bruce Lincoln, *Myth, Cosmos, and Society: Indo-European Themes of Creation and Destruction* (Cambridge, Mass.: Harvard University Press, 1986), 164–65.

76. Antonio Panaino, *The Lists of Names of Ahura Mazdā (Yašt I) and Vayu (Yašt XV)* (Rome: Istituto Italiano per l'Africa e l'Oriente, 2002), 45–48, with some minor changes.

77. For examples, see *Bund.* chapter 3.3 (Behramgore Tahmuras Anklesaria, *Zand-Ākāsīh: Iranian or Greater Bundahišn* [Bombay: Rahnumae Mazdayasnan Sabha, 1956], 36–37) on how Ohrmazd donned the white garment of priests and "possessed the splendor of the priesthood, because all knowledge is with the priests [*brāh ī āsrōnīh dāšt če hamē dānāgīh abāg āsrōnān*]"; *Bund.* chapter 36.4 (Anklesaria, *Zand-Ākāsīh*, 210–11), where Ohr-

mazd is called a priest (*āsrō*); *Zādsp.* chapter 35.17 (Philippe Gignoux and Ahmad Tafazzoli, *Anthologie de Zādspram* [Paris: Association pour l'Avancement des Études Iraniennes, 1993], 130–31), where Ohrmazd is called a *zōt*, a head officiating priest. The Pahlavi translation of *Yasna* 1 connects the *mowbedān mowbed* with the title "the most like Zarathustra" (Av. *zaraθuštrō.təma-*), the ideal priest, who memorized the entire Zand-Avesta (see Williams, *Pahlavi Rivāyat,* part 2, 183 n. 4). The *PRDīD* chapter 47.21–22 (ibid., 79) reports that Zardušt was *mowbedān mowbed* for thirty-five years. For more on the ideal priest, see Philip G. Kreyenbroek, "On the Concept of Spiritual Authority in Zoroastrianism," *Jerusalem Studies in Arabic and Islam* 17 (1994): 1–15, esp. 5–7 and 14.

78. See the assessment by Parvaneh Pourshariati, *Decline and Fall of the Sasanian Empire: The Sasanian-Parthian Confederacy and the Arab Conquest of Iran* (New York: I. B. Tauris, 2008), 347–48.

79. The information regarding the status of non-Zoroastrians in Sasanian courts provided in the *Mādayān ī Hazār Dādestān* is sparse, tending to center on issues of slavery, marriage, and conversion; on this topic, see Milka Levy-Rubin, *Non-Muslims in the Early Islamic Empire: From Surrender to Coexistence* (New York: Cambridge University Press, 2011), 119: "Apart from the issues of marriage and slave ownership, there does not seem to have been a consistent policy regarding the non-Zoroastrian communities living under Sasanian rule."

80. János Jany, "Private Litigation in Sasanian Law," *Iranica Antiqua* 45 (2010): 395–418, esp. 398.

81. Frye, *History,* 315. See also Daryaee, *Sasanian Persia,* 97.

82. For more on the status of non-Iranians in Sasanian law, see Maria Macuch, "Legal Constructions of Identity in the Sasanian Period," in *Iranian Identity in the Course of History: Proceedings of the Conference Held in Rome, 21–24 September 2005*, ed. Carlo G. Cereti (Rome: Istituto Italiano per l'Africa e l'Oriente, 2010), 193–212.

83. See János Jany, "Criminal Justice in Sasanian Persia," *Iranica Antiqua* 42 (2007): 347–86, esp. 349.

84. See, for example, the discussion in *b. Giṭ.* 88b.

85. Macuch, "Judicial and Legal Systems."

86. Macuch, "Legal Constructions," 200.

87. Ibid. 201.

88. See Wiesehöfer, *Ancient Persia,* 188; de Jong, "Contribution," 92; Jany, "Criminal Justice," 375–77.

89. Macuch, "Legal Constructions," 199.

90. Ibid. 200 (author's emphasis).

91. Ibid. 202–3.

92. Ibid. 201.

93. Ibid. 209.

94. See Jason Sion Mokhtarian, "The Boundaries of an Infidel in Zoroastrianism: A Middle Persian Term of Otherness for Jews, Christians, and Muslims," *Iranian Studies* 48 (2015): 99–115.

95. See *Hērb.* chapter 11.1 (Firoze M. Kotwal and Philip G. Kreyenbroek, *The Hērbedestān and Nērangestān*, vol. 1 [Paris: Association pour l'Avancement des Études Iraniennes, 1992], 58–59); *MHD* chapters 38.2 and 44.7 (Anahit Perikhanian, *Mādayān ī Hazār Dādestān: The*

Book of a Thousand Judgements, a Sasanian Law-Book [Costa Mesa: Mazda Publishers, 1997], 104–5 and 118–19).

96. See Shaked, "Religion," 106–9, asking similar questions about Armenians, Arabs, and the owners of the bowls.

97. Touraj Daryaee, "The Idea of Ērānšahr: Jewish, Christian and Manichaean Views in Late Antiquity," in *Iranian Identity in the Course of History: Proceedings of the Conference Held in Rome, 21–24 September 2005*, ed. Carlo G. Cereti (Rome: Istituto Italiano per l'Africa e l'Oriente, 2010), 91–108, esp. 94, has rightly asked in this regard: "Could this mean that there could have been a **mard ī ēr ī agdēn* 'Iranian man of evil religion'?" See also ibid. 95–96 on competing views of Ērānšahr in the fourth century, but noting that by the fifth century the monarchy saw non-Zoroastrians, including the Jews, as part of its citizenry. On page 97, the author conjectures: "It would then be plausible that Jews within the heartland of Persia, in Xūzestān, Fārs, and Media, would have considered themselves part of the state and loyal subjects, thus *ēr*." Unfortunately, there is no information about the Jews of these regions. In any case, it is hard to know whether the Jews would even have conceived of their own identity according to the Sasanian worldview.

98. See Seth Schwartz, "The Political Geography of Rabbinic Texts," in *The Cambridge Companion to the Talmud and Rabbinic Literature*, ed. Charlotte Elisheva Fonrobert and Martin S. Jaffee (Cambridge: Cambridge University Press, 2007), 75–96, esp. 81–82, and *Imperialism and Jewish Society, 200 B.C.E to 640 C.E* (Princeton: Princeton University Press, 2001), 5–6.

99. Shaye J. D. Cohen, "The Rabbi in Second-Century Jewish Society," in *The Cambridge History of Judaism*, vol. 3, *The Early Roman Period*, ed. William Horbury, W. D. Davies, and John Sturdy (New York: Cambridge University Press, 1999), 922–90, esp. 975. For more on the Palestinian rabbis as a marginal elite group, see also Schwartz, *Imperialism*, 103–28; the historiographical overview in Stuart Miller, *Sages and Commoners in Late Antique 'Ereẓ Israel: A Philological Inquiry into Local Traditions in Talmud Yerushalmi* (Tübingen: Mohr Siebeck, 2006), 7–17; and Steven Fine, *Art and Judaism in the Greco-Roman World: Toward a New Jewish Archaeology* (New York: Cambridge University Press, 2005), 35–46. Fine's work is particularly noteworthy for our purposes in its attentiveness to the role of archaeology and marginal texts in destabilizing rabbinic normativity, a topic that I discuss further in chapter 6 of this book.

100. See Shaye J. D. Cohen, "Rabbi," 971; Schwartz, *Imperialism*, 120 and n. 57.

101. For example, see the list of judges in *b. Sanh.* 17b, which says that the judge of the exile is Qarna; the judge of Pumbedita is Rav Pappa bar Shmuel; and the judge of Nehardea is Rav Adda bar Minyomi. Another text in *b. Šabb.* 10a describes Rav Ḥisda and Rabbah bar Rav Huna sitting all day in judgment. There are scattered throughout the Bavli similar characterizations of other sages; see also *b. Sanh.* 4b–5a on Rav Naḥman and R. Ḥiyya.

102. The quotation is from Richard Kalmin, *The Sage in Jewish Society of Late Antiquity* (New York: Routledge, 1999), 12, and see also *Sages, Stories, Authors, and Editors in Rabbinic Babylonia* (Atlanta: Scholars Press, 1994), 175–212.

103. This quotation and the next are cited from Richard Hidary, *Dispute for the Sake of Heaven: Legal Pluralism in the Talmud* (Providence: Brown University Press, 2010), 158–60.

104. Such policies need not, however, be deemed tolerant. In seeking a historical explanation to the Bavli's pluralistic, localized character, see ibid. 374–75, drawing on the *Epistles of Manuščihr* and concluding that the "Babylonian Amoraim mirror the tolerance of their

Sasanian Zoroastrian neighbors." Despite the author's claims in n. 30, this text should be treated as a reflection of later realities.

105. Jacob Neusner, *School, Court, Public Administration: Judaism and Its Institutions in Talmudic Babylonia* (Atlanta: Scholars Press, 1987), esp. 130–31; and see also pp. 85–152, including the list of court cases.

106. For more on the rabbinic courts, see Shalom Albeck, *Law Courts in Talmudic Times* (Ramat Gan: Bar-Ilan University Press, 1980; Hebrew). For a comparative study of judicial systems, see János Jany, *Judging in the Islamic, Jewish, and Zoroastrian Legal Traditions: A Comparison of Theory and Practice* (Burlington: Ashgate, 2012). On the ties between rabbinic study circles and courts of law, see Isaiah Gafni, "Yeshiva and Metivta," *Zion* 43 (1978): 12–37 (Hebrew).

107. Albeck, *Law Courts*, 15 (my translation).

108. See Geoffrey Herman, *A Prince without a Kingdom: The Exilarch in the Sasanian Era* (Tübingen: Mohr Siebeck, 2012), 181–209, esp. 186–87 and 209.

109. See Hanina Ben-Menahem, "Talmudic Law: A Jurisprudential Perspective," in *The Cambridge History of Judaism*, vol. 4, *The Late Roman–Rabbinic Period*, ed. Steven T. Katz (New York: Cambridge University Press, 2006), 877–98, esp. 892–93.

110. See Eliezer Segal, "Anthological Dimensions of the Babylonian Talmud," in *The Anthology in Jewish Literature*, ed. David Stern (New York: Oxford University Press, 2004), 81–107, and the other studies on this topic by this author; Isaiah Gafni, "Court Cases in the Babylonian Talmud: Literary Forms and Historical Implications," *Proceedings of the American Academy for Jewish Research* 49 (1982): 23–40 (Hebrew).

111. For one passage on judicial procedures, see *b. Sanh.* 7b–8a. See also the discussion in Hanina Ben-Menahem, *Judicial Deviation in Talmudic Law: Governed by Men, Not by Rules* (New York: Harwood Academic Publishers, 1991), 19–40.

112. On the Sasanian Jewish seals, see the studies by Shaul Shaked, "Jewish and Christian Seals of the Sasanian Period," in *Studies in Memory of Gaston Wiet*, ed. M. Rosen-Ayalon (Jerusalem: Institute of Asian and African Studies, Hebrew University of Jerusalem, 1977), 17–31; idem, "Epigraphica Judaeo-Iranica," in *Studies in Judaism and Islam Presented to S. D. Goitein*, ed. Shelomo Morag, Issachar Ben-Ami, and Norman A. Stillman (Jerusalem: Magnes Press, 1981), 65–82; and idem, "Jewish Sasanian Sigillography," in *Au carrefour des religions: Mélanges offerts à Philippe Gignoux*, ed. Rika Gyselen (Bures-sur-Yvette: Groupe pour l'Étude de la Civilisation du Moyen-Orient, 1995), 239–56. See also Moshe Beer, "Three Seals of Jews in Babylonia and Their Date," *Tarbiz* 52 (1983): 434–45 (Hebrew). There are also numerous Christian seals from the Sasanian era, on which see Judith A. Lerner, *Christian Seals of the Sasanian Period* (Istanbul: Nederlands Historisch-Archaeologisch Instituut te Istanbul, 1977).

113. Prudence O. Harper, *In Search of a Cultural Identity: Monuments and Artifacts of the Sasanian Near East, 3rd to 7th Century A.D.* (New York: Bibliotheca Persica, 2006), 63, suggests that the seals, with their national imagery, could be expressing "the rise of Jewish political aspirations within the Sasanian kingdom at certain times."

114. Judith A. Lerner, "Considerations on an Aspect of Jewish Culture under the Sasanians: The Matter of Jewish Sigillography," *Journal of the American Oriental Society* 129 (2009): 653-64, esp. 653 (review of Daniel M. Friedenberg, *Sasanian Jewry and Its Culture: A Lexicon of Jewish and Related Seals* [Urbana: University of Illinois Press, 2009]).

115. See Rika Gyselen, "Notes de glyptique sassanide. 5. Un sceau sassanide à l'iconographie juive," *Studia Iranica* 25 (1996): 249–51.

116. See Shaked, "Epigraphica Judaeo-Iranica," 65–68, and "Jewish Sasanian Sigillography," 242 no. 9. The name reads Ḥuna bar Nathan.

117. Shaul Shaked, "'No Talking During a Meal': Zoroastrian Themes in the Babylonian Talmud," in *The Talmud in Its Iranian Context*, ed. Carol Bakhos and M. Rahim Shayegan (Tübingen: Mohr Siebeck, 2010), 161–77, esp. 169.

118. See Geoffrey Herman, *Prince*, 328–29 and esp. n. 119.

119. Shaked, "Jewish Sasanian Sigillography," 240.

120. Lerner, "Considerations," 655.

121. *B. B. Meṣiʿa* 73b. Cf. the same tradition in *b. Yebam.* 46a. On these two loanwords, see *DJBA* 646 and 824. Just after this tradition, another loanword is found: גוהרקא, "litter," with which compare Middle Persian *gāhwārag*, "cot, cradle" (see *DJBA* 262).

122. Rika Gyselen, *Sasanian Seals and Sealings in the A. Saeedi Collection* (Leuven: Peeters, 2007), 13.

123. Maria Macuch, "Iranian Legal Terminology in the Babylonian Talmud in Light of Sasanian Jurisprudence," in *Irano-Judaica IV: Studies Relating to Jewish Contacts with Persian Culture throughout the Ages.* ed. Shaul Shaked and Amnon Netzer (Jerusalem: Ben-Zvi Institute, 1999), 91–101, esp. 97.

124. See, for example, *b. B. Bat.* 138b and *b. Giṭ.* 33a.

125. What follow are only examples of texts on these positions. On the distinguished man, see *b. Hor.* 4b and 7a–b; on lay judges, see *b. Meg.* 12b; and on court judges, see *b. Ḥag.* 14a, which replaces the biblical title for a judge *šôpeṭ* with *dayyān*. The latter title also appears with reference to the exilarch in *b. B. Bat.* 65a: "Rav Huna said to Rav Naḥman: the law follows you since you are close to the court of the exilarch, where judges are frequent."

126. For more on the מומחה, see Albeck, *Law Courts*, 76–82; and the synthesis in Shlomo Josef Zevin, ed., *Encyclopedia Talmudica: A Digest of Halachic Literature and Jewish Law from the Tannaitic Period to the Present Time, Alphabetically Arranged*, vol. 6 (Jerusalem: Yad Harav Herzog Press, 1992), 28–30. In addition to the texts cited below, see also *b. Sanh.* 23a and *b. Sanh.* 2b–3a, which probes the Mishnah's requirement for three judges in monetary cases, save for loans, in light of the Babylonian context of public experts.

127. See Zevin, *Encyclopedia Talmudica*, 28-29.

128. On ordination in rabbinic Palestine, see Catherine Hezser, *The Social Structure of the Rabbinic Movement in Roman Palestine* (Tübingen: Mohr Siebeck, 1997), 79-93. See *b. Sanh.* 13b, where the Talmud connects ordination to cases involving fines: "Rav Aḥa the son of Rava said to Rav Ashi: Do they ordain him with hands, literally? He said to him: They ordain him by name, they call him 'Rabbi,' and they give him the right to adjudicate cases involving fines" (trans. ibid. 91). *Bavli Sanh.* 14a contains a debate over whether ordination could occur outside Palestine. Cf. also *b. B. Qam.* 84a–b. For more on this complicated topic, see Albeck, *Law Courts*, 84–99; Michael S. Berger, *Rabbinic Authority*, 50–67; Julius Newman, *Semikhah (Ordination): A Study of Its Origin, History, and Function in Rabbinic Literature* (Manchester: University of Manchester Press, 1950).

129. See *b. Sanh.* 33a and *b. Sanh.* 4b–5a.

130. *B. Sanh.* 4b–5a. The translation is adopted from the critical edition of this source with manuscript variants in Geoffrey Herman, *Prince,* 196–97, with some minor changes. I have divided this text into three extracts.

131. Yaakov Elman has demonstrated that Rav Naḥman is one of the most Iranized rabbis in the Talmud, a fact that encourages us to read this source in its Sasanian context; see Elman, "Talmud, ii: Rabbinic Literature and Middle Persian Texts," *Encyclopaedia Iranica,* online ed., 2010: www.iranica.com/articles/talmud-ii, for a lengthy discussion of all the evidence.

132. *B. Sanh.* 4b–5a, trans. Geoffrey Herman, *Prince,* 196–97, modified.

133. See also ibid. 197–99.

134. See ibid. 38.

135. *B. Sanh.* 4b–5a, trans. Geoffrey Herman, *Prince,* 196–97, modified.

136. See Beth Berkowitz, *Execution and Invention: Death Penalty Discourse in Early Rabbinic and Christian Cultures* (New York: Oxford University Press, 2006).

137. See also *b. Ta'an.* 24b, where Ifra Hormizd saves Rava from the punishment of King Shapur after the monarch discovers that the sage has flogged someone for a sex crime; *b. B. Bat.* 58a–b, where R. Banaah is made a judge by the Persians; and *b. Giṭ.* 14a–b. On this last text, see Jacob Neusner, "Arda and Arta and Pyly Bryš"; Geoffrey Herman, *Prince,* 66–76.

138. See, e.g., *Lamentations Rabbah* 3.3 and 6.24, and Ephraim E. Urbach, "Redemption and Repentance in Talmudic Judaism," in *Types of Redemption,* ed. R. J. Zwi Werblowsky and C. Jouco Bleeker (Leiden: Brill, 1970), 190–206, esp. 198.

139. Ibid.

140. The word הרמנא means "command, order, authority" (*DJBA* 390–91). On the loanword, see MP *framān,* "command, order, authority," and its usage in *b. Giṭ.* 57b ("royal command"), in yet another passage on a Roman emperor; and *b. 'Erub.* 59a's term "local ruler" (< MP *kār-framān*), in reference to the exilarch (treated in Geoffrey Herman, *Prince,* 137–38). In the *Mādayān ī Hazār Dādestān,* the word *framān* means "royal edict" (e.g., *framān ī dahibedān*); see *MHD* chapters 2.17–3.1 and A27.5-7 (Anahit Perikhanian, *Mādayān ī Hazār Dādestān: The Book of a Thousand Judgements, a Sasanian Law-Book* [Costa Mesa: Mazda Publishers, 1997], 30–31 and 294-95). *MHD* chapters A37.3-4 and A37.9 (Perikhanian, *Mādayān,* 314–15) use it with reference to an order from a *mowbed.*

141. Cf. MP *frēstag* (*DJBA* 933). In Middle Persian it can also mean "angel, apostle," as seen in *Zādsp.* chapters 7.1 and 8.4 (*frēstag ī Ohrmazd*) (Philippe Gignoux and Ahmad Tafazzoli, *Anthologie de Zādspram* [Paris: Association pour l'Avancement des Études Iraniennes, 1993], 62–63), or as a title of the messenger-priest named Ērman (*Ērman frēstag*) who releases sinners from hell at the end of time, in chapter 34.38 (Gignoux and Tafazzoli, *Anthologie,* 122–23). See also *DīD* chapter 38.30 (Mahmoud Jaafari-Dehaghi, *Dādestān ī Dēnīg,* part 1, *Transcription, Translation, and Commentary* [Paris: Association pour l'Avancement des Études Iraniennes, 1998], 162–63) regarding how when the *kustīg* is fastened it becomes surrounded with "the command of the rulers and the decisions of angels" (*framān ī dahibedān ud wizīr ī frēstagān*). The first word in this Middle Persian text also contains the Middle Persian cognate of the loanword "authority" (הרמנא), which appears in *b. Ber.* 58a.

142. See Steingass, *A Comprehensive Persian-English Dictionary,* 1058, s.v. *kūpāl,* "mace." MS Oxford Opp. Add. fol. 23 adds: "Give him a club at the entrance of the lictors and let him

make judgment. They placed him at the entrance of the lictors, and he sat at the entrance and was rendering judgment" (see *DJBA* 1066).

143. On this tale and its protagonist, R. Shila, see Jonah Fraenkel, "The Story of Rabbi Shila (Bavli Berakhot 58a)," *Tarbiz* 40 (1970–71): 33–40, esp. 35 n. 2 (Hebrew); David Goodblatt, *Rabbinic Instruction in Sasanian Babylonia* (Leiden: Brill, 1975), 21–22, 51–54, and 137–42 on the name Shila and title *rêš sîdrā;* and Neusner, *History,* vol. 2, 109, who argues: "R. Shila was a civil authority in Babylonian Jewry," on a par with Rav and Shmuel, and "he was a judge by appointment of the exilarch." There are probably two sages with the name R. Shila, the first a third-generation Tanna and the other a first-generation Babylonian Amora in Nehardea.

144. Neusner, *History,* vol. 2, 32–35 (esp. 33) and 108–11.

145. *B. Ber.* 58a. For a critical edition of this story with manuscript variants, see Fraenkel, "Story," 33–34.

146. The MSS read "gentile."

147. Here or subsequently, the witnesses reference Caesar (e.g., בי קיסר).

148. On rabbinic references to non-Jews as donkeys, including the sexual implications of bestiality, see Sacha Stern, *Jewish Identity in Early Rabbinic Writings* (New York: Brill, 1994), 37–39.

149. Cf. MS Paris 671: קולפא דפרזלא, "iron staff."

150. *B. Ketub.* 105b.

151. *B. Sanh.* 98a and *b. Šabb.* 139a.

152. See Joseph Blenkinsopp, *Isaiah 1–39: A New Translation, with Introduction and Commentary* (New York: Doubleday, 2000), 86.

153. Cf. Deut. 16:18.

154. The word גזירפטי has been interpreted as either a Semitic-Iranian compound (see *DJBA* 274) from the Hebrew root *GZR,* "to decree, cut, guard," plus Iranian suffix *-pati,* or as an Iranian word altogether, from MP *wizīr,* "decision; judgment," according to Telegdi, "Essai," 237, and Shaul Shaked, "Aramaic, iii: Iranian Loanwords in Middle Aramaic," in *Encyclopaedia Iranica,* online ed., 1986: www.iranicaonline.org/articles/aramaic-#pt3.

155. *B. Šabb.* 139a.

156. Macuch, "Judicial and Legal Systems."

157. *MHD* chapter A38.12–16 (Anahit Perikhanian, *Mādayān ī Hazār Dādestān: The Book of a Thousand Judgements, a Sasanian Law-Book* [Costa Mesa: Mazda Publishers, 1997], 316–17). For a transliteration, see Maria Macuch, *Das sasanidische Rechtsbuch "Mātakdān ī hazār dātistān,"* part 2 (Wiesbaden: Deutsche Morgenländische Gesellschaft, Kommissionsverlag F. Steiner, 1981), 65.

158. Macuch, "Iranian Legal Terminology," 98.

159. Macuch, "Use," 82.

160. *MHD* chapter A35.3–5 (Anahit Perikhanian, *Mādayān ī Hazār Dādestān: The Book of a Thousand Judgements, a Sasanian Law-Book* [Costa Mesa: Mazda Publishers, 1997], 310–11).

161. *MHD* chapter A34.9–10 (Perikhanian, *Mādayān,* 310–11).

162. *MHD* chapter A34.6–9 (Perikhanian, *Mādayān,* 310–11).

163. *MHD* chapter 78.2–11 (Perikhanian, *Mādayān,* 190–91).

164. *B. Giṭ.* 28b (MS Vatican 130).

165. On Sasanian persecutions of Jews, see esp. Geoffrey Herman, *Prince*, 42–49; Richard Kalmin, *Jewish Babylonia between Persia and Roman Palestine* (New York: Oxford University Press, 2006), 121–47; Robert Brody, "Judaism in the Sasanian Empire: A Case Study in Religious Coexistence," in *Irano-Judaica II: Studies Relating to Jewish Contacts with Persian Culture throughout the Ages*, ed. Shaul Shaked and Amnon Netzer (Jerusalem: Ben-Zvi Institute, 1990), 52–62.

166. For a detailed analysis of this text, see Kalmin, *Jewish Babylonia*, 131–38 (with translation on p. 132).

167. Ibid. 133. See also Brody, "Judaism," 58; Moshe Beer, "On Three Edicts against the Jews of Babylonia in the Third Century C.E," in *Irano-Judaica: Studies Relating to Jewish Contacts with Persian Culture throughout the Ages*, ed. Shaul Shaked (Jerusalem: Ben-Zvi Institute, 1982), 30–35 (Hebrew).

168. Kalmin, *Jewish Babylonia*, 137.

169. Ibid. 131–33.

6. RABBIS, SORCERERS, AND PRIESTS

1. On the examples of food and sex in the complex issue of rabbinic regulations against interactions with gentiles, see David M. Freidenreich, *Foreigners and Their Food: Constructing Otherness in Jewish, Christian, and Islamic Law* (Berkeley and Los Angeles: University of California Press, 2011), 76, on how the Babylonian sages curbed interactions with gentiles in the realm of food because of "their elevated concern about the danger of assimilation." The author continues by stating that social history of Jewish Babylonia is one useful approach toward proving such theses. Relevant literature on the topic of Jewish-gentile social relations is plentiful; see, for instance, Christine Hayes, *Between the Babylonian and Palestinian Talmuds: Accounting for Halakhic Difference in Selected Sugyot from Tractate Avodah Zarah* (New York: Oxford University Press, 1997), 127–70 on how the Bavli is more stringent than the Jerusalem Talmud regarding social contact with idolaters. For restrictions against food-related and sexual contact with outsiders in post-Sasanian Zoroastrianism, see Albert de Jong, *Traditions of the Magi: Zoroastrianism in Greek and Latin Literature* (Leiden: Brill, 1997), 409, and "Animal Sacrifice in Ancient Zoroastrianism: A Ritual and Its Interpretations," in *Sacrifice in Religious Experience*, ed. Albert I. Baumgarten (Boston: Brill, 2002), 127–50, esp. 141 on how the religions of Sasanian Babylonia prohibited eating meat killed by outsiders. See also *Dēnk. III* chapter 288, which equates Dahāg's practice of slaughtering cattle before they reach maturity "according to the custom of the Jews [*jahūd ēwēn*]" (trans. Shaul Shaked, "Zoroastrian Polemics against Jews in the Sasanian and Early Islamic Period," in *Irano-Judaica II: Studies Relating to Jewish Contacts with Persian Culture throughout the Ages*, ed. Shaul Shaked and Amnon Netzer [Jerusalem: Ben-Zvi Institute, 1990], 85–104, esp. 101–3).

2. Joshua Levinson, "Enchanting Rabbis: Contest Narratives between Rabbis and Magicians in Late Antiquity," *Jewish Quarterly Review* 100 (2010): 54–94, esp. 74.

3. Ibid. 55. For a take on the impact of the presence of Sasanian priests on the Babylonian Talmud's posture toward magic, see Kimberly B. Stratton, "Imagining Power: Magic, Miracle, and the Social Context of Rabbinic Self-Representation," *Journal of the American Academy of Religion* 73 (2005): 361–93, esp. 382–85.

4. See, e.g., the similar statement by Adiel Schremer, "Stammaitic Historiography," in *Creation and Composition: The Contribution of the Bavli Redactors (Stammaim) to the Aggada*, ed. Jeffrey L. Rubenstein (Tübingen: Mohr Siebeck, 2005), 219–36, esp. 228.

5. On the influence of Hellenism in Jewish Babylonia, see Daniel Boyarin, "Hellenism in Jewish Babylonia," in *The Cambridge Companion to the Talmud and Rabbinic Literature*, ed. Charlotte Elisheva Fonrobert and Martin S. Jaffee (Cambridge: Cambridge University Press, 2007), 336–63, and *Socrates and the Fat Rabbis* (Chicago: University of Chicago Press, 2009), 133–35 on how such arguments do not preclude Iranian influences. On the status of the magi in Second Temple sources such as Josephus, Philo, and the New Testament, see Geza Vermes, *The Nativity: History and Legend* (New York: Doubleday, 2006), esp. 99-104. In my view, it seems unlikely that the Bavli's images of the Zoroastrian priests as sorcerers were strongly influenced by these sources.

6. See Shaul Shaked, *Dualism in Transformation: Varieties of Religion in Sasanian Iran* (London: School of Oriental and African Studies, 1994), 86.

7. See *Ecclesiastes Rabbah* 3.2.3 and *y. Yoma* 3:8 (40d), where Shmuel hears Persians cursing their son and knows that he will die.

8. See Abraham Goldberg, "The Babylonian Talmud," *The Literature of the Sages*, part 1, *Oral Tora, Halakha, Mishna, Tosefta, Talmud, External Tractates*, ed. Shmuel Safrai (Philadelphia: Fortress Press, 1987), 323–45, esp. 336. There is other evidence which supports reading this tale in its Persian setting. The identification of Pharaoh as an Iranian from Isfahan or elsewhere may have also penetrated Arabic descriptions, such as those of Ṭabarī, according to Adam Silverstein, "The Qur'ānic Pharaoh," in *New Perspectives on the Qur'ān: The Qur'ān in Its Historical Context*, vol. 2, ed. Gabriel Said Reynolds (New York: Routledge, 2011), 467–77, esp. 472–73. Finally, this setting of the Pharaoh tale is supported by the broader literary context of *b. Mo'ed Qaṭ.* 18a, which discusses the burial of nails, a demonological notion found also in Zoroastrianism; on this, see Yaakov Elman, "Middle Persian Culture and Babylonian Sages: Accommodation and Resistance in the Shaping of Rabbinic Legal Tradition," in *The Cambridge Companion to the Talmud and Rabbinic Literature*, ed. Charlotte Elisheva Fonrobert and Martin S. Jaffee (Cambridge: Cambridge University Press, 2007), 165–97, esp. 173, and Isaiah Gafni, "Babylonian Rabbinic Culture," In *Cultures of the Jews*, vol. 1, *Mediterranean Origins*, ed. David Biale (New York: Schocken Books, 2002), 223–66, esp. 246. For a primary source on this, see *Pahl. Vīdēv.* chapter 17 (Mahnaz Moazami, *Wrestling with the Demons of the Pahlavi Widēwdād: Transcription, Translation, and Commentary* [Leiden: Brill, 2014], 390–97).

9. On the Iranian etymology of this word, see James R. Russell, "A Note on Armenian hrmštk-el," in *Festschrift Garnik Asatryan*, ed. Uwe Bläsing (Leiden: Brill, forthcoming), 1–7.

10. The date and provenance of *Targum Pseudo-Jonathan* are obscure, with a range of scholarly opinions ranging from the Islamic period down to the Tannaitic era; on this, see the summary and literature cited in Robert Hayward, "Red Heifer and Golden Calf: Dating Targum Pseudo-Jonathan," in *Targums and the Transmission of Scripture into Judaism and Christianity* (Leiden: Brill, 2010), 234–58. See also Paul V. M. Flesher and Bruce D. Chilton, *The Targums: A Critical Introduction* (Waco: Baylor University Press, 2011), 151–67.

11. *B. Šabb.* 74b–75a (MS Oxford Opp. Add. fol. 23). For recent scholarship on this text, see Shai Secunda, *The Iranian Talmud: Reading the Bavli in Its Sasanian Context* (Philadelphia: University of Pennsylvania Press, 2013), 43–47 and 70–75; Jenny R. Labendz, *Socratic*

Torah: Non-Jews in Rabbinic Intellectual Culture (New York: Oxford University Press, 2013), 193–94.

12. MS Munich 95 and Soncino Print Family: "Rava."

13. MS Munich 95: "Mar Zutra bar Ṭoviyah" (both times).

14. The witnesses add the word "one" both times that this line appears in this text, except for MS Oxford Opp. Add. fol., which only adds it the second time.

15. The juxtaposition of the sins of violating the Sabbath and sorcery is also found in *b. Sanh.* 67b.

16. Cf. Printed editions: מגושתא. MS Vatican 108: אמגושא.

17. For more on this root, meaning "denigrate, ridicule; blasphemy," see *DJBA* 262 and 278. Occurrences of the term in the Bavli are associated with statements of disapproval (e.g., "R. Abbahu denigrated" in *b. Šabb.* 62b).

18. MS Munich 95 and MS Vatican 108 begin this line with the conjunction "and."

19. The title *ha-māgôš* appears only in *b. Šabb.* 75a. The closest form to this is *māgôš* in *b. Soṭah* 22a. For more on the variants of this word, see above, chapter 5, note 7.

20. See *b. Sanh.* 17a, which states that members of the Sanhedrin should have knowledge of magic.

21. For more on the sorcerer as other in the Hebrew Bible, see S. D. Ricks, "The Magician as Outsider: The Evidence of the Hebrew Bible," in *New Perspectives on Ancient Judaism*, vol. 5, ed. P. Flesher (Lanham: University Press of America, 1990), 125–34. For a further analysis of Deut. 18, see Brian Schmidt, "Canaanite Magic vs. Israelite Religion: Deuteronomy 18 and the Taxonomy of Taboo," in *Magic and Ritual in the Ancient World*, part 4, ed. Paul Allan Mirecki and Marvin W. Meyer (Leiden: Brill, 2002), 243–62, esp. 244–45 on the four stages of the text's redaction.

22. On the rabbinic distinction between magical practices and illusions, and a sketch of the different phases of ancient Judaism's attitudes toward magic, see Philip S. Alexander, "The Talmudic Concept of Conjuring (*'Ahizat 'Einayim*) and the Problem of the Definition of Magic (*Kishuf*)," in *Creation and Re-Creation in Jewish Thought: Festschrift in Honor of Joseph Dan on the Occasion of His Seventieth Birthday*, ed. Rachel Elior and Peter Schäfer (Tübingen: Mohr Siebeck, 2005), 7–26, esp. 10–15 and 26. Middle Persian literature defines sorcery (*jādūgīh*) in similar ways; see *Dēnk. VI* chapter 256 (Shaul Shaked, *The Wisdom of the Sasanian Sages: Dēnkard VI* [Boulder: Westview Press, 1979], 100–101): "This is sorcery: having secretive character (*nihān xēmīh*) and displaying oneself as different from what one is (*tan ī xwēš juttar nimūdan*)."

23. *B. Sanh.* 68a.

24. The phrase in brackets appears in the printed editions.

25. On magic as a form of knowledge in Babylonia, see Levinson, "Enchanting Rabbis," 70–71 and 92.

26. See Michael Morony, "Magic and Society in Late Sasanian Iraq," in *Prayer, Magic, and the Stars in the Ancient and Late Antique World*, ed. Scott Noegel, Joel Walker, and Brannon Wheeler (University Park: Pennsylvania State University, 2003), 83–107, esp. the very useful quantitative data of the bowls' sociolinguistic and physical variables in tables IA, IB, II, and III; Shaul Shaked, "Popular Religion in Sasanian Babylonia," *Jerusalem Studies in Arabic and Islam* 21 (1997): 103–17.

27. On magic in Jewish Babylonia, see Gideon Bohak, *Ancient Jewish Magic: A History* (New York: Cambridge University Press, 2008); Michael D. Swartz, "Jewish Magic in Late

Antiquity," in *The Cambridge History of Judaism*, vol. 4, *The Late Roman-Rabbinic Period*, ed. Steven T. Katz (New York: Cambridge University Press, 2006), 699–720, esp. 702–8 and 711–13; Kimberly B. Stratton, *Naming the Witch: Magic, Ideology, and Stereotype in the Ancient World* (New York: Columbia University Press, 2007), 143–76; Jonathan Seidel, "Charming Criminals: Classification of Magic in the Babylonian Talmud," in *Ancient Magic and Ritual Power*, ed. Marvin W. Meyer and Paul Mirecki (Leiden: Brill, 1995), 145–66. On the Jewish bowls, see most recently Shaul Shaked, James Nathan Ford, and Siam Bhayro, eds., with Matthew Morgenstern and Naama Vilozny, *Aramaic Bowl Spells: Jewish Babylonian Aramaic Bowls* (Boston: Brill, 2013), 1–27. On Mandaic magic, see my discussion below. For an overview of magic in late antique Zoroastrianism, especially as recorded in material sources, see Pierfrancesco Callieri, "In the Land of the Magi: Demons and Magic in the Everyday Life of Pre-Islamic Iran," in *Démons et merveilles d'Orient*, ed. Rika Gyselen (Leuven: Peeters, 2001), 11–36; Rika Gyselen, *Sceaux magiques en Iran sassanide* (Paris: Association pour l'Avancement des Études Iraniennes, 1995). On magic bowls and Manichaeism, see Jason BeDuhn, "Magical Bowls and Manichaeans," in *Ancient Magic and Ritual Power*, ed. Marvin Meyer and Paul Mirecki (New York: Brill, 1985), 419–34, including 429 on how there are Jewish elements in them that would normally be forbidden in the faith.

28. Bohak, *Ancient Jewish Magic*, 193–94. For more on the skulls, see James Montgomery, *Aramaic Incantation Texts from Nippur* (Philadelphia: University Museum, 1913), 256–57; Dan Levene, "Calvariae Magicae: The Berlin, Philadelphia and Moussaieff Skulls," *Orientalia* 75 (2006): 359–79. The skulls do not attest to interaction between groups.

29. Cyrus H. Gordon, "Aramaic Magical Bowls in the Istanbul and Baghdad Museums," *Archiv Orientální* 6 (1934): 319–34, esp. 328–29, with some changes to the translation.

30. Shaked, "Popular Religion," 106.

31. On polythetic definitions of religion, see Jonathan Z. Smith, *Imagining Religion: From Babylon to Jonestown* (Chicago: University of Chicago Press, 1982), 1–18; Michael L. Satlow, "Defining Judaism: Accounting for 'Religions' in the Study of Religion," *Journal of the American Academy of Religion* 74 (2006): 837–60.

32. See Dan Levene, *A Corpus of Magic Bowls: Incantation Texts in Jewish Aramaic from Late Antiquity* (New York: Kegan Paul, 2003), 21–23.

33. On the surprising lack of Zoroastrian penetration into Jewish magic, see Shaul Shaked, "Bagdāna, King of the Demons, and Other Iranian Terms in Babylonian Aramaic Magic," in *Papers in Honour of Professor Mary Boyce*, vol. 1 (Leiden: Brill, 1985), 511–25, esp. 511. Zoroastrian literature contains a plethora of terms for sorcery, including *jādūg*, "sorcerer," *kundāg*, "soothsayer," and *parīg*, "witch," as well as mythic storylines regarding evil sorcerers who battle the religious heroes by contesting the rise of the Good Religion. For examples of such stories, see the narrative about the demonic priests called *karps* (or *karbs*) who attack Zarathustra as a child, found in *Dēnk. VII* chapter 3 (Marijan Molé, *La légende de Zoroastre selon les textes pehlevis* [Paris: Klincksieck, 1967], 28–41), and cf. also *Zādsp.* chs. 10–12 (Philippe Gignoux and Ahmad Tafazzoli, *Anthologie de Zādspram* [Paris: Association pour l'Avancement des Études Iraniennes, 1993], 66–73); the story of Wīdrafš the sorcerer who slays Zarēr, the brother of Wištāsp, in battle, found in the *Ayādgār ī Zarērān*, an epic poem that likely circulated throughout the Sasanian period (see Davoud Monchi-Zadeh, *Die Geschichte Zarēr's* [Uppsala: Almqvist and Wiksell International, 1981]); the dialogue of riddles between the Avestan hero Jōišt ī Friyān and the evil wizard Axt, found in the *Mādayān*

ī Jōišt ī Friyān, ed. M. Weinreich, "Die Geschichte von Jōišt ī Frīyan," *Altorientalische Forschungen* 19 (1992): 44–101, as well as in *Dēnk. III* chapter 196 (Jean de Menasce, *Le troisième livre du Dēnkart, traduit du pehlevi* [Paris: Klincksieck, 1973], 203–5).

34. The Iranian derivation of Bagdāna is controversial in part because the title does not appear in Iranian sources. See Shaked, "Bagdāna"; Jonas C. Greenfield, "Notes on Some Aramaic and Mandaic Magic Bowls," *Journal of the Ancient Near Eastern Society* 5 (1973): 149–56, esp. 153 and n. 27. For examples of primary texts, see Joseph Naveh and Shaul Shaked, *Amulets and Magic Bowls: Aramaic Incantations of Late Antiquity*, 3rd ed. (Jerusalem: Magnes Press, 1998), 198–205; Montgomery, *Aramaic Incantation Texts*, 195–97.

35. See Erica C. D. Hunter, "Aramaic-Speaking Communities of Sasanid Mesopotamia," *Aram* 7 (1995): 319–35.

36. On orality, see Christa Müller-Kessler, "Puzzling Words and Spellings in Babylonian Aramaic Magic Bowls," *Bulletin of the School of Oriental and African Studies* 62 (1999): 111–14, esp. 113 on how "the recorded interchanges of labials and dentals from Mandaic into Babylonian Aramaic suggest an oral transmission of the magical texts," including through memorized formulas. It seems likely that there existed recipe books to which magicians had access, on which see Shaul Shaked, "Transmission and Transformation of Spells: The Case of the Jewish Babylonian Aramaic Bowls," in *Continuity and Innovation in the Magical Tradition*, ed. Gideon Bohak, Yuval Harari, and Shaul Shaked (Leiden, Brill, 2011), 187–218, esp. 205–6. On how studies of duplicate texts by the same or different scribes, sometimes in diverse languages, demonstrate that magical formulas crossed cultural boundaries, see Levene, *Corpus*, 24–30, and the detailed study of one example of this phenomenon by Erica C. D. Hunter, "Manipulating Incantation Texts: Excursions in Refrain A," *Iraq* 64 (2002): 259–73.

37. Hunter, "Aramaic-Speaking Communities," 332–33.

38. See Jonas C. Greenfield and Joseph Naveh, "A Mandaic Lead Amulet with Four Incantations," *Eretz Israel* 18 (1985): 97–107 (Hebrew); Jonas C. Greenfield, "The Use of the Targum in a Mandaic Incantation Text," in *"Open Thou Mine Eyes . . .": Essays on Aggadah and Judaica Presented to Rabbi William G. Braude on His Eightieth Birthday and Dedicated to His Memory*, ed. Herman J. Blumberg et al. (Hoboken: Ktav, 1992), 79–82, on the Mandaic text's use of Exodus 32:18; Greenfield, "Notes on Some Aramaic and Mandaic Magic Bowls," *Journal of the Ancient Near Eastern Society* 5 (1973): 149–56, esp. 154–55, on McCullough Text D (W. S. McCullough, *Jewish and Mandaean Incantation Bowls in the Royal Ontario Museum* [Toronto, 1967]), of which the author says "although it was written in Mandaic, possibly for a Mandaean, it was clearly the work of a Jewish scribe" and "is the most Jewish of Mandaean bowls." This text's mixture of Mandaic and Jewish elements, including from Merkavah mysticism, makes it difficult to determine "whether this text was written by a Jewish magician who happened to know Mandaean, or by a Mandaean who drew on Jewish sources," as described in Philip S. Alexander, "Incantations and Books of Magic," in *The History of the Jewish People in the Age of Jesus Christ (175 B.C.–A.D. 135)*, vol. 3.1, ed. Emil Schürer; rev. Geza Vermes, Fergus Millar, and Martin Goodman (Edinburgh: T. and T. Clark, 1986), 342–79, esp. 353.

39. On Mandaeans' negative attitude toward Judaism, see Tapani Harviainen, "Syncretistic and Confessional Features in Mesopotamian Incantation Bowls," *Studia Orientalia* 70 (1993): 29–37, esp. 30; Edwin M. Yamauchi, *Mandaic Incantation Texts* (New Haven: American Oriental Society, 1967), 44–45: "A striking testimony to the strength of the anti-Jewish

feeling of the Mandaeans even in the eclectic area of magic is the absence of any citations from the Hebrew Scriptures, although the words 'Amen' and 'Selah' occur (26:25). This is in marked contrast to the frequent use of Scripture verses in the Aramaic bowl texts."

40. On Adonai as the chief of the evil spirits in Mandaic, see Yamauchi, *Mandaic Incantation Texts,* 36, 154–55, 194–95, and the entry in glossary B on page 364. On El-Shaddai the sorcerer, who appears to be a positive force against evil spirits, see M. J. Geller, "Four Aramaic Incantation Bowls," in *The Bible World: Essays in Honor of Cyrus H. Gordon,* ed. Gary Rendsburg, Ruth Adler, Milton Arfa, and Nathan H. Winter (New York: Ktav, 1980), 47–60, esp. 49–50 on a bowl for a client named Metaniš bar Azarmiduk and his wife, Eve.

41. See Harviainen, "Syncretistic and Confessional Features"; Shaked, "Popular Religion," 107. It is important to note that not all bowls are syncretistic: see, for example, a bowl discovered in 1935–36 in excavations of Tell Khafaje, edited by Edward M. Cook, "An Aramaic Incantation Bowl from Khafaje," *Bulletin of the American Schools of Oriental Research* 285 (1992): 79–81, esp. 80: "Its strongly Jewish terminology runs counter to the syncretism and eclecticism characteristic of many of the bowl texts."

42. See the series of articles on this topic in a special edition of the journal *Historical Reflections/Réflexions Historiques* 27 (2001): 365–509.

43. See Gustavo Benavides, "Power, Intelligibility and the Boundaries of Religion," ibid. 481–98, esp. 486.

44. Robert D. Baird, *Category Formation and the History of Religions* (Paris: Mouton, 1971), 147.

45. See Rosalind Shaw and Charles Stewart, "Introduction: Problematizing Syncretism," in *Syncretism/Anti-Syncretism: The Politics of Religious Synthesis,* ed. Rosalind Shaw and Charles Stewart (New York: Routledge, 1994), 1–24, esp. 7.

46. M. J. Geller, "Jesus' Theurgic Powers: Parallels in the Talmud and Incantation Bowls," *Journal of Jewish Studies* 28 (1977): 141–55, esp. 149–50.

47. On these important features of the bowl texts, see the analysis by Shaul Shaked, "Manichaean Incantation Bowls in Syriac," *Jerusalem Studies in Arabic and Islam* 24 (2000): 58–92, esp. 64:

> Another interesting feature consists of the fact that on the outside we have two labels indicating the room in the house where the bowl is to be placed. One of these is done in the same Manichaean-type script as the main body of the bowl, and the other in Pahlavi. Both indicate the same thing: the bowl is to be placed in the inner dining room. The dining hall is also mentioned in the main text, and it makes sense that the bowl should be placed there. It seems reasonable to suppose that the scribe of the bowl wrote the label in Syriac, and he or some one else on his behalf wrote the Pahlavi label for the benefit of the client, so that the latter should know, when he got home, where the bowl should be placed.

Ibid. 64–65, provides another case:

> One bowl has a bilingual label, written in Pahlavi and Syriac. The Pahlavi label says: BBA Y LBA [=*dar ī wuzurg*] "the great court" (or "door"). This is followed by a label in Syriac: *Busa* son of Gušnai, Marqonta, Barukh, Zardoi, Yanti. These are the names of the clients who ordered the bowl, and they are also mentioned in the body of the

text. The first name, Busa, is written in Pahlavi, and the rest of the names in Syriac. It seems that the writer of the labels was the same person who wrote the text of the bowl. He wrote the Pahlavi label, indicating where in the house the bowl should be placed, for the convenience of his clients. He then turned over to writing the Syriac label, where the names of the clients are mentioned. The Syriac label is presumably for the benefit of the practitioner himself, who wrote the bowl, in order to be able to quickly identify the bowl ordered by these customers when they came to claim their order.

48. Ibid. 65.

49. See the examples given in Shaul Shaked, "Form and Purpose in Aramaic Spells: Some Jewish Themes (The Poetics of Magic Texts)," in *Officina Magica: Essays on the Practice of Magic in Antiquity*, ed. Shaul Shaked (Boston: Brill, 2005), 1–30, esp. 6 and 10.

50. For some examples of male Iranian names among Jews as attested in the Bavli, see Tal Ilan, with Kerstin Hünefeld, *Lexicon of Jewish Names in Late Antiquity*, part 4, *The Eastern Diaspora, 330 BCE–650 CE* (Tübingen: Mohr Siebeck, 2011), 171 on Bahrām (the name of five Sasanian kings) in *b. Ḥul.* 38a; ibid. 179 on Hamdakh in *b. Mo'ed Qaṭ.* 4b; ibid. 188 on Xudāī (literally "lord") in *b. Yoma* 44a; ibid. 189 on Mahbūxt" (literally "moon," with suffix) in *b. Zebaḥ.* 9b.

51. Shaked, "Manichaean Incantation Bowls," 65–66.

52. See Dan Levene, *Jewish Aramaic Curse Texts from Late-Antique Mesopotamia: "May These Curses Go Out and Flee"* (Boston: Brill, 2013), 1.

53. Ibid. 99.

54. Ibid. 97.

55. Ibid. 98.

56. Harviainen, "Syncretistic and Confessional Features," 36 (emphasis original).

57. Hunter, "Aramaic-Speaking Communities," 332.

58. Dan Levene and Gideon Bohak, "A Babylonian Jewish Aramaic Incantation Bowl with a List of Deities and Toponyms," *Jewish Studies Quarterly* 19 (2012): 56–72, esp. 71.

59. Shaul Shaked, "Jesus in the Magic Bowls: Apropos Dan Levene's '. . . and by the name of Jesus. . .'," *Jewish Studies Quarterly* 6 (1999): 309–19, esp. 315.

60. Ibid. 315–16.

61. Rebecca Lesses, "Exe(o)rcising Power: Women as Sorceresses, Exorcists, and Demonesses in Babylonian Jewish Society of Late Antiquity," *Journal of the American Academy of Religion* 69 (2001): 343–75, esp. 353–54 and 366–67.

62. Shaul Shaked, "Parole des anges, parole des démons: À propos des coupes magiques de la Babylonie sassanide," in *Union Académique Internationale: Soixante-treizième session annuelle du Comité, Cracovie, du 20 au 26 juin 1999* (Brussels: Secrétariat Administratif de l'UAI, 1999), 17–33, esp. 28, summarizes this issue well.

63. Dina Stein, "Let the 'People' Go? The 'Folk' and Their 'Lore' as Tropes in the Reconstruction of Rabbinic Culture," *Prooftexts: A Journal of Jewish Literary History* 29 (2009): 206–41. See also Galit Hasan-Rokem, *Web of Life: Folklore and Midrash in Rabbinic Literature*, trans. Batya Stein (Stanford: Stanford University Press, 2000).

64. See James Nathan Ford and Alon Ten-Ami, "An Incantation Bowl for Rav Mešaršia son of Qaqay," *Tarbiz* 80 (2012): 219–30 (Hebrew). The name Qaqay is probably Iranian, according to Naveh and Shaked, *Amulets*, 197.

65. Lesses, "Exe(o)rcising," 361.

66. For an example from Mandaic texts, see Dan D. Y. Shapira, "Manichaeans (*Marmanaiia*), Zoroastrians (*Iazuqaiia*), Jews, Christians and Other Heretics: A Study in the Redaction of Mandaic Texts," *Le Muséon* 117 (2004): 243–80, on Mandaic texts on heretics, including the texts' use of the appellation *Iazuqaiia* for Zoroastrians.

67. Alexander, "Talmudic Concept," 9.

68. See Levene, *Corpus*, 48–49.

69. Bohak, *Ancient Jewish Magic*, 423.

70. See Shaked, Ford, and Bharyo, *Aramaic Bowl Spells*, 7. On the Bavli's references to bowls and amulets, see Yaakov Elman, "Saffron, Spices, and Sorceresses: Magic Bowls and the Bavli," in *Daughters of Hecate: Women and Magic in the Ancient World*, ed. Kimberly B. Stratton, with Dayna S. Kalleres (New York: Oxford University Press, 2014), 365–85, esp. 366–73.

71. On this term, for which there is a large literature, see Richard Kalmin, "Christians and Heretics in Rabbinic Literature of Late Antiquity," *Harvard Theological Review* 87 (1994): 155–69; Daniel Boyarin, *Border Lines: The Partition of Judaeo-Christianity* (Philadelphia: University of Pennsylvania Press, 2004), 54–58, 220–25.

72. See Yaakov Elman, "The Socioeconomics of Babylonian Heresy," *Jewish Law Association Studies* 17 (2007): 80–127, esp. 121–22 for an interpretation of a heretic as a Zoroastrian.

73. On this topic, see Gideon Bohak, "Magical Means for Handling *Minim* in Rabbinic Literature," in *The Image of the Judaeo-Christians in Ancient Jewish and Christian Literature*, ed. Peter J. Tomson and Doris Lambers-Petry (Tübingen: Mohr Siebeck, 2003), 267–79, esp. 267–68.

74. Albert de Jong, "Zoroastrian Religious Polemics and Their Contexts: Interconfessional Relations in the Sasanian Empire," in *Religious Polemics in Context: Papers Presented to the Second International Conference of the Leiden Institute for the Study of Religions (LISOR), Held at Leiden 27-28 April 2000*, ed. T.L. Hettema and A. van der Kooij (Assen: Royal van Gorcum, 2004), 48–63, esp. 60–61.

75. On this term's meaning, see Marijan Molé, "Le problème des sectes zoroastriennes dans les livres pehlevis," *Oriens* 13–14 (1960–61): 1–28, esp. 1–2, 9–20. In an important article on the Middle Iranian inscriptions in the Dura-Europos synagogue, Bernhard Geiger, "The Middle Iranian Texts," in *The Excavations at Dura-Europos, Final Report*, vol. 8, part 1, ed. M.I. Rostovtzeff, A.R. Bellinger, F.E. Brown, and C.B. Welles (New Haven: Yale University Press, 1956), 283–317, esp. 299–300 and 303–5, the author interprets the Middle Persian word *zndky* in the line "this zndky of the Jews to his edifice of the God [of] the Gods of the Jews," as *zandakē*, which, in consultation with Saul Lieberman and following the earlier work of Ginzberg, has a parallel word in the *Aggadat Esther*, which Ginzberg connects with Middle Persian *zandīg*, "heretic," as a "term of abuse" (ibid. 300). This reading is, however, incorrect, for a variety of reasons. See Touraj Daryaee, "To Learn and to Remember from Others: Persians Visiting the Dura-Europos Synagogue," *Scripta Judaica Cracoviensia* 8 (2010): 29–37, esp. 32, who reads it as Middle Persian *zandag*, "district," which is plausible.

76. Harviainen, "Syncretistic and Confessional Features," 33.

77. On this idea, see Jacques Berlinerblau, "Toward a Sociology of Heresy, Orthodoxy, and *Doxa*," *History of Religions* 40 (2001): 327–51, esp. 350–51.

78. This description of orthodoxy versus heterodoxy is guided by Pierre Bourdieu, *Outline of a Theory of Practice* (New York: Cambridge University Press, 1977), 159–97, esp. 167–71.

79. See Shaked, Ford, and Bharyo, *Aramaic Bowl Spells,* 18–27; Levene, *Corpus,* 10–17.

80. Dan Levene, "'If You Appear as a Pig': Another Incantation Bowl (Moussaieff 164)," *Journal of Jewish Studies* 52 (2007): 59–70, esp. 66-67.

81. See Stephen A. Kaufman, "A Unique Magic Bowl from Nippur," *Journal of Near Eastern Studies* 32 (1973): 170–74.

82. On these two figures, see Baruch M. Bokser, "Wonder-Working and the Rabbinic Tradition: The Case of Ḥanina ben Dosa," *Journal for the Study of Judaism* 16 (1985): 49–92; Shaked, Ford, and Bharyo, *Aramaic Bowl Spells,* 53–96 (on Ḥanina ben Dosa) and 103–54 (on Rabbi Yehoshua bar Peraḥia).

83. Shaked, "Form and Purpose," 19–22.

84. For more on this theme, see Shaul Shaked, "The Poetics of Spells: Language and Structure in Aramaic Incantations of Late Antiquity, 1—The Divorce Formula and Its Ramifications," in *Mesopotamian Magic: Textual, Historical, and Interpretative Perspectives,* ed. Tzvi Abusch and Karel van der Toorn (Groningen: Styx Publications, 1999), 173–95; Shaked, Ford, and Bharyo, *Aramaic Bowl Spells,* 99–100; Levene, *Corpus,* 18–21.

85. Shaked, Ford, and Bharyo, *Aramaic Bowl Spells,* 137–38 (JBA 24), with some minor changes. I have not reproduced all the text's sigla.

86. See ibid. 100, and Levene, *Jewish Aramaic Curse Texts,* 96. See another bowl made for this family in Shaked, Ford, and Bharyo, *Aramaic Bowl Spells,* 208–9 (JBA 46), which threatens the demons with "the curses that are written in the Torah and in Deuteronomy," before quoting Deuteronomy 28:57.

87. See Shaul Shaked, "*Dramatis Personae* in the Jewish Magic Texts: Some Differences between Incantation Bowls and Geniza Magic," *Jewish Studies Quarterly* 13 (2006): 363–87, esp. 383–84.

88. The names Palḥas and Palḥadad appear in other bowls for Persian-named clients, such as JBA 19 (Shaked, Ford, and Bharyo, *Aramaic Bowl Spells,* 123–24), for Hormiz son of Imma and his wife, Šabuhrdukh daughter of Ṭuṭay.

89. See the image in Shaked, Ford, and Bharyo, *Aramaic Bowl Spells,* 152.

90. Ibid. 153 (JBA 26).

91. For an analysis of the demonic power of pairs in *b. Pesaḥ.* 110a, see Yaakov Elman, "The World of the 'Sabboraim': Cultural Aspects of Post-Redactional Additions to the Bavli," in *Creation and Composition: The Contribution of the Bavli Redactors (Stammaim) to the Aggada,* ed. Jeffrey L. Rubenstein (Tübingen: Mohr Siebeck, 2005), 383–416, esp. 402.

92. On the assessments regarding the overlap in language between the bowls and the dialects of Aramaic in the Babylonian Talmud, see Christa Müller-Kessler and Theodore Kwasman, "A Unique Talmudic Aramaic Incantation Bowl," *Journal of the American Oriental Society* 120 (2000): 159–65, esp. 159: "The idiom of the Babylonian Jews attested in the Talmud, however, is not used in the texts of the magic bowls," save for BM 135563, which they discuss. See also the conclusions made by Hannu Juusola, *Linguistic Peculiarities in the Aramaic Magic Bowl Texts* (Helsinki: Finnish Oriental Society, 1999), 245–54, esp. the statement on page 248 that with respect to morphology and phonology "the Aramaic in the bowl texts is clearly more archaic than standard BTA and Mandaic."

93. Jonas C. Greenfield, "Ratin Magosha," in *Joshua Finkel Festschrift: In Honor of Dr. Joshua Finkel*, ed. Sydney B. Hoenig and Leon D. Stitskin (New York: Yeshiva University Press, 1974), 63–69, esp. 63. See also Moulie Vidas, *Tradition and the Formation of the Talmud* (Princeton: Princeton University Press, 2014), 136–66.

94. Israel Drazin, *Targum Onkelos to Deuteronomy: An English Translation of the Text, with Analysis and Commentary* (New York: Ktav, 1982), 181.

95. See, for example, JBA 45 line 7 in Shaked, Ford, and Bharyo, *Aramaic Bowl Spells*, 205.

96. *B. B. Meṣiʿa* 29b (MS Florence II-I-8).

97. See Müller-Kessler and Kwasman, "Unique Talmudic Aramaic Incantation Bowl," 162–64.

98. See Dan Levene, "'This Is a *Qybl*' for Overturning Sorceries': Form, Formula—Threads in a Web of Transmission," in *Continuity and Innovation in Magical Tradition*, ed. Gideon Bohak, Yuval Harari, and Shaul Shaked (Leiden: Brill, 2011), 219–44, esp. 221–23.

99. See the recently published book by Marco Moriggi, *A Corpus of Syriac Incantation Bowls: Syriac Magical Texts from Late-Antique Mesopotamia* (Boston: Brill, 2014), where this word for "sorcery" is ubiquitous and is used similarly as in the Jewish bowls. For one example, see Bowl No. 12 (p. 71): "Prepared is this amulet for the pressing and for the binding of all evil sorcery and of hateful magical acts."

BIBLIOGRAPHY

Aberbach, Moses. "Did Alexander Yannai Negotiate an Alliance with the Parthians?" In *Biblical and Related Studies Presented to Samuel Iwry*, ed. Ann Kort and Scott Morschauser, 1–4. Winona Lake: Eisenbrauns, 1985.

Adams, Robert McCormick. *Land behind Baghdad: A History of Settlement on the Diyala Plains*. Chicago: University of Chicago Press, 1965.

Albeck, Shalom. *Law Courts in Talmudic Times*. Ramat Gan: Bar-Ilan University Press, 1980. [Hebrew.]

Alexander, Philip S. "Bavli Berakhot 55a–57b: The Talmudic Dreambook in Context." *Journal of Jewish Studies* 46 (1995): 230–48.

———. "Incantations and Books of Magic." In *The History of the Jewish People in the Age of Jesus Christ (175 B.C.–A.D. 135)*, ed. Emil Schürer, vol. 3, part 1, 342–79. Edinburgh: T. and T. Clark, 1986. [Rev. ed. Geza Vermes, Fergus Millar, and Martin Goodman.]

———. "The Talmudic Concept of Conjuring (*'Ahizat 'Einayim*) and the Problem of the Definition of Magic (*Kishuf*)." In *Creation and Re-Creation in Jewish Thought: Festschrift in Honor of Joseph Dan on the Occasion of His Seventieth Birthday*, ed. Rachel Elior and Peter Schäfer, 7–26. Tübingen: Mohr Siebeck, 2005.

———. *The Targum of Lamentations: Translated, with a Critical Introduction, Apparatus, and Notes*. Collegeville: Liturgical Press, 2007.

Allen, Douglas. "Eliade and History." *Journal of Religion* 68 (1988): 545–65.

Amouzgar, Jaleh, and Ahmad Tafazzoli. *Le cinquième livre du Dēnkard*. Paris: Association pour l'Avancement des Études Iraniennes, 2000.

Anklesaria, Behramgore Tahmuras. *The Pahlavi Rivāyat of Āturfarnbag and Farnbag-Srōš*. Part 1, *Text and Transcription*. Bombay: Cama Athornan Institute, 1969.

———. *Pahlavi Vendidâd: (Zand-î Jvîṭ-dêv-dâṭ): Transliteration and Translation in English*. Bombay: K. R. Cama Oriental Institute, 1949.

———. *Zand-Ākāsīh: Iranian or Greater Bundahišn—Transliteration and Translation in English.* Bombay: Rahnumae Mazdayasnan Sabha, 1956.

Anklesaria, Tehmuras Dinshaw. *Dânâk-u Mainyô-i Khard: Pahlavi, Pazand, and Sanskrit Texts.* Bombay: The Fort Printing Press, 1913.

Avi-Yonah, Michael, with Shmuel Safrai. *Carta's Atlas of the Period of the Second Temple, the Mishnah, and the Talmud.* Jerusalem: Carta, 1966. [Hebrew.]

Azarpay, Guitty, with Catherine Demos, Edward Gans, Lydia Gans, Wolfgang Heimpel, Anne Draffkorn Kilmer, Sanjyot Mehendale, and Jeanette Zerneke. "Sasanian Seals from the Collection of the Late Edward Gans, at the University of California, Berkeley." Online: www.ecai.org/sasanianweb/docs/sasanianseals.html.

Back, Michael. *Die sassanidischen Staatsinschriften: Studien zur Orthographie und Phonologie des Mittelpersischen der Inschriften zusammen mit einem etymologischen Index des mittelpersischen Wortgutes und einem Textcorpus der behandelten Inschriften.* Leiden: Brill, 1978.

Bailey, Harold W. "To the Zamasp-Namak, I." *Bulletin of the School of Oriental Studies* 6, no.1 (1930): 55–85.

———. "To the Zamasp-Namak, II." *Bulletin of the School of Oriental Studies* 6, no. 3 (1931): 581–600.

Baird, Robert D. *Category Formation and the History of Religions.* Paris: Mouton, 1971.

Bakhos, Carol. *Ishmael on the Border: Rabbinic Portrayals of the First Arab.* Albany: State University of New York Press, 2006.

Bakhos, Carol, and M. Rahim Shayegan, eds. *The Talmud in Its Iranian Context.* Tübingen: Mohr Siebeck, 2010.

Bassett, James. *Persia, the Land of the Imams: A Narrative of Travel and Residence, 1871–1885.* New York: Charles Scriber's Sons, 1886.

Bausani, Alessandro. "Gabr." In *Encyclopedia of Islam,* 2nd ed., online: referenceworks.brillonline.com/entries/encyclopaedia-of-islam-2/gabr-SIM_2413.

Beck, Roger. "Thus Spake Not Zarathuštra: Zoroastrian Pseudepigrapha of the Greco-Roman World." In Mary Boyce and Frantz Grenet, with Roger Beck, *A History of Zoroastrianism,* vol. 3, *Zoroastrianism under Macedonian and Roman Rule,* 491–565. Leiden: Brill, 1991.

Becker, Adam H. "The Comparative Study of 'Scholasticism' in Late Antique Mesopotamia: Rabbis and East Syrians." *Association for Jewish Studies Review* 34 (2010): 91–113.

BeDuhn, Jason. "Magical Bowls and Manichaeans." In *Ancient Magic and Ritual Power,* ed. Marvin Meyer and Paul Mirecki, 419–34. New York: Brill, 1985.

Beer, Moshe. *The Babylonian Amoraim: Aspects of Economic Life.* Ramat Gan: Bar-Ilan University Press, 1974. [Hebrew.]

———. *The Babylonian Exilarchate in the Arsacid and Sasanian Periods.* Tel Aviv: Devir, 1976. [Hebrew.]

———. "The Decrees of Kartir on the Babylonian Jews." *Tarbiz* 55 (1986): 525–39. [Hebrew.]

———. "On Three Edicts against the Jews of Babylonia in the Third Century C.E." In *Irano-Judaica: Studies Relating to Jewish Contacts with Persian Culture throughout the Ages,* ed. Shaul Shaked, 25–37. Jerusalem: Ben-Zvi Institute, 1982. [Hebrew.]

———. "Three Seals of Jews in Babylonia and Their Date." *Tarbiz* 52 (1983): 434–45. [Hebrew.]

Behl, Aditya. "Pages from the Book of Religions: Comparing Self and Other in Mughal India." In *Notes from a Maṇḍala: Essays in the History of Indian Religions in Honor of Wendy Doniger*, ed. Laurie L. Patton and David L. Haberman, 113–49. Newark: University of Delaware Press, 2010.

Ben-Menahem, Hanina. *Judicial Deviation in Talmudic Law: Governed by Men, Not by Rules.* New York: Harwood Academic Publishers, 1991.

———. "Talmudic Law: A Jurisprudential Perspective." In *The Cambridge History of Judaism*, vol. 4, *The Late Roman–Rabbinic Period*, ed. Steven T. Katz, 877–98. New York: Cambridge University Press, 2006.

Benavides, Gustavo. "Power, Intelligibility and the Boundaries of Religion." *Historical Reflections/Réflexions Historiques* 27 (2001): 481–98.

Benveniste, Émile. *Les mages dans l'ancien Iran.* Paris: Maisonneuve, 1938.

Berger, Michael S. *Rabbinic Authority.* New York: Oxford University Press, 1998.

Berkowitz, Beth. *Execution and Invention: Death Penalty Discourse in Early Rabbinic and Christian Cultures.* New York: Oxford University Press, 2006.

Berlinerblau, Jacques. "Toward a Sociology of Heresy, Orthodoxy, and *Doxa.*" *History of Religions* 40 (2001): 327–51.

Bianchi, Ugo. *The History of Religions.* Leiden: Brill, 1975.

Bidez, Joseph, and Franz Cumont. *Les mages hellénisés: Zoroastre, Ostanès et Hystaspe d'après la tradition grecque.* 2 vols. Paris: Société d'Éditions "Les Belles Lettres," 1938.

Blenkinsopp, Joseph. *Isaiah 1–39: A New Translation, with Introduction and Commentary.* New York: Doubleday, 2000.

Blidstein, Gerald J. "Method in the Study of Talmud." *Journal of the American Academy of Religion* 39 (1971): 186–92.

Bohak, Gideon. *Ancient Jewish Magic: A History.* New York: Cambridge University Press, 2008.

———. "Magical Means for Handling *Minim* in Rabbinic Literature." In *The Image of the Judaeo-Christians in Ancient Jewish and Christian Literature*, ed. Peter J. Tomson and Doris Lambers-Petry, 267–79. Tübingen: Mohr Siebeck, 2003.

Bokser, Baruch M. "Talmudic Names of the Iranian Festivals." *Journal of the American Oriental Society* 95 (1975): 261–62.

———. "Wonder-Working and the Rabbinic Tradition: The Case of Hanina ben Dosa." *Journal for the Study of Judaism* 16 (1985): 42–92.

Bourdieu, Pierre. *The Field of Cultural Production: Essays on Art and Literature.* Ed. Randal Johnson. New York: Columbia University Press, 1993.

———. *Outline of a Theory of Practice.* New York: Cambridge University Press, 1977.

Boustan, Ra'anan S., Martha Himmelfarb, and Peter Schäfer, eds. *Hekhalot Literature in Context: Between Byzantium and Babylonia.* Tübingen: Mohr Siebeck, 2013.

Boustan, Ra'anan S., Oren Kosansky, and Marina Rustow, eds. *Jewish Studies at the Crossroads of Anthropology and History: Authority, Diaspora, Tradition.* Philadelphia: University of Pennsylvania Press, 2011.

Boyarin, Daniel. *Border Lines: The Partition of Judaeo-Christianity.* Philadelphia: University of Pennsylvania Press, 2004.

———. *Carnal Israel: Reading Sex in Talmudic Culture.* Berkeley and Los Angeles: University of California Press, 1993.

———. *Dying for God: Martyrdom and the Making of Christianity and Judaism.* Stanford: Stanford University Press, 1999.

———. "Hellenism in Jewish Babylonia." In *The Cambridge Companion to the Talmud and Rabbinic Literature,* ed. Charlotte Elisheva Fonrobert and Martin S. Jaffee, 336–63. Cambridge: Cambridge University Press, 2007.

———. *Socrates and the Fat Rabbis.* Chicago: University of Chicago Press, 2009.

Boyce, Mary. *The Letter of Tansar.* Rome: Istituto Italiano per il Medio ed Estremo Oriente, 1968.

———. "On the Orthodoxy of Sasanian Zoroastrianism." *Bulletin of the School of Oriental and African Studies* 59 (1996): 11–28.

———. *Zoroastrianism: Its Antiquity and Constant Vigour.* Costa Mesa: Mazda Publishers, 1992.

———. *Zoroastrians: Their Religious Beliefs and Practices.* Boston: Routledge, 1979.

Boyce, Mary, and Frantz Grenet. *A History of Zoroastrianism.* Volume 3, *Zoroastrianism under Macedonian and Roman Rule.* New York: Brill, 1991.

Braude, William G., and Israel J. Kapstein. *Tanna dĕḇe Eliyyahu: The Lore of the School of Elijah.* Philadelphia: Jewish Publication Society, 1981.

Brodsky, David. *A Bride without a Blessing: A Study in the Redaction and Content of Massekhet Kallah and Its Gemara.* Tübingen: Mohr Siebeck, 2006.

Brody, Robert. "The Anonymous Talmud and the Words of the Amoraim." In *Iggud: Selected Essays in Jewish Studies,* vol. 1, *The Bible and Its World: Rabbinic Literature and Jewish Thought,* ed. Baruch J. Schwartz, Aharon Shemesh, and Abraham Melamed, 213–32. Jerusalem: World Union of Jewish Studies, 2008. [Hebrew.]

———. *The Geonim of Babylonia and the Shaping of Medieval Jewish Culture.* New Haven: Yale University Press, 1998.

———. "Judaism in the Sasanian Empire: A Case Study in Religious Coexistence." In *Irano-Judaica II: Studies Relating to Jewish Contacts with Persian Culture throughout the Ages,* ed. Shaul Shaked and Amnon Netzer, 52–62. Jerusalem: Ben-Zvi Institute, 1990.

Brown, Francis, with S. R. Driver, and Charles A. Briggs. *The Brown-Driver-Briggs Hebrew and English Lexicon: With an Appendix Containing the Biblical Aramaic.* Peabody: Hendrickson, 2001.

Brown, Theodore L. *Imperfect Oracle: The Epistemic and Moral Authority of Science.* University Park: Pennsylvania State University Press, 2009.

Brunner, Christopher J. *Sasanian Stamp Seals in the Metropolitan Museum of Art.* New York: The Metropolitan Museum of Art, 1978.

Callieri, Pierfrancesco. "In the Land of the Magi: Demons and Magic in the Everyday Life of Pre-Islamic Iran." In *Démons et merveilles d'Orient,* ed. Rika Gyselen, 11–36. Leuven: Peeters, 2001.

Cantera, Alberto. "Lost in Transmission: The Case of the Pahlavi-Vīdēvdād Manuscripts." *Bulletin of the School of Oriental and African Studies* 73 (2010): 179–205.

———. *Studien zur Pahlavi-Übersetzung des Avesta.* Wiesbaden: Harrassowitz, 2004.

Carter, George William. *Zoroastrianism and Judaism.* New York: AMS Press, 1918.

Cereti, Carlo G. "Middle Persian Literature, i: Pahlavi Literature." *Encyclopaedia Iranica,* online ed., 2009: www.iranica.com/articles/middle-persian-literature-1-pahlavi.

———. "On the Date of the Zand ī Wahman Yasn." In *K. R. Cama Oriental Institute, Second International Congress Proceedings*, ed. H.J.M. Desai and H.N. Modi, 243–58. Bombay: K. R. Cama Institute, 1996.

———. "Primary Sources for the History of Inner and Outer Iran in the Sasanian Period (Third-Seventh Centuries)." *Archivum Eurasiae Medii Aevi* 9 (1997): 17–71.

———. *The Zand ī Wahman Yasn: A Zoroastrian Apocalypse*. Rome: Istituto Italiano per il Medio ed Estremo Oriente, 1995.

Chacha, Homi F. *Gajastak Abâlish: Pahlavi Text: Pahlavi Text with Transliteration, English Translation, Notes and Glossary*. Bombay: The Trustees of the Parsi Punchayet Funds and Properties, 1936.

Chaumont, Marie Louise. "Bōē." *Encyclopaedia Iranica*, online ed., 1989: www.iranica.com/articles/boe-gk.

———. "Recherches sur le clergé zoroastrien: Le hērbad." *Revue de l'Histoire des Religions* 158 (1960): 55–80.

Choksy, Jamsheed K. *Conflict and Cooperation: Zoroastrian Subalterns and Muslim Elites in Medieval Iranian Society*. New York: Columbia University Press, 1997.

———. "Reassessing the Material Contexts of Ritual Fires in Ancient Iran." *Iranica Antiqua* 42 (2007): 229–69.

Christensen, Arthur. *L'Iran sous les Sassanides*. 2nd ed. Copenhagen: Munksgaard, 1944.

Ciancaglini, Claudia A. *Iranian Loanwords in Syriac*. Wiesbaden: Reichert, 2008.

———. "Iranian Loanwords in Syriac: Some Problems in Chronology and Cultural History." In *Middle Iranian Lexicography: Proceedings of the Conference Held in Rome, 9–11 April 2001*, 253–76. Rome: Istituto Italiano per l'Africa e l'Oriente, 2005.

Cohen, Abraham, ed. *The Minor Tractates of the Talmud*. 2 vols. London: Soncino Press, 1966.

Cohen, Barak S. *The Legal Methodology of Late Nehardean Sages in Sasanian Babylonia*. Leiden: Brill, 2011.

Cohen, Shaye J. D. "The Rabbi in Second-Century Jewish Society." In *The Cambridge History of Judaism*, vol. 3, *The Early Roman Period*, ed. William Horbury, W. D. Davies, and John Sturdy, 922–90. New York: Cambridge University Press, 1999.

Cohn, Robert L. "Before Israel: The Canaanites as Other in Biblical Tradition." In *The Other in Jewish Thought: Constructions of Jewish Culture and Identity*, ed. Laurence J. Silberstein and Robert L. Cohn, 74–90. New York: New York University Press, 1994.

Cook, Edward M. "An Aramaic Incantation Bowl from Khafaje." *Bulletin of the American Schools of Oriental Research* 285 (1992): 79–81.

Crone, Patricia. "Kavād's Heresy and Mazdak's Revolt." *Iran* 29 (1991): 21–42.

Dandamayev, Muhammad, and V. A. Livshits. "Zattumēšu, a Magus in Babylonia." In *A Green Leaf: Papers in Honour of Professor Jes P. Asmussen*, 457–59. Leiden: Brill, 1988.

Daryaee, Touraj. "Apocalypse Now: Zoroastrian Reflections on the Early Islamic Centuries." *Medieval Encounters* 4 (1998): 188–202.

———. "The Idea of Ērānšahr: Jewish, Christian and Manichaean Views in Late Antiquity." In *Iranian Identity in the Course of History: Proceedings of the Conference Held in Rome, 21–24 September 2005*, ed. Carlo G. Cereti, 91–108. Rome: Istituto Italiano per l'Africa e l'Oriente, 2010.

———. "National History or Keyanid History?: The Nature of Sasanid Zoroastrian Historiography." *Iranian Studies* 28 (1995): 121–41.

———. *Šahrestānīhā ī Ērānšahr: A Middle Persian Text on Late Antique Geography, Epic, and History.* Costa Mesa: Mazda Publishers, 2002.
———. *Sasanian Persia: The Rise and Fall of an Empire.* New York: I. B. Tauris, 2009.
———. "To Learn and to Remember from Others: Persians Visiting the Dura-Europos Synagogue." *Scripta Judaica Cracoviensia* 8 (2010): 29–37.
Dhabhar, Bamanji Nusserwanji. *The Epistles of Mânûshchîhar.* Bombay: The Trustees of the Parsee Panchayat Funds and Properties, 1912.
———. *The Persian Rivayats of Hormazyar Framarz and Others.* Bombay: K. R. Cama Oriental Institute, 1932.
———. *Translation of Zand-i Khūrtak Avistāk.* Bombay: K. R. Cama Oriental Institute, 1963.
Doniger, Wendy. "Minimyths and Maximyths and Political Points of View." In *Myth and Method,* ed. Laurie L. Patton and Wendy Doniger, 109–27. Charlottesville: University Press of Virginia, 1996.
———. "Post-modern and -colonial -structural Comparisons." In *A Magic Still Dwells: Comparative Religion in the Postmodern Age,* ed. Kimberley C. Patton and Benjamin C. Ray, 63–74. Berkeley and Los Angeles: University of California Press, 2000.
Donovan, Peter. "Neutrality in Religious Studies." In *The Insider/Outsider Problem in the Study of Religion: A Reader,* ed. Russell T. McCuthcheon, 235–47. New York: Cassell, 1999.
Drazin, Israel. *Targum Onkelos to Deuteronomy: An English Translation of the Text, with Analysis and Commentary.* New York: Ktav, 1982.
Dresden, M. J., ed. *Dēnkart: A Pahlavi Text.* Wiesbaden: Harrassowitz, 1966.
Duchesne-Guillemin, Jacques. *The Western Response to Zoroaster.* Oxford: Clarendon Press, 1958.
Dudley, Guilford. "Mircea Eliade as the 'Anti-Historian' of Religions." *Journal of the American Academy of Religion* 44 (1976): 345–59.
Durkin-Meisterernst, Desmond. "Huzwāreš." *Encyclopaedia Iranica,* online ed., 2004: www.iranicaonline.org/articles/huzwares.
Eliade, Mircea. *Patterns in Comparative Religion.* Trans. Rosemary Sheed. New York: Sheed and Ward, 1958.
———. *The Quest: History and Meaning in Religion.* Chicago: University of Chicago Press, 1969.
Elman, Yaakov. "Acculturation to Elite Persian Norms and Modes of Thought in the Babylonian Jewish Community of Late Antiquity." In *Neti'ot le-David: Jubilee Volume for David Weiss Halivni,* ed. Ephraim B. Halivni, Zvi A. Steinfeld, and Yaakov Elman, 31–56. Jerusalem: Orhot, 2004.
———. "The Babylonian Talmud in Its Historical Context." In *Printing the Talmud: From Bomberg to Schottenstein,* ed. Sharon Liberman Mintz and Gabriel M. Goldstein, 19–27. New York: Yeshiva University Museum, 2005.
———. "'He in His Cloak and She in Her Cloak': Conflicting Images of Sexuality in Sasanian Mesopotamia." In *Discussing Cultural Influences: Text, Context, and Non-Text in Rabbinic Judaism—Proceedings of a Conference on Rabbinic Judaism at Bucknell University,* ed. Rivka Ulmer, 129–64. Lanham: University Press of America, 2007.
———. "Marriage and Marital Property in Rabbinic and Sasanian Law." In *Rabbinic Law in Its Roman and Near Eastern Context,* ed. Catherine Hezser, 227–76. Tübingen: Mohr Siebeck, 2003.

———. "Middle Persian Culture and Babylonian Sages: Accommodation and Resistance in the Shaping of Rabbinic Legal Tradition." In *The Cambridge Companion to the Talmud and Rabbinic Literature,* ed. Charlotte Elisheva Fonrobert and Martin S. Jaffee, 165–97. Cambridge: Cambridge University Press, 2007.

———. "Orality and the Redaction of the Babylonian Talmud." *Oral Tradition* 14 (1999): 52–99.

———. "The Other in the Mirror: Iranians and Jews View One Another—Questions of Identity, Conversion, and Exogamy in the Fifth-Century Iranian Empire (Part One)." In Carol Altman Bromberg, Nicholas Sims-Williams, and Ursula Sims-Williams, eds., *Iranian and Zoroastrian Studies in Honor of Prods Oktor Skjærvø. Bulletin of the Asia Institute* 19 (2009): 15–25.

———. "Saffron, Spices, and Sorceresses: Magic Bowls and the Bavli." In *Daughters of Hecate: Women and Magic in the Ancient World,* ed. Kimberly B. Stratton, with Dayna S. Kalleres, 365–85. New York: Oxford University Press, 2014.

———. "The Socioeconomics of Babylonian Heresy." *Jewish Law Association Studies* 17 (2007): 80–127.

———. "Talmud, ii: Rabbinic Literature and Middle Persian Texts." *Encyclopaedia Iranica,* online ed., 2010: www.iranica.com/articles/talmud-ii.

———. "Toward an Intellectual History of Sasanian Law: An Intergenerational Dispute in *Hērbedestān* 9 and Its Rabbinic and Roman Parallels." In *The Talmud in Its Iranian Context,* ed. Carol Bakhos and M. Rahim Shayegan, 21–57. Tübingen: Mohr Siebeck, 2010.

———. "'Up to the Ears' in Horses' Necks (B.M. 108a): On Sasanian Agricultural Policy and Private 'Eminent Domain.'" *Jewish Studies: An Internet Journal* 3 (2004): 95–149.

———. "Why Is There No Zoroastrian Central Temple? A Thought Experiment." In *The Temple of Jerusalem: From Moses to the Messiah—In Honor of Professor Louis H. Feldman,* ed. Steven Fine, 151–70. Boston: Brill, 2011.

———. "The World of the 'Sabboraim': Cultural Aspects of Post-Redactional Additions to the Bavli." In *Creation and Composition: The Contribution of the Bavli Redactors (Stammaim) to the Aggada,* ed. Jeffrey L. Rubenstein, 383–416. Tübingen: Mohr Siebeck, 2005.

Elman, Yaakov, and Mahnaz Moazami. "*Zand ī Fragard ī Jud-dēw-dād.*" *Encyclopaedia Iranica,* online ed., 2014: www.iranicaonline.org/articles/zand-fragard-jud-dew-dad.

Eshel, Ben-Zion. *Jewish Settlements in Babylonia during Talmudic Times: Talmudic Onomasticon, Including Geographical Locations, Historical Notes, and Indices of Place-Names.* Jerusalem: Magnes Press, 1979. [Hebrew.]

Fessler, Siegmund. *Mar Samuel, der bedeutendste Amora.* Breslau: Frank, 1879.

Fiey, J. M. "Topographie chrétienne de Mahozé." *L'Orient Syrien* 12 (1967): 397–420.

Fine, Steven. *Art and Judaism in the Greco-Roman World: Toward a New Jewish Archaeology.* New York: Cambridge University Press, 2005.

Fishman, Talya. *Becoming the People of the Talmud: Oral Torah as Written Tradition in Medieval Jewish Cultures.* Philadelphia: University of Pennsylvania Press, 2011.

Fitzgerald, Timothy. *The Ideology of Religious Studies.* New York: Oxford University Press, 2000.

Flesher, Paul V. M., and Bruce D. Chilton. *The Targums: A Critical Introduction.* Waco: Baylor University Press, 2011.

Flood, Gavin. "Reflections on Tradition and Inquiry in the Study of Religions." *Journal of the American Academy of Religion* 74 (2006): 47–58.

Ford, James Nathan, and Alon Ten-Ami. "An Incantation Bowl for Rav Mešaršia son of Qaqay." *Tarbiz* 80 (2012): 219–30. [Hebrew.]

Fraade, Steven D. *From Tradition to Commentary: Torah and Its Interpretation in the Midrash Sifre to Deuteronomy.* Albany: State University of New York Press, 1991.

Fraenkel, Jonah. "The Story of Rabbi Shila (Bavli Berakhot 58a)." *Tarbiz* 40 (1970–71): 33–40. [Hebrew.]

———. "The Study of Aggadic Literature: A View into the Future." *Jewish Studies* 30 (1990): 21–30. [Hebrew.]

———. "Time and Its Role in the Aggadic Story." In *Binah: Jewish Intellectual History in the Middle Ages*, vol. 2, ed. Joseph Dan, 31–56. Westport: Praeger, 1989.

Freidenreich, David M. *Foreigners and Their Food: Constructing Otherness in Jewish, Christian, and Islamic Law.* Berkeley and Los Angeles: University of California Press, 2011.

Friedman, Shamma. "On the Historical Aggada in the Babylonian Talmud." In *Saul Lieberman Memorial Volume*, ed. Shamma Friedman, 119–63. New York: Jewish Theological Seminary, 1993. [Hebrew.]

———. "The Orthography of the Names Rabbah and Rava in the Babylonian Talmud." *Sinai* 110 (1992): 140–64. [Hebrew.]

Frye, Richard N. *The History of Ancient Iran.* Munich: Beck, 1984.

———. "The Political History of Iran under the Sasanians." In *The Cambridge History of Iran*, vol. 3.1, *The Seleucid, Parthian, and Sasanian Periods*, ed. Ehsan Yarshater, 116–80. Cambridge: Cambridge University Press, 1983.

Gafni, Isaiah. "Babylonian Rabbinic Culture." In *Cultures of the Jews*, vol. 1, *Mediterranean Origins*, ed. David Biale, 223–66. New York: Schocken Books, 2002.

———. "Court Cases in the Babylonian Talmud: Literary Forms and Historical Implications." *Proceedings of the American Academy of Jewish Research* 49 (1982): 23–40. [Hebrew.]

———. "How Babylonia Became 'Zion': Shifting Identities in Late Antiquity." In *Jewish Identities in Antiquity: Studies in Memory of Menahem Stern*, ed. Lee I. Levine and Daniel R. Schwartz, 333–48. Tübingen: Mohr Siebeck, 2009.

———. *The Jews of Babylonia in the Talmudic Era: A Social and Cultural History.* Jerusalem: Merkaz Zalman Shazar, 1990. [Hebrew.]

———. "The Modern Study of Rabbinics and Historical Questions: The Tale of the Text." In *The New Testament and Rabbinic Literature*, ed. Reimund Bieringer, Florentino García Martínez, Didier Pollefeyt, and Peter J. Tomson, 43–61. Boston: Brill, 2010.

———. "The Political, Social, and Economic History of Babylonian Jewry, 224–628 CE." In *The Cambridge History of Judaism*, vol. 4, *The Late Roman–Rabbinic Period*, ed. Steven T. Katz, 792–820. New York: Cambridge University Press, 2006.

———. "Rabbinic Historiography and Representations of the Past." In *The Cambridge Companion to the Talmud and Rabbinic Literature*, ed. Charlotte Elisheva Fonrobert and Martin S. Jaffee, 295–312. Cambridge: Cambridge University Press, 2007.

———. "Rethinking Talmudic History: The Challenge of Literary and Redaction Criticism." *Jewish History* 25 (2011): 355–75.

———. "Synagogues in Babylonia in the Talmudic Period." In *Ancient Synagogues: Historical Analysis and Archaeological Discovery*, vol. 1, ed. Dan Urman and Paul V. M. Flesher, 221–31. Leiden: Brill, 1998.

———. "Yeshiva and Metivta." *Zion* 43 (1978): 12–37. [Hebrew.]

Garfinkel, Stephen. "Applied *Peshat:* Historical-Critical Method and Religious Meaning." *Journal of the Ancient Near Eastern Society* 22 (1993): 19–28.

Gehman, Henry S. "Notes on the Persian Words in the Book of Esther." *Journal of Biblical Literature* 43 (1924), 321–28.

Geiger, Bernhard. "The Middle Iranian Texts." In *The Excavations at Dura-Europos, Final Report,* vol. 8, part 1, ed. M. I. Rostovtzeff, A. R. Bellinger, F. E. Brown, and C. B. Welles, 283–317. New Haven: Yale University Press, 1956.

Geller, M. J. "Four Aramaic Incantation Bowls." In *The Bible World: Essays in Honor of Cyrus H. Gordon,* ed. Gary Rensdburg, Ruth Adler, Milton Arfa, and Nathan H. Winter, 47–60. New York: Ktav, 1980.

———. "Jesus' Theurgic Powers: Parallels in the Talmud and Incantation Bowls." *Journal of Jewish Studies* 28 (1977): 141–55.

Ghirshman, Roman. *Persian Art: The Parthian and Sassanian Dynasties, 249 B.C.–A.D. 651.* Trans. Stuart Gilbert and James Emmons. New York: Golden Press, 1962.

Gignoux, Philippe. "Une catégorie de mages à la fin de l'époque sasanide: Les *mogvēh.*" *Jerusalem Studies in Arabic and Islam* 9 (1987): 19–23.

———. "Church-State Relations in the Sasanian Period." In *Monarchies and Socio-religious Traditions in the Ancient Near East: Papers Read at the 31st International Congress of Human Sciences in Asia and North Africa,* ed. HIH Prince Takahito Mikasa, 72–80. Wiesbaden: Harrassowitz, 1984.

———. "Dēnkard." *Encyclopaedia Iranica,* online ed., 1994: www.iranicaonline.org/articles/denkard.

———. "Éléments de prosopographie de quelques *mōbad*s sasanides." *Journal Asiatique* 270 (1982): 257–69.

———. *Le livre d'Ardā Vīrāz: Translittération, transcription et traduction du texte pehlevi.* Paris: Éditions Recherche sur les Civilisations, 1984.

———. "Pour une esquisse des fonctions religieuses sous les Sasanides." *Jerusalem Studies in Arabic and Islam* 7 (1986): 93–108.

———. "Pour une nouvelle histoire de l'Iran sasanide." In *Middle Iranian Studies: Proceedings of the International Symposium Organized by the Katholieke Universiteit Leuven from the 17th to the 20th of May 1982*, ed. Wojciech Skalmowski and Alois Van Tongerloo, 253–62. Leuven: Peeters, 1984.

———. "Problèmes de distinction et de priorité des sources." In *Prolegomena to the Sources on the History of Pre-Islamic Central Asia,* ed. János Harmatta, 137–41. Budapest: Akadémiai Kiadó, 1979.

———. *Les quatre inscriptions du mage Kirdīr: Textes et concordances.* Paris: Association pour l'Avancement des Études Iraniennes, 1991.

———. "Die religiöse Administration in sasanidischer Zeit: Ein Überblick." In *Kunst, Kultur und Geschichte der Achämenidenzeit und ihr Fortleben,* ed. Heidemarie Koch and David Neil MacKenzie, 253–66. Berlin: Reimer, 1983.

———. "Un témoin du syncrétisme mazdéen tardif: Le traité pehlevi des 'Sélections de Zādsparam.'" In *Transition Periods in Iranian History: Actes du Symposium de Fribourg-en-Brisgau (22–24 Mai 1985)*, 59–72. Paris: Association pour l'Avancement des Études Iraniennes, 1987.

———. "Titres et fonctions religieuses sasanides d'après les sources syriaques hagiographiques." *Acta Antiqua Academiae Scientiarum Hungaricae* 28 (1983): 191–203.

Gignoux, Philippe, and Rika Gyselen, eds. *Bulles et sceaux sassanides de diverses collections*. Paris: Association pour l'Avancement des Études Iraniennes, 1987.

Gignoux, Philippe, and Ahmad Tafazzoli. *Anthologie de Zādspram: Édition critique du texte pehlevi, traduit et commenté*. Paris: Association pour l'Avancement des Études Iraniennes, 1993.

Ginzberg, Louis. *Introductory Essay: The Palestinian Talmud*. New York: The Jewish Theological Seminary of America, 1941.

Gnoli, Gherardo. *The Idea of Iran: An Essay on Its Origin*. Rome: Istituto Italiano per il Medio ed Estremo Oriente. [Distributed by Brill (Leiden), 1989.]

Göbl, Robert. "Šābuhr, König der Könige von Iran." *Quaderni Ticinesi di Numismatica e Antichità Classiche* 20 (1991): 239–45.

———. *Sasanian Numismatics*. Würzburg: Braunschweig, Klinkhardt, and Biermann, 1971.

Goldberg, Abraham. "The Babylonian Talmud." In *The Literature of the Sages*, part 1, *Oral Tora, Halakha, Mishna, Tosefta, Talmud, External Tractates*, ed. Shmuel Safrai, 323–45. Philadelphia: Fortress Press, 1987.

Goodblatt, David. "The Jews in Babylonia, 66–c. 235 CE." In *The Cambridge History of Judaism*, vol. 4, *The Late Roman–Rabbinic Period*, ed. Steven T. Katz, 82–92. New York: Cambridge University Press, 2006.

———. "The Poll Tax in Sasanian Babylonia." *Journal of the Economic and Social History of the Orient* 22 (1979): 233–95.

———. *Rabbinic Instruction in Sasanian Babylonia*. Leiden: Brill, 1975.

———. "Towards the Rehabilitation of Talmudic History." In *History of Judaism: The Next Ten Years*, ed. Baruch M. Bokser, 31–44. Chico: Scholars Press, 1980.

Gordon, Cyrus H. "Aramaic Magical Bowls in the Istanbul and Baghdad Museums." *Archiv Orientální* 6 (1934): 319–34.

Gray, Alyssa. "The Power Conferred by Distance from Power: Redaction and Meaning in b. A.Z. 10a–11a." In *Creation and Composition: The Contribution of the Bavli Redactors (Stammaim) to the Aggada*, ed. Jeffrey L. Rubenstein, 26–72. Tübingen: Mohr Siebeck, 2005.

Green, William Scott. "Otherness Within: Towards a Theory of Difference in Rabbinic Judaism." In *"To See Ourselves as Others See Us": Christians, Jews, "Others" in Late Antiquity*, ed. Jacob Neusner and Ernest S. Frerichs, 49–69. Chico: Scholars Press, 1985.

———. "What's in a Name? The Problematic of Rabbinic 'Biography.'" In *Approaches to Ancient Judaism: Theory and Practice*, ed. William Scott Green, 77–96. Missoula: Scholars Press, 1978.

Greenfield, Jonas C. "Notes on Some Aramaic and Mandaic Magic Bowls." *Journal of the Ancient Near Eastern Society* 5 (1973): 149–56.

———. "Ratin Magosha." In *Joshua Finkel Festschrift: In Honor of Dr. Joshua Finkel,* ed. Sydney B. Hoenig and Leon D. Stitskin, 63–69. New York: Yeshiva University Press, 1974.

———. "The Use of the Targum in a Mandaic Incantation Text." In *"Open Thou Mine Eyes . . .": Essays on Aggadah and Judaica Presented to Rabbi William G. Braude on His Eightieth Birthday and Dedicated to His Memory,* ed. Herman J. Blumberg et al., 79–82. Hoboken: Ktav, 1992.

Greenfield, Jonas C., and Joseph Naveh. "A Mandaic Lead Amulet with Four Incantations." *Eretz Israel* 18 (1985): 97–107. [Hebrew.]

Grenet, Frantz. *La geste d'Ardashir fils de Pâbag: Kārnāmag ī Ardaxšēr ī Pābagān.* Die: Éditions A Die, 2003.

Grignaschi, M. "Quelques spécimens de la littérature sassanide conservés dans les bibliothèques d'Istanbul." *Journal Asiatique* 254 (1966): 1–142.

Gyselen, Rika. *La géographie administrative de l'empire sassanide: Les témoignages sigillographiques.* Leuven: Peeters, 1989.

———. "Note de glyptique sassanide: Les cachets personnels de l'Ohrmazd-mogbed." In *Études irano-aryennes offertes à Gilbert Lazard,* 185–92. Paris: Association pour l'Avancement des Études Iraniennes, 1989.

———. "Note de glyptique sassanide: Quelques éléments d'iconographie religieuse." In *Contribution à l'histoire de l'Iran: Mélanges offerts à Jean Perrot,* ed. François Vallat, 253–67. Paris: Éditions Recherche sur les Civilisations, 1990.

———. "Primary Sources and Historiography on the Sasanian Empire." *Studia Iranica* 38 (2009): 163–90.

———. *Sasanian Seals and Sealings in the A. Saeedi Collection.* Leuven Peeters, 2007.

———. "Les sceaux des mages de l'Iran sassanide." In *Au carrefour des religions: Mélanges offerts à Philippe Gignoux,* ed. Rika Gyselen, 121–50. Bures-sur-Yvette: Groupe pour l'Étude de la Civilisation du Moyen-Orient, 1995.

———. *Sceaux magiques en Iran sassanide.* Paris: Association pour l'Avancement des Études Iraniennes, 1995.

Halbwachs, Maurice. *The Collective Memory.* Trans. Francis J. Ditter, Jr., and Vida Yazdi Ditte. New York: Harper and Row, 1980.

Halivni, David Weiss. "Aspects of the Formation of the Talmud." In *Creation and Composition: The Contribution of the Bavli Redactors (Stammaim) to the Aggada,* ed. and trans. Jeffrey L. Rubenstein, 339–60. Tübingen: Mohr Siebeck, 2005.

———. *The Book and the Sword: A Life of Learning in the Shadow of Destruction.* New York: Farrar, Straus, and Giroux, 1996.

———. *The Formation of the Babylonian Talmud.* Trans. Jeffrey L. Rubenstein. New York: Oxford University Press, 2013.

———. *Midrash, Mishnah, and Gemara: The Jewish Predilection for Justified Law.* Cambridge, Mass.: Harvard University Press, 1986.

———. *Sources and Traditions: A Source-Critical Commentary on the Talmud Tractate Baba Bathra.* Jerusalem: Magnes Press, 2007. [Hebrew.]

Hallock, Richard Treadwell. *Persepolis Fortification Tablets.* Chicago: University of Chicago Press, 1969.

Harper, Prudence O. *In Search of a Cultural Identity: Monuments and Artifacts of the Sasanian Near East, 3rd to 7th Century A.D.* New York: Bibliotheca Persica, 2006.

Harviainen, Tapani. "Syncretistic and Confessional Features in Mesopotamian Incantation Bowls." *Studia Orientalia* 70 (1993): 29–37.

Hasan-Rokem, Galit. *Web of Life: Folklore and Midrash in Rabbinic Literature.* Trans. Batya Stein. Stanford: Stanford University Press, 2000.

Hassan, Ihab H. "The Problem of Influence in Literary History: Notes towards a Definition." *The Journal of Aesthetics and Art Criticism* 14 (1955): 66–76.

Hayes, Christine. *Between the Babylonian and Palestinian Talmuds: Accounting for Halakhic Difference in Selected Sugyot from Tractate Avodah Zarah.* New York: Oxford University Press, 1997.

———. *Gentile Impurities and Jewish Identities: Intermarriage and Conversion from the Bible to the Talmud.* New York: Oxford University Press, 2002.

———. "The 'Other' in Rabbinic Literature." In *The Cambridge Companion to the Talmud and Rabbinic Literature,* ed. Charlotte Elisheva Fonrobert and Martin S. Jaffee, 243–69. Cambridge: Cambridge University Press, 2007.

Hayward, Robert. *Targums and the Transmission of Scripture into Judaism and Christianity.* Leiden: Brill, 2010.

Heinemann, Joseph. *Aggadah and Its Development.* Jerusalem: Keter, 1974. [Hebrew.]

———. "The Nature of the Aggadah." In *Midrash and Literature,* ed. Geoffrey H. Hartman and Sanford Budick, 41–55. New Haven: Yale University Press, 1986.

Herman, Geoffrey. "The Story of Rav Kahana (BT Baba Qamma 117a–b) in Light of Armeno-Persian Sources." In *Irano-Judaica VI: Studies Relating to Jewish Contacts with Persian Culture throughout the Ages,* ed. Shaul Shaked and Amnon Netzer, 53–68. Jerusalem: Ben-Zvi Institute, 2008.

———. "Ahasuerus, the Former Stable-Master of Belshazzar, and the Wicked Alexander of Macedon: Two Parallels between the Babylonian Talmud and Persian Sources." *Association for Jewish Studies Review* 29 (2005): 283–97.

———. "'*One Day David Went Out for the Hunt of the Falconers*': Persian Themes in the Babylonian Talmud." In *Shoshannat Yaakov: Jewish and Iranian Studies in Honor of Yaakov Elman,* ed. Shai Secunda and Steven Fine, 111–36. Boston: Brill, 2012.

———. "Persia in Light of the Babylonian Talmud—Echoes of Contemporary Society and Politics: *hargbed* and *bidaxš.*" In *The Talmud in Its Iranian Context,* ed. Carol Bakhos and M. Rahim Shayegan, 58–82. Tübingen: Mohr Siebeck, 2010.

———. *A Prince without a Kingdom: The Exilarch in the Sasanian Era.* Tübingen: Mohr Siebeck, 2012.

Herman, Luc, and Bart Vervaeck. "Ideology." In *The Cambridge Companion to Narrative,* ed. David Herman, 217–30. New York: Cambridge University Press, 2007.

Hermann, Georgina. "The Rock Reliefs of Sasanian Iran." In *Mesopotamia and Iran in the Parthian and Sasanian Periods: Rejection and Revival c. 238 BC–AD 642—Proceedings of a Seminar in Memory of Vladimir G. Lukonin,* ed. John Curtis, 35–45. London: British Museum, 2000.

Herr, Moshe. "The Conception of History among the Sages." In *Proceedings of the Sixth World Congress of Jewish Studies, Jerusalem, August 13–19, 1973,* vol. C, div. C, 129–42. Jerusalem: World Union of Jewish Studies, 1977. [Hebrew.]

Hezser, Catherine. *The Social Structure of the Rabbinic Movement in Roman Palestine.* Tübingen: Mohr Siebeck, 1997.

Hidary, Richard. *Dispute for the Sake of Heaven: Legal Pluralism in the Talmud.* Providence: Brown University Press, 2010.

Hintze, Almut. "The Avesta in the Parthian Period." In *Das Partherreich und seine Zeugnisse,* ed. Josef Wiesehöfer, 147–62. Stuttgart: Steiner, 1998.

Hirshman, Marc. "Aggadic Midrash." In *The Literature of the Sages,* part 2, *Midrash and Targum, Liturgy, Poetry, Mysticism, Contracts, Inscriptions, Ancient Science, and the Languages of Rabbinic Literature,* ed. Shmuel Safrai, Zeev Safrai, Joshua Schwartz, and Peter J. Tomson, 107–32. Assen: Royal Van Gorcum and Fortress Press, 2006.

———. *The Stabilization of Rabbinic Culture, 100 C.E.–350 C.E.: Texts on Education and Their Late Antique Context.* New York: Oxford University Press, 2009.

Hoffman, David Zvi. *Mar Samuel, Rector der jüdischen Akademie zu Nehardea in Babylonien: Lebensbild eines talmudischen Weisen der ersten Hälfte des dritten Jahrhunderts, nach den Quellen dargestellt* Leipzig: Leiner, 1873.

Horovitz, Jakob. *Mar Samuel und Schabur I: Zur Erklärung der letzten Zeilen des Talmudtraktats Baba Mezia.* Breslau: Marcus, 1936.

Humbach, Helmut, with Josef Elfenbein and Prods Oktor Skjærvø. *The Gāthās of Zarathustra and the Other Old Avestan Texts.* Part 1, *Introduction: Text and Translation.* Heidelberg: Winter, 1991.

Hunter, Erica C. D. "Aramaic-Speaking Communities of Sasanid Mesopotamia." *Aram* 7 (1995): 319–35.

———. "Manipulating Incantation Texts: Excursions in Refrain A." *Iraq* 64 (2002): 259–73.

Hutter, Manfred. *Manis kosmogonische Šābuhragān-Texte: Edition, Kommentar und literaturgeschichtliche Einordnung der manichäisch-mittelpersischen Handschriften M 98/99 I und M 7980–7984.* Wiesbaden: Harrassowitz, 1992.

Hutton, Patrick H. *History as an Art of Memory.* Hanover: University Press of New England, 1993.

Huyse, Philip. *Die dreisprachige Inschrift Šābuhrs I. an der Ka'ba-i Zardušt' (ŠKZ). Corpus Inscriptionum Iranicarum.* Part 3, *Pahlavi Inscriptions.* Volume 1, *Royal Inscriptions, with Their Parthian and Greek Versions.* London: School of Oriental and African Studies, 1999.

———. "Kerdīr and the First Sasanians." In *Proceedings of the Third European Conference of Iranian Studies, Held in Cambridge, 11–15 September 1995,* part 1, *Old and Middle Iranian Studies,* ed. Nicholas Sims-Williams, 109–20. Wiesbaden: Reichert, 1998.

Idel, Moshe. *Golem: Jewish Magical and Mystical Traditions on the Artificial Anthropoid.* Albany: State University of New York Press, 1990.

Ilan, Tal, with Kerstin Hünefeld. *Lexicon of Jewish Names in Late Antiquity.* Part 4, *The Eastern Diaspora, 330 BCE–650 CE.* Tübingen: Mohr Siebeck, 2011.

Iricinschi, Eduard, and Holger M. Zellentin. "Making Selves and Marking Others: Identity and Late Antique Heresiologies." In *Heresy and Identity in Late Antiquity,* ed. Eduard Iricinschi and Holger M. Zellentin, 1–27. Tübingen: Mohr Siebeck, 2008.

Jaafari-Dehaghi, Mahmoud. *Dādestān ī Dēnīg.* Part 1, *Transcription, Translation, and Commentary.* Paris: Association pour l'Avancement des Études Iraniennes, 1998.

Jamaspasa, Kaikhusroo M., and Helmut Humbach, eds. *Pursišnīhā: A Zoroastrian Catechism.* Part 1, *Text, Translation, Notes.* Wiesbaden: Harrassowitz, 1971.

Jany, János. "Criminal Justice in Sasanian Persia." *Iranica Antiqua* 42 (2007): 347–86.

———. *Judging in the Islamic, Jewish, and Zoroastrian Legal Traditions: A Comparison of Theory and Practice*. Burlington: Ashgate, 2012.

———. "Private Litigation in Sasanian Law." *Iranica Antiqua* 45 (2010): 395–418.

Jastrow, Marcus. *Dictionary of the Targumim, Talmud Bavli, Talmud Yerushalmi, and Midrashic Literature*. New York: Judaica Treasury, 1971.

de Jong, Albert. "Animal Sacrifice in Ancient Zoroastrianism: A Ritual and Its Interpretations." In *Sacrifice in Religious Experience*, ed. Albert I. Baumgarten, 127–50. Boston: Brill, 2002.

———. "The Contribution of the Magi." In *Birth of the Persian Empire*, vol. 1 of *The Idea of Iran*, ed. Vesta Sarkhosh Curtis and Sarah Stewart, 85–99. New York: I. B. Tauris, 2005.

———. *Traditions of the Magi: Zoroastrianism in Greek and Latin Literature*. Leiden: Brill, 1997.

———. "Zoroastrian Religious Polemics and Their Contexts: Interconfessional Relations in the Sasanian Empire." In *Religious Polemics in Context: Papers Presented to the Second International Conference of the Leiden Institute for the Study of Religions (LISOR), Held at Leiden 27–28 April 2000*, ed. T. L. Hettema and A. van der Kooij, 48–63. Assen: Royal van Gorcum, 2004.

Josephson, Judith. *The Pahlavi Translation Technique as Illustrated by the Hōm Yašt*. Uppsala: Uppsala Universitetsbibliotek, 1997.

Jullien, Christelle. "Kaškar 'la sublime' et sa singulière prééminence sur le siège patriarcal de Séleucie-Ctésiphon." In *Proceedings of the Fifth Conference of the Societas Iranologica Europaea, Held in Ravenna, 6–11 October 2003*, vol. 1, *Ancient and Middle Iranian Studies*, ed. Antonio C. D. Panaino and Andrea Piras, 543–52. Milan: Mimesis, 2006.

———. "La minorité chrétienne 'grecque' en terre d'Iran à l'époque sassanide." In *Chrétiens en terre d'Iran: Implantation et acculturation*, ed. Rika Gyselen, 105–42. Paris: Association pour l'Avancement des Études Iraniennes, 2006.

Juusola, Hannu. *Linguistic Peculiarities in the Aramaic Magic Bowl Texts*. Helsinki: Finnish Oriental Society, 1999.

Kalmin, Richard. "Christians and Heretics in Rabbinic Literature of Late Antiquity." *Harvard Theological Review* 87 (1994): 155–69.

———. "The Formation and Character of the Babylonian Talmud." In *The Cambridge History of Judaism*, vol. 4, *The Late Roman–Rabbinic Period*, ed. Steven T. Katz, 840–76. New York: Cambridge University Press, 2006.

———. *Jewish Babylonia between Persia and Roman Palestine*. New York: Oxford University Press, 2006.

———. "Midrash and Social History." In *Current Trends in the Study of Midrash*, ed. Carol Bakhos, 133–59. Leiden: Brill, 2006.

———. *Migrating Tales: The Talmud's Narratives and Their Historical Context*. Berkeley and Los Angeles: University of California Press, 2014.

———. "Rabbinic Literature of Late Antiquity as a Source for Historical Study." In *Judaism in Late Antiquity*, vol. 2, ed. Jacob Neusner and Alan J. Avery-Peck, 187–99. Leiden: Brill, 1999.

———. *The Sage in Jewish Society of Late Antiquity*. New York: Routledge, 1999.

———. "Talmudic Attitudes toward Dream Interpreters: Preliminary Thoughts on Their Iranian Cultural Context." In *The Talmud in Its Iranian Context*, ed. Carol Bakhos and M. Rahim Shayegan, 83–99. Tübingen: Mohr Siebeck, 2010.

Kanga, Maneck Fardunji. *Čītak Handarž i Pōryōtkēšān: A Pahlavi Text Edited, Transcribed, and Translated into English, with Introduction and a Critical Glossary, and with a Foreword by Professor H. W. Bailey.* Bombay: M. F. Kanga, 1960.

Kaufman, Stephen A. "A Unique Magic Bowl from Nippur." *Journal of Near Eastern Studies* 32 (1973): 170–74.

Kennedy, Hugh. "Survival of Iranianness." In *The Rise of Islam*, vol. 4 of *The Idea of Iran*, ed. Vesta Sarkhosh Curtis and Sarah Stewart, 13–29. New York, I. B. Tauris, 2009.

Kent, Roland. *Old Persian: Grammar, Texts, Lexicon.* New Haven: American Oriental Society, 1959.

Khanbaghi, Aptin. "De-Zoroastrianization and Islamization: The Two Phases of Iran's Religious Transition, 747–837 CE." *Comparative Studies of South Asia, Africa, and the Middle East* 29 (2009): 201–12.

Kiel, Yishai. "Redesigning *Tzitzit* in the Babylonian Talmud in Light of Literary Depictions of the Zoroastrian *kustīg*." In *Shoshannat Yaakov: Jewish and Iranian Studies in Honor of Yaakov Elman*, ed. Shai Secunda and Steven Fine, 185–202. Boston: Brill, 2012.

———. "Selected Topics in Laws of Ritual Defilement: Between the Babylonian Talmud and Pahlavi Literature." Ph.D. dissertation, Hebrew University of Jerusalem, 2011. [Hebrew.]

Kingsley, Peter. "Greeks, Shamans and Magi." *Studia Iranica* 23 (1994): 187–98.

Kiperwasser, Reuven. "Rabba bar bar Channa's Voyages." *Jerusalem Studies in Hebrew Literature* 22 (2008): 215–42. [Hebrew.]

Kiperwasser, Reuven, and Dan D. Y. Shapira. "Irano-Talmudica I: The Three-Legged Ass and *Ridyā* in B. Ta'anith—Some Observations about Mythic Hydrology in the Babylonian Talmud and in Ancient Iran." *Association for Jewish Studies Review* 32 (2008): 101–16.

———. "Irano-Talmudica II: Leviathan, Behemoth, and the 'Domestication' of Iranian Mythological Creatures in Eschatological Narratives of the Babylonian Talmud." In *Shoshannat Yaakov: Jewish and Iranian Studies in Honor of Yaakov Elman*, ed. Shai Secunda and Steven Fine, 203–25. Boston: Brill, 2012.

Kiperwasser, Reuven, and Serge Ruzer. "To Convert a Persian and Teach Him the Holy Scriptures: A Zoroastrian Proselyte in Rabbinic and Syriac Christian Narratives." In *Jews, Christians and Zoroastrians: Religious Dynamics in a Sasanian Context*, ed. Geoffrey Herman, 101–38. Piscataway: Gorgias Press, 2014.

———. "Zoroastrian Proselytes in Rabbinic and Syriac Christian Narratives: Orality-Related Markers of Cultural Identity." *History of Religions* 51 (2012): 197–218.

Kohut, Alexander. "Les fêtes persanes et babyloniennes dans les Talmuds de Babylon et de Jerusalem." *Revue des Études Juives* 24 (1892): 256–71.

———. "Parsic and Jewish Legends of the First Man." *Jewish Quarterly Review* 3 (1891): 231–50.

———. *Ueber die jüdische Angelologie und Daemonologie in ihrer Abhängigkeit vom Parsismus.* Leipzig: Brockhaus, 1866.

König, Götz. "Der Pahlavi-Text *Zand ī Fragard ī Juddēvdād*." In *Ancient and Middle Iranian Studies: Proceedings of the 6th European Conference of Iranian Studies, Held in Vienna, 18–22 September 2007*, ed. Maria Macuch, Dieter Weber, and Desmond Durkin-Meisterernst, 115–32. Wiesbaden: Harrassowitz, 2010.

Kossmann, Maarten. "Borrowing." In *The Oxford Handbook of Arabic Linguistics*, ed. Jonathan Owens, 349–68. New York: Oxford University Press, 2013.

Kotwal, Firoze M., and Philip G. Kreyenbroek, with James R. Russell. *The Hērbedestān and Nērangestān.* 4 vols. Paris: Association pour l'Avancement des Études Iraniennes, 1992–2009.

Krauss, Samuel. *Griechische und lateinische Lehnwörter im Talmud, Midrasch und Targum.* 2 vols. Berlin: Calvary, 1898–99.

———. *Persia and Rome in the Talmud and Midrashim.* Jerusalem: Mossad Harav Kook, 1948. [Hebrew.]

Krauss, Samuel, Bernhardo Geiger, Ludovico Ginzberg, Immanuele Löw, and Benjamino Murmelstein, eds. *Additamenta ad Librum Aruch Completum Alexandri Kohut.* Vienna: The Alexander Kohut Memorial Foundation, 1937.

Kreyenbroek, Philip G. "The *Dādestān ī Dēnīg* on Priests." *Indo-Iranian Journal* 30 (1987): 185–208.

———. "How Pious was Shapur I? Religion, Church and Propaganda under the Early Sasanians." In *The Sasanian Era,* vol. 3 of *The Idea of Iran,* ed. Vesta Sarkhosh Curtis and Sarah Stewart, 7–16. New York: I. B. Tauris, 2008.

———. "On the Concept of Spiritual Authority in Zoroastrianism." *Jerusalem Studies in Arabic and Islam* 17 (1994): 1–15.

———. "Review: J. K. Choksy, *Conflict and Cooperation: Zoroastrian Subalterns and Muslim Elites in Medieval Iranian Society* (New York: Columbia University Press, 1997)." *Indo-Iranian Journal* 42 (1999): 387–92.

———. "The Zoroastrian Priesthood after the Fall of the Sasanian Empire." In *Transition Periods in Iranian History: Actes du Symposium de Fribourg-en-Brisgau, 22–24 Mai 1985,* 151–66. Paris: Association pour l'Avancement des Études Iraniennes, 1987.

———. "The Zoroastrian Tradition from an Oralist's Point of View." In *K. R. Cama Oriental Institute, Second International Congress Proceedings,* ed. H. J. M. Desai and H. N. Modi, 231–37. Bombay: K. R. Cama Oriental Institute, 1996.

Krupp, Michael. "Manuscripts of the Babylonian Talmud." In *The Literature of the Sages,* part 1, *Oral Tora, Halakha, Mishna, Tosefta, Talmud, External Tractates,* ed. Shmuel Safrai, 346–66. Philadelphia: Fortress Press, 1987.

Labendz, Jenny R. *Socratic Torah: Non-Jews in Rabbinic Intellectual Culture.* New York: Oxford University Press, 2013.

de Lagarde, Paul. *Gesammelte Abhandlungen.* Leipzig: Brockhaus, 1866.

Lerner, Judith A. *Christian Seals of the Sasanian Period.* Istanbul: Nederlands Historisch-Archaeologisch Instituut te Istanbul, 1977.

———. "Considerations on an Aspect of Jewish Culture under the Sasanians: The Matter of Jewish Sigillography." *Journal of the American Oriental Society* 129 (2009): 653-64. [Review of Daniel M. Friedenberg, *Sasanian Jewry and Its Culture: A Lexicon of Jewish and Related Seals* (Urbana: University of Illinois Press, 2009).]

Leslau, Wolf. *Comparative Dictionary of Geʿez (Classical Ethiopic).* Wiesbaden: Harrassowitz, 1987.

Lesses, Rebecca. "Exe(o)rcising Power: Women as Sorceresses, Exorcists, and Demonesses in Babylonian Jewish Society of Late Antiquity." *Journal of the American Academy of Religion* 69 (2001): 343–75.

Levene, Dan. "Calvariae Magicae: The Berlin, Philadelphia and Moussaieff Skulls." *Orientalia* 75 (2006): 359–79.

———. *A Corpus of Magic Bowls: Incantation Texts in Jewish Aramaic from Late Antiquity.* New York: Kegan Paul, 2003.

———. *Curse or Blessing: What's in the Magic Bowl?* Southampton: University of Southampton, 2002. Online: www.southampton.ac.uk/vmba/documents/curse_or_blessing.pdf. [Ian Karten Lecture, 2002.]

———. "'If You Appear as a Pig': Another Incantation Bowl (Moussaieff 164)." *Journal of Jewish Studies* 52 (2007): 59–70.

———. *Jewish Aramaic Curse Texts from Late-Antique Mesopotamia: "May These Curses Go Out and Flee."* Boston: Brill, 2013.

———. "'This Is a *Qybl'* for Overturning Sorceries': Form, Formula—Threads in a Web of Transmission." In *Continuity and Innovation in Magical Tradition,* ed. Gideon Bohak, Yuval Harari, and Shaul Shaked, 219–44. Leiden: Brill, 2011.

Levene, Dan, and Siam Bhayro. "'Bring to the Gates . . . upon a Good Smell and upon Good Fragrances': An Aramaic Incantation Bowl for Success in Business." *Archiv für Orientforschung* 51 (2005–6): 242–46.

Levene, Dan, and Gideon Bohak. "A Babylonian Jewish Aramaic Incantation Bowl with a List of Deities and Toponyms." *Jewish Studies Quarterly* 19 (2012): 56–72.

Levinson, Joshua. "Enchanting Rabbis: Contest Narratives between Rabbis and Magicians in Late Antiquity." *Jewish Quarterly Review* 100 (2010): 54–94.

Levy, André, and Alex Weingrod, eds. *Homelands and Diasporas: Holy Lands and Other Places.* Stanford: Stanford University Press, 2005.

Levy, Jacob. *Neuhebräisches und chaldäisches Wörterbuch über die Talmudim und Midraschim.* 4 vols. Leipzig: Brockhaus, 1876–89.

———. *Wörterbuch über die Talmudim und Midraschim.* 4 vols. 2nd ed. Ed. Lazarus Goldschmidt. Berlin: Harz, 1924.

Levy-Rubin, Milka. *Non-Muslims in the Early Islamic Empire: From Surrender to Coexistence.* New York: Cambridge University Press, 2011.

Lieberman, Saul. *Greek in Jewish Palestine.* New York: Jewish Theological Seminary, 1942.

———. *Hellenism in Jewish Palestine.* New York: Jewish Theological Seminary, 1950.

Lincoln, Bruce. *Authority: Construction and Corrosion.* Chicago: University of Chicago Press, 1994.

———. *Myth, Cosmos, and Society: Indo-European Themes of Creation and Destruction.* Cambridge, Mass.: Harvard University Press, 1986.

———. "Theses on Method." *Method and Theory in the Study of Religion* 8 (1996): 225–27.

Löw, Leopold. "Dina de-Malekhuta Dina." *Ben Chananja* 5 (1862): 36–40.

MacKenzie, David Neil. "Bundahišn." *Encyclopaedia Iranica,* online ed., 1989: www.iranicaonline.org/articles/bundahisn-primal-creation.

———. *A Concise Pahlavi Dictionary.* Oxford: Oxford University Press, 1971.

———. "Mani's Šābuhragān, I." *Bulletin of the School of Oriental and African Studies* 42 (1979): 500–534

———. "Mani's Šābuhragān, II." *Bulletin of the School of Oriental and African Studies* 43 (1980): 288–310.

Macuch, Maria. "An Iranian Legal Term in the Babylonian Talmud and in Sasanian Jurisprudence: *dastwar(īh).*" In *Irano-Judaica VI: Studies Relating to Jewish Contacts with

Persian Culture throughout the Ages, ed. Shaul Shaked and Amnon Netzer, 126–38. Jerusalem: Ben-Zvi Institute, 2008.

———. "Iranian Legal Terminology in the Babylonian Talmud in Light of Sasanian Jurisprudence." In *Irano-Judaica IV: Studies Relating to Jewish Contacts with Persian Culture throughout the Ages*, ed. Shaul Shaked and Amnon Netzer, 91–101. Jerusalem: Ben-Zvi Institute, 1999.

———. "Judicial and Legal Systems, iii: Sasanian Legal System." *Encyclopaedia Iranica*, online ed., 2012: www.iranicaonline.org/articles/judicial-and-legal-systems-iii-sasanian-legal-system.

———. "Legal Constructions of Identity in the Sasanian Period." In *Iranian Identity in the Course of History: Proceedings of the Conference Held in Rome, 21–24 September 2005*, ed. Carlo G. Cereti, 193–212. Rome: Istituto Italiano per l'Africa e l'Oriente, 2010.

———. "Pahlavi Literature." In *The Literature of Pre-Islamic Iran*, ed. Ronald E. Emmerick and Maria Macuch, 116–96. New York: I. B. Tauris, 2009.

———. *Das sasanidische Rechtsbuch "Mātakdān ī hazār dātistān."* Part 2. Wiesbaden: Deutsche Morgenländische Gesellschaft, Kommissionsverlag F. Steiner, 1981.

———. "The Use of Seals in Sasanian Jurisprudence." In *Sceaux d'Orient et leur emploi*, ed. Rika Gyselen and Pierre Amiet, 79–87. Leuven: Peeters; 1997.

Madan, Dhanjishah Meherjibhai, ed. *The Complete Text of the Pahlavi Dinkart.* 2 vols. Bombay: Society for the Promotion of Researches into the Zoroastrian Religion, 1911.

Malandra, William W., and Pallan Ichaporia. *The Pahlavi Yasna of the Gāthās and Yasna Haptaŋhāiti.* Wiesbaden: Reichert, 2013.

Martin, Luther H. "Comparison." In *Guide to the Study of Religion*, ed. Willi Braun and Russell T. McCutcheon, 45–56. New York: Cassell, 2000.

McCutcheon, Russell T. "'It's a Lie. There's no Truth in It! It's a Sin!': On the Limits of the Humanistic Study of Religion and the Costs of Saving Others from Themselves." *Journal of the American Academy of Religion* 74 (2006): 720–50.

de Menasce, Jean. *Une apologétique mazdéenne du IXe siècle: Škand-gumānīk vičār, la solution décisive des doutes.* Fribourg: Librairie de l'Université, 1945.

———. *Le troisième livre du Dēnkart, traduit du pehlevi.* Paris: Klincksieck, 1973.

Mendes-Flohr, Paul, and Jehuda Reinharz, eds. *The Jew in the Modern World: A Documentary History.* 3rd ed. New York: Oxford University Press, 2011.

Messina, Giuseppe. *Libro apocalittico persiano Ayātkār i Žāmāspīk: Testo pehlevico, pārsi e pāzend restituito, tradotto e commentato.* Rome: Pontificio Istituto Biblico, 1939.

Milikowsky, Chaim. "The Status Quaestionis of Research in Rabbinic Literature." *Journal of Jewish Studies* 39 (1988): 201–11.

Miller, Stuart. *Sages and Commoners in Late Antique 'Ereẓ Israel: A Philological Inquiry into Local Traditions in Talmud Yerushalmi.* Tübingen: Mohr Siebeck, 2006.

Milner, Vincent L. *Religious Denominations of the World: Comprising a General View of the Origin, History, and Condition of the Various Sects of Christians, the Jews, and Mahometans, as Well as the Pagan Forms of Religion Existing in the Different Countries of the Earth.* Philadelphia: Garretson, 1871.

Miri, Negin. *Sasanian Pārs: Historical Geography and Administrative Organization.* Costa Mesa: Mazda Publishers, 2012.

Moazami, Mahnaz. *Wrestling with the Demons of the Pahlavi Widēwdād: Transcription, Translation, and Commentary.* Leiden: Brill, 2014.
Modi, Jivanji Jamshedji. "An Avesta Amulet for Contracting Friendship." In *Anthropological Papers,* vol. 1, 131–39. Bombay: British India Press, 1911.
———. *The Religious Ceremonies and Customs of the Parsees.* Bombay: J. B. Karani's Sons, 1922.
Mokhtarian, Jason Sion. "The Boundaries of an Infidel in Zoroastrianism: A Middle Persian Term of Otherness for Jews, Christians, and Muslims." *Iranian Studies* 48 (2015): 99–115.
———. "Rabbinic Depictions of the Achaemenid King Cyrus the Great: The *Babylonian Esther Midrash* (bMeg. 10b–17a) in Its Iranian Context." In *The Talmud in Its Iranian Context,* ed. Carol Bakhos and M. Rahim Shayegan, 112–39. Tübingen: Mohr Siebeck, 2010.
Molé, Marijan. *La légende de Zoroastre selon les textes pehlevis.* Paris: Klincksieck, 1967.
———. "Le problème des sectes zoroastriennes dans les livres pehlevis." *Oriens* 13–14 (1960–61): 1–28.
Monchi-Zadeh, Davoud. *Die Geschichte Zarēr's.* Uppsala: Almqvist and Wiksell International, 1981.
———. "Xusrōv i Kavātān ut Rētak: Pahlavi Text, Transcription and Translation." In *Monumentum Georg Morgenstierne,* vol. 2, 47–92. Leiden: Brill, 1982.
Montgomery, James. *Aramaic Incantation Texts from Nippur.* Philadelphia: University Museum, 1913.
Morag, Shelomo, and Yechiel Kara. *Babylonian Aramaic in Yemenite Tradition: The Noun.* Jerusalem: Magnes Press, 2002. [Hebrew.]
Moriggi, Marco. *A Corpus of Syriac Incantation Bowls: Syriac Magical Texts from Late-Antique Mesopotamia.* Boston: Brill, 2014.
Morony, Michael. *Iraq after the Muslim Conquest.* Princeton: Princeton University Press, 1984.
———. "Magic and Society in Late Sasanian Iraq." In *Prayer, Magic, and the Stars in the Ancient and Late Antique World,* ed. Scott Noegel, Joel Walker, and Brannon Wheeler, 83–107. University Park: Pennsylvania State University Press, 2003.
Moscovitz, Leib. *Talmudic Reasoning: From Casuistics to Conceptualization.* Tübingen: Mohr Siebeck, 2002.
Müller-Kessler, Christa. "Puzzling Words and Spellings in Babylonian Aramaic Magic Bowls." *Bulletin of the School of Oriental and African Studies* 62 (1999): 111–14.
Müller-Kessler, Christa, and Theodore Kwasman. "A Unique Talmudic Aramaic Incantation Bowl." *Journal of the American Oriental Society* 120 (2000): 159–65.
Naveh, Joseph, and Shaul Shaked. *Amulets and Magic Bowls: Aramaic Incantations of Late Antiquity.* 3rd ed. Jerusalem: Magnes Press, 1998.
Neale, Harry Stuart. "Sufism Godliness and Popular Islamic Storytelling in Farīd al-Dīn 'Aṭṭār's *Tadkiratu-l-'awliyā'.*" Ph.D. dissertation, University of California, Berkeley, 2007.
Neubauer, Adolphe. *La géographie du Talmud.* Hildesheim: Olms, 1967.
Neusner, Jacob. "Arda and Arta and Pyly Bryš." *Jewish Quarterly Review* 53 (1963): 298–305.
———. *A History of the Jews in Babylonia.* 5 vols. Leiden: Brill, 1965–70.
———. "How Much Iranian in Jewish Babylonia?" *Journal of the American Oriental Society* 95 (1975): 184–90.

———. *Judaism and Zoroastrianism at the Dusk of Late Antiquity: How Two Ancient Faiths Wrote Down Their Great Traditions.* Atlanta: Scholars Press, 1993.

———. *Persia and Rome in Classical Judaism.* Lanham: University Press of America, 2008.

———. "Rabbi and Magus in Third-Century Sasanian Babylonia." *History of Religions* 6 (1966): 169–78.

———. *School, Court, Public Administration: Judaism and Its Institutions in Talmudic Babylonia.* Atlanta: Scholars Press, 1987.

———. "Talmud, Persian Elements in." *Encyclopaedia Iranica,* online ed., 2005: www.iranicaonline.org/articles/talmud-persian-elements-in-2.

———. "A Zoroastrian Critique of Judaism (Škand Gumanik Vičar, Chapters Thirteen and Fourteen: A New Translation and Exposition)." *Journal of the American Oriental Society* 83 (1963): 283–94.

Neusner, Jacob, and Alan J. Avery-Peck, eds. *Judaism in Late Antiquity.* 5 vols. Leiden: Brill, 1995–2001.

Neusner, Jacob, and Jonathan Z. Smith. "Archaeology and Babylonian Jewry." In *Near Eastern Archaeology in the Twentieth Century: Essays in Honor of Nelson Glueck,* ed. James A. Sanders, 331–47. Garden City: Doubleday, 1970.

Newman, Hillel. "Closing the Circle: Yonah Fraenkel, the Talmudic Story, and Rabbinic History." In *How Should Rabbinic Literature Be Read in the Modern World?* ed. Matthew Kraus, 105–13. Piscataway: Gorgias Press, 2006.

Newman, Julius. *The Agricultural Life of the Jews in Babylonia between the years 200 C.E. and 500 C.E.* London: Oxford University Press, 1932.

———. *Semikhah (Ordination): A Study of Its Origin, History, and Function in Rabbinic Literature.* Manchester: University of Manchester Press, 1950.

Nöldeke, Theodor. *Geschichte der Perser und Araber zur Zeit der Sasaniden: Aus der arabischen Chronik des Tabari.* Leiden: Brill, 1879.

Nyberg, Henrik Samuel. *A Manual of Pahlavi.* 2 vols. Wiesbaden: Harrassowitz, 1964–74.

Obermann, Julian. "Two Magic Bowls: New Incantation Texts from Mesopotamia." *The American Journal of Semitic Languages and Literatures* 57 (1940): 1–31.

Olson, Carl. *The Allure of Decadent Thinking: Religious Studies and the Challenge of Postmodernism.* New York: Oxford University Press, 2013.

Oppenheim, David. "Die Namen der persischen und babylonischen Feste im Talmud." *Monatsschrift für Geschichte und Wissenschaft des Judentums* 7 (1854): 347–52.

Oppenheimer, Aharon. "Babylonian Synagogues with Historical Associations." In *Ancient Synagogues: Historical Analysis and Archaeological Discovery,* ed. Dan Urman and Paul V. M. Flesher, 40–48. Leiden: Brill, 1995.

Oppenheimer, Aharon, and Michael Lecker. "The Genealogical Boundaries of Jewish Babylonia." In Aharon Oppenheimer, *Between Rome and Babylon: Studies in Jewish Leadership and Society,* ed. Nili Oppenheimer, 339–55. Tübingen: Mohr Siebeck: 2005.

Oppenheimer, Aharon, with Benjamin Isaac and Michael Lecker. *Babylonia Judaica in the Talmudic Period.* Wiesbaden: Reichert, 1983.

Paden, William E. "Elements of a New Comparativism." In *A Magic Still Dwells: Comparative Religion in the Postmodern Age,* ed. Kimberley C. Patton and Benjamin C. Ray, 182–92. Berkeley and Los Angeles: University of California Press, 2000.

Pakzad, Fazlollah. *Bundahišn—Zoroastriche Kosmogonie und Kosmologie.* Volume 1, *Kritische Edition.* Tehran: Centre for the Great Islamic Encyclopaedia, 2005.

Panaino, Antonio. *The Lists of Names of Ahura Mazdā (Yašt I) and Vayu (Yašt XV).* Rome: Istituto Italiano per l'Africa e l'Oriente, 2002.

Perikhanian, Anahit. *Mādayān ī Hazār Dādestān: The Book of a Thousand Judgements, a Sasanian Law-Book.* Costa Mesa: Mazda Publishers, 1997.

Perles, Joseph. *Etymologische Studien zur Kunde der rabbinischen Sprache und Alterthümer.* Breslau: Schletter, 1871.

Perry, John R. "Lexical Areas and Semantic Fields of Arabic Loanwords in Persian and Beyond." In *Linguistic Convergence and Areal Diffusion: Case Studies from Iranian, Semitic, and Turkic,* ed. Éva Ágnes Csató, Bo Isaksson, and Carina Jahani, 97–110. New York: RoutledgeCurzon, 2005.

Porada, Edith. *Art of Ancient Iran.* New York: Greystone Press, 1965.

Porton, Gary. *Goyim: Gentiles and Israelites in the Mishnah-Tosefta.* Atlanta: Scholars Press, 1988.

Pourshariati, Parvaneh. *Decline and Fall of the Sasanian Empire: The Sasanian-Parthian Confederacy and the Arab Conquest of Iran.* New York: I. B. Tauris, 2008.

Rabbinowicz, R. N. N. *Variae Lectiones in Mischnam et in Talmud Babylonicum.* Volume 13, *Baba Mezia.* Munich: Huber, 1883.

Raffaelli, Enrico G. *The Sīh-rōzag in Zoroastrianism: A Textual and Historico-Religious Analysis.* New York: Routledge, 2014.

Rennie, Bryan S. *Reconstructing Eliade: Making Sense of Religion.* Albany: State University of New York Press, 1996.

Ricks, S. D. "The Magician as Outsider: The Evidence of the Hebrew Bible." In *New Perspectives on Ancient Judaism,* vol. 5, ed. P. Flesher, 125–34. Lanham: University Press of America, 1990.

Rosensweig, Michael. "The Study of the Talmud in Contemporary Yeshivot." In *Printing the Talmud: From Bomberg to Schottenstein,* ed. Sharon Liberman Mintz and Gabriel M. Goldstein, 111–20. New York: Yeshiva University Museum, 2005.

Rosenthal, E. S. "For the Talmudic Dictionary—Talmudica Iranica." In *Irano-Judaica: Studies Relating to Jewish Contacts with Persian Culture throughout the Ages,* ed. Shaul Shaked, 38–134. Jerusalem: Ben-Zvi Institute, 1982. [Hebrew.]

Rosenthal, Franz. *A History of Muslim Historiography.* Leiden: Brill, 1952.

Rubenstein, Jeffrey L. "Astrology and the Head of the Academy." In *Shoshannat Yaakov: Jewish and Iranian Studies in Honor of Yaakov Elman,* ed. Shai Secunda and Steven Fine, 301–21. Boston: Brill, 2012.

———. "Criteria of Stammaitic Intervention in Aggada." In *Creation and Composition: The Contribution of the Bavli Redactors (Stammaim) to the Aggada,* ed. Jeffrey L. Rubenstein, 417–40. Tübingen: Mohr Siebeck, 2005.

———. *The Culture of the Babylonian Talmud.* Baltimore: The Johns Hopkins University Press, 2003.

———. *Talmudic Stories: Narrative Art, Composition, and Culture.* Baltimore: The Johns Hopkins University Press, 1999.

———. "Translator's Introduction." In David Weiss Halivni, *The Formation of the Babylonian Talmud,* xvii–xxx. New York: Oxford University Press, 2013.

Russell, James R. "A Note on Armenian hrmštk-el." In *Festschrift Garnik Asatryan*, ed. Uwe Bläsing, 1–7. Leiden: Brill, forthcoming.

———. "The Sage in Ancient Iranian Literature." In *Armenian and Iranian Studies*, 389–400. Cambridge, Mass.: Harvard University Press, 2004.

———. *Zoroastrianism in Armenia*. Cambridge, Mass.: Harvard University Press, 1987.

Sabato, Mordechai. *A Yemenite Manuscript of Tractate Sanhedrin and Its Place in the Text Tradition*. Jerusalem: Ben-Zvi Institute, 1998. [Hebrew.]

Safa-Isfehani, Nezhat. *Rivāyat-i Hēmīt-i Ašawahištān: Edition, Transcription and Translation—A Study in Zoroastrian Law*. Cambridge, Mass.: Harvard University Press, 1980.

Sandmel, Samuel. "Parallelomania." *Journal of Biblical Literature* 81 (1962): 1–13.

Satlow, Michael L. "Beyond Influence: Toward a New Historiographic Paradigm." In *Jewish Literatures and Cultures: Context and Intertext*, ed. Yaron Eliav and Anita Norich, 37–53. Providence: Brown University Press, 2008.

———. "Defining Judaism: Accounting for 'Religions' in the Study of Religion." *Journal of the American Academy of Religion* 74 (2006): 837–60.

Schäfer, Peter. *Jesus in the Talmud*. Princeton: Princeton University Press, 2007.

———. "Research into Rabbinic Literature: An Attempt to Define the Status Quaestionis." *Journal of Jewish Studies* 37 (1986): 139–52.

———, ed. *The Yerushalmi Talmud and Graeco-Roman Culture*. Volumes 1 and 3. Tübingen: Mohr Siebeck, 1998 and 2002.

Schäfer, Peter, and Catherine Hezser, eds. *The Yerushalmi Talmud and Graeco-Roman Culture*. Volume 2. Tübingen: Mohr Siebeck, 1999.

Scheftelowitz, Isidor. *Die altpersische Religion und das Judentum: Unterschiede, Übereinstimmungen und gegenseitige Beeinflussungen*. Giessen: Verlag von Alfred Töpelmann, 1920.

Schiffman, Lawrence H. "Medium and Message: The Talmud as a Transmitter of Jewish Culture." In *Printing the Talmud: From Bomberg to Schottenstein*, ed. Sharon Liberman Mintz and Gabriel M. Goldstein, 163–67. New York: Yeshiva University Museum, 2005.

Schippmann, Klaus. *Grundzüge der Geschichte des sasanidischen Reiches*. Darmstadt: Wissenschaftliche Buchgesellscahft, 1990.

———. *Die iranischen Feuerheiligtümer*. New York: De Gruyter, 1971.

Schmidt, Brian. "Canaanite Magic vs. Israelite Religion: Deuteronomy 18 and the Taxonomy of Taboo." In *Magic and Ritual in the Ancient World*, part 4, ed. Paul Allan Mirecki and Marvin W. Meyer, 243–62. Leiden: Brill, 2002.

Schmidt, Hanns-Peter. "Gathic *maga* and Vedic *maghá*." In *K. R. Cama Oriental Institute, International Congress Proceedings*, 220–39. Bombay: H. J. M. Desai and H. N. Modi, 1991.

Schremer, Adiel. "Stammaitic Historiography." In *Creation and Composition: The Contribution of the Bavli Redactors (Stammaim) to the Aggada*, ed. Jeffrey L. Rubenstein, 219–36. Tübingen: Mohr Siebeck, 2005.

Schwartz, Seth. "Historiography on the Jews in the Talmudic Period." In *The Oxford Handbook for Jewish Studies*, ed. Martin Goodman, Jeremy Cohen, and David Sorkin, 79–114. Oxford: Oxford University Press, 2002.

———. *Imperialism and Jewish Society, 200 B.C.E. to 640 C.E.* Princeton: Princeton University Press, 2001.

———. "The Political Geography of Rabbinic Texts." In *The Cambridge Companion to the Talmud and Rabbinic Literature,* ed. Charlotte Elisheva Fonrobert and Martin S. Jaffee, 75–96. Cambridge: Cambridge University Press, 2007.

Scott, James M. *Paul and the Nations: The Old Testament and Jewish Background of Paul's Mission to the Nations, with Special Reference to the Destination of Galatians.* Tübingen: Mohr Siebeck, 1995.

Secunda, Shai. "*Dashtana—'Ki Derekh Nashim Li'*: A Study of the Babylonian Rabbinic Laws of Menstruation in Relation to Corresponding Zoroastrian Texts." Ph.D. dissertation, Yeshiva University, 2007.

———. *The Iranian Talmud: Reading the Bavli in Its Sasanian Context.* Philadelphia: University of Pennsylvania Press, 2013.

———. "On the Age of the Zoroastrian Sages of the Zand." *Iranica Antiqua* 47 (2012): 317–49.

———. "Parva—A Magus." In *Shoshannat Yaakov: Jewish and Iranian Studies in Honor of Yaakov Elman,* ed. Shai Secunda and Steven Fine, 391–402. Leiden: Brill, 2012.

———. "Reading the Bavli in Iran." *Jewish Quarterly Review* 100 (2010): 310–42.

———. "The Sasanian '*Stam*': Orality and the Composition of Babylonian Rabbinic and Zoroastrian Legal Literature." In *The Talmud in Its Iranian Context,* ed. Carol Bakhos and M. Rahim Shayegan, 140–60. Tübingen: Mohr Siebeck, 2010.

———. "Studying with a Magus/Like Giving a Tongue to a Wolf." In *Iranian and Zoroastrian Studies in Honor of Prods Oktor Skjærvø,* ed. Carol Altman Bromberg, Nicholas Sims-Williams, and Ursula Sims-Williams, *Bulletin of the Asia Institute* 19 (2009): 151–57.

———. "Talmudic Text and Iranian Context: On the Development of Two Talmudic Narratives." *Association for Jewish Studies Review* 33 (2009): 45–69.

Segal, Eliezer. "Anthological Dimensions of the Babylonian Talmud." In *The Anthology in Jewish Literature,* ed. David Stern, 81–107. New York: Oxford University Press, 2004.

Segal, Robert. "All Generalizations Are Bad: Postmodernism on Theories." *Journal of the American Academy of Religion* 74 (2006): 157–71.

———. "How Historical Is the History of Religions?" *Method and Theory in the Study of Religion* 1 (1989): 2–17.

Seidel, Jonathan. "Charming Criminals: Classification of Magic in the Babylonian Talmud." In *Ancient Magic and Ritual Power,* ed. Marvin W. Meyer and Paul Mirecki, 145–66. Leiden: Brill, 1995.

Shahbazi, Shapur. "On the *Xwadāy-Nāmag*." In *Papers in Honor of Professor Ehsan Yarshater,* 208–29. Leiden: Brill, 1990.

———. "Shapur I." *Encyclopaedia Iranica,* online ed., 2002: www.iranica.com/articles/shapur-i.

Shaked, Shaul. "Administrative Functions of Priests." In *Proceedings of the First European Conference of Iranian Studies,* part 1, ed. Gherardo Gnoli and Antonio Panaino, 261–73. Rome: Istituto Italiano per il Medio ed Estremo Oriente, 1990.

———. "Aramaic, iii: Iranian Loanwords in Middle Aramaic." *Encyclopaedia Iranica,* online ed., 1986: www.iranicaonline.org/articles/aramaic-#pt3.

———. "Bagdāna, King of the Demons, and Other Iranian Terms in Babylonian Aramaic Magic." In *Papers in Honour of Professor Mary Boyce,* vol. 1, 511–25. Leiden: Brill, 1985.

———. "Between Iranian and Aramaic: Iranian Words Concerning Food in Jewish Babylonian Aramaic, with Some Notes on the Aramaic Heterograms in Iranian." In *Irano-Judaica V: Studies Relating to Jewish Contacts with Persian Culture throughout the Ages,* ed. Shaul Shaked and Amnon Netzer, 120–37. Jerusalem: Ben-Zvi Institute, 2003.

———. "*Dramatis Personae* in the Jewish Magic Texts: Some Differences between Incantation Bowls and Geniza Magic." *Jewish Studies Quarterly* 13 (2006): 363–87.

———. *Dualism in Transformation: Varieties of Religion in Sasanian Iran.* London: School of Oriental and African Studies, 1994.

———. "Epigraphica Judaeo-Iranica." In *Studies in Judaism and Islam Presented to S. D. Goitein,* ed. Shelomo Morag, Issachar Ben-Ami, and Norman A. Stillman, 65–82. Jerusalem: Magnes Press, 1981.

———. "Form and Purpose in Aramaic Spells: Some Jewish Themes (The Poetics of Magic Texts)." In *Officina Magica: Essays on the Practice of Magic in Antiquity,* ed. Shaul Shaked, 1–30. Boston: Brill, 2005.

———. "Iranian Elements in Middle Aramaic: Some Particles and Verbs." In *Medioiranica: Proceedings of the International Colloquium Organized by the Katholieke Universiteit Leuven from the 21st to the 23rd of May 1990,* ed. Wojciech Skalmowski and Alois Van Tongerloo, 147–56. Leuven: Uitgeverij Peeters and Departement Orientalistiek, 1993.

———. "Iranian Influence on Judaism: First Century B.C.E. to Second Century C.E." In *The Cambridge History of Judaism,* vol. 1, *Introduction; The Persian Period,* ed. W. D. Davies and Louis Finkelstein, 308–25. New York: Cambridge University Press, 1984.

———. "Items of Dress and Other Objects in Common Use: Iranian Loanwords in Jewish Babylonian Aramaic." In *Irano-Judaica III: Studies Relating to Jewish Contacts with Persian Culture throughout the Ages,* ed. Shaul Shaked and Amnon Netzer, 106–17. Jerusalem: Ben-Zvi Institute, 1994.

———. "Jesus in the Magic Bowls: Apropos Dan Levene's '. . . and by the name of Jesus. . .'" *Jewish Studies Quarterly* 6 (1999): 309–19.

———. "Jewish and Christian Seals of the Sasanian Period." In *Studies in Memory of Gaston Wiet,* ed. M. Rosen-Ayalon, 17–31. Jerusalem: Institute of Asian and African Studies, Hebrew University of Jerusalem, 1977.

———. "Jewish Sasanian Sigillography." In *Au carrefour des religions: Mélanges offerts à Philippe Gignoux,* ed. Rika Gyselen, 239–56. Bures-sur-Yvette: Groupe pour l'Étude de la Civilisation du Moyen-Orient, 1995.

———. "Manichaean Incantation Bowls in Syriac." *Jerusalem Studies in Arabic and Islam* 24 (2000): 58–92.

———. "The Myth of Zurvan: Cosmogony and Eschatology." In *Messiah and Christos: Studies in the Jewish Origins of Christianity, Presented to David Flusser on the Occasion of His Seventy-Fifth Birthday,* ed. I. Gruenwald, S. Shaked, and G. G. Stroumsa, 219–40. Tübingen: Mohr Siebeck, 1992.

———. "'No Talking During a Meal': Zoroastrian Themes in the Babylonian Talmud." In *The Talmud in Its Iranian Context,* ed. Carol Bakhos and M. Rahim Shayegan, 161–77. Tübingen: Mohr Siebeck, 2010.

———. "Notes on the Pahlavi Amulet and Sasanian Courts of Law." *Bulletin of the Asia Institute* 7 (1993): 165–72.

———. "Parole des anges, parole des démons: À propos des coupes magiques de la Babylonie sassanide." In *Union Académique Internationale: Soixante-treizième session annuelle du Comité, Cracovie, du 20 au 26 juin 1999*, 17–33. Brussels: Secrétariat Administratif de l'UAI, 1999.

———. "The Poetics of Spells: Language and Structure in Aramaic Incantations of Late Antiquity, 1—The Divorce Formula and Its Ramifications." In *Mesopotamian Magic: Textual, Historical, and Interpretative Perspectives*, ed. Tzvi Abusch and Karel van der Toorn, 173–95. Groningen: Styx Publications, 1999.

———. "Popular Religion in Sasanian Babylonia." *Jerusalem Studies in Arabic and Islam* 21 (1997): 103–17.

———. "Religion in the Late Sasanian Period: Eran, Aneran, and Other Religious Designations." In *The Sasanian Era*, vol. 3 of *The Idea of Iran*, ed. Vesta Sarkhosh Curtis and Sarah Stewart, 103–17. New York: I. B. Tauris, 2008.

———. "Towards a Middle Persian Dictionary." In *Iran: Questions et connaissances—Actes du IVe Congrès européen des études iraniennes, organisé par la Societas Iranologica Europaea, Paris, 6–10 septembre 1999*, vol. 1, *La période ancienne*, ed. Philip Huyse, 121–34. Paris: Association pour l'Avancement des Études Iraniennes, 2002.

———. "Transmission and Transformation of Spells: The Case of the Jewish Babylonian Aramaic Bowls." In *Continuity and Innovation in the Magical Tradition*, ed. Gideon Bohak, Yuval Harari, and Shaul Shaked, 187–218. Leiden, Brill, 2011.

———. *The Wisdom of the Sasanian Sages: Dēnkard VI*. Boulder: Westview Press, 1979.

———. "Zoroastrian Polemics against Jews in the Sasanian and Early Islamic Period." In *Irano-Judaica II: Studies Relating to Jewish Contacts with Persian Culture throughout the Ages*, ed. Shaul Shaked and Amnon Netzer, 85–104. Jerusalem: Ben-Zvi Institute, 1990.

Shaked, Shaul, James Nathan Ford, and Siam Bhayro, eds., with Matthew Morgenstern and Naama Vilozny. *Aramaic Bowl Spells: Jewish Babylonian Aramaic Bowls*. Boston: Brill, 2013.

Shaki, Mansour. "Class System, iii: In the Parthian and Sasanian Periods." *Encyclopaedia Iranica*, online ed., 1992: www.iranicaonline.org/articles/class-system-iii.

———. "The Dēnkard Account of the History of the Zoroastrian Scriptures." *Archiv Orientální* 49 (1981): 114–25.

———. "A Few Unrecognized Middle Persian Terms and Phrases." In *Middle Iranian Studies: Proceedings of the International Symposium Organized by the Katholieke Universiteit Leuven from the 17th to the 20th of May 1982*, ed. Wojciech Skalmowski and Alois Van Tongerloo, 95–102. Leuven: Peeters, 1984.

———. "Gabr." *Encyclopaedia Iranica*, online ed., 2000: www.iranicaonline.org/articles/gabr-.

Shapira, Dan D. Y. "Manichaeans (*Marmanaiia*), Zoroastrians (*Iazuqaiia*), Jews, Christians and Other Heretics: A Study in the Redaction of Mandaic Texts." *Le Muséon* 117 (2004): 243–80.

———. "Studies in Zoroastrian Exegesis: *Zand*." Ph.D. dissertation, Hebrew University of Jerusalem, 1998.

Shapiro, Marc B. "Talmud Study in the Modern Era: From *Wissenschaft* and Brisk to *Daf Yomi*." In *Printing the Talmud: From Bomberg to Schottenstein*, ed. Sharon Liberman Mintz and Gabriel M. Goldstein, 103–10. New York: Yeshiva University Museum, 2005.

———. "The Brisker Method Reconsidered: Review Essay." *Tradition* 31 (1997): 78-102.

Sharpe, Eric J. *Comparative Religion: A History.* 2nd ed. La Salle: Open Court Publishing, 1986.

Shaw, Rosalind, and Charles Stewart. "Introduction: Problematizing Syncretism." In *Syncretism/Anti-Syncretism: The Politics of Religious Synthesis,* ed. Rosalind Shaw and Charles Stewart, 1–24. New York: Routledge, 1994.

Shilo, Shmuel. *Dina De-Malkhuta Dina.* Jerusalem: Jerusalem Academic Press, 1974. [Hebrew.]

Siegal, Michal Bar-Asher. *Early Christian Monastic Literature and the Babylonian Talmud.* New York: Cambridge University Press, 2013.

Silverstein, Adam. "The Qur'ānic Pharaoh." In *New Perspectives on the Qur'ān: The Qur'ān in Its Historical Context,* vol. 2, ed. Gabriel Said Reynolds, 467–77. New York: Routledge, 2011.

Simpson, St John. "Mesopotamia in the Sasanian Period: Settlement Patterns, Arts and Crafts." In *Mesopotamia and Iran in the Parthian and Sasanian Periods: Rejection and Revival c. 238 BC–AD 642—Proceedings of a Seminar in Memory of Vladimir G. Lukonin,* ed. John Curtis, 57–66. London: British Museum Press, 2000.

Skjærvø, Prods Oktor. "Aramaic in Iran." *Aram* 7 (1995 [1998]): 283–318.

———."Review: Cantera, *Pahlavi-Übersetzung des Avesta.*" *Kratylos* 53 (2008): 1–20.

———. "Class System, i: In the Avesta." *Encyclopaedia Iranica,* online ed., 1991: www.iranica.com/articles/class-system-i.

———. "The Importance of Orality for the Study of Old Iranian Literature and Myth." *Nāme-ye Irān-e Bāstān: The International Journal of Ancient Iranian Studies* 5 (2005–6): 1–23.

———. "'Kirdir's Vision': Translation and Analysis." *Archäologische Mitteilungen aus Iran* 16 (1983): 269–306.

———. "On the Terminology and Style of the Pahlavi Scholastic Literature." In *The Talmud in Its Iranian Context,* ed. Carol Bakhos and M. Rahim Shayegan, 178–205. Tübingen: Mohr Siebeck, 2010.

Smith, Jonathan Z. *Drudgery Divine: On the Comparison of Early Christianities and the Religions of Late Antiquity.* Chicago: University of Chicago Press, 1990.

———. "The 'End' of Comparison: Redescription and Rectification." In *A Magic Still Dwells: Comparative Religion in the Postmodern Age,* ed. Kimberley C. Patton and Benjamin C. Ray, 237–41. Berkeley and Los Angeles: University of California Press, 2000.

———. "The Eternal Deferral." In *Hermeneutics, Politics, and the History of Religions: The Contested Legacies of Joachim Wach and Mircea Eliade,* ed. Christian K. Wedemeyer and Wendy Doniger, 215–37. New York: Oxford University Press, 2010.

———. *Imagining Religion: From Babylon to Jonestown.* Chicago: University of Chicago Press, 1982.

———. *Relating Religion: Essays in the Study of Religion.* Chicago: University of Chicago Press, 2004.

Sokoloff, Michael. *A Dictionary of Jewish Babylonian Aramaic.* Ramat Gan: Bar-Ilan University Press, 2002.

———. *A Dictionary of Jewish Palestinian Aramaic of the Byzantine Period.* Ramat Gan: Bar-Ilan University Press, 1990.

Sperber, Daniel. "Bab Nahara." *Iranica Antiqua* 8 (1968): 70–73.

———. “On the Unfortunate Adventures of Rav Kahana: A Passage of Saboraic Polemic from Sasanian Persia.” In *Irano-Judaica: Studies Relating to Jewish Contacts with Persian Culture throughout the Ages*, ed. Shaul Shaked, 83–100. Jerusalem: Ben-Zvi Institute, 1982.

Spicehandler, Ezra. “Dina de Magista and Bei Dawar: Notes on Gentile Courts in Talmudic Babylonia.” *Hebrew Union College Annual* 26 (1955): 333–54.

———. “Joshua Heschel Schorr—The Mature Years.” *Hebrew Union College Annual* 40–41 (1969–70): 503–28.

Stausberg, Michael. “The Invention of a Canon: The Case of Zoroastrianism.” In *Canonization and Decanonization: Papers Presented to the International Conference of the Leiden Institute for the Study of Religions (LISOR), Held at Leiden 9–10 January 1997*, ed. A. van der Kooij and K. van der Toorn, 257–78. Leiden: Brill, 1998.

———. “The Significance of the *kusti:* A History of Its Zoroastrian Interpretations.” *East and West* 54 (2004): 9–29.

Stein, Dina. “Let the ‘People’ Go? The ‘Folk’ and Their ‘Lore’ as Tropes in the Reconstruction of Rabbinic Culture.” *Prooftexts: A Journal of Jewish Literary History* 29 (2009): 206–41.

Steingass, Francis Joseph. *A Comprehensive Persian-English Dictionary.* London: Routledge, 1892.

Stern, Sacha. *Jewish Identity in Early Rabbinic Writings.* New York: Brill, 1994.

Stewart, Charles, and Rosalind Shaw, eds. *Syncretism/Anti-Syncretism: The Politics of Religious Synthesis.* New York: Routledge, 1994.

Strack, H. L., and Günter Stemberger. *Introduction to the Talmud and Midrash.* 2nd ed. Minneapolis: Fortress Press, 1996.

Stratton, Kimberly B. “Imagining Power: Magic, Miracle, and the Social Context of Rabbinic Self-Representation.” *Journal of the American Academy of Religion* 73 (2005): 361–93.

———. *Naming the Witch: Magic, Ideology, and Stereotype in the Ancient World.* New York: Columbia University Press, 2007.

Strenski, Ivan. *Thinking about Religion: An Historical Introduction to Theories of Religion.* Malden: Blackwell Publishing, 2006.

Stroumsa, Guy G. *A New Science: The Discovery of Religion in the Age of Reason.* Cambridge, Mass.: Harvard University Press, 2010.

Sussmann, Yaacov. “Returning to Yerushalmi Nezikin.” *Talmudic Studies* 1 (1990): 55–134. [Hebrew.]

———, ed. *Talmud Yerushalmi: According to Ms. Or. 4720 (Scal. 3) of the Leiden University Library, with Restorations and Corrections.* Jerusalem: The Academy of the Hebrew Language, 2001.

Swartz, Michael D. “Jewish Magic in Late Antiquity.” In *The Cambridge History of Judaism*, vol. 4, *The Late Roman–Rabbinic Period*, ed. Steven T. Katz, 699–720. New York: Cambridge University Press, 2006.

Székely, Edmond Bordeaux. *The Essene Teachings of Zarathustra.* Cartago: International Biogenic Society, 1973.

Tafazzoli, Ahmad. *Sasanian Society.* New York: Bibliotheca Persica Press, 2000.

———. *Vāža-nāma-ye mīnū-ye ḵarad.* Tehran: Iranian Culture Foundation, 1969.

Taqizadeh, S. H. “The Iranian Festivals Adopted by the Christians and Condemned by the Jews.” *Bulletin of the School of Oriental Studies* 10 (1940–42): 632–53.

———. "The Old Iranian Calendars Again." *Bulletin of the School of Oriental and African Studies* 14 (1952): 603–11.

Tarapore, J.C. *Pahlavi Andarz-Nāmak, Containing Chītak Andarz ī Pōryōtkaêshān; or, The Selected Admonitions of the Pōryōtkaêshān and Five Other Andarz Texts.* Bombay: The Trustees of the Parsee Punchayet Funds and Properties, 1933.

Tavadia, Jehangir C. *Šāyast-nē-šāyast: A Pahlavi Text on Religious Customs.* Hamburg: De Gruyter, 1930.

Taylor, Mark C. "Introduction." In *Critical Terms for Religious Studies,* ed. Mark C. Taylor, 1–19. Chicago: University of Chicago Press, 1988.

Telegdi, Zsigmond. "Essai sur la phonétique des emprunts iraniens en araméen talmudique." *Journal Asiatique* 226 (1935): 177–256.

Tracy, David. "Western Hermeneutics and Interreligious Dialogue." In *Interreligious Hermeneutics,* ed. Catherine Cornille and Christopher Conway, 1–43. Eugene: Cascade Books, 2010.

Tropper, Amram D. "Roman Contexts in Jewish Texts: On Diatagma and Prostagma in Rabbinic Literature." *Jewish Quarterly Review* 95 (2005): 207–27.

Urbach, Ephraim E. "Redemption and Repentance in Talmudic Judaism." In *Types of Redemption,* ed. R.J. Zwi Werblowsky and C. Jouco Bleeker, 190–206. Leiden: Brill, 1970.

Utas, Bo, ed. *Frahang ī Pahlavīk: Edited, with Transliteration, Transcription, and Commentary from the Posthumous Papers of Henrik Samuel Nyberg.* Wiesbaden: Harrassowitz, 1988.

———. "The Pahlavi Treatise *Avdēh u Sahīkēh ī Sakistān;* or, 'Wonders and Magnificence of Sistan.'" In *From Hecataeus to Al-Huwarizmi: Bactrian, Pahlavi, Sogdian, Persian, Sanskrit, Syriac, Arabic, Chinese, Greek and Latin Sources for the History of Pre-Islamic Central Asia,* ed. J. Harmatta, 259–67. Budapest: Akadémiai Kiadó, 1984.

———. "Verbal Ideograms in the *Frahang ī Pahlavik.*" In *Middle Iranian Studies: Proceedings of the International Symposium Organized by the Katholieke Universiteit Leuven from the 17th to the 20th of May 1982,* ed. Wojciech Skalmowski and Alois Van Tongerloo, 57–67. Leuven: Peeters, 1984.

Vahman, Fereydun. *Ardā Wirāz Nāmag: The Iranian "Divina Commedia."* London: Curzon Press, 1986.

Vermes, Geza. *The Nativity: History and Legend.* New York: Doubleday, 2006.

Vevaina, Yuhan Sohrab-Dinshaw. "Miscegenation, 'Mixture,' and 'Mixed Iron': The Hermeneutics, Historiography, and Cultural Poesis of the 'Four Ages' in Zoroastrianism." In *Revelation, Literature, and Community in Late Antiquity,* ed. Philippa Townsend and Moulie Vidas, 237–69. Tübingen: Mohr Siebeck, 2011.

———. "Relentless Allusion: Intertextuality and the Reading of Zoroastrian Interpretive Literature." In *The Talmud in Its Iranian Context,* ed. Carol Bakhos and M. Rahim Shayegan, 206–32. Tübingen: Mohr Siebeck, 2010.

———. "Studies in Zoroastrian Exegesis and Hermeneutics, with a Critical Edition of the *Sūdgar Nask* of *Dēnkard* Book 9." Ph.D. dissertation, Harvard University, 2007.

Vidas, Moulie. *Tradition and the Formation of the Talmud.* Princeton: Princeton University Press, 2014.

Visotzky, Burton L. *Golden Bells and Pomegranates: Studies in Midrash Leviticus Rabbah.* Tübingen: Mohr Siebeck, 2003.

———. "Review Article: Leaning Literary, Reading Rabbinics." *Prooftexts: A Journal of Jewish Literary History* 28 (2008): 85–99.

Weinreich, M. "Die Geschichte von Jōišt ī Frīyan." *Altorientalische Forschungen* 19 (1992): 44–101.

Weitzman, Steven. *Surviving Sacrilege: Cultural Persistence in Jewish Antiquity.* Cambridge, Mass.: Harvard University Press, 2005.

West, E. W. *The Book of the Mainyo-i-Khard: The Pazand and Sanskrit Texts (in Roman Characters) as Arranged by Neriosengh Dhaval in the Fifteenth Century, with an English Translation, a Glossary of the Pazand Text, Containing the Sanskrit, Persian and Pahlavi Equivalents, a Sketch of Pazand Grammar, and an Introduction.* Stuttgart: Grüninger, 1871.

Wewers, Gerd A. "Israel zwischen den Mächten: Die rabbinischen Traditionen über König Schabhor." *Kairos* 22 (1980): 77–100.

Weryho, J. W. "Syriac Influence on Islamic Iran." *Folia Orientalia* 13 (1971): 299–321.

White, David Gordon. "The Scholar as Mythographer: Comparative Indo-European Myth and Postmodern Concerns." In *A Magic Still Dwells: Comparative Religion in the Postmodern Age,* ed. Kimberley C. Patton and Benjamin C. Ray, 47–54. Berkeley and Los Angeles: University of California Press, 2000.

Widengren, Geo. "Iran and Israel in Parthian Times with Special Regard to the Ethiopic *Book of Enoch.*" In *Religious Syncretism in Antiquity: Essays in Conversation with Geo Widengren,* ed. Birger A. Pearson, 85–129. Missoula: Scholars Press, 1975.

———. "Some Remarks on Riding Costume and Articles of Dress among Iranian Peoples in Antiquity." *Studia Ethnographica Upsaliensia* 11 (1956): 228–76.

———. "The Status of the Jews in the Sassanian Empire." *Iranica Antiqua* 1 (1961): 117–62.

Wiesehöfer, Josef. *Ancient Persia from 550 B.C. to 650 A.D.* Trans. Azizeh Azodi. New York: I. B. Tauris, 1996.

Wikander, Stig. *Feuerpriester in Kleinasien und Iran.* Lund: Gleerup, 1946.

Williams, A. V. *The Pahlavi Rivāyat Accompanying the Dādestān ī Dēnīg.* Part 1, *Transliteration, Transcription and Glossary.* Copenhagen: Munksgaard, 1990.

———. *The Pahlavi Rivāyat Accompanying the Dādestān ī Dēnīg.* Part 2, *Translation, Commentary and Pahlavi Text.* Copenhagen: Munksgaard, 1990.

Williams-Jackson, A. V. "The Religion of the Achaemenids." In *Indo-Iranian Studies: Being Commemorative Papers Contributed by European, American and Indian Scholars in Honour of Shams-Ul-Ullema Dastur Darab Peshotan Sanjana,* trans. D. Mackichan, 31–60. New York: Routledge Library Editions, 1925. [Reprint, London: Routledge, 2011.]

Winston, David. "The Iranian Component in the Bible, Apocrypha, and Qumran: A Review of the Evidence." *History of Religions* 5 (1966): 183–216.

Wood, Philip. The *Chronicle of Seert: Christian Historical Imagination in Late Antique Iraq.* Oxford: Oxford University Press, 2013.

Wright, Rick. *Linguistic Evidence for the Pre-Exilic Date of the Yahwistic Source.* New York: T. and T. Clark International, 2005.

Yamauchi, Edwin M. *Mandaic Incantation Texts.* New Haven: American Oriental Society, 1967.

Yarshater, Ehsan. "Iranian National History." In *The Cambridge History of Iran,* vol. 3.1, *The Seleucid, Parthian, and Sasanian Periods,* ed. Ehsan Yarshater, 359–480. Cambridge: Cambridge University Press, 1983.

Yassif, Eli. *The Hebrew Folktale: History, Genre, Meaning.* Trans. Jacqueline S. Teitelbaum. Bloomington: Indiana University Press, 2009.

Zaehner, Robert C. *At Sundry Times: An Essay in the Comparison of Religions.* London: Faber and Faber, 1958.

———. *Zurvan: A Zoroastrian Dilemma.* Oxford: Clarendon Press, 1955.

Zevin, Shlomo Josef. *Encyclopedia Talmudica: A Digest of Halachic Literature and Jewish Law from the Tannaitic Period to the Present Time, Alphabetically Arranged.* Volume 6. Jerusalem: Yad Harav Herzog Press, 1992.

SOURCE INDEX

HEBREW BIBLE

Genesis
- 9:27–10:12 68–69
- 11:4–9 71
- 31:4 51
- 31:35 63
- 49:10 113

Exodus
- 7:15 125
- 12:9 44
- 15:3 72
- 21:10 51
- 23:13 71
- 32:18 223n38

Leviticus
- 6:6 182n36

Numbers
- 30:2 111

Deuteronomy
- 4:44 72
- 18:9–12 126, 128, 142
- 21:23 79–80
- 32:21 122
- 33:1 193n149

Judges
- 1:11 63

1 Samuel
- 12:15 122

1 Kings
- 5:9 51

Isaiah
- 1:25–27 117–19
- 13:3 51–52, 73, 184n58
- 14:5 119–20
- 59:3 119–20

Jeremiah
- 39:13 205n13
- 48:11 59
- 49:20 195n167
- 2:1–3 139

Ezekiel
- 21:21–23 139
- 23:20 116

Zephaniah
- 3:11–15 52, 117–19, 184n58

Zechariah
9:9 77

Malachi
11:9 118

Psalms
137 67

Proverbs
3:15 81
6:22 81

Lamentations
1:13 183n40

Ecclesiastes
7:8 53, 184n58

Esther
1:20 58

Daniel
2:29–30 88
3:23–38 133
7:5 71–73, 190n125
7:13 77
11:45 191n125

1 Chronicles
29:11 115

TARGUM

Pseudo-Jonathan
Exodus 7:1 125

Onqelos
Deuteronomy 18:10–11 142

MISHNAH

Šabbat
2:1 59
7:2 126
10:5 52
2:1 59

'Erubin
3:1 43

Giṭṭin
8:5 69

Baba Meṣi'a
10:6 83

Sanhedrin
7:11 127–28
10:3 70

'Abodah Zarah
5:12 91

Šebu'ot
4:13 139

JERUSALEM TALMUD

Berakot
7:2 (11b) 182n40
6:2 (10b) 54

Pe'ah
1:1 (15d) 80

Šabbat
16:8 (15d) 54
6:1 (7d) 186n90

'Erubin
6:3 (23c) 185n73

Yoma
3:8 (40d) 220n7

Megillah
1:8 (71b) 194n159

Nedarim
3:2 (37d) 196n1

Nazir
5:5 (54b) 182n40

'Abodah Zarah
1:3 (39c) 66

Šebu'ot
3:8 (34d) 196n1

MIDRASH

Genesis Rabbah
36.8 69
37 194n159
74.2 51
91.3 182n40

Ecclesiastes Rabbah
3.2.3 220n7
7.8.1 53–55
7.23.1 51

Leviticus Rabbah
13:5 195n179

Deuteronomy Rabbah
11:4 193n149

Song of Songs Rabbah
4.8.1 186n90
8.9.3 183n40

Lamentations Rabbah
1.13.41 183n40
3.3 217n138
6.24 217n138

BABYLONIAN TALMUD

Berakot
8b 51–52
40a 59
46b 182n38
55b–56a 87–89
56a 191n125, 196n1
58a 114–16

Šabbat
10a 185n82, 214n101
11a 204n7, 205n16, 205n18, 193n158
20b 59
31a 53, 55
36a 70
45a 204n7
59b 56
62b 221n17
66b 188n112
74b–75a 125–28, 142, 204n7, 221n19
94a 52, 62, 184n58, 190n125
110a 191n134
110b 182n39
113b 79, 196n1
115a 191n128
122b 55
139a 204n7, 118–20

'Erubin
28a 179n9
29b 43–44
59a 188n109, 217n140
62a 111

Pesaḥim
41a 44
54a 78, 196n1
110a 141
113b 204n7, 207n35

Yoma
9b–10a 51–52, 68–69, 183n44, 195n167
35a 203n6, 204n7
44a 225n50
77a 190n125, 195n179

Sukkah
18a 45
34a 70
53a 77, 196n1

Beṣah
6a 204n7

Roš Haššanah
13b 204n7
25b 111–12

Ta'anit
20b–24a 61
20a 118
24a 55
24b 196n1, 217n137

Megillah
6b 188n109
10b–17a 51
11a 195n179
12b 59, 216n125
16a 188n109
18a 191n128
26a 193n158
29a 67–68

Mo'ed Qaṭan
4b 225n49
7b 201n41
18a 125, 204n7, 220n8
26a 196n1

Ḥagigah
5b 182n38, 196n1
14a 216n125
25a 204n7

Yebamot
25b 111
46a 216n121
63b 121–22, 204n7, 205n18

Ketubbot
48a 51
59a–b 188n113
60b–61a 196n1
61a–b 196n3
105b 116

Nedarim
8a–9a 111
25a 196n1
28a 198n20
62b 204n7
77a 111

Soṭah
22a 142, 204n7, 221n19
49b 192n136

Giṭṭin
10b 198n20
11a 192n137
14a–b 186n87, 217n137
16b–17a 122, 183n44, 204n7, 205n15, 205n18
19b 64
28b 121
33a 216n124
56b 201n41
57a 191n125
57b 217n140
58b 209n46
70a 182n39
80b 69
88b 213n84

Qiddušin
33a 179n8
60b 181n31
72a 52, 71, 204n7, 205nn15–16, 207n35,

Baba Qamma
55a 182n39, 195n181
58b 182n39
83a 192n136
84a–b 216n128
96b 79, 196n1
113a 198n20
114a 209n46
117a 201n41

Baba Meṣi'a
8b 201n41
28b 182n39
29b 142
38b 203n63
59a–b 127
70b 79, 196n1
73b 110
83a–86a 61
85a 79
118b–119a 75, 83–84

Baba Batra
8a 79, 184n57, 196n1
10b 79
12b 193n158
46a 201n41
54b 198n20
55a 198n20
55a 190n125
58a 204n7
58a–b 217n137
65a 216n125
73a–b 193n153
115b 196n1, 198n16
120b–121a 111
136a 58
138b 216n124
168a 201n41
172b 79
173b 182n39

Sanhedrin
2b–3a 216n126
4b–5a 112–14, 123, 150, 214n101, 216n129, 216n129

7b–8a 215n111
13b–14a 216n128
17a 221n20
17b 78, 214n101
23a 216n126
33a 216n129
39a 66–67, 204n7
46b 79, 196n1
65b 204n7
67b 221n15
68a 127
74b 59, 204n7
94b 62, 189n121
95a 184n59
97b 114
98a 77, 117, 184n58, 190n125, 196n1
109a 70, 191n125

ʿAbodah Zarah
2b 52, 72, 183n44
10b–11a 81
11b 65–66, 70
24b 63
26a 209n46
30a 190n125
71a 61, 184n58
76b 75, 91, 196n1

Horayot
4b 216n125
7a–b 216n125

Šebuʿot
10a 201n41
29b 196n1
34b 182n39

Zebaḥim
9b 225n49
19a 196n3

Ḥullin
38a 225n50
59b 201n41
62b 196n3, 203n6, 204n7

Bekorot
25b 111
60a 191n131

ʿArakin
28a 181n31

Tamid
32b 188n104

Niddah
20a 188n113
20b 196n1
25a 188n109

ARAMAIC BOWLS (SELECTED)

Geller, "Four Aramaic Incantation Bowls"
Bowl A 224n40

Gordon, "Aramaic Magical Bowls"
Text D (No. 6519) 128–29, 222n29

Levene, *A Corpus of Magic Bowls*
M102 137

Levene, *Jewish Aramaic Curse Texts*
SD27 133–34, 225n55

Levene, "'This Is a Qybl'"
039A (BM 91771) 142, 228n98

Montgomery, *Aramaic Incantation Texts*
No. 19 (CBS 16018) 224n40

Moriggi, *A Corpus of Syriac Incantation Bowls*
No. 12 228n99

Naveh and Shaked, *Amulets and Magic Bowls*
Bowl 13 223n34

Shaked et al., *Aramaic Bowl Spells*
JBA 24 140–41
JBA 26 141

MIDDLE PERSIAN LITERATURE

Ardā Wirāz Nāmag
6 211n66
10:18–11:8 190n123

Bundahišn
0.2 173n83
1.1–3 193n154
3.3 212n76
14.38 173n83
31.37 173n83

33.1–22 173n83
33.21–22 197n9
35.1 210n54
35.56 210n58
36.0 173n83
36.4 212n77
36.9 173n83

Dādestān ī Dēnīg
2.13 190n123
38.30 217n141
38.31 186n86

Dēnkard III
80 211n63
176 173n83
196 223n33
288 210n60, 219n1
308 173n83
420 173n83

Dēnkard V
22 197n9
24.16C 192n148

Dēnkard VI
13–14 189n123
256 221n22
D2–D5 211n66

Dēnkard VII
1.34 173n83
3 222n33
4.63–7.38 172n66
8.47 173n83

Dēnkard VIII
27 210n61

Dēnkard IX
2.20 189n123
13.9 189n123

Frahang ī Pahlavīk
4.11 191n125
11.4 206n27
13.2 206n24
13.5 209n41

Gizistag Abāliš
7 186n84

Hērbedestān
11.1 213n95
12 210n62
18–19 211n62
19 211n62

Kārnāmag ī Ardaxšēr ī Pābagān
10 82, 200n34

Mādayān ī Hazār Dādestān
2.17–3.1 217n140
5.13 211n66
38.2 213n95
44.7 213n95
65.9 195n170
78.2–11 218n163
84.13–15 190n125
93.4–9 209n49
95.16–96.3 208n41
A26.11–16 209n43
A27 195n170
A27.4–5 210n55
A27.5–7 217n140
A28.5–7 210n56
A34.6–9 218n162
A34.6–35.3 210n57
A34.9–10 218n161
A35.3–5 218n160
A36.3–12 210n57
A37.1–6 209n41
A37.3–4 217n140
A37.9 217n140
A38.12–16 120

Nērangestān
13.5 212n71
67–69 186n84
72.9 211n66

Pahlavi Rivāyat Accompanying the Dādestān ī Dēnīg
47.21–22 213n77
48.49 210n59

Pahlavi Vīdēvdād
17 220n8

Pahlavi Zand
Yašt 1:12 103

Pursišnīhā
Questions 6–7 211n62

Šahrestānīhā ī Ērānšahr
— 194n160, 196n3

Šāyest nē Šāyest
4 186n84

Wizīdagīhā ī Zādspram
3.13 173n83
7.1 217n141
8.4 217n141
10–12 222n33
35.17 213n77

Zand ī Wahman Yasn
4.59 173n83
6.10 173n83
9.10 173n83

GENERAL INDEX

Abarag, 30, 169n42
Abaye, 43–44, 52, 59–60, 67, 79, 121, 179n8
academies, rabbinic: and the Babylonian Jewish court system, 108, 123; in comparison to Persian society, 98; insularity and cultural horizon outside of, 2, 15, 145–46; location of, 19–20; relations with the exilarch, 109
Achaemenids, portrayals of, in the Babylonian Talmud, 49; in comparison to Rome, 50–51, 68–69, 73, 88; political continuity with the Sasanian empire, 51, 80–82, 104; social and political histories of, 39
acculturation. *See* rabbis, Babylonian, acculturation to Persian culture; rabbis, Babylonian, acculturation to Zoroastrianism, lack of
Ādurbād Ēmēdān, 36
Ādurbād son of Mahrspandān, 101
Ādurfarnbag ī Farroxzādān, 36, 174n94
agdēn, 104–6, 138
Aggadah: similarities with Middle Persian texts and culture, 32, 49; textual and historical analysis of, 10–12, 146–47
Agzar bar Dibšata, Rav, 141
Aḥa bar Rav Huna, Rav, 140
Aḥma son of Aḥat, Rav, 140
Ahriman, 66–67
Akiva, R., 51, 127
Alexander, Philip, 137
Alexandri, R., 77
Alon, Gedalyahu, 14, 106
Ameimar, 61–62, 64–67
amgûšā (Zoroastrian priest): association with magic, in Hellenism and in the Babylonian Talmud, 95, 125–26, 128; origins of Talmudic term, 95. *See also* priests, Zoroastrian, portrayals of, in the Babylonian Talmud
andarz (wisdom literature), 32, 36, 77, 101
anēr, 104–6, 138
anērān, 82, 211n62
Arabs. *See* Islam
Aramaic: cultural koiné of, in Sasanian Mesopotamia, 19, 135–36; relationship between dialects and speakers, in Sasanian Mesopotamia, 19, 58, 98, 130, 141–42, 147. *See also* bowls, Aramaic magic; Syriac; Targum; loanwords, Iranian, in the Babylonian Talmud
Ardā Wirāz Nāmag, 33
Ardawān IV (Parthian king), 75, 80–82
Ardashir (Sasanian king), 33, 76, 80, 82, 86–87
Ashi, Rav, 13–14, 57, 61–65, 68
Ashmedai, 141, 184n57
Assi, R., 71
authority. *See* priests, Zoroastrian, role of, in Sasanian society, as judges, administrators, and scholar-priests; rabbis, Babylonian, authority of, in judicial settings; rabbis, Babylonian, authority of, in comparison to the Zoroastrian priests

Avesta: status of, in Sasanian politics, 101–4; transmission of, 37–38, 85–87, 200n38, 211n67. *See also* Zand
Avot de-Rabbi Nathan, 53
Ayādgār ī Jāmāspīg, 33
Ayādgār ī Wuzurgmihr, 32
Ayādgār ī Zarērān, 32–33

Babylonian Esther Midrash, 51
Bagdāna, 129–30
Baird, Robert, 130
bans: in the Aramaic magic bowls, 139–41, 151; in rabbinic literature, 107, 111, 127
Bati bar Tovi, 90–91
Bausani, Alessandro, 96
bears. *See* Persians, portrayals of, in the Babylonian Talmud, and bears, motif of
Beer, Moshe, 121
bei dāwar, 188n113, 209n46
Bidez, Joseph, 102
blasphemy (*ḤRŠ*): in the Aramaic magic bowls, 141–42; in the Babylonian Talmud, 125–26, 221n17
Bohak, Gideon, 135, 137
bowls, Aramaic magic, 39, 124–43; and the amalgamation of identities, 124, 129–33; in comparison to Talmudic culture, 39, 128, 139–43; as evidence of social contact between groups, 49, 106, 128–29, 133–34; Jewish sources used in, 139; onomastic evidence of, 49, 132; in Pahlavi, 39; provenance of, in Nippur and elsewhere, 39, 129–30, 139; rabbis referred to in, 139–41; references to, in the Babylonian Talmud, 142; the relationship between sorcerers and clients, 131–32; relationship to official religions, 136–39; the religious identity of sorcerers and clients, 131–36; syncretism of, 129–31. *See also* bans, in the Aramaic magic bowls; blasphemy (*ḤRŠ*), in the Aramaic magic bowls; Christianity, in the Aramaic magic bowls; Daniel, in the Aramaic magic bowls; divorce deeds, in the Aramaic magic bowls; Mandaeism, in the Aramaic magic bowls; *Targum,* cited in the Aramaic magic bowls; vows, in the Aramaic magic bowls
Boyce, Mary, 38, 86, 102
Brody, Robert, 16–17, 63
Bundahišn, 29, 33, 35, 67, 87, 101
burial, 31, 79–80, 95, 122

Caesar, 88–89, 114–15, 182n38
Cantera, Alberto, 32
capital punishment. *See* corporal punishment
Catholikoi, 69
censorship, of the Bavli, of Romans with Persians, 114–15
Cereti, Carlo, 29, 37
Christianity: in the Aramaic magic bowls, 132–33; context of, relevance for the study of Palestinian rabbinic Judaism, 2–3; referenced in Middle Persian sources, 170n54; Syriac, context of, relevance for study of the Babylonian Talmud, 20–21; Zoroastrian polemics against, 35
Čīdag Andarz ī Pōryōtkēšān, 32
Cohen, Shaye, 106–7
comparison, of Sasanian religions: 22–42; emphasis on differences and historical context, 22–24, 26–28; emphasis on similarities, 23–26, 40–42; and the historical boon of interaction, 25–26; and textual parallelomania, 23. *See also* Middle Persian literature, in comparison to the Babylonian Talmud; Smith, Jonathan Z.; Talmud, Babylonian, in comparison to Middle Persian sources
conversion, from Zoroastrianism to Christianity or Islam, 33–34, 104–5, 174n90
corporal punishment, 114–16, 121, 126
corpses. *See* burial
courts. *See* judges, in Jewish Babylonia; rabbis, Babylonian, attitude of, toward Jewish and Persian courts; rabbis, Babylonian, authority of, in judicial settings; Sasanian empire, courts of law
Ctesiphon, 19–20, 68–69
culture. *See* Persians, portrayals of, in the Babylonian Talmud, as evidence of rabbinic knowledge of Persian culture; rabbis, Babylonian, culture of, as influenced by the Persian world; rabbis, Babylonian, culture of, shared with the Aramaic magic bowls
Cumont, Franz, 102
Cyrus the Great, 51, 69

dādwar, 100, 150. *See also* bei dāwar
Dahāg, 101, 219n1
Daniel (Hebrew Bible): in the Aramaic magic bowls, 133–34; in the Babylonian Talmud, portrayals of Persians, 71–73, 77, 88, 190n125; image of, in the lions' den, on Jewish-Sasanian seals, 109
dastwar, 33–34
death penalty. *See* corporal punishment
Dēnkard, 30, 33–35, 76; editors of, 36

Dēnkard III, 34–35, 101
Dēnkard IV, 84–87, 200n37
Dēnkard VI, 62
Dēnkard VIII, 105
Dēnkard IX, 30, 36
dînā de-malḥûtā dînā, 80–83
disciples: *hāwišt*, 101–2; *hāwišt*, economic tensions with *hērbed*, 173n75; in rabbinic and Zoroastrian societies, 98
Divine Presence, 67–69, 118–20, 139
divorce deeds: in the Aramaic magic bowls, 131, 133, 136, 139–41; in the Babylonian Talmud, 64, 69–70, 111
dream-interpretation, 88–90, 100
Duchesne-Guillemin, Jacques, 28

Ecclesiastes Rabbah: influenced by the Babylonian Talmud, 50–53; portrayals of Persians in, 53–55, 125, 220n7
Elephantine papyri, 95
Eliade, Mircea, 24–25
Eliezer, R., 127–28
Elman, Yaakov, 2, 20, 47–48, 73
Esther, 49, 51
ethrog, 91, 109–10, 203n67
excommunication. *See* bans
exilarch: in Maḥoza, 20; role of, in Jewish judicial system, 104, 108–15, 123, 216n125. *See also* academies, rabbinic, relations with the exilarch; judges, in Jewish Babylonia, public experts
Ezra, 45, 49, 51

Fārs, 17, 32–33, 36, 80, 104
festivals, Persian, 65–66
fire temples, Zoroastrian, 19, 99–102, 176n108; in the Babylonian Talmud, 204n7
Fishman, Talya, 16
forced explanation, 14–15
Fraenkel, Jonah, 10, 12, 18
Friedman, Shamma, 8–10, 12
Frye, Richard, 104

gabr. *See* ḥabarei
Gafni, Isaiah, 11, 49, 62, 96
Gamaliel, Rabban, 51–52
Geller, Markham, 131
Geonim: Babylonian Talmud, status of among, 8, 15–17, 97–98; Persian language, status of among, 63
gĕzîrpatei, 117–20
gift-giving, Persian practice of, 61–62, 80–81
Gignoux, Philippe, 38, 99
Ginzberg, Louis, 14, 45
Gizistag Abāliš, 36
Goldberg, Abraham, 125
Guebers. *See* ḥabarei
Gyselen, Rika, 39, 109–11

ḥabarei: and *amgûšā*, 95, 125; derived from Deuteronomy 18, 126–28, 142; portrayals of, in the Babylonian Talmud, 71–72, 122–23, 193n158; Rashi on, 96; similarities with *hērbeds*, 96; as sorcerers, 95, 125–27; translated as Guebers, from New Persian *gabr*, 96–97. *See also* priests, Zoroastrian, portrayals of, in the Babylonian Talmud
Hadith, 30
Halivni, David Weiss, 8–9, 14–16, 18
Ḥama, Rav, 79–80
Ḥanah, Rabbah bar bar, 49, 122
Ḥanina ben Dosa, 139
Harviainen, Tapani, 134, 138
hāwišt. *See* disciples
Hayes, Christine, 12–14
Heinemann, Joseph, 11
hērbed: relationship with *mowbeds*, 98, 102, 114; as scholar-priests, in comparison to the Babylonian rabbis, 96, 101–02, 123, 148
Hērbedestān, 29, 31–32, 99, 106
heresy: punishment of, in Sasanian courts, 104, 120–21; as a term of otherness, in rabbinic and Middle Persian literatures, 124, 137–38; within the Zoroastrian priesthood, 37. *See also* zandīg
Herman, Geoffrey, 7, 10, 20, 32, 62, 109–10, 113, 155n6
heterodoxy, religious, in Sasanian religions, 17, 37, 139, 151. *See also* orthodoxy
heterograms, Aramaic, in Pahlavi script, 96–97
Hidary, Richard, 107–8
Hirshman, Marc, 53–54
Hormizd I (Sasanian king), 56
Hunter, Erica, 129–30, 134
Hyde, Thomas, 27–28

Ifra Hormiz, 52, 75, 79
Indo-European studies, 29, 103
inscriptions, Sasanian, 19, 31, 38, 56, 76, 89; of Kirder, 99, 102, 122
insularity, of Sasanian religious texts, 10, 18–19, 23–24, 50, 129, 137–39, 146–48, 150–51
intermarriage, 49, 104, 106, 132. *See also* marriage

Iranian studies, 2, 28–29
Islam, impact of, on Middle Persian literature, 33–37

Jany, János, 104
Japheth. *See* Tiras
de Jong, Albert, 23, 34, 50, 100
Josephson, Judith, 29
Joshua b. Peraḥia, R., 139–41
Judah the Prince, R., 80–81
judges, in Jewish Babylonia: public experts, 109–14, 123, 150; lay and court judges, 111. *See also* exilarch, role of, in Jewish judicial system; rabbis, Babylonian, authority of, in judicial settings

Kahana, Rav, 49, 91
Kalmin, Richard, 7, 10, 19, 92, 107, 122
Kārnāmag ī Ardaxšēr ī Pābagān, 32, 76, 82, 101
Kashkar, 68–70
Kawad son of Peroz (Sasanian king), 100
Khusrow I (Sasanian king): and the dating of Sasanian seals, 100; and the dating of Zoroastrian literature, 32, 37–38, 85–87. *See also* Xusrow and the Page
Kiel, Yishai, 48
kings, Sasanian, portrayals of, in the Babylonian Talmud: 74–93, 149; bribery, motif of, 79. *See also* Ardashir; Ardawān IV (Parthian king); Peroz; Shapur I, portrayals of, as symbol of authority, in the Babylonian Talmud; Shapur II, portrayals of, in the Babylonian Talmud; Yazdegird I
Kirder, 56, 82, 99, 102, 122
Kohut, Alexander, 44
Krauss, Samuel, 57
Kreyenbroek, Philip, 34
Kwasman, Theodore, 142

Lesses, Rebecca, 136
Letter of Tansar, 33, 99
Levene, Dan, 133, 135, 139
Levi, 56–57
Levinson, Joshua, 124
Lieberman, Saul, 15, 62
loanwords, Aramaic, in Middle and New Persian, 97, 207n32
loanwords, Iranian, in the Babylonian Talmud: 49, 57–66, with examples of, discussed in this book, 43–44, 52, 55–63, 77–78, 83, 100–101, 110, 115, 120–21, 125, 182n38, 184n59, 185n80, 185n82, 201n41, 216n121; classification of, 60; as a common topic of study in Irano-Talmudica, 44; in comparison to Middle Persian cognates, 61–62; errors in transmission of, 65–66; as evidence of Babylonian rabbinic provenance, 60–61, 125; in the form of verbs and adverbs, 60; Old Persian loanwords, 58, 95, 187n99; origins and etymologies of, 58–59, 187n96; rabbinic folk etymologies of, 63; rabbis associated with traditions containing, 61; similarities with Iranian loanwords in Syriac and other languages, 58, 115, 187n101; in Talmudic exegesis of the Mishnah, 59–60; in texts about Romans, 191n125; total number and relative dearth of, 57, 59–60, 187n96; as unique data for Iranian linguists, 152; used in lieu of Aramaic synonyms, 55, 59, 188n104; used in reference to the exilarch, 59–60, 62, 217n140; used to signal Persian otherness, 62, 148, 190n125
loanwords, Iranian, in Geonic literature and Aramaic magic bowls: 60, 187n96, 188n107, 188n113
loanwords, Iranian, in Syriac, 58, 186n85

Macuch, Maria, 35–36, 38, 48, 100, 104–6, 109, 111, 120–21
Mādayān ī Hazār Dādestān, 31, 45, 47, 69, 99–101, 104, 106, 109, 111, 120–21
mages hellénisés, les, 102
magians. *See* mowbed
magic. *See* bowls, Aramaic magic
Maḥlafa son of Khwardukh, Rav, 140
Maḥoza, 20, 39, 57, 116
Ma'mūn, al-, 36
Mandaeism, in the Aramaic magic bowls, 128–31, 135
Manichaeism: and magic, 128, 132–33; *zandīg*, designation for, 120, 138
Mardānfarrox son of Ohrmazddād, 35
Manūščihr, 34, 36
marriage, rabbinic jurisdiction over, 104, 108, 111, 150. *See also* intermarriage
Mata Meḥasya, 68
Mazdakism, 37
Medes, 51–52, 66
de Menasce, Jean, 101
Mēnōg ī Xrad, 32
menstruation, 31, 48, 63, 191n134
Mesharshiya b. Qaqay, Rav, 136
měšîkâ, 61–62
Messiah, 77, 118
Middle Persian (language), rabbinic and Geonic knowledge of, 62–65

Middle Persian literature: 28–38; authors of, ninth- and tenth-century Pahlavi books, 36–37; challenges of dating, 33–35, 38; in comparison to the Babylonian Talmud, 29–30, 33, 36, 40–42, 145–48; genres of, 31–35; inaccurate reflection of diversity in pre-Islamic Iran, 36–37. *See also* Islam, impact of, on Middle Persian literature; Khusrow I, and the dating of Zoroastrian literature; Shapur I, in Middle Persian sources; Talmud, Babylonian, in comparison to Middle Persian sources
mog, 34, 95, 100, 150
mog-mard (mwg-GBRA), 96–97
mowbed: in comparison to the Babylonian rabbis, 96, 98–99, 102, 123, 148; role of, in Sasanian society, 33, 99–100, 102, 104, 150
mowbedān mowbed, 36, 82, 101–2, 121
Müller-Kessler, Christa, 142

Naḥman, Rav, 20, 45, 61, 78–79
Nāmagīhā ī Manūščihr, 36
Nehardea, 20, 56–57, 68, 107, 115
Nērangestān, 31–32, 99
Neusner, Jacob, 4, 11, 46–47, 65, 73, 94, 108, 115
Nippur. *See* bowls, Aramaic magic, provenance of, in Nippur and elsewhere
numismatics, Sasanian, 38, 76, 99

oaths, 139
Ohrmazd, 66–67, 104
Oppenheimer, Aharon, 70
orality: comparison of rabbinic and Zoroastrian, 17, 30, 49; as a mode of exchange between sorcerers, 129
ordination, rabbinic, 112
orthodoxy, religious, in Sasanian religions, 17, 138–39, 151. *See also* heterodoxy
ōstāndār, 69–70
otherness: study of, in rabbinic literature, 3, 74. *See also* kings, Sasanian, portrayals of, in the Babylonian Talmud; Persians, portrayals of, in the Babylonian Talmud; priests, Zoroastrian, portrayals of, in the Babylonian Talmud

Pahlavi literature. *See* Middle Persian literature
Pahlavi Rivāyat Accompanying the Dādestān ī Dēnīg, 101
Pahlavi Vīdēvdād, 29–32
Pahlavi Yasna, 31–32
Pappa, Rav, 64–65, 78, 117–20
Parthians, portrayals of, in rabbinic literature, 49–50, 80–82
Peroz (Sasanian king), 75
Persians, portrayals of, in the Babylonian Talmud: 43–73, 148–49; and bears, motif of, 71–73, 195n179; and the biblical origins of Persia, 67–71; and diet, 43–44, 51, 58; as evidence of rabbinic knowledge of Persian culture, 46–47, 49–50, 65–66; and fashion, 55–57; and festivals, list of, 65–66; and horses, motif of, 52, 62, 73, 77–78, 148, 184n59, 193n153; and modesty and pride, motifs of, 51–53; as references to the Achaemenid, Parthian, or Sasanian empire, 49–51; and sex, 51
Persians, portrayals of, in Palestinian rabbinic literature: 50–51, 53–55, 66, 69, 80–81, 125, 182n40, 185n73, 186n90, 194n159, 196n1, 194n159, 220n7
polemics: and discourses of magic, 124, 127, 130, 138; as a means of gaining power, 150; Zoroastrian, against Jews, 101
public expert. *See* judges, in Jewish Babylonia
Pumbedita, 20, 39, 43, 51
pursišn-nāmag, 101, 120–21
priests, Zoroastrian, portrayals of, in the Babylonian Talmud, as sorcerers and corrupt administrators, 94–98, 116–23, 124–28, 142, 149–51, 204n7; bribery, motif of, 122; role of, in Sasanian society, in comparison to the Babylonian rabbis in Jewish society, 98–99; role of, in Sasanian society, as judges, administrators, and scholar-priests, 99–106, 120–21. *See also* amgûšā; dādwar; dastwar; ḥabarei; hērbed; mog; mowbed; rad

Qarna, 107

Rabbah, 43, 70
rabbis, Babylonian: acculturation to Persian culture, 20, 44, 47–48; acculturation to Zoroastrianism, lack of, 56, 60, 188n112; attitude of, toward Jewish and Persian courts, 116–20; authority of, in comparison to the Zoroastrian priests, 94–95, 98, 123, 149–50; authority of, in judicial settings, 106–16; authority of, rabbinic claims to, and the utility of second-order, contextual research, 3, 18, 143, 145–47; culture of, as influenced by the Persian world, 1–2, 10, 43–57, 61, 148–49; culture of, shared with the Aramaic magic bowls, 139–42

rad, 33, 36, 100–101, 105, 120–21
Rashi, 14, 16, 52; on Persians, 63, 69, 89, 96, 193n153, 204n7, 205n16
Rav, 44, 50, 53–54, 61, 71, 81, 112–14, 125–26, 128
Rava, 20, 61, 63, 78–79, 88–91, 111, 116–17
Ravina, 57, 61
Rivāyat ī Ēmēd ī Ašawahištān, 36
Romans. *See* Achaemenids, portrayals of, in the Babylonian Talmud, in comparison to Rome
Rosensweig, Michael, 16
Rosenthal, E. S., 2, 44, 121
Rubenstein, Jeffrey, 14, 32

Saboraim, 8
Safra, Rav, 57
Šāhnāme, 33, 82, 96
Sasanian empire: courts of law, 31, 99–101, 120; courts of law, bribery, motif of, in the Babylonian Talmud, 116, 121–22; policies toward non-Zoroastrians, 104–6. *See also* priests, Zoroastrian, role of, in Sasanian society
Šāyest nē Šāyest, 32
Scheftelowitz, Isidor, 44
Schorr, Joshua Heschel, 44
Schremer, Adiel, 8
Schwartz, Seth, 2, 106
seals, Sasanian, 3, 19–20, 31, 34, 38–39, 99–101; discussion of, in the Babylonian Talmud, 110–11; Jewish-Sasanian seals, 109–10
Secunda, Shai, 2, 23, 40–42, 48
Segal, Eliezer, 109
Shahbazi, Shapur, 33
Shaked, Shaul, 37, 44, 56, 60, 65, 110, 129, 132, 135–36, 139–40
Shaki, Mansour, 87, 96–97
Shapur I (Sasanian king): in Middle Persian sources, 80–87; portrayals of, as symbol of authority, in the Babylonian Talmud, 74–79, 87–92; and Shmuel, associated with, in the Babylonian Talmud, 77–78, 87–89
Shapur II (Sasanian king), portrayals of, in the Babylonian Talmud, 74, 78–80
Sheshet, Rav, 110–11
Shila, R., 70–71, 114–16
Shmuel, 55, 125–26; Iranian loanwords attributed to, 61, 77–78; in Palestinian rabbinic texts about Persians, 50, 53–55, 125. *See also* dînā de-malḥûtā dînā; Shapur I
silence during meals, Zoroastrian practice of, 49, 182n38
Škand Gumānīg Wizār, 35, 47, 89–90
Skjærvø, Prods Oktor, 2, 47
skulls, magic, 128
Smith, Jonathan Z., 22, 26–27, 161n52
Soloveitchik, Haym, 16, 161n49
sorcerers. *See* bowls, Aramaic magic
Sōšāns, 30, 169n42
Sōšyans, 101
Sperber, Daniel, 44–45
Spicehandler, Ezra, 44
Stammaim, 7–9
Stausberg, Michael, 86
Stern, Sacha, 50, 72
Sura, 68, 107
Sussmann, Yaacov, 8
syncretism. *See* bowls, Aramaic magic
Syriac, language and literature: in the Aramaic magic bowls, 132–33, 135, 142–43, 224n47; references to Zoroastrian priests in, 95; as a source for Sasanian history, 38–39, 101, 105; value of, in comparison with the Babylonian Talmud, 20–21, 25

Table of Nations, 67–70, 194n159
Talmud, Babylonian: in comparison to Middle Persian sources, 29–30, 33, 36, 40–42, 145–48; exegetical and internal approaches toward, 7–10, 12–15; formation of, 7–9; in its Iranian context, past studies on, 1–2, 15–26, 40–49, 94–95, 125, 128–29, 145–48; in its Iranian context, reasons it is an understudied topic, 2, 15–16, 28–29, 40, 47, 97–98; normativity of, 16–18; as a source for Babylonian Jewish history, 10–12, 17–18, 109; as a source for Sasanian history, 46, 58, 151–52
Talmud, Jerusalem. *See* Persians, portrayals of, in Palestinian rabbinic literature
Tanna de-be Eliyahu, portrayals of Persians in, 182n36
Tansar, 86, 102
Targum: cited in the Aramaic magic bowls, 130, 139; in comparison to Zand, 31; *Onqelos*, as Babylonian composition, 49; and the Zoroastrian priests, 125, 142
taxes, 46, 65, 82, 110
Telegdi, Zsigmond, 44
Testament of Ardashir, 33
Tiras, 68–69, 194n159, 195n167
Tosafists, 16, 147
Tower of Babylon, 67, 70–71

Urbach, Ephraim, 114
ur-texts, 14–15, 48

Vevaina, Yuhan, 35
Vidas, Moulie, 9
vows, in the Aramaic magic bowls, 136; in the Babylonian Talmud, 111, 123

Wahram II (Sasanian king), 102
Widengren, Geo, 56
Winston, David, 89
Wissenschaft des Judentums, 11
Wizīdagīhā ī Zādspram, 37

Xusrow and the Page, 77
Xwadāy-Nāmag, 33

Yannai (Hasmonean king), 50
Yazdegird I (Sasanian king), 75, 196n3
Yeshivot, modern, 16, 161n46, 161n49
Yosef, Rav: baraitot of, 52, 68–69, 71–72; and capital cases in gentile courts, 121; connection to Persians, in the Babylonian Talmud, 43–44, 51–52, 79; and exegesis of the Table of Nations and Tower of Babylon, 68–69, 71; and exegesis of Daniel, for Persians as bears, 71–72; position on the public expert, 111–14, 123
Yosef Šeda, Rav, 140–41

Zādspram, 36
Zand: composition, date, and technique of, 29–33, 38, 170n55; as encyclopedia of wisdom, 85–87; as part of Sasanian social ideology, 103; transmitted by *hērbeds*, 101, 211n67. *See also* Middle Persian literature
Zand ī Fragard ī Juddēvdād, 31
Zand ī Wahman Yasn, 29, 33
Zand ī Xorde Avesta, 31
zandīg, 120, 138, 226n75. *See also* Manichaeism
Zoroastrianism: in comparison to Talmudic Judaism, 4, 23–25, 66–67, 145; orientalization of, 27–28. *See also* Middle Persian literature; priests, Zoroastrian; Sasanian empire
Zutra bar Ṭoviyah, Rav, 126

www.ingramcontent.com/pod-product-compliance
Lightning Source LLC
Chambersburg PA
CBHW030529230426
43665CB00010B/819
9780520385726